SIAMESE
MELTING
POT

SIAMESE MELTING POT

ETHNIC MINORITIES IN THE MAKING OF BANGKOK

EDWARD VAN ROY

Silkworm Books

ISEAS YUSOF ISHAK INSTITUTE

First published in Singapore in 2017 by
ISEAS Publishing
30 Heng Mui Keng Terrace
Singapore 119614

For worldwide distribution except Thailand.

E-mail: publish@iseas.edu.sg
Website: <http://bookshop.iseas.edu.sg>

First published in Thailand in 2017 by
Silkworm Books
104/5 M. 7, Chiang Mai–Hot Road, T. Suthep, Chiang Mai 50200 Thailand
P.O. Box 296 Phra Singh Post Office Chiang Mai 50205

For distribution in Thailand.

E-mail: info@silkwormbooks.com
Website: <http://www.silkwormbooks.com>

The responsibility for facts and opinions in this publication rests exclusively with the author and his interpretations do not necessarily reflect the views or the policy of the publishers or their supporters.

ISEAS Library Cataloguing-in-Publication Data

Van Roy, Edward, 1937–
  Siamese Melting Pot : Ethnic Minorities in the Making of Bangkok.
  1. Minorities—Thailand—Bangkok.
  2. Bangkok (Thailand)—Social life and customs.
  3. Bangkok (Thailand)—History.
DS589 B2V21   2017

ISEAS ISBN 978-981-4762-83-0 (paperback)
ISEAS ISBN 978-981-4762-84-7 (e-book PDF)
Silkworm ISBN 978-616-215-139-2 (paperback)

Typeset by Superskill Graphics Pte Ltd
Printed in Singapore by Markono Print Media Pte Ltd

Contents

List of Maps

List of Tables

Preface

More than half a century ago, upon my initial encounter with Bangkok, I discovered a labyrinthine city of joyous confusion, the exotic Orient in all its enigmatic splendor. From my well-situated home base on Worachak Road I first explored, always on foot, my neighbourhood from Wat Saket to Wang Burapha and then gradually stretched my reconnoiterings across an ever-expanding urban terrain, reaching from the Grand Palace and Sanam Luang to Sampheng's raucous waterfront. Wandering the city's dusty byways I sought to find the order behind the clutter but was stymied at every turn. In the process of negotiating the baffling metropolis I found that many locals faced as much difficulty as I in directing me to my destination. Few street signs — and those few only in indecipherable Thai — were available to guide my way, and house numbers were aligned in no apparent sequence; even a reasonable city map was unavailable. Only many years later was I able to acquire my first reliable Bangkok street-guide (Tanya 1984), which still occupies its cherished place on my bookshelf as a memorial to those bygone days. That unforgettable experience inspired me, in my abiding conviction in the innate rationality of mankind, to continue to the present day my search for the logical underpinnings of Bangkok's apparent spatial chaos.

Similar dissonance met my efforts to identify the guiding principles of Thai culture and society. A clear sense of easy acquaintance, happy camaraderie, and calm self-effacement overrode less affable undertones of nationalist sensitivity, class prejudice, and an elemental dialectic of seniority and servility. Bangkok's social cacophony was a pervasive presence. From dancing the *ramwong* (a formerly popular Thai dance form) at a sumptuous charity ball where the capital's elite flaunted their wealth, to sharing bamboo-joints of *khao lam* (steamed sweetened sticky rice) and tin cups of *nam tan sot* (watered palm sugar) at a roadside stall with a gang of *sam-lo* (three-wheeler) taxi drivers was tantamount to crossing civilizations. Yet all were Bangkok natives, and proud of it. Searching the city's few English-language bookshops for clarification of that jumbled scenario, all I could find was an assortment of esoteric monographs on the "loosely structured" Thai social order (Evers 1969), elaborating on a curiously chaotic theory of the amiable incongruities of Thai life so evident all around me. Scholarly research on traditional Thai social organization and its continuing evolution has progressed significantly since those days, as the subsequent chapters show, but it surely still has far to go.

Some years later, having made some progress in my grasp of Bangkok's spatial and social contours, I was fortuitously posted to temporary office quarters in the midst of the inner city's Bang Lamphu district (long before the backpacker invasion of that neighbourhood's Khao San Road). Two dramatically contrasting royal temples bracketed that market locale. The sparkling grandeur of one, Wat Bowon Niwet, put to shame the sadly squalid state of the other, Wat Chana Songkhram, where mangy dogs, scrabbling chickens, and the occasional scrawny bullock strayed the unkempt grounds. Yet both temples, I learned, were closely associated with Bangkok's former division between king (*maharat*) and viceroy (*uparat*). The baffling contrast between those two royal landmarks whetted my appetite for uncovering their untold backstory. Some of my findings on the far-reaching implications of that political anomaly of Old Bangkok are contained in the following chapters.

Roaming Bang Lamphu's maze of lanes and alleys (many of them long since eradicated in the district's ongoing modernization), I discovered the remnants of its past human geography, including residual elements of a number of old palaces, lingering signs of an old Mon community, whispers of a past Khmer presence, and vestiges of a nearby Lao settlement, not to mention the neighbourhood's still-vigorous Malay village and bustling Sino-Thai marketplace. That remarkable diversity of what I had initially thought to be nothing more than a simple Thai urban precinct raised further enticing mysteries. It soon became evident that the ethnic mélange so evident in Bang Lamphu's history permeated the entire city. Only many years later, having mastered Thai (to some degree) and having gained the freedom to pursue these interests full-time and across the entire cityscape, have I been able to construct a logical solution to what originally posed such a riddle.

* * *

And so this book, the result of a half-century's participant-observer immersion in the urban melting pot that has become my hometown, a city hiding a fascinating human past. The book presents an ethnohistory — a socio-cultural biography — of Old Bangkok (1782–1910), otherwise known as Ratanakosin, the capital of Siam. It traces the synergy between the city's evolving spatial design, social organization, and political plot from its eighteenth-century origins to its early-twentieth-century modernization.

It deals with a set of closely related thematic threads woven around a single topic — Old Bangkok's ethnically plural society — reaching from the former Siamese feudal state to its transformation into today's Thai nation-state.

Among those themes are the following: First, the function of the city, from its beginnings in the wake of the fall of Ayutthaya, as a haven for refugees, detention centre for war captives, and magnet for entrepreneurs and wage workers of diverse ethnicity; the contributions made by the respective ethnic communities to the city's growth and development; and the social and spatial autonomy long maintained by those ethnic groups despite their close proximity with one another and intimate relations with their elite Thai patrons. Second, the feudal structure of Old Bangkok, with the respective ethnic communities linking hierarchically to the Thai elite through a variety of functional reciprocities; the forces that in the closing decades of the nineteenth century led to the city's meteoric transformation from feudalism to nationalism, from a policy regime of "benign neglect" to one of "active intervention," and from ethnic pluralism to ideological factionalism. Third, the factors, such as economic opportunity, social proximity, intermarriage, and mass education, that facilitated cultural assimilation, in opposition to those such as religious partisanship, communal endogamy, and social isolation which supported or reinforced the retention of ethnic identity in the face of integrative pressures. And fourth, the manner in which Old Bangkok's physical design, conforming to the metaphysical, aesthetic, and utilitarian principles of the mandala, complemented the city's ethnically plural social organization; and the process whereby that symbolic schema disintegrated, just as its social corollary withered away under conditions of growing royal absolutism, intensifying bureaucratic centralization, and rising nationalism.

The ethnic constituencies of Old Bangkok covered in this book range from the Thai (elite and commons), Portuguese-Thai, Mon, Lao, Muslims (Cham, Persians, Arabs, Indians, Malays, Indonesians), and Chinese (Taechiu, Hokkien, Hakka, Hainanese, Cantonese) to a congeries of lesser groups (Khmer, Vietnamese, Thai Yuan, Sikh, *farang*). The following chapters treat those various groups seriatim. They can be read together to gain an appreciation of the city's unfolding human history, or individually as the reader's interests in specific ethnicities may dictate. In either case, they provide a bottom-up perspective on Bangkok's evolving human tapestry to complement the top-down vision conveyed by the conventional historical literature.

* * *

Several of the following chapters contain revised versions, in whole or in part, of previously published papers on those themes. The respective publishers are thanked for their permission to reuse those materials here:

- "The Portuguese in Siam: A Quinquacentennial Retrospect", *Asian Review* 20 (2007), pp. 125–64.
- "Sampheng: From Ethnic Isolation to National Integration", *Sojourn: Journal of Social Issues in Southeast Asia* 23, no. 1 (2008), pp. 1–29.
- "Under Duress: Lao War Captives at Bangkok in the Nineteenth Century", *Journal of the Siam Society* 97 (2009), pp. 43–68.
- "Safe Haven: Mon Refugees at Ayutthaya, Thonburi, and Bangkok from the 1500s to the 1800s", *Journal of the Siam Society* 98 (2010), pp. 151–84.
- "Rise and Fall of the Bangkok Mandala", *Journal of Asian History* 45, nos. 1–2 (2011), pp. 85–118.
- "Contending Identities: Islam and Ethnicity in Old Bangkok", *Journal of the Siam Society* 104 (2016), pp. 169–202.

* * *

This book owes much to my former mentors, role models, and facilitators, particularly Ben Higgins, Terry Neale, John B. Cornell, June and Jane Hanks, Pradit Cheosakul, Hiroshi Kitamura, and Denis Sinor; and to Kantasilo Bhikkhu of Wat Bowon Niwet and Phra Khru Somsak Subhalert of Wat Chakrawat for their years of friendship and good counsel.

Without Michael Montesano's unstinting motivational support, technical guidance, and eagle-eyed editorial aid, this book would not have seen the light of day; to him my gratitude is boundless. At various stages in the development of this project Supang Chantavanich, Thanapol Limapichart, Chalong Soontravanich, Naengnoi Suksri, Piyanart Bunnag, and Chatri Prakitnonthakhan provided invaluable appraisals, conceptual insights, and leads to further research. Varah Rochanavibhata and Parate Attavipach; Manatham Phothong, Srawut Aree, and Imtiyaz Yusuf; Sisak Walliphodom; N. Seshagiri; Khrui and Temsiri Bunyasing, and Ginny and Jim Di Crocco offered helpful information and advice on a variety of specific issues and ethnicities dealt with in the text.

The staffs of the Chulalongkorn University Political Science Library, Arts Library, and Central Library; Siam Society Library; National Library and National Archives; and National Museum Library extended ever-smiling assistance. Suthee Boonmi of Chulalongkorn University's Institute of Asian

Studies produced this volume's many maps. Somjit Uluchanyong, Sanit Akhamit, Phongpak Satianpak, and Olarn Wachirodom provided essential interpretation and translation services at various stages in the fieldwork. Thanaroj Vanasrisawasd, Craig Johnson, and Thipa Asvarak proved their lasting friendship in shepherding this relic of a former technological era through the minefields of word processing, computer mapping, and internet exploration.

Heartfelt thanks are extended to the host of Bangkok government officials, business people, shopkeepers, artisans, schoolteachers, wage workers, housewives, and retirees, as well as the many temple abbots, mosque imams, church pastors, and shrine wardens, among others, who so willingly offered their hospitality, fellowship, and much time in informal discussion reminiscing about their community and family histories, often through the tales and documents passed down to them by their forebears.

Lastly, the support provided over the years by my wife, Amporn, and her now-long-departed parents, Seri Wirarat (Tan Buan-seng) and Loean Binsri, is beyond words. To them I owe a debt of gratitude to which this book stands in humble testimony.

1

Old Bangkok:
An Ethnohistorical Overview

B angkok, the capital of Siam since 1782, served from the outset as the kingdom's ceremonial, administrative, commercial, and demographic centre — a primate city in every sense of the term. In speaking of its "premodern" phase, 1782–1910, covering the first five reigns of the Chakri dynasty, the city is conventionally referred to as Old Bangkok, or more formally, Ratanakosin. Thus, the 129-year time span from 1782 to 1910 may be termed the Ratanakosin period. As Ratanakosin, the city is often visualized as the walled and moated artificial island that still carries its name, but the physical contours of Old Bangkok reached well beyond those confines to incorporate the densely populated urban periphery. From the very outset, the Bangkok conurbation expanded progressively in area and population, attracting a diverse citizenry representing a multiplicity of ethnic communities while expediting Siam's growing prosperity and accelerating modernization. Yet, until the rise of the absolute monarchy and nationalism in the decades crossing into the twentieth century, Old Bangkok retained much of the feudal political and social alignment that had in former centuries characterized the ancestral capital of Ayutthaya. This introductory chapter briefly surveys Old Bangkok's spatial design, political structure, social organization, and ethnic diversity in their historical context as background to the five historical studies of the city's principal ethnic minorities that follow in Chapters 2 to 6, plus the five summary ethnohistories of lesser communities contained in Chapter 7. In fact, the present chapter can be considered to add yet a further ethnohistory in its discussion of the role played by Old Bangkok's Thai ruling elite and Thai commons in the city's nineteenth–twentieth century modernization.

RATANAKOSIN, THE JEWEL OF INDRA

City of Angels, Great Metropolis, Excellent Jewel of Indra [demiurge of the Vedic heavens], Capital of the World, Endowed with the Nine Precious Gems [divine virtues], Happy City Abounding in Great Royal Palaces, Replica of the Celestial City Founded by Indra and Built by Vishvakarman [Indra's architect], City Wherein Dwell Vishnu's Avatars [the Chakri dynasty kings, also associated with such kindred celestial avatars as Rama and Buddha] (Thipakorawong 2009a, p. 75).

Celestial Metaphor

At a grand celebration in mid-1785, culminating three years of painstaking planning, preparation, and construction, the royal city of Bangkok was formally consecrated with the above-cited grandiose, densely metaphorical title. In conformance with the traditional Thai interpretation of the Brahman cosmos (Lithai 1985; Ivarsson 1995), that majestic Sanskrit-based appellation envisaged the Siamese capital as an earthly replica of the supernal city of Sudarsana ("Suthat" in Thai), abode of the thirty-three deities ruled by Indra, lord of the Tavatimsa Heaven ("Dawadoeng Sawan" in Thai), at the summit of the cosmic Mount Meru. Not merely in name but far more substantively in its physical layout, political structure, and social organization, Ratanakosin was designed to evoke Indra's celestial city. Sparse surviving evidence suggests that Bangkok's precursor, Ayutthaya, had early on been laid out along similar lines, only to deviate progressively from its cosmic design as the city evolved over the course of its four centuries' lifetime (1351–1767). Reviving the ancient mystique, the new capital as well as the kingdom over which it presided came to be known as Ratanakosin — "the Jewel of Indra". Even today, with Ratanakosin a quaint reference to bygone days, Bangkok continues to be popularly known as Krung Thep — "the City of Angels". Quite unintentionally but strangely prescient, that subtle shift in emphasis from Indra's magisterial pre-eminence to the ascendancy of a contentious gaggle of lesser deities expresses much of Bangkok's storied history.

Following the tradition firmly established at the ancestral capital of Ayutthaya, the founders of Ratanakosin sought to associate themselves metaphorically with the Brahman deities by exploiting numerous allusions to Mount Meru's supreme habitants: Indra, Vishnu, Rama, and Buddha. As self-professed avatars of those heavenly beings, they retained the customary title of "celestial prince" (*chao fa*). They found it fitting to meld Brahman and Buddhist iconography in their selection of the Emerald Buddha image, set upon its soaring dais suggestive of Mount Meru, as the kingdom's palladium, in large part for its emerald green hue, the color of Indra, bespeaking the fertility of the rice fields, the bounty of Indra's rain-making might. The image of Indra's mount, the celestial elephant Airavata ("Erawan" in Thai), with Indra mounted upon its shoulders, was installed as a featured symbol on many of Bangkok's royal edifices and was in due course adopted as the official emblem of the Bangkok Municipality. Indra's weapon, the lightning bolt (*vajra*, or *wachira* in Thai, iconographically represented as a trident), became a popular motif of Thai royalty and was eventually incorporated in the title and royal regalia of Rama VI (King Wachirawut). In parallel fashion, Vishnu's weapon, the bladed discus (*chakra*, or *chak* in Thai, also associated with the dynasty's founder in his former capacity as minister of civil affairs) was adopted as the Chakri dynasty's crest and continues to be proudly displayed as the privileged emblem of the kingdom's armed forces. And Rama was eventually selected as the personal avatar of the Chakri kings, with episodes from the Ramakien (the Thai version of the Ramayana epic) adorning the mural-clad inner wall of the Chapel Royal (Wat Phra Si Sasadaram, popularly known as Wat Phra Kaew), and his heroic statue today gracing the forecourt of the former Front Palace (the viceroy's stronghold, sited some 200 metres due north of the Grand Palace). Such examples of the ruling elite's affinity for the celestial symbolism embodied in the gods and accouterments of Indra's heaven could be extended endlessly (Wales 1931; Smith 1978).

The interminable associations between Thai sovereignty, Brahman cosmology, and Buddhist ethics served as an essential validation of the Thai elite's rule over the loosely structured, ethnically diverse feudal Siamese kingdom. As the defining mystique surrounding a new and insecure dynasty reigning over a kingdom only recently shattered by war, the celestial imagery penetrated deep into the Ratanakosin psyche. Most elaborate of all those allusions was the physical design of Bangkok itself in the form of a mandala (*monthon* in Thai), simulating the layout of Indra's celestial city (see "The Mandala as Urban Template" in the concluding chapter). As depicted in tapestries, murals, and illustrated manuscripts, the mandala image simplifies the three-dimensionality of Mount Meru onto a two-dimensional topography — in effect an aerial projection of Indra's heaven atop Mount Meru, dividing the celestial city into an octagonal ring of precincts surrounding the pre-eminent ninth precinct, the citadel, at the pinnacle — each precinct identified with a Brahman deity possessing specific auspicious attributes, contributing to the integrity of the whole. That propitiously symmetrical arrangement was applied purposefully in Old Bangkok, a city radiating from the centrally positioned City Pillar (*lak moeang*), surrounded by the royal palaces and temples, encircled in turn by

partitioning water channels and roadways, all surrounded by the city wall
with its sixteen bastions and major gates (eight each for the Grand Palace
and Front Palace zones) and by the City Moat (*khu moeang*) (Naengnoi
1991, pp. 18–25). Overlooking all was the great celebratory monument (*phra
prang*) of Wat Arun, erected in the Second Reign as a visionary rendering
of Mount Meru in glorification of Ratanakosin and its reigning dynasty
(Wat Arun Rachaworaram 1983; Chatri 2013).

Earthly Design

The 1767 relocation of Siam's capital from devastated Ayutthaya to Thonburi,
some sixty kilometres downriver, marked a turning point in Thai history.
The new stronghold, founded in haste to defend a fledgling regime under
threat of imminent attack, soon showed its deficiencies in its constricted
confines, inadequate fortifications, and crumbling shoreline, as well as its
inauspicious asymmetry. The city's cross-river expansion a decade later
to incorporate "East Thonburi" — more than doubling the dimensions of
the whole from 0.9 to 2.2 square kilometres — sought to remedy those
shortcomings, though the cross-river bifurcation contributed to the city's
defensive vulnerability (Map 1.1). Efforts to formalize Thonburi's riparian
unity by adding a moat and wall to the east-side precinct (Amphan 1994)
did little to ease the disquiet. It appears that toward the end of the Thonburi
reign a plan was thus mooted to move the royal redoubt to the east bank.
But realization of that plan had to await the coup of 1782, which brought
to power the Chakri dynasty.

Within the two weeks immediately following the 1782 coup, the decision
to recentre the city from the west bank of the river to the east was confirmed.
The new, enlarged riverine capital — more than redoubling its former area to
4.6 square kilometres — was laid out as a cosmically demarcated stronghold
for the ruling elite, the inner citadel for the aristocracy and the outer
precincts for the nobility, with the commons relegated to the "wilderness"
beyond the walled and moated bounds. The expanded city's basic parameters
were quickly marked out (Map 1.2): the City Pillar was ritually planted at
the riparian site's precise centre; a sizeable Chinese immigrant community
was evicted from the delimited area; the precise positions of the new
royal palaces were determined (Thipakorawong 2009*a*, p. 6). The new city
was laid out to accommodate the southern and northern zones of royal
occupation and authority, demarcated by its latitudinal axis. Under the
dual supervision of the king and viceroy (*uparat*, or heir presumptive), a
workforce was mobilized and construction materials were acquired; the new
city's waterlogged terrain was drained, cleared, levelled, and raised; a new

MAP 1.1
The Thonburi mandala, pre-1782

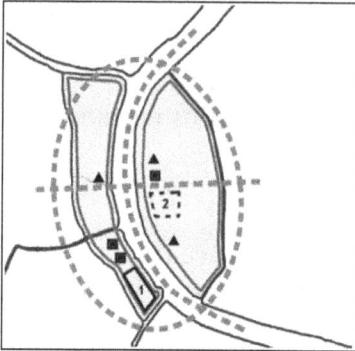

MAP 1.2
The original Bangkok mandala, 1782–85

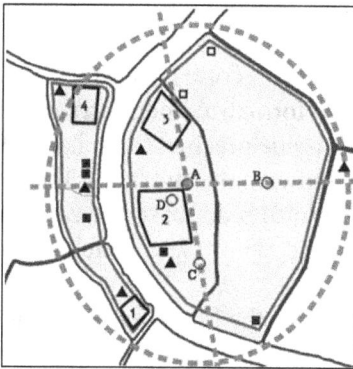

	= Thonburi/Bangkok
	= Bangkok citadel
	= Mandala perimeter, axes
A	= City Pillar
B	= Brahman temple and ritual swing
C	= Spirit shrines
D	= Emerald Buddha image
E	= Royal cremation ground
F	= Sinhalese Buddha image
1	= Thonburi Grand Palace
2	= Bangkok Grand Palace
3	= Front Palace
4	= Rear Palace
■	= King's entourage palaces
□	= Viceroy's entourage palaces
▲	= Major royal temples

MAP 1.3
The revised Bangkok mandala, 1809

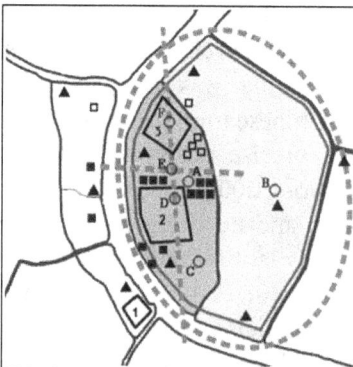

moat was excavated to circle the city; a new city wall was erected; the newly appointed aristocracy's palaces and nobility's mansions were built; and the existing temples were rebuilt to meet royal specifications (Thipakorawong 2009a, pp. 59–60). The thousands of Khmer, Lao, and other war captives conscripted to implement that massive task were assigned settlement sites along the new city's sparsely populated outskirts.

Whereas Bangkok was founded with great fanfare, its subsequent evolution proceeded at a gradual, largely unpublicized pace. Imperceptibly, the political significance of Thonburi as the city's west-bank precinct slipped steadily toward obscurity. After the construction of Thonburi's Rear Palace (residence of the short-lived adjunct viceroy) in 1785, no further palace was built on the west bank over the remainder of the new dynasty's First Reign. In the following years the deaths of several senior royal family members residing along the Thonburi riverfront opened opportunities for the downgrading of their palaces. Particularly telling was the dissolution of the Rear Palace in 1806. That incremental downgrading of the west bank as a royal quarter truncated the original Bangkok design to the 3.7 square kilometres east-bank walled and moated city, eliminating Ratanakosin's cross-river vulnerability and leaving the capital a distinct island — but unaesthetically asymmetrical in its elemental design (Map 1.3).

The citadel's south-north division between the king's and viceroy's zones became increasingly apparent over the course of the First Reign as the sons of the king and viceroy were awarded their own palaces upon their coming of age. (To be sure, there was little outward evidence to distinguish the princes' "palaces" from the nobility's "mansions". The rank and status of their occupants were their essential differentiating characteristic.) Fourteen princely palaces were built between 1785 and the close of the First Reign, ten within the southern zone (for nine of the king's sons and one grandson) and the other four in the northern zone (for the viceroy's four senior sons) (Table 1.3). Accentuating that division was the recentring of the city from the City Pillar (Map 1.2, site A) to the newly instated Royal Cremation Ground (*thung phra men [= meru]*, that Thai term referring to the towering crematory monuments erected there for the funerals of ranking royals) (Map 1.3, site E). That crystallization of the citadel's south-north divide was further confirmed by the pairing of two great royal monasteries, the former — Wat Photaram (later renamed Wat Phra Chetuphon) — standing directly behind the Grand Palace as the king's signature temple and the latter — Wat Mahathat — adjoining the Front Palace under the viceroy's patronage. The parallel association of those royal temples with the Grand Palace and Front Palace was corroborated not only by their position as

TABLE 1.1
Bangkok palaces: Locations over the course of the
first five Chakri reigns, 1782–1910

Reign	Citadel	City (outside the citadel)	Outside (outside the walled city)	Total
First Reign (1782–1809)				
1782–1785				
King's entourage	2	4[a]	–	6
Viceroy's entourage	1	4[a]	–	5
1785–1809				
King's entourage	10	–	–	10
Viceroy's entourage	4	–	–	4
Second Reign (1809–1824)				
King's entourage	10	4	–	14
Viceroy's entourage	–	1	1	2
Third Reign (1824–1851)				
King's entourage	9	9	–	18
Viceroy's entourage	4	7	3	14
Fourth Reign (1851–1868)				
King's entourage	1	–	5	6
Viceroy's entourage	2	4	–	6
Fifth Reign (1868–1910)				
1868–85				
King's entourage	2	14	3	19
Viceroy's entourage	–		1	1
1885–1910				
King's entourage	1	2	19	22
Viceroy's entourage[b]	–	2	5	7
Total	46	51	37	134[c]

Notes: [a] Palaces located in Thonburi and established during the Thonburi period (1767–1782), included in the original Bangkok mandala.
[b] Because of the early deaths of the successive viceroys of the Chakri dynasty, a number of viceroys' sons' palaces were established for them by the respective kings. Thus, seven viceroys' sons' palaces are listed as having been established after 1885, following the death of the last viceroy and abolition of his post.
[c] Not all these palaces survived to 1910.

Sources: Derived from Damrong (1964) and Naengnoi (1991), supplemented by a number of individual princes' commemorative biographies (funeral souvenir volumes).

virtual palace annexes but also by their many elements of internal symbolism associated with the king and viceroy, respectively.

Under the Thai elite's conspicuously polygynous marital norms, the proliferation of princes, each of whom required his own palace upon attaining maturity, intensified space constraints within the citadel over the successive reigns, ultimately leading it to burst its aristocratic bounds. Thus, nineteen out of thirty-two new princely palaces were built outside the citadel in the Third Reign, nine out of twelve in the Fourth Reign, and forty-seven out of forty-eight in the Fifth Reign (Table 1.1). Even with the growing dispersion of palaces and also the establishment of discrete ministry headquarters, however, the city's north-south divide was retained (Maps 1.4 and 1.5). Beyond the declining relevance of the citadel as the aristocratic enclave, the spread of royal residence and ministry headquarters into the noble quarter contributed to the gradual easing of status consciousness that accompanied the opening up of the walled city during the later decades of the nineteenth century. With growing dynastic self-assurance and an increasingly outward-oriented worldview, entry and exit through the city gates was eased for commoners, with the traditional 9 p.m. to 6 a.m. city gate curfew being abolished early in the Fourth Reign. The urban expansion of "metropolitan Bangkok" accelerated in the Fourth and Fifth Reigns with the addition of an outer moat, the Phadung Krung Kasem Canal — again more than doubling the cityscape, to 8.6 square kilometres — and a network of new roadways bounded by rental shophouses and tenements that facilitated the intrusion of commerce and commoners into the walled city. By the 1880s, the emerging Bangkok metropolis including both the west bank and the city's southern riverine extension covered an inexact oval with latitudinal and longitudinal dimensions of some five and ten kilometres, respectively (Thailand, Post and Telegraph Department 1883; Wilson 1989). By the turn of the century, that ovoid urban expanse had come to consist of "a vast agglomeration of villages" some thirty kilometres in circumference (Jottrand 1995, pp. 28, 438; Antonio 1997, pp. 13–30).

Over the course of the Fifth Reign, Old Bangkok's utilitarian, earthly design diverged ever further from its symbolic, celestial template with the substitution of Western imperial grandeur for Eastern cosmic metaphor as the cityscape's defining mystique. The citadel was profoundly reshaped with the decommissioning of the Front Palace, creation of the Great Esplanade (*sanam luang*, a major expansion of the old Cremation Ground), and cut-through of Rachadamnoen Avenue (the King's Promenade) to the new Dusit Palace and its surrounding cluster of princely villas several

MAP 1.4
Bangkok: The king's and viceroy's zones, 1782–1885

A	= Grand Palace
B	= Front Palace
C	= Former Grand Palace
D	= Rear Palace
E	= Wat Phra Chetuphon
F	= Wat Mahathat
G	= Wat Chana Songkhram
H	= Wat Bowon Niwet
I	= Wat Suthat
▦	= Kings' and sons' palaces
☐	= Viceroys' and sons' palaces
▲	= Temples
▦	= Royal Cremation Ground/ Great Esplanade
x	= City Pillar
✱	= Giant Swing
+	= Spirit shrines
- - -	= Main roadways
▱	= City wall
● ● ●	= King's zone/viceroy's zone boundary
○	= Ministry headquarters

1. War
2. Interior
3. Foreign Affairs
4. Finance
5. Capital
6. Agriculture
7. Royal Household
8. Justice
9. Education
10. Public Works

● = Other major government facilities

MAP 1.5
Bangkok: The post-mandala city, 1910

kilometres to the north. Adding to the proliferation of royal residences, various ministries and other government offices were stationed at convenient locations within the walled city, and later without as well, as Western-style public administration replaced the old personalized feudal arrangements. At the same time, Chinese, Western, and Indian business enterprises along with Lao, Malay, Khmer, Vietnamese, and other artisans' and wage workers' neighbourhoods penetrated the Old City in ever-greater numbers. The very idea of Ratanakosin as an elitist stronghold paled with its merger into the greater metropolitan area through the improvement of transport routes, bridging of the City Moat, demolition of the city wall, gates, and bastions, and construction of commoners' housing and marketplaces. The cosmic metaphor of Ratanakosin was thus increasingly attenuated as the greater presence of metropolitan Bangkok gained prominence, until finally, after more than a century of escalating deviation from the celestial archetype, it was laid to rest as obsolete myth. Today, after decades of mounting urban modernization, a newly conceived "Ratanakosin Island conservation movement" seeks quixotically to revive prominent physical features of the nineteenth-century city's royal heritage, introduce new elements to enhance the Old City's imagined historical image, and eliminate non-royal traces considered to be inappropriate intrusions (Chatri 2012, pp. 129–45). After a century-long interval of relentless urban modernization, that anachronistic, misconceived campaign to resurrect as a monarchist monument a selectively refashioned image of the former Ratanakosin cityscape comes as much too little, far too late.

Political Space and Social Place
Simply and cogently stated, "the landscape of Old Bangkok was a visible representation of the structure of society" (Tomosugi 1991, p. 127). As an aerial projection of the Jewel of Indra atop the cosmic cone of Mount Meru, Old Bangkok's political space was a bounded topography of its privileged precincts; correspondingly, its social place was a vertical projection of its people's status hierarchy along the cosmic slopes. Particularly important in the nobility's social positioning for political advantage was their spatial location relative to the king and viceroy, and correspondingly, the commons' location near their noble patrons. The confluence of social status and political rank within the city's physical confines formed "a single architectural-cosmological scheme ... in which territorial and functional aspects ... [were] incidental and derivative" (Tambiah 1976, pp. 141ff). The vision of political space as a symmetrical plane, expressed primarily through centricity and radiation, meshed with the notion of the feudal lord and his retinue of vassals

and servants as a social unit. The first aspect of Bangkok's spatial symmetry concerned the siting of the city's precincts, wards, quarters, and districts in concentric rings of successively lesser status spreading from the city's sacred centre to its profane outskirts. The second aspect was axiality, direction, and orientation, which referred to the positioning of settlements, villages, and neighbourhoods north and south of the city's ritual core, reaching to its most peripheral upstream and downstream extensions.

It has been said, in reference to the graded radiation of premodern Siam's feudal polity from the sacral centre to the secular periphery, that "Siam has always been a hierarchical domain, differentiated not only by class and status, but by ethno-geography as well" (Thongchai 2000a, p. 41). The Bangkok microcosm from the outset conformed to that broad social design. As a miniature likeness of the kingdom, the capital was laid out in a series of concentric zones of habitation radiating from the royal citadel in successively diminishing degrees of eminence: Within, the aristocracy and nobility gathered in the citadel and surrounding walled city. Without, along the urban periphery, the settlements of the lower social strata — freemen, debt bondsmen, war captives, and hereditary slaves of diverse ethnicities. In principle, and to a diminishing degree in practice as time and circumstance eroded the original vision, those valorized inner and outer zones of habitation were reserved for the elite and the commons, respectively. With rare exceptions — those exceptions becoming increasingly less rare as time went by (as later discussion will amplify) — no member of the elite would deign to live without; without special sanction, no commoner household or village would dare settle within.

Complementing the hierarchical radiation of settlements from the sacral centre was their placement above and below the city's lateral axis, running between the king's and viceroy's respective strongholds and thus separating the city's upstream and downstream precincts. Under Siam's feudal institutions, the viceroy maintained a political presence considerably more influential than simply the king's factotum, which was why he was considered virtually the "second sovereign"; he headed an administration which, though of lesser authority than the king's, boasted its own nobility militia, revenue base, and subject population (Englehart 2001, p. 80). Though ranking beneath the king in the formal status hierarchy, he habitually emphasized his equivalent royal spiritual power (*saksit*) and charisma (*barami*) (see the "Thai Yuan" discussion in Chapter 7). He contested often quite blatantly for power (Nidhi 2002), and in so doing, he often exercised virtually independent authority over what he considered his share of the kingdom's peoples and territories. Within Bangkok, his zone of occupation and control lay to the north of the city's lateral axis, while the king's lay to the south. Not only the palaces of his princely sons and the mansions of his noble subordinates but the many commoner settlements occupying the city's northern outskirts lay within his ambit of authority.

The second half of the nineteenth century saw Bangkok's demographic fulcrum slip downstream with the growing presence of the international market economy. The commercially minded, maritime-oriented districts stretching downriver flourished with the establishment of scores of foreign-invested enterprises — rice mills, sawmills, workshops, shipping firms, agency houses — and the accelerated immigration of wage workers to staff those ventures. That buoyant expansion stood in contrast to the economic stagnation of the city's northern, inland-oriented precincts as the viceroy's power, status, and wealth faded. The viceroy's feudal command over his hinterland client communities withered as the traditional redistributive economy gave way to capitalism, as refugee and captive arrivals declined, as Chinese merchants and tax farmers gained control of the inland markets, as state revenues were centralized increasingly in the hands of the king. With the political eclipse of Siam's last viceroy in 1875, followed by his death a decade later, the city's north-south dualism came to an end, and the remaining vestiges of the former viceroy's political authority were appropriated by the now absolute monarch. More than any other single development, that event signalled the formal end of Siam's feudal order and ultimately marked the onset of Old Bangkok's demise.

RULERS AND RULED

Siamese rulers saw their own position as far ahead of, or high above their subjects, those under the shadow of their protection. It is difficult to measure the distance, but the extent of the gap was sufficient to enable the élite to "look back" or "look down"… on their subjects and the marginal minorities, not as They, yet not as We, but perhaps as Theirs (Thongchai 2000b, p. 55).

Much like Old Bangkok's physical design, its political structure and social organization, viewed as an aerial projection of the cosmic social order (Lithai 1985, pp. 494–501), comprised a series of concentric rings of descending power and status spreading from centre (peak) to periphery (base). Beyond Bangkok, the rural hinterlands were inhabited by peasant villages, Thai and non-Thai. Many districts and even entire regions of lesser fertility were settled by ethnic minorities: war captives forcibly carried off to domesticate formerly uninhabitable tracts, refugees from oppression in neighbouring states granted permission to settle marginal lands under a hospitable regime, indigenous tribal groups relegated to servile subsistence in the remote uplands. Minority communities with special qualifications — warriors, artisans, scholars, merchants, administrators — were invited to establish their settlements close to the capital; a few, exceptionally, even within the walled city itself. Within the city wall, the exclusive residential zones of aristocracy and nobility complemented and confirmed the strictly segregated social strata of feudal Siam. The easing of those spatial constraints as the nineteenth century wore on corresponded, in turn, with the gradual liberalization of the kingdom's social hierarchy.

The Ruling Elite

In their self-justified rule over the lower social strata, Old Bangkok's ruling class saw itself as an organic society of unique merit in the cosmic order, a select upper crust imbued with a sense of immutable political authority, social superiority, and moral righteousness. The gap between the Thai ruling elite and the Thai commons was sufficiently wide that the elite verged on a distinct sub-culture. As of the close of the nineteenth century, it has been observed, the Thai ruling elite, "Regarding themselves subjectively as almost a supra-ethnic or supranational cosmopolitan ruling caste, ... lorded it over the Siamese nation-people as colonial masters with a royal Thai face" (Kasian 2001, p. 6, quoted in Harrison and Jackson 2010, p. 14). As in other premodern civilizations both East and West, "the idea that the aristocracy belonged to the same culture as the peasants must have seemed abominable to the former and incomprehensible to the latter" (Eriksen 2010, p. 123). The two social worlds distinguished themselves discernibly in terms of such disparate culture traits as dialect (though collectively Thai), religious conviction and practice (though jointly Theravada Buddhist), gender relations and marriage, sources of income and wealth, diet, dress, and locus and style of habitation. Despite their common ethnicity as "Thai," the social bounds separating elite from commons were strictly observed, and infringements were punished through both judicial sanction and social censure. In sum, the Thai commons (visualized as an ethnic entity in its own right) was dealt with by its masters no differently than the other ethnic constituencies.

The ruling elite comprised the aristocracy (*chaonai*) and nobility (*khunnang*), their heads of household invariably holding titled rank (*yot, bandasak*). Irrespective of personal qualifications, virtually all occupied executive government positions, albeit often no more than pro forma. In theory, the king (abetted by his viceroy) held unfettered power to tax, to conscript labour, to appoint officials, to reward and punish. In practice, however, he had limited ability to govern at a distance. As a second-best option under those circumstances, it was considered advantageous for him to allow his surrogates broad autonomy (Englehart 2001, pp. 13–14, 33). Was the king therefore "an absolute monarch whose every whim was law" or was he "comparatively helpless" in the clutches of his vassals (Englehart 2001, p. 12)? Both views carry an aura of validity: the king may have exercised "absolute control" within the restricted ambit of court and capital, but he was relatively "helpless" in his reliance on his self-interested minions beyond that. That spatial diffusion of authority speaks directly to the kingdom's feudal political structure.

Beyond the king (the *maharat*), the highest office in the land was held by the viceroy (the *uparat*), conventionally the king's younger brother or eldest son. The intimate association between king and viceroy was symbolically validated in the court's preoccupation with the Ramakien (the Thai Ramayana). That intricately plotted, multi-layered tale of ancient statecraft, valour, and chivalry has as one of its essential themes the bond between Rama ("Phra Ram"), prince of Ayodhya (patronymic of Ayutthaya), and his younger brother, Lakshman ("Phra Lak"). Lakshman's loyalty, devotion, obedience, respect, and deference to Rama were virtues historically associated with the Thai viceroy's fealty to his king (Goss 2008), despite the fact that those ideals were repeatedly sacrificed to the ambitions of Siam's colorful series of viceroys. That fraternal, elder-younger royal pairing animated the Thai cultural (spatial, political, social) theme of dualism — higher-lower, inner-outer, right-left, south-north.

It has been conservatively reckoned that the ruling elite at the Thai capital during the decades before the move from Ayutthaya to Thonburi/ Bangkok constituted no more than 2,000 persons out of Siam's total population of perhaps two million (and Ayutthaya's possible 200,000) (Turton 1980, p. 253). Of Bangkok's initial population, it may thus be inferred that about 1,000 (less than 1.5 per cent) constituted the ruling elite as of 1782. That number probably doubled by 1851, and it more than doubled again to reach about 6,000 persons by 1910, reflecting a decline to well below 1 per cent of Bangkok's total inhabitants. (By comparison, no more than 1.7 per cent of China's total population in the late 1800s is said to have belonged to the gentry (Wakeman 1975, p. 22).) The growth of Old Bangkok's ruling elite was slower than that of the capital's overall population growth partly due to the accelerated urban in-migration of commoners (a large share of whom were Chinese) with the easing of feudal constraints on mobility and the city's rising economic opportunities as the nineteenth century wore on, and partly due to the steady rise in upcountry government postings for the nobility as the kingdom's national integration proceeded.

The ruling elite was ethnically Thai by default; entrants of non-Thai ethnicity automatically became "Thai" by virtue of their enhanced status affiliation and were expected to assimilate fully into elite Thai culture, though that expectation was not always wholly fulfilled. Two principal routes of entry into, as well as rise within, the ruling elite presented themselves: for men, advancement through the ranks of the military or civil service to positions of command; for women, marriage (or concubinage). "In essence, [inter-ethnic relations between the elite and commons] centred upon the ... elite's exchange of administrative protection and facility for an income of rents, interest and bribes; it was reinforced by inter-marriage and, ultimately, by ... cultural assimilation" (Brown 1988, p. 172). An old Thai saying had it that "women strive upward, men reach down", referring to the use of women as a medium of exchange in the kindred's struggle for upward social mobility (Loos 2005). Attesting to that social convention are multiple documented cases of Mon, Lao, Khmer, Vietnamese, Cham, Thai Yuan, and Chinese female contributors to the Chakri royal lineage. Even the Chakri dynasty's founders were of mixed Mon-Chinese-Thai ancestry; many of their close collaborators, awarded senior positions in the new regime, were non-Thai; and many of their royal descendants could boast ethnic minority maternal descent. As a result, the ruling elite, traced to its ancestral roots, was actually the kingdom's most ethnically diverse social group (with the possible exception of the Buddhist clergy).

The Commons

The overwhelming preponderance of Siam's population were commoners. Nearly all of those lesser subjects of the crown were subsistence-oriented farmers, whose surplus output was regularly siphoned off to fill the state coffers, support the ruling elite, and sustain the monkhood. However, the commoner presence in Old Bangkok, as at the kingdom's lesser urban centres, constituted a special case, consisting primarily of traders, artisans, military personnel, minor functionaries, and others with specialized skills, as well as staff and servants in the retinues of the ruling elite — all of whom were subjected to relatively lenient rates of taxation and were exempted from corvée service. In particular, the Chinese, Persians, Portuguese, and certain other immigrant-descent groups were technically considered temporary sojourners even after generations of residency and were thus treated as a separate case from the commoner class at large.

Until the abolition of slavery and corvée — a gradual, stepwise process that lasted from 1874 to 1905 — the commons comprised freemen (*phrai*) and slaves (*that* or *kha*), and their dependants, of all ethnicities. (Resident "sojourners" — mainly Chinese, Indian, and Westerners — formed a separate category.) Freemen were divided into two categories: *phrai luang*, serving the king; and *phrai som*, awarded to individual princes or nobles. That division was not as straightforward as it appears: "The varieties [of freemen] were often mutually overlapping and sometimes contradictory.... The categories were ad hoc, locally defined, and coined for administrative convenience" (Englehart 2001, p. 111). Though nominally free, the king's men were bound in periodic service (*rachakan*, commonly translated as corvée) to government departments (*krom*) under the direction of the senior nobility and their provincial subalterns (*nai*) (Akin 1975, p. 105). Those bound to princes or nobles were generally subjected to relatively lenient treatment, making for much slippage between categories. To cope with that issue, a comprehensive procedure of manpower registration, tattooing, and direct oversight was exerted over the king's men, and the individual princes' and nobles' men may in many cases have been similarly controlled. The agrarian commons was thus not far removed from serfdom, leaving reference to *phrai* as "freemen" something of a misnomer (Khachon 1976; Chatchai 1988).

Even more serf-like were the various forms of slavery, which ranged from debt bondsmen and war captives, both technically redeemable (though rarely possessing the resources to purchase their freedom), to non-redeemable slaves (Cruikshank 1975; Turton 1980; Chatchai 1982). Obtained through capture in war or through abduction, purchase, indebtedness, birth, or other means, slaves — Thai as well as other ethnicities — formed a far greater portion of the kingdom's population, and particularly its urban population, than is ordinarily recognized. While the permanent, irredeemable enslavement of war captives (many of them Khmer, Lao, Mon, and Malay) and abducted outlanders (primarily tribals from the frontier uplands) had been a principal source of manpower acquisition in earlier centuries, the preponderance of slaves during the Ratanakosin period appear to have been debt slaves (a status akin to indenture), most of them destitute Thai peasants. "Figures for the proportion of the population with the status of [slaves] are either non-existent or disputed for every period of Thai history. Even approximate orders of magnitude ... are difficult to assess, let alone the proportions of different types [or ethnicities] of slave" (Turton 1980, p. 274). Yet, it has been conservatively conjectured that in the mid-nineteenth century around a quarter of the kingdom's population were slaves, while perhaps nine-tenths of Bangkok's non-Chinese population were slaves (Turton 1980, p. 275).

The position of slaves was generally inferior to that of freemen. By and large, calls on their labour services were more frequent and onerous; rates of in-kind revenue extraction were higher; security of productive land tenure was lower; freedom of movement was more tightly restricted; access to patronage was less readily available and less benevolent. In short, they were generally condemned to a lower standard of living. In addition to their toil as agricultural workers on the royal lands and the private estates of the ruling elite, as conscript labour in the construction and maintenance of pubic works and in military service, and as craftsmen in personal service to their patrons, a privileged minority of slaves were household servants and personal attendants to the ruling elite, forming the major part of many titled officials' retinues at public events. War captives as well as frontier villagers "swept up" (*kwat*) in the course of slave-raiding forays fell under the direct control of the king and viceroy; many groups of those captives were in turn deployed to senior royals and favoured nobles for use on their own estates. And so, a number of captive ethnic minority settlements came to be scattered along the Bangkok periphery. An 1805 decree incorporated war captives into the total mass of redeemable slaves, but there is no evidence that any of those unfortunates ever resorted to (or were able to avail themselves of) that means of regaining their freedom over the subsequent generations.

Throughout Siam, ethnic minorities formed a major part of the commons. They comprised five social categories: refugees from oppression in neighbouring states, war captives from armed conflicts with nearby kingdoms, tribals abducted from the frontier uplands by raiding parties, destitute immigrant labourers from foreign ports, and economic adventurers from near and far. Tribal captives were relegated to the bottom rung of the social pyramid as hereditary slaves; war prisoners were accorded a higher standing within the slave category with the prospect of eventual release to freeman status; and refugees were provided a standing equivalent to, but not within, the Thai freeman population. Both economic adventurers and wage workers from overseas, finally, were held at arms-length, even if resident over several generations. At Bangkok, as throughout the kingdom, that status hierarchy was associated with residential location, with the general pattern of settlement radiating from the city in accordance with declining social standing.

Masters-Minions, Patrons-Clients

Under Siam's feudal regime, the social hierarchy coalesced around a continuing flow of goods and services passing between superiors (*phu yai*, or *nai*) and inferiors (*phu noi*, or *phrai*) — primarily goods and labour flowing upward, protection and privilege down (Akin 1975, pp. 108–13, Akin 1996, pp. 96–114; see also "Feudalism in Comparative Perspective" in the concluding chapter). Those superior-inferior, master-minion ties were embedded in a formal administrative apparatus joining designated officials and their charges in a "relationship [that superficially] resembled that between a medieval lord and his serfs" (Englehart 2001, p. 36). The hierarchy of formal links for each ministry or department (*krom*) ran sequentially from the many villages under its authority up the administrative ladder through village headmen, district chiefs, and provincial functionaries to the central authorities. At each succeeding level, each official had under his supervision a cohort of subordinates who were bound to do his bidding. Whether that mechanism was essentially benevolent or coercive probably differed greatly from case to case and in any event cannot be determined from the scattered anecdotal evidence. Certainly, it was often oppressive, tension-filled, and fragile. However, a persistent impulse runs through Thai historical writings stressing the benevolence of superiors to their inferiors. That is nowhere better expressed than in the standard euphemistic translation of "*nai-phrai*" (superior-inferior, or master-minion) as "patron-client". The dynastic apologists and many later historians defended the system by spinning a fantasy of the happy peasant, the grateful servant, the satisfied slave. Alternative appraisals (e.g., Somsamai 1987; Chaiyan 1994; Chatthip 1999) have been slow in emerging and have generally not been well received.

As formally instituted, hierarchical relations under the *nai-phrai* system were prescribed from the top down, leaving few options open to the *phrai* to negotiate their obligations, change their place in the system, or escape it entirely. Under that arrangement the minority communities, dealing with their masters (*nai*) across ethnic boundaries, stood at a particular disadvantage. Supplementary to the formal *nai-phrai* system, however, was a parallel network of informal, socially embedded patron-client relations, a system featuring interpersonal bonds built on close association and mutual consent (Akin 1975, pp. 114–16). "Unlike feudal relations of lord to vassal [the link] between patron and client is voluntary and may be terminated unilaterally by either party" (Hanks 1975, p. 199). The informal patron-client system, based on universal social principles of reciprocity, mutuality, and trust, mitigated the authoritarian, coercive, oppressive inclination of the formal *nai-phrai* system. It is only after the unravelling of the feudal "social contract" between rulers and ruled in the closing decades of the Ratanakosin period that informal patron-client relations rose to dominance as a social institution. In hindsight, students of Thai social history have sown much confusion through their unwarranted conflation of the two systems, one formal, the other informal; one centrist, the other localized; one administrative, the other communal; one authoritarian, the other consensual.

The informal patron-client system was, and continues to be, built on "connections" (*sen*). It was initially nurtured by the inadequacies of the formal *nai-phrai* system in meeting the commons' basic needs. Its chains of informal social links, coalescing into entourages, alliances, factions, and "circles of affiliation" within which benevolence and self-interest merge seamlessly, remain a pervasive presence in Thai social and political life (Hanks 1975, pp. 200–207). Major patrons in local patron-client networks today continue to include such community leaders as village headmen, landowners, employers, moneylenders, temple abbots, and village toughs and political bosses (*nakleng, chao pho, tua hia*, etc.) (Akin 1978). Not well attuned or sympathetic to the impersonal efficiencies of the market system, Thai society continues to rely on such socially embedded relations in daily life as a conventional means of smoothing business transactions, gaining political favour, ensuring preferential treatment, claiming protection, and the like, a lingering vestige of an earlier era.

Ethnic Minorities

There [on Bangkok's rickety trams] will be found sitting together yellow robed Siamese monks, long bearded Arabs, sarong clad Malays, voluble Chinese ..., dark-skinned Tamils, Burmese, Mon, the panung-clad Thai and members of a host of other races [including the occasional starched-shirted, ruddy-faced, heavily sweating European gentleman] (Seidenfaden 1927, p. 35).

Bangkok's vibrant multi-ethnic street scene in the early twentieth century was not simply the exotic sideshow of harmonious coexistence that the abovementioned imaginative rendering of the port-city's comings and goings seeks to convey, but lay at the very heart of the city's social and political dynamics. The ethnic diversity infusing the capital's everyday existence enlivened the evolving synergy between indigenous Siam and the encroaching cosmopolitan world well into the era of the nation-state, but the Thai effort to accommodate the West was not its essential driving force. It has been suggested that "alongside the colonial enterprise, the

Siamese rulers had an equivalent project of their own, concerning their own subjects, a project which reaffirmed their superiority, hence justifying their rule…. It was a project on the 'Others Within' " (Thongchai 2000*a*, p. 41). In fact, Siam's policy toward ethnic pluralism, on open display in Bangkok, differed from the coercive Western colonial model in its benign impact on the ethnic minorities (see "The Port-City's Plural Society" in the concluding chapter). Unlike the Western colonial establishment, the Thai ruling elite over the course of the first five Chakri reigns pursued a strategy of indirect rule over Bangkok's ethnic minorities, a feudal practice that did not systematically intrude upon or discriminate among the respective ethnic communities and thus had far fewer and far less disruptive implications for the capital's minorities than was the case in the neighbouring Western-ruled colonies. Some of the vital aspects of that policy frame and its urban implications are examined below.

Some Demographics
Who were Siam's and Bangkok's ethnic minorities, and how prominent a place did they occupy in the kingdom and its capital? The norm of population estimates from late eighteenth to mid-nineteenth century Siam — at that time a loosely defined amalgam of central state, provincial hinterlands, and peripheral dependencies — rose from about three million to some six million inhabitants (Sternstein 1984, p. 45, fig. 1; Grabowsky 1996, p. 75). Within that rising total, the many non-Thai ethnic groups settled in central Siam may well have collectively equalled, or possibly even exceeded, the number of self-styled Thai (Lieberman 2003, vol. 1, p. 319). Broadly speaking, the ethnically Thai peasantry was concentrated in the highly productive wet-rice floodplain of the lower Chaophraya River basin, while Chinese merchant communities were concentrated in the market centres. Large elements of the other major ethnic minorities were settled along the lower-yielding periphery of the kingdom's agrarian heartland. In the kingdom's outer regions — the north, northeast, south, and southeast, as well as the western highlands — non-Thai ethnic groups significantly exceeded the Thai. Thus, within the kingdom as a whole, only a plurality of the population consisted of ethnic Thai. To gain an impression of the kingdom's changing ethnic composition over the course of the Ratanakosin period it is useful to review the sequence of contemporary population estimates (Table 1.2). Those estimates are highly variable, but the overall trend shows a fairly steady rate of increase from less than three million as of 1782 to a benchmark figure of eight million

TABLE 1.2
Population of Siam, by ethnic group, 1822–1904
(contemporary estimates, in thousands)

Year	Source	Thai	Lao	Chinese	Malay	Khmer	Mon	Karen	Other	Total
1822	Crawfurd	4,200	...	700	15	50	42	...	...	5,007
1835	Roberts	1,600	1,200	500	320	...	...	...	...	3,620
1839	Malcolm	1,500	800	450	195	...	...	...	...	2,945
1854	Pallegoix	1,900	1,000	1,500	1,000	500	50	50	...	6,000
1864	Mouhot	2,000	1,000	1,500	1,000	350	50	...	...	5,900
1885a	de Rosny	1,600	1,000	1,500	1,000	600	40	160	...	5,900
1885b	de Rosny	3,500	1,000	1,520	1,200	620	40	35	...	7,915
1890	Rautier	3,000	1,300	3,000	1,000	1,000	...	400	...	9,700
1899	v. Hesse-	3,000	1,500	3,000	1,000	1,000	...	500	...	10,000
1901	Aymonier	3,000	1,000	2,000	1,000	800	100	100	...	8,000
1903	Little	1,700	2,000	700	600	...	...	...	...	5,000
1904	Lunet ...	1,766	1,354	523	753	490	130	130	51	5,197

Source: Grabowsky 1996, p. 75 (source citations listed in Grabowsky 1996, pp. 84–85).

for 1910 (Sternstein 1984, p. 45, Fig. 1), with the ethnic Thai component slipping, percentage-wise, from about half the total to around a third over that thirteen-decade time frame.

As a microcosm of the Siamese kingdom, Old Bangkok could well be described as a city dominated by non-Thai ethnic minorities, ruled by a tiny Thai ruling class. The city's colourful reputation rested heavily on its diverse assortment of Chinese, Mon, Lao, Khmer, Malay, Cham, South and West Asian, Vietnamese, Burmese, and indigenized Portuguese communities, plus a sprinkling of Western expatriate newcomers. (Chapters 2 through 7 provide individual ethnohistories of a number of those Old Bangkok ethnic minorities.) The Chinese, by far the largest of those minorities, were themselves composed of five cultural sub-species: Taechiu, Hokkien, Hakka, Hainanese, and Cantonese. The small Western community could similarly be divided among its oft-contentious ethno-national constituencies, led by the British, French, Germans, and Americans. Less well defined was a category termed "*khaek*", consisting mainly of South, West, and Southeast Asian Muslims (though the term *khaek* was extended "racially" to include, indiscriminately, South Asian Hindus, Buddhists, Sikhs, and Christians). Despite their shared religion, Bangkok's nineteenth-century Muslims were of diverse language, sect, custom, and origin, ranging from Arab, Persian, and Indian traders to Malay and Cham war captives and more recently arrived bonded labour from the troubled colonial empires of British India and the Netherlands Indies. Similar complexities governed the classification of other ethnic constituencies. What is clear is that Bangkok's various ethnic minorities did not interact easily; they coexisted in the port-city severally as discrete client communities under the patronage of the Thai ruling elite, each being allowed internal administrative autonomy in return for guarantees of political tranquility and economic cooperation. Old Bangkok was thus very much a plural society.

Within Bangkok, as for Siam as a whole, the ethnic minorities collectively far outnumbered the ethnic Thai. Contemporary estimates of the capital's population vary widely, due in large part to observers' widely differing conceptions of the territorial extent of the Bangkok conurbation (as distinct from Ratanakosin, the walled and moated inner city); a comprehensive review of fifty-nine contemporary estimates of "built-up" Bangkok's 1780–1900 population rises from 75,000 to 800,000 (Sternstein 1984, pp. 43–45, ft. 4). Those figures suggest a remarkable more-than-doubling in Bangkok's share of the kingdom's population over the course of the Ratanakosin period. As late as 1908, however, it could still be reliably reported that "no satisfactory official census has yet been taken in Bangkok, and it is difficult to estimate, even approximately, what the population may be" (Wright and Breakspeare 1908, p. 248). Despite those cautionary words, it is possible to hazard some broad estimates of Old Bangkok's evolving population and ethnic composition. (The estimates provided here refer to the built-up, relatively densely populated urban-village area of Bangkok-Thonburi, covering both sides of the river.) Tables 1.3, 1.4, and 1.5 present such estimates for the start, midpoint, and close of the Ratanakosin period. However, be warned! In the absence of firm census or survey data, those figures are no more than best-fit approximations. Their rounding to thousands or higher orders of magnitude is meant to suggest as much; such rounding also avoids the spurious accuracy intimated by the common practice of presenting patently inexact figures down to the single digit.

Development Phases
Irrespective of the uncertainties clouding the evolving magnitude and composition of Old Bangkok's multi-ethnic population, it is evident that the city's many minority communities constituted a lively panoply of individual villages (*ban, bang*), settlements (*nikhom*), communes (*tambon*), neighbourhoods (*chumchon*), and districts (*yan*). Together, in the shadow of the city's many palaces, mansions, temples, and marketplaces, and later its proliferating numbers of shophouses, government offices, and entertainment locales, they set the tone and character of Bangkok's social and economic life. Bangkok's urban agglomeration grew throughout the Ratanakosin period as a dispersion of ethnic clusters radiating outward from the royal citadel, strung north-south along the river and east-west along its major side-channels and feeder canals, and later along its growing grid of carriageways. Maps 1.6, 1.7, and 1.8 identify the evolving distribution of those minority settlements over three successive phases: (a) the recovery from Ayutthaya's destruction during the brief Thonburi period (1767–1782); (b) Bangkok's establishment and expansion over the first three Chakri reigns (1782–1851); and (c) the capital's accelerated growth and incipient modernization through the fourth and fifth Chakri reigns (1851–1910). Though an oversimplification, it may be said for heuristic purposes that in their ethnic make-up the first phase was marked by Ayutthaya refugees, the second was identified with war captives, and the third was characterized by economic adventurers and wage workers.

The first phase (1767–1782), spurred initially by an inflow of Ayutthaya refugees of diverse ethnicity (Map 1.6), saw the start of a sustained revival of the Siamese kingdom. A scattering of Mon, South Asian, indigenized Portuguese, and Hokkien Chinese settlements had since the late Ayutthaya

TABLE 1.3
Bangkok population: Major ethnic constituencies, 1782, 1851, 1910
(approximations)

Major ethnic constituencies	1782	%	1851	%	1910	%
Thai	20,000	26.7	75,000	25.0	240,000	30.0
Chinese	25,000	33.3	150,000	50.0	400,000	50.0
Other	30,000	40.0	75,000	35.0	160,000	20.0
Totals	75,000	100.0	300,000	100.0	800,000	100.0

Sources: Author's approximations, based on Skinner (1957); Sternstein (1982); Sternstein (1984); and the various other sources cited in Chapters 2–7.

TABLE 1.4
Bangkok population: Chinese speech groups, 1782, 1851, 1910 (approximations)

Chinese speech groups	1782	%	1851	%	1910	%
Taechiu	15,000	60.0	110,000	73.3	240,000	60.0
Hokkien	8,000	32.0	20,000	13.3	60,000	15.0
Hakka	...	...	8,000	5.3	40,000	10.0
Hainanese	...	...	8,000	5.3	40,000	10.0
Cantonese	2,000	8.0	4,000	2.7	20,000	5.0
Total Chinese	25,000	100.0	150,000	100.0	400,000	100.0

Sources: Author's approximations, based on Skinner (1957) and the other sources cited in Chapter 6.

TABLE 1.5
Bangkok population: Non-Chinese ethnic minorities, 1782, 1851, 1910
(approximations)

Ethnic minorities	1782	%	1851	%	1910	%
Mon	8,000	26.7	15,000	20.0	30,000	18.7
Lao	6,000	20.0	18,000	24.0	30,000	18.7
Malay	5,000	16.7	15,000	20.0	32,000	20.0
Cham	3,000	10.0	8,000	10.7	12,000	7.5
Persian	3,000	10.0	4,000	5.3	8,000	5.0
Arab	1,000	3.3	2,000	2.7	3,000	1.9
Indian	...	...	3,000	4.0	15,000	9.4
Indonesian	...	...	1,000	1.3	5,000	3.1
Portuguese	2,000	6.7	3,000	4.0	6,000	3.8
Khmer	2,000	6.7	6,000	8.0	10,000	6.3
Vietnamese	...	...	...	...	7,000	4.4
Westerners	...	...	...	...	2,000	1.3
Totals	30,000	100.0	75,000	100.0	160,000	100.0

Sources: Author's approximations, based on Tomlin (1831); Crawfurd (1967); Pallegoix (2000); and the various other sources cited in Chapters 2–7.

MAP 1.6
Thonburi: Notable ethnic minority settlements, 1767–1782

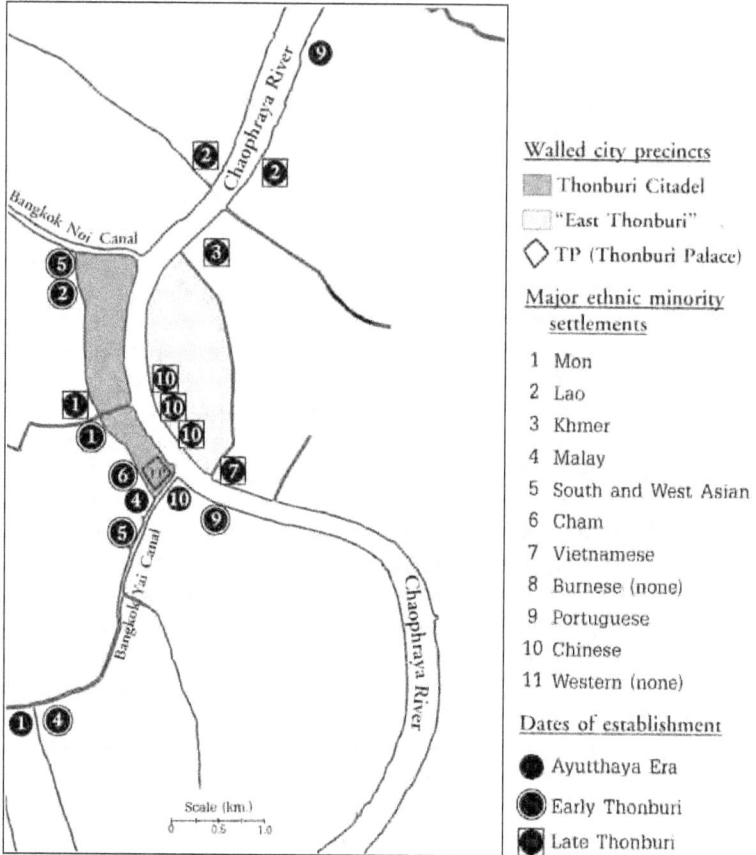

Walled city precincts

░ Thonburi Citadel

☐ "East Thonburi"

◇ TP (Thonburi Palace)

Major ethnic minority
   settlements

1 Mon
2 Lao
3 Khmer
4 Malay
5 South and West Asian
6 Cham
7 Vietnamese
8 Burmese (none)
9 Portuguese
10 Chinese
11 Western (none)

Dates of establishment

● Ayutthaya Era

◉ Early Thonburi

◉ Late Thonburi

era dappled the banks of the lower Chaophraya River and its offshoot Bangkok Yai Canal in the vicinity of the Thonburi fort and customs post (later rebuilt as the Thonburi Grand Palace). In the months and years immediately following the 1767 fall of Ayutthaya, a straggle of new communities arrived at Thonburi in response to King Taksin's efforts to populate his stronghold with the surviving remnants of Ayutthaya's population. The Thonburi citadel was quickly filled with the residential compounds of the old Thai elite who had managed to survive the slaughter, avoid Burmese captivity, and return from their hinterlands dispersal. The early years of Taksin's reign also witnessed the establishment of a ring of Mon, Malay, Persian, Arab, Cham, Lao, Portuguese, and Chinese refugee

MAP 1.7
Bangkok: Notable ethnic minority settlements, 1782–1851

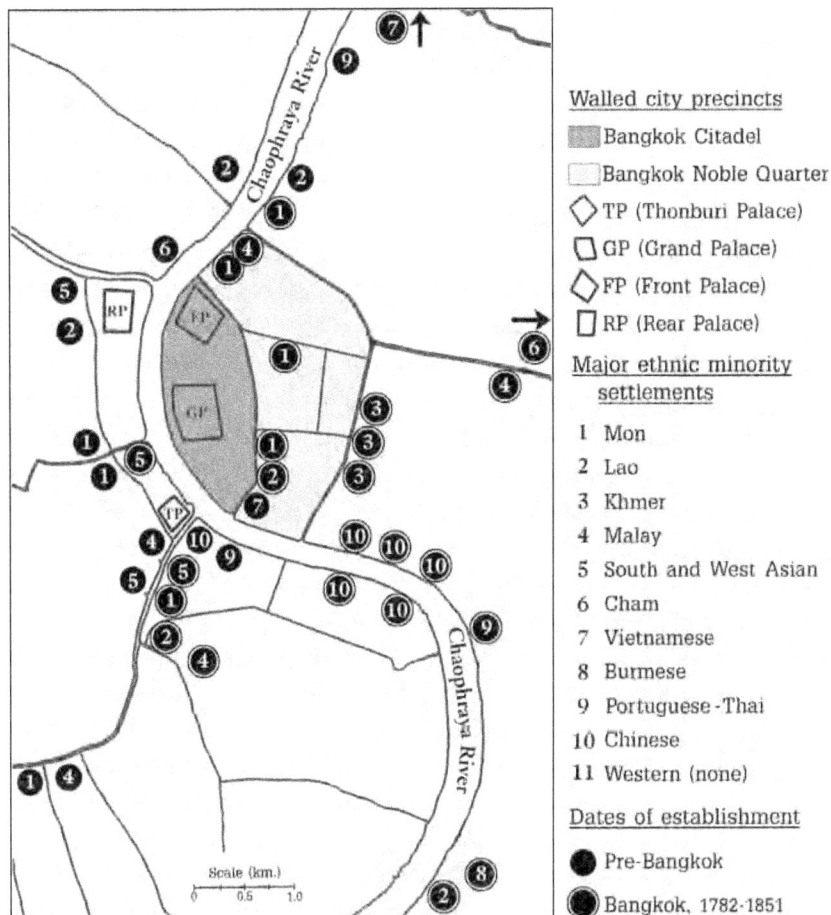

Walled city precincts

▓ Bangkok Citadel

☐ Bangkok Noble Quarter

◇ TP (Thonburi Palace)

◖ GP (Grand Palace)

◇ FP (Front Palace)

☐ RP (Rear Palace)

Major ethnic minority
  settlements

1 Mon
2 Lao
3 Khmer
4 Malay
5 South and West Asian
6 Cham
7 Vietnamese
8 Burmese
9 Portuguese-Thai
10 Chinese
11 Western (none)

Dates of establishment

● Pre-Bangkok

● Bangkok, 1782-1851

settlements along the outer edge of the Thonburi citadel. Over the ensuing years, Taksin's continuing policy of strengthening Thonburi's military and mercantile position turned to the gathering of immigrants from further afield. A substantial number of Chinese settlers were recruited from Siam's eastern seaboard provinces and from Taksin's ancestral Taechiu homeland; they were provided a privileged residential tract directly across the river from the Thonburi citadel. Additional convoys of fugitives from civil war in southern Vietnam were afforded sanctuary at a site directly downstream. In the closing years of the reign, arriving contingents of Khmer and Lao

MAP 1.8
Bangkok: Notable ethnic minority settlements, 1851–1910

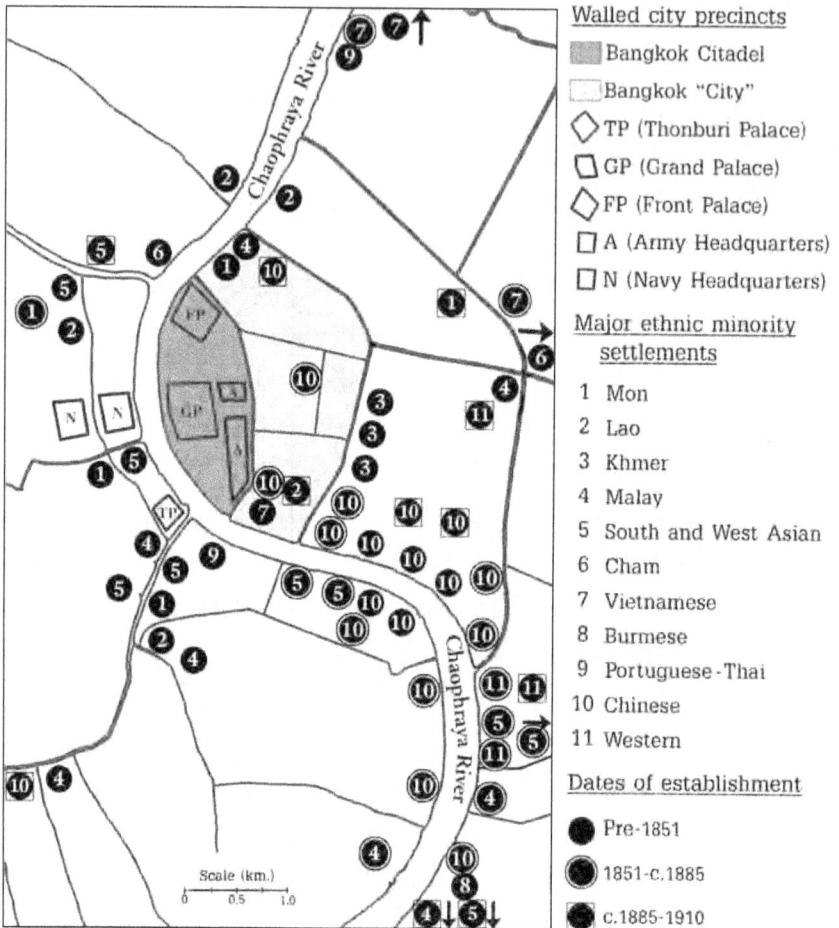

Walled city precincts

▨ Bangkok Citadel

▢ Bangkok "City"

◇ TP (Thonburi Palace)

◻ GP (Grand Palace)

◇ FP (Front Palace)

◻ A (Army Headquarters)

◻ N (Navy Headquarters)

Major ethnic minority
  settlements

1 Mon
2 Lao
3 Khmer
4 Malay
5 South and West Asian
6 Cham
7 Vietnamese
8 Burmese
9 Portuguese - Thai
10 Chinese
11 Western

Dates of establishment

● Pre-1851

◕ 1851-c.1885

◑ c.1885-1910

war captives were provided settlement sites directly cross-river and upriver from the Thonburi citadel. By the close of the Thonburi reign, the capital boasted perhaps 75,000 inhabitants, containing elements of over twelve ethnic minorities.

Over the course of the second phase (1782–1851), after the capital's cross-river relocation and territorial extension, the number of minority settlements scattered about the Bangkok periphery grew rapidly (Map 1.7). Immediately after the 1782 decision to move the citadel to the east bank, the Chinese settlement occupying that precinct was evicted, to be re-established several kilometres downstream along the Sampheng waterfront. That new downriver Chinese presence quickly coalesced into Bangkok's main commercial anchorage and bazaar. In addition, soon after the new capital's founding, the residential compounds of several ranking Mon and Malay leaders and the associated dwellings of their entourages were established within the city's noble precincts. On the other hand, with the departure of the Cambodian refugee elite settlement formerly situated within the city wall back to their homeland, the associated Khmer commoner village was relocated to a less eminent site without. Growth of the established Mon, Indian, Persian, Cham, Portuguese, and Chinese communities prompted the hiving off of a number of settlements toward the urban fringe. In addition, a cordon of new settlements of freshly arrived Lao, Malay, and Cham war captives materialized along the urban outskirts during the first and second Chakri reigns. The process of relocating war captives to Siam's agrarian hinterlands, and their leaderships to the Bangkok outskirts, culminated during the Third Reign. First, the Lao war (the so-called Chao Anu Rebellion) of 1827–1828; second, the extended Vietnamese/Cambodian conflict of 1831–1845; and third, the Patani campaigns of 1832 and 1838 gained Siam a multitude of Lao, Khmer, Cham, Vietnamese, and Malay war captives, with contingents of their elites and leading artisans being diverted to the Bangkok periphery.

Throughout the third phase (1851–1910), the city's ethnic diversity evolved along liberalized lines and at an accelerated pace (Map 1.8). Siam's negotiation in 1855 of a Treaty of Friendship and Commerce with Great Britain (the Bowring Treaty), followed by a series of virtually identical treaties with other Western powers, opened Bangkok to free trade and extraterritorial privileges for resident Western nationals and their Asian subjects. Although the privileged position of the Chinese merchants who had formerly handled the royal monopoly trade was thereby destroyed, the anticipated decline in the China trade did not occur. Instead, Chinese participation in Bangkok's export economy continued to expand, in tandem with the Western commercial incursion. With the trade boom, the city's cosmopolitan population increased rapidly, along with the formation of new Chinese, South Asian, and Western "sojourner" neighbourhoods, inhabited predominantly by hardworking, savings-focused, self-employed, ethnically differentiated entrepreneurs. At the same time, the hardening of Siam's land borders in the face of encroaching Western imperialism ended the influx of refugees, war captives, and abducted slaves from adjacent states and the peripheral uplands, strangling the cultural vigour of Bangkok's Lao, Khmer, and other inland-oriented settlements. The changing demographic balance between hinterlands manpower sources and market-oriented overseas immigrants caused the weight of Bangkok's non-Thai population to drift downriver. Furthermore, with the relaxation of residential constraints and upgrading of the urban infrastructure, the walled city's noble precincts — now generally referred to by the Western community as the "City" — were invaded by bourgeois neighbourhoods of Chinese, South Asian, and Western shopkeepers, artisans, and professionals. Through all that, however, the Bangkok citadel remained a Thai royal ceremonial centre and residential enclave until the closing decades of the Fifth Reign and continued even thereafter to resist non-aristocratic intrusion.

The Politics of Diversity

"Not only was [the] profusion of ethnicities not a problem in the old system, kings positively gloried in it" (Englehart 2001, p. 50). Bangkok's ethnic diversity advertised the kingdom's vitality. It spoke to the ruling elite's success in resolving the traditional manpower problem. Locating the leadership of Siam's various ethnic minorities at the centre of power, furthermore, facilitated the rulers' control and patronage of the minorities while providing for their self-representation and the effective negotiation of their concerns.

For purposes of administrative expediency, the Siamese feudal state customarily allowed its respective ethnic minorities a high degree of internal autonomy, or self-governance (though — with some exceptions, particularly the "sojourner" communities — they were not thereby absolved of their contributions to the state's periodic tax or corvée levies). That political strategy, strikingly evident in Old Bangkok, links with the broader proposition that "Bangkok's political structure was 'segmentary' rather than functionally differentiated and organically unified" (Chaiyan 1994, pp. 4–5). It bespoke the rulers' purposeful "benign neglect" of their minority communities, a policy that persisted until the major government reforms of the 1890s. Under premodern Siam's feudal policy of indirect rule, the minority communities were allowed to govern their internal affairs under the administration of their own leaders, who were in affirmation thereof awarded senior positions in the nobility — typically at the rank of *phraya*, roughly equivalent to army colonel, departmental director-general, or provincial governor. Those officials represented their constituencies at court, dealing directly with the state ministers on behalf of their ethnic communities both within the capital and far beyond, extending to the kingdom's very frontiers. For instance, Chaophraya Mahayotha, head of Siam's Mon community, served as intermediary for the many Mon settlements of the

Meklong River basin and the Kanchanaburi upland districts reaching to the Burmese border; the Vientiane princes residing along Bangkok's Bang Yi-khan riverfront represented the Lao population centre at Saraburi and the many Lao-peopled districts scattered across the Siamese northeast; Phraya Chula Rachamontri, head of the Persian community, served as putative interlocutor for the various Muslim minorities concentrated at Bangkok and its hinterlands as well as Siam's deep south; and Phraya Chodoek Rachasethi held responsibility for the Chinese-populated districts at Bangkok and also served as liaison with other Chinese population centres throughout the kingdom. Under that arrangement, the respective ethnic group leaders were responsible for maintaining their communities' internal law and order as well as ensuring their compliance with tax impositions in addition to periodic manpower levies for military campaigns, public works projects, state ceremonies, and the like. Many of their daughters were married off into the highest echelons of the ruling elite, ensuring the political integration of their kindreds, and more broadly their ethnic constituencies, into the Siamese state.

Bangkok's minority communities were assigned settlement sites near to or distant from the city centre not so much in keeping with ethnic considerations per se as in correspondence with their political ranking, social status, and occupational skills. First, a ring of leading refugee settlements (Mon, Portuguese, Cham, Persian, Vietnamese, and Hokkien) occupied preferred sites directly adjacent to the Thonburi and Bangkok citadels. Second, ranking settlements of war captives (Lao, Khmer, Malay, and Cham) were situated along the outer periphery of the Thonburi and Bangkok city precincts. Third, a string of "sojourner" settlements (Chinese, South Asian, and Western) stretched along the river well downstream from the walled city. And lastly, small settlements of hereditary slaves (Karen, Khmu, and other nondescript "tribals") were relegated to the more distant hinterlands, though small groups were assigned to menial service in individual elite households and some of the city's royal temples.

That concentric pattern of ethnic dispersion along the Bangkok periphery was closely paralleled by the dispersal of occupational specializations. In its original conception, Thonburi had been intended specifically to function as a military strongpoint, and early Bangkok continued that emphasis. The river, moats, walls, bastions, and surrounding armed camps all combined to serve as defensive works for the royal redoubt (Naengnoi 1991, pp. 18–25). Surrounding the growing citadel, ethnic minority militias were assigned to serve as the backbone of Bangkok's defences: Mon gunners and marines were assigned to the fortifications downstream from the capital, and Mon land forces upstream; the Portuguese and Vietnamese provided artillery battalions; the Cham manned the freshwater navy; Lao, Khmer, and Malay contingents contributed musketry, sapper, elephantry, and other specialized combat units. Thai infantry cohorts, supported by foot soldiers drawn from other ethnic constituencies comprising the bulk of the army, were conscripted from peasant villages scattered far and wide about the Siamese countryside (Battye 1974, pp. 1–63; Snit and Breazeale 1988, pp. 125–26). The loyalty of that military assemblage in warfare was ensured by the dependants left behind in their villages.

As artisans, Bangkok's ethnic minority communities ensured their economic viability by differentiating their occupational skills and products. The Mon were known for brick- and pottery-making; the Khmer were adept at producing ritual paraphernalia such as monks' alms bowls and funerary fireworks, as well as dance masks, costumes, and musical instruments for pubic entertainments in which they performed; the Lao were master boat-builders and woodworkers; the Cham were expert silk weavers; the Portuguese served the crown as gunsmiths, ships' chandlers, compradors, and interpreters; the Vietnamese were talented in the decorative arts of stained-glass, niello, mother-of-pearl, and lacquerware; some of the Malays were skilled as boatmen and pilots, and others as gold and silver jewellers. Many of those craftsmen had been brought to Bangkok in the first place specifically to serve in the Royal Artisans Department (*krom chang sip mu*) (Phromphong 2004).

Trade and maritime transport, supported by a broad range of mercantile services, were the traditional specialties of the Chinese and South Asian communities. Over the course of the early Chakri reigns and culminating in the Fourth Reign their mercantile influence spread inexorably beyond the city wall to the riparian districts of Sampheng, Khlong San, and Bang Rak. Later they were joined by an assortment of Western firms reaching downstream to the Yan Nawa and Bang Ko Laem districts. The shoreline downstream from the city came to be pockmarked initially with their lime kilns and then with their rice mills, sawmills, dockyards, and warehouses.

Lastly, along the outermost urban periphery, the ethnic minorities cleared tracts for market gardens, fruit orchards, piggeries and poultry runs, livestock pasturelands, freshwater fisheries, and charcoal smoulderies to satisfy the city dwellers' daily demand for fresh produce and cooking fuel. The dominant presence of ethnic minority hawkers and shopkeepers in the city's many strategically placed land- and water-based farmers' markets reflects their enthusiastic participation in the urban-oriented agrarian trades, reaching from production to consumption, while Thai peasants, most of them located further from the city and specializing in wet-rice cultivation, shared less interest in exploring the economic opportunities presented by Bangkok's growing consumer market.

FROM OLD BANGKOK TO NEW

Ethnicity serves as the womb in which a putative nationality slumbers until some societal impetus causes it to be awakened. It would assist the study of nationalism if it could be ascertained what precisely those societal impulses are, and to determine at which exact point in time or development it is possible to speak of nationality instead of ethnicity (Spira, 2004, p. 263).

The Law of Entropy

In physics, entropy denotes the inexorable, systematic degradation of cosmic matter and energy to an ultimate state of inert uniformity. In the social sciences, it refers to the ineluctable, cumulative intensification of societal complexity from an initial state of systemic order toward an ultimate state of chaos. Linking those two quite dissimilar physical and social principles, a free-thinking physicist has averred that "entropy inevitably disrupts mankind's best-laid plans" (West 2011). Entropy lay at the very heart of Old Bangkok's evolution over the course of the nineteenth century, culminating in the increasingly densely populated and ethnically variegated city's physical, political, and social transformation over the turn of the twentieth century and beyond. Bangkok had been conceived in accordance with a clear and consistent vision of its place in the cosmic order, expressed as a body of primordial propositions that were thought to ensure the city's propitious destiny. As the city grew in physical scale, demographic density, social intricacy, economic sophistication, and cultural vitality, however, it became increasingly difficult to adhere to that primeval design, and in the rush to prosperity as the nineteenth century wore on, the original vision faded and was eventually forgotten. The result was growing urban disorder, disorganization, and systemic dissonance.

Successive reigns witnessed the progressive deviation of Bangkok's urban design from its ideal symmetry under the influence of accelerating social change. With that, the myth of Ratanakosin as a sacred city reserved for the habitation of "deities" inevitably vaporized. Increasingly, the outward-oriented pressure of residential crowding at the centre complemented the inward pull of commercial opportunity to override the ritual concerns for cosmic conformity and the political concerns for dynastic legitimacy in the shaping of the Bangkok cityscape. Within the walled city, the cumulative spread of palaces beyond the confines of the citadel corroded the original conception of a capital spatially stratified between royal and noble zones of occupation (Map 1.4). Under the practice of unfettered royal polygyny, the multi-generational households of the successive Chakri kings and viceroys grew exponentially. As each of the successive rulers' many adult sons formed their own households, growing pressure on the available terrain encouraged the construction of twenty-five palaces outside the citadel bounds by the end of the Third Reign and eighty-eight by the end of the Fifth. Though outside the citadel, nearly all those palaces continued to be sited in conformity with the south-north dualism of the king's and viceroy's respective zones of occupation and control (Map 1.4). An analogous tendency to overcrowding and resultant expansion beyond the city wall arose in the precincts populated by the city's similarly polygynous nobility.

Adding to the walled city's rising density over the successive reigns was the emergence of a number of commoners' settlements in the interstices between the elite's residential tracts. Select coteries of both Thai and non-Thai slaves and freemen had from the start formed a substratum of servants, staff, and other subordinates nested within the sprawling residential compounds of the city's elite. Added to that initial presence, constraints on access to the walled city eased during the Fourth and Fifth Reigns with the relaxation of curfew, residency, and landholding regulations, construction of metalled roads and sturdy bridges, drainage of remaining waterlogged tracts, and introduction of rental shophouses and tenements. Increasingly, prosperity, changing fashions, and the accompanying demand for new luxury goods and specialized services induced an influx of artisans' workshops, shopfronts, and peddlers along the walled city's streets and alleys, waterways and crossings. With them appeared a number of new commercial neighbourhoods and marketplaces (Tomosugi 1993, pp. 13–15; Prani 2002). Under those swelling impulses, the city wall and moat were gradually reduced to a vaguely emblematic social boundary in the mind of the Thai elite; to many commoners they came to be seen as a threshold into a world of economic opportunity. Those evolving circumstances wore the aristocratic mystique of Ratanakosin increasingly thin, and the memory of the walled city's sacral configuration as a replica of Indra's heaven melted away.

That entropic decline of the Bangkok mandala was complemented by rising dissatisfaction with the spiritual potency and metaphorical applicability of Brahman cosmography as the kingdom's elite sought to accommodate the intellectual challenge of Western scientific rationalism (Reynolds 2006b, pp. 171–80). Spearheaded by the efforts of King Mongkut (Rama IV) and his minions to liberate Buddhism from the Brahman mythos, the metaphysical trappings of Bangkok's spatial symmetry were systematically deconstructed. In the process, and in line with the Chakri dynasty's consistent Buddhist fundamentalism, the influential role of the Brahman adepts at the Thai court was gradually marginalized while the place of Buddhist ritual in royal ceremony was brought to the fore (Tambiah 1976, pp. 227–28). All that goes far toward explaining why the king's closest confederates in the revisionist enterprise omitted reference to Bangkok's celestial template from their compilation of the dynastic chronicles.

Dismantling Ratanakosin

The Fifth Reign residential spread of Bangkok's ruling elite beyond the crowded confines of the walled city, combined with the commons' penetration into the inner city's emerging commercial neighbourhoods, proceeded relentlessly, to the point where the physical integrity of Bangkok's inner precincts became seriously compromised. Bangkok's first postal directory (Thailand, Post and Telegraph Department 1883) illustrates the issue in its formative stage. The four-volume register of mailing addresses was compiled to accommodate the spatial distribution of the capital's social order. The first volume lists the addresses of Bangkok's royalty and senior nobility (covering the walled city), while the subsequent three volumes list the addresses of the commoners residing at successive degrees of distance from the centre — the inner, built-up precincts featuring streets and lanes while the outer suburbs are identified in terms of villages and other residential nodes along the river, transport canals, and irrigation, drainage, and boundary ditches. But the physical realities refused to comport precisely with the social status presumption, as substantial numbers of officials had already by the 1880s moved beyond the city wall, and many commoners' residences were already listed within. The spatial mingling of the major social strata had thus by the early 1880s already proceeded to a point preventing any definitive linking of the walled city with the ruling elite.

Relations between the successive Chakri kings and viceroys, and thus between the city's southern and northern zones, had often been strained. Early in the Fifth Reign they reached the breaking point with an armed confrontation that proved disastrous for the viceroy (Mead 2004, pp. 60–64). His defeat culminated in his political eclipse and set King Chulalongkorn (Rama V) on the path to monarchist absolutism. The discredited viceroy's death in 1885 provided the king with a unique opportunity to abolish the ancient viceregal office and dissolve the power base it represented. The Front Palace was abandoned as a royal residence; by 1898 it had been reduced by over half its former expanse to make way for the creation of the Great Esplanade (*sanam luang*) (Map 1.5). The viceroy's signature temples (Wat

Mahathat, Wat Chana Songkhram, Wat Phra Kaew Wang Na) were also reduced in size and standing. Similarly, the princely palaces within the Front Palace zone, left vulnerable following the loss of their chief source of support and security, declined in number over the ensuing years as they reverted to the crown with the death or eviction of their occupants (Maps 1.4 and 1.5). The Front Palace nobility and lesser staff were reassigned, many to minor postings upcountry within the reorganized state bureaucracy. With that restructuring, the division of the city between the king's and viceroy's respective zones of occupation and control came to an end.

Just as the divide between the king's and viceroy's south-north zones was eliminated, so was the east-west demarcation between the city's royal and noble precincts progressively obscured. Of the 134 palaces built over the course of the first five Chakri reigns (Table 1.1), only fifty were still serving in that capacity as of 1910, and only half of those were located within the walled city (Map 1.5). That dispersal of royal residence was accompanied by the scattering of seats of ministerial power. The Western custom of separation of place of work from place of residence in government service was introduced to Bangkok in the early 1880s and was institutionalized over the following decade. The procedure of converting old palaces to ministry headquarters and affiliated offices proved both a convenient and cost-effective means of housing the modern bureaucracy. By 1910 four of Siam's ten ministries as well as many subsidiary departments were quartered in such converted premises outside the citadel (the other six ministries were still situated within the citadel) (Map 1.5). That dispersion of the administrative apparatus quickened in subsequent years, first beyond the citadel and then further, beyond the city wall.

Over the course of his forty-two-year reign, King Chulalongkorn became increasingly engaged in the kingdom's modernization, or "civilizing process" (*kabuan kansiwilai*), through the adoption and adaptation of selective attributes of Western culture (Thongchai 2000*b*). In his effort to cope with the menace of Western imperialism he came to envisage the kingdom's political salvation in nineteenth-century European terms, within the context of royal authoritarianism. A major step in his campaign toward absolutism was a comprehensive bureaucratic reform, first mooted in 1888 (Chulalongkorn 1989), culminating four years later in the concentration of administrative control in his hands (Mead 2004, pp. 94–104). In the aftermath, his 1897 grand tour of fourteen European capitals provided him with long-anticipated personal exposure to the elaborate protocol and opulent lifestyle of the European aristocracy that glorified the cult of absolute monarchy, which was adopted as his own (Stengs 2009, pp. 30–77). Immediately upon his return he set in motion a comprehensive programme to replicate that Western style of stately grandeur in Bangkok (Peleggi 2002, pp. 84–90).

Initial steps toward the capital's modernization had been taken in the early 1890s with the upgrading of the transport infrastructure in Bangkok's chief commercial districts. That mobilization of bureaucratic resources in the cause of urban development marked a significant departure from the former convention of benign neglect of the city's ethnic minority communities. A supporting factor in the municipal development programme was the expropriation of right-of-way for the construction of royally sponsored streetside shophouse and tenement lines, markets, and tram lines, both within the walled city and in the built-up outer districts. Those new commercial relations between the ruling elite and the commons systematically ignored the former distinction between the walled city and the outer districts in favour of indiscriminate property development both within and beyond the walled city bounds.

After the king's 1897 European excursion, that work was relegated to lower priority to accommodate the redesign of the capital's royal precincts. The capstone of that project was the construction of the Dusit Palace, a new grand palace more than three times the size of the old, sited one-and-a-half kilometres northeast of the walled city (Map 1.9). The Dusit Palace was set in the midst of the Dusit Garden (*suan dusit*) district, a new royal quarter embellished with a number of sumptuous European-style royal villas and two royal temples. The Dusit district construction project, particularly the Dusit Palace itself, featured the import of scores of shiploads of costly European construction materials, furnishings, and statuary, plus the hiring of teams of Italian architects, civil engineers, artists, and artisans (Lazara and Piazzardi 1996). The overall cost was never disclosed but is known to have had dire consequences for the state budget (Brown 1992, pp. 57, 117).

Of the nineteen palaces that King Chulalongkorn built outside the walled city for his sons (Table 1.1), eleven were established in the immediate vicinity of the Dusit Palace (Map 1.9). The surrounding district, formerly an exurban agrarian tract known for little more than its scattering of fruit orchards, was overrun by the residences of lesser royals, court attendants, and government functionaries relocated from the walled city, opening space within the inner city for the accelerated infiltration of commercial establishments. Chulalongkorn himself finally abandoned the crowded, antiquated Grand Palace in 1907 in favour of the modern, far more spacious Dusit Palace. With the majestic prospect of Rachadamnoen Avenue serving as the umbilicus between the old citadel and the new royal quarter, Bangkok — at least from the royalist perspective — was transformed at the turn of

MAP 1.9
Bangkok: The metropolitan cityscape, 1910

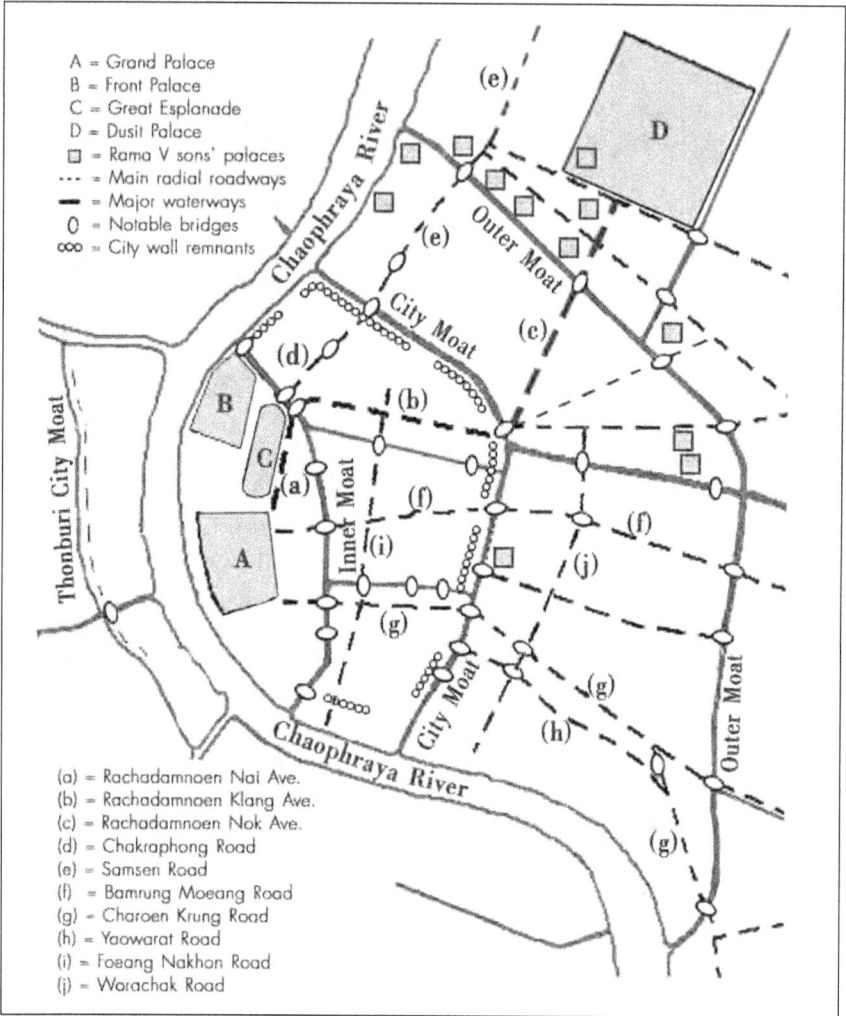

A = Grand Palace
B = Front Palace
C = Great Esplanade
D = Dusit Palace
□ = Rama V sons' palaces
··· = Main radial roadways
▬ = Major waterways
0 = Notable bridges
∞ = City wall remnants

(a) = Rachadamnoen Nai Ave.
(b) = Rachadamnoen Klang Ave.
(c) = Rachadamnoen Nok Ave.
(d) = Chakraphong Road
(e) = Samsen Road
(f) = Bamrung Moeang Road
(g) = Charoen Krung Road
(h) = Yaowarat Road
(i) = Foeang Nakhon Road
(j) = Worachak Road

the century into a metropolis unbound, euphemistically termed a "city of magnificent distances" (Sternstein 1982).

Just as the Dusit project put the final obliterating touch on the former conceptual integrity of the Bangkok citadel as the capital's political, social, and cultural core, so did the piecemeal demolition of the city wall and its gates and bastions as well as the enhanced bridging of its moats effectively erase not only the physical bounds but also the celestial associations of the Old City (Map 1.9).

In a telling metaphor of Ratanakosin's transformation from bounded redoubt to open precinct within the greater Bangkok metropolis, the brick rubble from the city's demolished defences was carted off to surface the newly installed thoroughfares. The principal land routes radiating from the walled city to the greater Bangkok metropolis (Map 1.9) were greatly improved in the succeeding years to accommodate motorized traffic. In addition, they came to be served by a network of electrified tramlines radiating from the central tram terminus (located directly alongside the city pillar shrine) toward the metropolitan area's rapidly expanding outer commercial and residential districts (Wright and Breakspeare 1908, p. 242). Less interest was shown in the concentric perimeter roads circumscribing the old city centre. By the close of the Fifth Reign, Bangkok's former physical demarcation between rulers and ruled had been emphatically reversed. The transformation was cogently symbolized by the construction of many handsome vehicular bridges crossing the city's numerous waterways (Map 1.9). Some 2,000 bridges are said to have been erected to accommodate the rapidly spreading road network of this "Venice of the East" (Wright and Breakspeare 1908, p. 241).

Bangkok's unrestrained turn-of-the-century expansion thus spelled the end of the old royal redoubt of Ratanakosin. With that transformation the aesthetics of Indra's celestial city were abandoned in favour of the West's secular architectonics. A new, more public expression of sovereign power was introduced, with "monumental public spaces as suitable stage sets for the performance of [royal] spectacles" (Peleggi 2002, p. 94), serving the Fifth Reign cult of kingship (Stengs 2009) to fit the temper of the times. That double re-creation of the capital's royal space along with the metropolitan area's opening up — a reconfiguration both outward to accommodate the city's flourishing emporium and inward to celebrate its exuberant royal grandeur — effectively eradicated Old Bangkok. With those developments, the Ratanakosin era — the historical phase during which Bangkok's morphology had assumed the guise of Indra's celestial city — came resoundingly to a close.

With that physical transformation, the city became an arena for accelerated social change: a levelling of social strata, a homogenization of communal residence, a melting pot of ethnic identities. The increasingly compulsive pursuit of an improved, modern lifestyle through monetized transactions, mass-market-oriented artisanship and small-scale manufacture, wholesale and retail entrepreneurship, and wage work in the inner city's rapidly expanding commercial neighbourhoods and along its newly popular shoppers' walkways and dry-goods markets brought members of different ethnic groups into close and constant contact. Questions of ethnicity were submerged beneath the common quest for profits, rents, wages, and interest. A new achievement-oriented, Thai-centred national identity was being forged.

Thai Ethno-nationalism

Surrounded by a tightening ring of Western colonies as the nineteenth century wore on, Siam's multi-ethnic feudal polity sought to defend itself with its reinvention as a nation-state under an absolute monarchy (Mead 2004). With that strategic policy redirection at the culmination of a century and more of progress, imminent adversity was transformed into putative virtue. It is as if the Thai ruling elite took heed of the Shakespearian aphorism: "There is a tide in the affairs of men, which, taken at the flood, leads on to fortune." The kingdom's political transformation over the decades spanning the nineteenth-twentieth century divide involved, among its many far-reaching measures, territorial concessions and consolidation, administrative rationalization and centralization, ethnic integration and social levelling, accommodation to Western technology and cultural norms, and a secularized cult of kingship. It was the climax of Siam's metamorphosis from feudal state to nation-state. At the heart of that "political project" stood ethno-nationalism, an approach to nation building featuring a conscious effort to promote social inclusiveness (Conversi 2004). In the case of Siam's plural society, Thai ethnicity (*chat thai*) proved to be the cradle and abiding core of the emerging Thai nation (*moeang thai*); Thai "racial" identity and Thai national identity were mysteriously fused (Saichon 2003, pp. 59–82), leaving the ethnic minorities little option but to accommodate, integrate, and ultimately assimilate.

Under the impact of the Siamese state's nationalist policy, sizeable elements of Bangkok's plural society evaporated as recognizably distinct ethnic constituencies. Many ethnic place names lost their former significance as their residents blended into the broader community or moved out to be replaced by new occupants of nondescript origin. The association between particular ethnic groups and traditional livelihoods declined as formal patronage links with the old aristocracy and nobility unwound. Theravada Buddhism was promoted as a pillar of the Thai nation-state in legislation, the state budget, the schools, and the workplace. Minority kindreds were influenced to adopt Thai surnames, language, religion, and other culture markers, submerging their (former) ethnicity under a Thai veneer. Reference to ethnic minorities in official documents was terminated, just as allusion to the ethnic affiliations of individual localities, military units, and family lineages declined precipitously. Open recognition of the

maternal non-Thai ethnic pedigrees of major branches of the royal family
and other elements of the ruling elite dissolved. The double meaning of
"Thai" as both ethnic and national denotation came to be revitalized several
decades later in an effort to stamp out remaining resistance, following
the eclipse of the absolute monarchy, in the hands of a newly populist,
chauvinist regime (Streckfuss 1993; Barmé 1993, pp. 14–17, 138–44). By
the mid-1930s the process had proceeded sufficiently that official statistics
could submerge most of Bangkok's traditional ethnic diversity under the
"Thai" label (Table 1.6).

TABLE 1.6
Bangkok-Thonburi population, by ethnic group,
1933/34 and 1937/38

	1933/34[a]	1937/38[b]
Thai	572,186	593,162
Chinese	246,407	285,564
Khaek[c]	23,887	5,603
Western	1,542	1,040
Other	1,591	5,084
Total	845,613	890,453

Notes: [a] Ministry of Interior, 2.2.5/428 (2476 [1933/34]).
        [b] Population Census of 1937/38.
        [c] Indian and Malay. The dramatic fall in the "khaek" numbers
            between 1933/34 and 1937/38, entirely spurious, remains
            unexplained.
Source: Porphant (2013), p. 163 (1933/34 "Chinese" typographical
            error adjusted).

Ethnic integration is not a one-way process; it entails accommodation
from both parties involved, and rarely is it easily or entirely achieved. While
Bangkok's ethnic minorities have been extensively "Thai-ized", the city's
Thai core has selectively absorbed many of its ethnic neighbours' culture
traits — linguistic terms, social mannerisms, spiritual beliefs, dietary habits,
entertainment traditions, artistic and architectural motifs, etc. — to the
point where ethnic differentiation has been largely dissipated. Nevertheless,
a century after the waning of Bangkok's plural society, the metropolis
today — and even more perceptibly Thailand's upcountry provinces and
outlying regions — retains many traces of the kingdom's historical ethnic
diversity. Throughout the city today can still be found numerous religious,
linguistic, architectural, occupational, culinary, and other cultural traces of

the old plural society, and the city still harbours the remains of a number of long-established ethnic minority neighbourhoods — Chinese, Muslim, Portuguese-Thai, Western — that continue to resist full assimilation into the Thai cultural mainstream, despite the changing scale and texture of the city's urban society, despite the submersion of the former pattern of personalized elite patronage of individual minority communities beneath the nation-state's depersonalized social movements, class interests, political ideologies, and regional affiliations, vestiges of ethnic pluralism endure. Both within the capital and upcountry, the Thai government continues to pursue its policy of national integration, contending with the kingdom's diverse ethnic and ideological outliers through a succession of innovative programmes in its unending quest to blend all under a single "Thai" national identity. The chapters that follow trace some of the historical roots of Thailand's still-incomplete march toward that idealized ethnic homogenization. They underline the lingering relevance of ethnicity to any understanding of what it means today to be "Thai."

2

Interlopers: Portuguese Parishes

A dozen years after Vasco de Gama's epic voyage round the Cape of Good Hope to India's Malabar coast, the Portuguese in 1510 established a strongpoint at Goa, which thenceforth served as the linchpin of their eastern empire. Alfonso d'Albuquerque, the second Viceroy of Goa, extended the Portuguese presence further east a year later by leading a naval squadron across the Indian Ocean to seize the well-situated port of Malacca. Discovering that Malacca was a distant vassal of Siam, he immediately dispatched an envoy to Ayutthaya (by Chinese junk) to inform the king of Siam of the Portuguese *coup de main*. The envoy was well received at the Siamese court and was pleasantly surprised to find that no objections were raised against the Portuguese initiative. Returning to Malacca by the overland route from Ayutthaya to the Andaman coast, he officially apprised the Siamese vassal ports of Tenasserim and Martaban of the new Portuguese presence and friendly intentions. And so, Portuguese relations with the Siamese kingdom started off on the right foot (Bidya 1998, pp. 29–76; Campos 1959; Silva Rego 1982).

A second Portuguese mission visited Ayutthaya in 1512. After a two-year stay during which the envoy explored trade opportunities for the Portuguese Crown, he returned to Malacca and then Goa accompanied by a Thai embassy. In 1516, Malacca dispatched to Ayutthaya yet another ambassador, who managed to negotiate a treaty of "friendship and commerce" between the kingdoms of Siam and Portugal, the first Siamese compact with a European power. The treaty specified that the Portuguese would be permitted to set up trading posts at Ayutthaya and other Siamese ports, that they would supply Ayutthaya with guns and powder, and that they would be allowed to practise their religion openly and freely. The Portuguese settlement that subsequently emerged at Ayutthaya was headed by a series of captains-major (*capitanães-mor*), appointed — with the concurrence of the Siamese authorities — by the Estado Português da Índia, instituted in 1505 and headquartered at Goa. In practice, the Estado pursued a hands-off policy. Ayutthaya's Portuguese settlement was left largely to its own devices and, much to the liking of the Siamese authorities, frequently carried out its mercantile activities in defiance of Portuguese royal orders (D'Ávila Lourido 1996, p. 76).

Relations between Ayutthaya on the one side and Goa and Malacca on the other were disrupted upon Portugal's merger with Spain from 1580 to 1640. During that period Manila, Spain's main Asian base, replaced Goa as the centre of Iberian interests in the Orient, as is reflected in the several embassies that voyaged between Siam and Manila in those years. The sixty years of Spanish hegemony — during which the conjoined kingdoms of Spain and Portugal unleashed the Great Armada against England, with tragic consequences for Iberia — bled Portugal of manpower and treasure. They marked the turning point in Portugal's Asian fortunes (Boxer 1969, pp. 111, 114). In the wake of that "Spanish interlude" the Portuguese were in 1639 expelled from Japan, Malacca was taken by the Dutch in 1641, and Colombo fell to the Dutch in 1660. Some of the Portuguese traders evicted from those ports found their way to Siam, increasing the size of the Portuguese community at Ayutthaya at the very time when the Portuguese presence in Asia was on the wane. With the loss of those outposts, the role of Macao, Portugal's window to China, increased. From 1660 to 1680 Macao traded increasingly with Siam and became a well-known source of provisions, arms, and seamen. Early in the seventeenth century the Dutch and English established trading posts at Ayutthaya, and starting in 1673 the French sent several impressive missions that succeeded in building a strong French political presence. In an effort to revive Portuguese interests at Ayutthaya in the face of that growing international competition, an embassy led by Pero Vaz de Siqeira, one of Portuguese East Asia's wealthiest merchants and ship owners, was dispatched from Macao in 1684 (Seabra 2005). Though cordially received, the mission ultimately proved unsuccessful, and the Portuguese position at Ayutthaya languished.

While the Lisbon and Macao archives attest to the continuing close links between Portugal and Ayutthaya, Portugal's relations with Siam's vassals along the maritime trade routes are scarcely mentioned. From what little is known, however, there can be no doubt that they were significant nonetheless. As early as 1538, for instance, the trading post at Patani, a Siamese vassal port on the opposite shore of the Peninsula from Malacca, sheltered 300 Portuguese residents (Suthachai 1999, p. 44, citing Pinto 1989). Along the Andaman coast, the ports of Mergui/Tenasserim, Tavoy, Ye, and Martaban received many trade missions (Map 2.1). As important way-stations linking the Indian Ocean sea lanes with the overland routes — the "elephant roads" (*thanon khot*) — crossing the Tenasserim Cordillera to Ayutthaya, they developed strong alliances with both Malacca and Goa. Martaban, for instance, boasted ninety Portuguese residents and a number of brick warehouses as of 1568 (Harvey 1925, pp. 175, 178). "The trans-peninsular route .... was favored over the Straits because of pirates ... and contrary winds at certain times of the year, which could make a trip via the Straits six times longer than normal" (Andaya 1999, p. 133). However, the Burmese southward advance into the Irrawaddy Delta over the course of the sixteenth century made life in the Andaman ports increasingly insecure. Finally, with the Burmese assault of 1765, Siam permanently lost suzerainty over the Andaman coast, cutting Ayutthaya off from its overland route to the west and forcing the remaining Portuguese merchant-residents on that coast to flee to Goa, never to return (Sunait 1999, pp. 115–16).

MERCHANTS, MERCENARIES, MISSIONARIES, MESTIZOS

Merchants

Throughout its two-and-a-half centuries of trading relations with Western merchant-adventurers, the Ayutthaya entrepôt built up a well-deserved reputation for openness, tolerance, and adaptability. The arrival of the hairy, stinking, uncouth, bellicose, religiously intemperate Westerners (*feringi*, or *farang*) presented a challenge to those Thai cultural predispositions. But, unlike the later-arriving Castilians and Frenchmen, and to a lesser degree the Dutch and English, the Portuguese proved relatively well-disposed, honest, and intrepid, and not so haughty or obstinate as to dampen the spirit of compromise necessary for successful trade negotiations (Bidya 1998, pp. 194–223; D'Ávila Lourido 1996, pp. 84–94).

Ayutthaya had from the outset been an emporium straddling the cultural divide between the resource-rich inland reaches and the maritime transport routes to overseas markets. A number of itinerant Armenian, Turkish, and Italian traders — even, it has been said, the Venetian merchant-adventurer Marco Polo (1254–1324) — passed through the kingdom long before the Portuguese arrival. With the establishment of relations with the Portuguese, Siam's King Prachai Racha (r. 1534–1546) appears to have found the

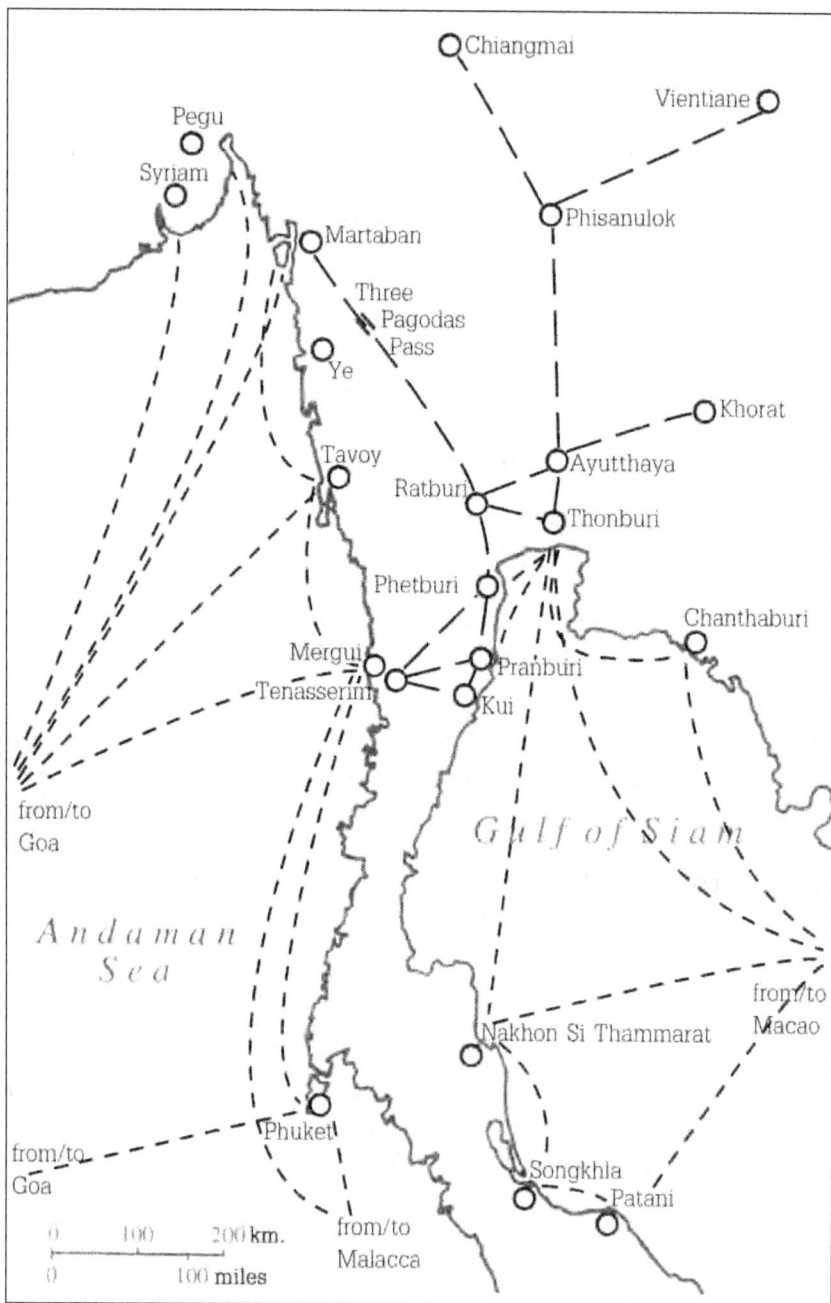

MAP 2.1
Portuguese trade routes to/from Siam, 1511–1767

Portuguese, in addition to the South Asian and Mid-Eastern Muslims as well as the Chinese, to be profitable trading partners, which decided him to improve Ayutthaya's access to the sea by having a number of shortcut transport canals excavated. Among them was a canal cutting across the great ox-bow bend later known as the Bangkok Yai/Bangkok Noi Canal — the river stretch that today separates Bangkok from Thonburi.

The initial Portuguese trading missions searched unsuccessfully in Siam for the rare spices, such as cloves, nutmeg, cardamom, mace, and pepper, that would maximize their return on the difficult and dangerous westward journey. "After an initial flurry of interest in the 1510s and 1520s, Portuguese officials concluded that Ayutthaya would not be an important source of goods for the Portuguese crown trade, and Portuguese involvement in Ayutthaya was left to private traders thereafter" (Breazeale 1999, p. 44). Taking advantage of the opportunity, growing numbers of "private and unauthorized merchants came to Ayutthaya from 1515 onwards. Mostly they came from the lower classes and wanted to try their luck in Ayutthaya. A Portuguese community was set up at Ayutthaya probably from these years...." (Suthachai 1999, p. 42).

Left in private hands, at least on the Portuguese side, the Siamese export trade flourished with a miscellany of agricultural and extractive goods, such as nipa-palm wine (arrack and jaggery), rice, tin, ivory, sappanwood, scented woods, sticklac, raw gemstones, deer hide, and occasionally elephants, as well as such transit wares as Chinese silks and ceramics. In return, the private traders found a ready market in Siam for a variety of manufactures and processed goods, including guns and gunpowder, printed cottons, cut and polished gemstones, opium, aromatics, medical concoctions, and even slaves. Like other European traders along the Andaman coast and at Ayutthaya, the Portuguese relied primarily on barter in their entrepôt commerce, with a great variety of silver and gold coinages serving as measures of value and residual mediums of exchange (Ferrand 1920). They sought unsuccessfully to corner the principal indigenous money market of the day, the cowrie "coinage" (*bia* in Thai), by seeking to wrest the cowrie trade from the sultanate of the Maldives, which held virtual monopoly control over the shells used in the marketplaces of Siam (Hogendorn and Johnson 1986, pp. 28–36). From Tenasserim, from the early 1500s, the Portuguese traders shipped across the Indian Ocean in large ceramic "Martaban jars" (*i-loeng* in Thai) the Andaman coast's fine nipa-palm wine. In the seventeenth century they were joined in that trade by the French and English, who were well acquainted with the Andaman ports as a convenient way-station along the route to Ayutthaya.

At Ayutthaya in the seventeenth and eighteenth centuries, Siam's Ministry of Trade and Foreign Affairs (*krom phra khlang*) was left largely in the hands of officials drawn from the resident non-Thai trading communities, including the Portuguese. The head of the Western Trade Department (*krom tha khwa*) was traditionally a resident Muslim of Persian descent carrying the rank and title of Phraya Chula Rachamontri. Under him served two "harbormasters" (*chao tha*), one dealing with the Muslim community — Arabs, Persians, Turks, Indians, and Malays (the wide array of coastal peoples ranging from the Malay Peninsula through the Indonesian Archipelago) — and the other dealing with the Christian community — Europeans (except the Dutch, who were classed with the Japanese), Vietnamese (who were classed with the French), Armenians, and South Asian Christians. The Portuguese resident captain-major was traditionally designated as harbour master for Ayutthaya's Christian (i.e., European, or *farang*) community (Breazeale 1999, pp. 11–12, 49–50). Malay served as the language of convenience in dealings with *farang* through the Western Trade Department; many of the local Portuguese serving the Siamese state as commercial agents, river pilots, cargo inspectors, and tax and fee collectors were proficient Malay interpreters (Breazeale 1999, p. 11).

With the fall of Malacca to the Dutch in 1641 and with subsequent Burmese encroachments along the Andaman coast, Siamese-Portuguese trade links swung from Goa to Macao. But Macao, too, entered a difficult period after the expulsion of its merchants from Japan in 1636, termination of its participation in the Manila trade in 1640, and disruptions of the China trade following the Ming-Ching dynastic transition of 1644, in addition to the unrelenting military-backed commercial pressure exerted by the Dutch. Under those increasingly difficult conditions both west and east, the Portuguese community at Ayutthaya fell on hard times. Thus, over the course of Ayutthaya's inward-oriented Ban Phlu Luang dynasty (1688–1767) there is little information on Portuguese trade with Siam.

Mercenaries

"[The] Portuguese soldiers who were sent out as cannon-fodder to the colonial battlefields during the whole of the seventeenth century were only too often forcibly recruited from gaol-birds and convicted criminals...." (Boxer 1969, pp. 116–17). They were widely disparaged as ill-trained and ill-disciplined. Nevertheless, Ayutthaya on several occasions negotiated with Portuguese envoys to secure the services of those mercenaries (Bidya 1998, pp. 171–93). The Andaman coast principalities may be presumed to have had a similar interest. The tale of Felipe de Brito y Nicote is symbolic of the early Portuguese mercenary influence along the Andaman coast. Initially stationed at Goa, de Brito entered the employ of the king of Arakan and in 1600 participated in the conquest of Syriam, a key seaport along the Irrawaddy delta coast. With a complement of fifty Portuguese comrades he was left in command of that strategic outpost, exacting a rich bounty of taxes and fees from passing ships. In due course he deputed his son to govern Martaban, extending his control from the delta to the Andaman coast. The landlocked Burmese chafed under de Brito's trade blockage and in 1613 retook Syriam, captured and killed de Brito, and carried his Portuguese troops off into slavery. Martaban also was besieged, and de Brito's son was assassinated. But the Siamese, aided by bands of Portuguese mercenaries eager to avenge de Brito's fall, were able to repel the Burmese advance and retain their suzerainty over the Andaman coast (Harvey 1925, pp. 185–89). All this intimates the sort of role that may have been played by the long-forgotten Portuguese adventurers at Ayutthaya.

Some 120 Portuguese mercenaries are said to have served as the bodyguard of Ayutthaya's King Prachai Racha. They and their successors functioned as instructors in the use of Western firearms — initially harquebuses (shoulder-fired matchlock guns) and jingals (light artillery, sometimes fired from elephant-back) and later muskets, mortars, and heavy cannon — and they also introduced cannon founding, gunpowder manufacture, and gunsmithing (Boxer 1965; Charney 2004). As a reward for their services they were provided with land for their residences and a church, the first one in Siam, at Ban Din, later known as Ban Portuket, 1.5 kilometres downriver from the walled city of Ayutthaya, where they produced weaponry and trained gunners (Harvey 1925, pp. 340–41; Pinto 1989, p. 400). In the 1549 Burmese siege of Ayutthaya, the weakest section of the city wall was manned by a contingent of fifty Portuguese mercenaries (Harvey 1925, p. 159). And again in later Burmese sieges of Ayutthaya, the use of Portuguese gunners — by both defenders and besiegers — is repeatedly mentioned (Damrong 2001, *passim*).

In addition to their material innovations, the Portuguese introduced the military tactic of "direct, fast, and efficient attack where troops were pushed to the limit and men killed indiscriminately in order to gain a victory" (Terwiel 2005, p. 38). But that ruthless tactic was adopted with greater effect by the Burmese than by the Thai, which aided the Burmese in overwhelming Ayutthaya twice in their military confrontations of the sixteenth and eighteenth centuries. Only under the generalship of Siam's King Taksin (r. 1767–1782) were those techniques perfected by the Thai. Through such contributions the Portuguese introduced a new phase in

Southeast Asian warfare, setting on course a sequence of cumulative changes in the region's military history over the succeeding centuries (Charney 2004; Lorge 2008).

Missionaries

With Ayutthaya's Portuguese settlers came Catholic friars and priests, first Franciscans and Dominicans and later, in the footsteps of Francis Xavier, who visited Malacca in 1545, Jesuits. The Franciscans were renowned for their humanism, the Dominicans for their fearsome zealotry, and the Jesuits for their intellectual excellence and tenacity. And so it was in Siam, with the Dominicans brushing aside the Franciscans, and the Jesuits — with French backing — ultimately outperforming the Dominicans (Bidya 1998, pp. 237–43; Pallegoix 2000, pp. 303–402).

The missionary presence was a fundamental element in the life of Ayutthaya's Portuguese community. The friars and priests were, in concert with the Portuguese captain-major, the effective heads of the community. In addition to their sacral duties they served as custodians of Portuguese custom, teachers of language and manners, arbiters in disputes, archivists of the rites of passage, and stewards of church and cemetery, school, convent, and orphanage. Their presence was considered so essential that both Goa and Macao regularly sponsored their recruitment and financed their travel to Siam. During periods of weak or absent clerical leadership, the Portuguese community at Ayutthaya languished, as is demonstrated by its persistent petitioning of Goa and Macao for assistance.

Following the investment of Goa with the archbishopric for East Asia in 1557, the Andaman route took on redoubled significance as the most convenient means of missionary passage between South and Southeast Asia. Initially, the government at Goa, and later Macao, sponsored the Franciscan and Dominican missionaries in Siam, but that material support to the Portuguese settlements evaporated with the empire's declining fortunes in the seventeenth century. The first Dominican missionaries arrived at Ayutthaya from Malacca in 1566; the first Jesuit missionary, also Portuguese, arrived overland from Tenasserim in 1606 (Suthachai 1999, pp. 49, 52). Thereafter, the union of Cross and Crown, which empowered Portuguese dominion worldwide, was progressively attenuated at Ayutthaya with the diminished interest of the Portuguese state in Siam's trade prospects (Boxer 1969, p. 228).

Three churches were built at Ayutthaya's Portuguese settlement (Map 2.2), a plethora reflecting the tensions between the respective clerical orders. The first, apparently dating back to at least the mid-1500s, was

St. Augustine's Church, established by Portuguese Franciscans. It was situated at the upstream end of the settlement tract, nearest the walled city. By the close of the sixteenth century it was well established, but it apparently floundered thereafter and was abandoned by mid-century. The second was St. Dominic's Church, under the stewardship of Portuguese Dominicans. It was probably built in the late 1500s, about 300 metres downstream from St. Augustine's, and became the community's most conspicuous landmark. Third was St. Paul's Church, built around 1606 or shortly thereafter by Portuguese Jesuits but taken over by French Jesuits sometime after 1662. It was located at the downstream end of the Portuguese settlement, some 500 metres south of St. Dominic's.

Clerics serving with the French politically-connected, well-financed Société des Missions Étrangères de Paris, established in 1658, revived the missionary spirit at Ayutthaya with the arrival of two bishops in 1662, accompanying the first French diplomatic mission, followed by another capable priest in 1664. They found eight Portuguese priests — four Jesuits, two Franciscans, and two Dominicans — as well as three lay missionaries already in residence (Suthachai 1999, p. 53). The French missionaries established a fourth church at Ayutthaya, St. Joseph's, in 1665 (Map 2.2). King Narai (r. 1656–1688) awarded them a plot of land and building materials for the construction of that church and seminary nearly four kilometres upstream from the Portuguese settlement. The well-situated site, along the Chaophraya River across from the Chakrai Yai (Persian Sheik's) City Gate, was awarded in appreciation of the brilliant services that the Catholic priests had provided in strengthening the fortifications at Ayutthaya and downstream at the Thonburi guardpost. Failing in their efforts to convert the Thai and attract the local Portuguese populace, the French priests expanded the mission school into a seminary catering to Vietnamese youths imported from Tonkin. Its fame overshadowed the lesser Portuguese churches downstream, which aggravated the enmity between the Portuguese and French, both laity and clergy, an irritant that persisted well into the Bangkok era.

Mestizos

Antonio van Diemen, Dutch Governor-General at Batavia from 1636 to 1645 and well experienced in combating Portuguese commercial hegemony in the Far East, observed that "most of the Portuguese in [Asia] look upon this region as their fatherland. They think no more about Portugal. They drive little or no trade thither, but content themselves with the interport trade of Asia, just as if they were natives thereof and had no other country"

MAP 2.2
Ayutthaya: Portuguese settlement and related sites, pre-1767

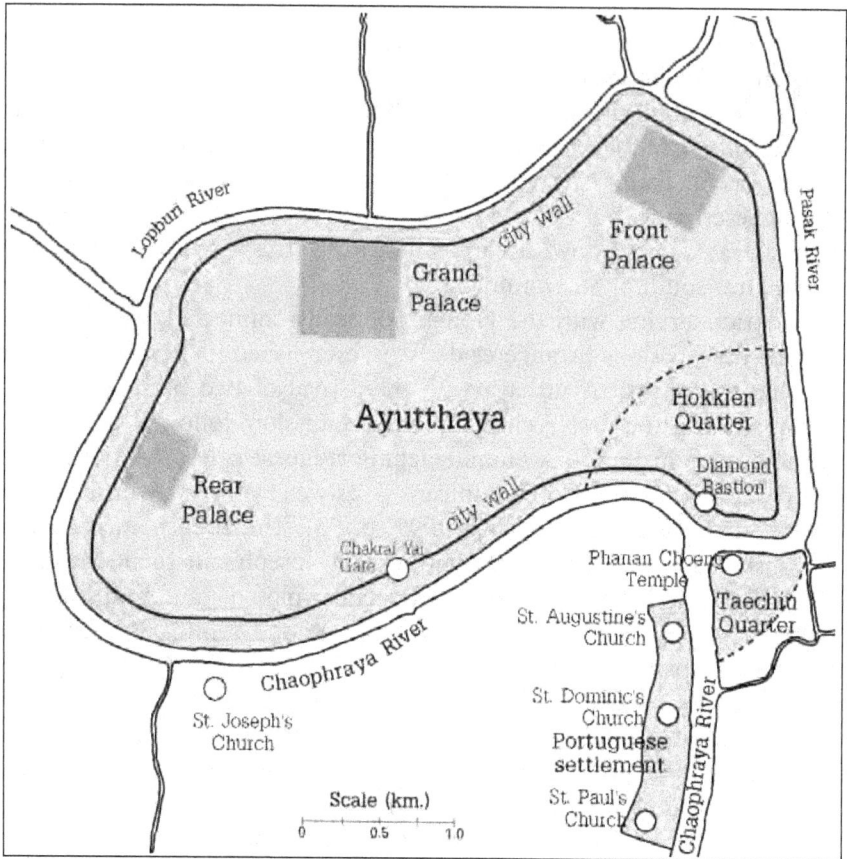

(Boxer 1969, p. 120, quoted in translation). Goodly numbers of the many young men brought east in the Portuguese royal service fled at the first opportunity to seek their fortune as private traders or mercenaries, or both, in the many port cities and inland kingdoms ringing the Indian Ocean.

The Portuguese settlers were termed "creoles" — migrants to the outposts of empire — for a single generation; "mestizos" — Eurasians, the product of local intermarriage — thereafter (Bidya 1998, pp. 77–170; Boxer 1963). The very prevalence of the word "*mestiço*", carrying all the pejorative overtones of its English equivalent, attests to the commonality of "miscegenation" between the Iberians and the "native" populations. The mestizo community grew through intermarriage with the "native races", through conversion (including "rice converts" — indigents in search of assured subsistence — as well as those seeking to avoid conscription, or *corvée*), through the "adoption" of orphans, slaves, seminarians, and the progeny of "sexual indulgence". Over successive generations, progressive loss of distinguishing physical traits, relaxation of custom and mannerism, and decline of Portuguese linguistic fluency left them virtually indistinguishable from the local population.

Some 200–300 Portuguese are said to have settled near Ayutthaya initially. By the mid-seventeenth century, through repeated intermarriage, the three parishes at the downriver site that came to be known as Ban Portuket (Portuguese Village) amounted to 400–500 members each (Map 2.2) (Pallegoix 2000, p. 303). Another estimate claims that by 1662 the Portuguese settlement was 2,000 strong (Suthachai 1999, p. 53). By the 1680s the number of households (containing an average of perhaps seven-eight members each) was reported to have risen to 700–800 (Bidya 1998, p. 138). In sum, it has been posited that Ayutthaya's Portuguese community grew from some 2,000 during 1516–1569, to 3,000 during 1569–1653, and then 6,000 during 1653–1767 (Bidya 1998, p. viii). Of the inhabitants, virtually all were mestizos.

Though the most prominent members of the community were merchants and mercenaries, the majority were artisans, men of lesser distinction but perhaps more lasting influence — iron founders, armourers, gunsmiths, ships' navigators, cartographers, able-bodied seamen, shipbuilders, sail-makers, rope-makers, interpreters, pharmacists, surgeons, to name only a few of their myriad skills. Among those mestizo artisans may well have been descendants of Portugal's *marranos*, Jews who had ostensibly converted to Catholicism to escape the Inquisition and Expulsion, some of whom had then joined the voyages of discovery and conquest to east and west. They carried with them the highest skills, such as mathematics, finance, linguistics, cartography, navigation, architecture, medicine, and metallurgy, and were sought after as valuable companions on the Iberian odysseys of exploration and commerce (Kaplan 1992). So a subtle irony underlying the zealous Catholicism and national pride of Siam's Portuguese community is that it included many members of patently non-Catholic, non-Portuguese ethnic background.

CATASTROPHE AND REVIVAL

The Sack of Ayutthaya

Ayutthaya in the seventeenth and eighteenth centuries was an exceptionally cosmopolitan city. Its far-reaching renown as "emporium of the Eastern

Seas" and "marvel of Oriental splendor" was evidently one of the envies that drove the Burmese on their course of pillage and destruction in the 1760s. In the initial, aborted assault on Ayutthaya in 1760 the Dutch trading post was "reduced to ashes" while "the Christian quarter alone was respected", possibly at the behest of Portuguese mercenaries serving in the Burmese army (Turpin 1997, pp. 86–87). In the 1766–1767 siege of Ayutthaya, however, such immunity was not extended; the Portuguese community was left abandoned to mount its own desperate resistance. On 7 March 1767 the Burmese attacked Saint Joseph's parish, but the defenders succeeded in holding them off. "The Portuguese, at a distance of two leagues from [St. Joseph's Church,] gave signal proof of their courage [and ethnic solidarity]. They sabred a crowd of Burmese who had attempted to storm [St. Joseph's] college" (Turpin 1997, p. 107). The Portuguese success was partly due to the fact that the main Burmese force in that sector had been deployed to attack the Chinese port, which they took despite the combined strength of the Chinese and Portuguese defenders. Ban Portuket, the Portuguese settlement, capitulated two weeks later. Those of its residents who had not already fled were placed in captivity and carried off to Pegu and Ava, never to return. The Portuguese settlement, including its churches, was annihilated (Pallegoix 2000, pp. 377–80).

Much the same happened at the downriver Thonburi guardpost in 1766. From at least 1680, the defences at Thonburi, much strengthened with the assistance of the French clerics who had arrived with the diplomatic mission of 1662, was manned by some 400 soldiers, of whom about 100 were local Portuguese. It has been speculated that Thonburi's garrison was drawn from the Portuguese village at Samsen (Ban Portuket Samsen), some four kilometres upstream from the Thonburi fortress (Tomosugi 1993, pp. 228–29). The village households there were clustered around the Church of the Immaculate Conception, which had been founded in 1674 (Pallegoix 2000, p. 332). The Portuguese military contingent that had served with the garrison at Thonburi was extinguished in that calamitous year of 1766, and the village at Samsen was razed to the ground (Turpin 1997, p. 103).

In the turmoil following the fall of Ayutthaya on 7 April 1767, the Portuguese community was not spared (Turpin 1997, pp. 98, 113). Those who managed to escape did so by the skin of their teeth. One group managed to commandeer a Chinese junk and slip away to Cambodian exile (Turpin 1997, pp. 112–13; Pallegoix 2000, p. 380). Most, however, were not so fortunate. Those who were captured were tortured mercilessly to disclose their hidden wealth. Their daughters were taken (though a strange quirk of Burmese chivalry, it is said, prevented the conquerors from interfering with those who were already married). The Burmese treated Ayutthaya's Buddhist monks especially harshly, killing many of them, and the Catholic priests of the city fared little better. The temples were destroyed and their grounds were piled high with corpses. The rivers were filled with putrid cadavers giving off a revolting stench and breeding myriads of flies that tormented the Burmese troops and their enslaved captives alike (Turpin 1997, pp. 109–15). A senior Thai Buddhist monk later recalled in vivid terms the dire straits in which those who remained were left:

> Some wandered about, starving, searching for food. They were bereft of their families, their children and wives, and stripped of their possessions and tools.... They had no rice, no fish, no clothing.... They found only the leaves of trees and grass to eat.... In desperation many turned to dacoity.... They gathered in bands, and plundered for rice and paddy and salt. Some found food, and others could not. They grew thinner, and their flesh and blood wasted away. Afflicted with a thousand ills, some died and some lived on (Wyatt 1984, pp. 136–37, quoting Wanarat 1923, pp. 409–10; quoted in translation).

Survivors at Thonburi

Those of the Portuguese fugitives who managed to find their way to Cambodia received sanctuary with the small local Christian community that had emerged there under the tutelage of French missionaries. Phraya Taksin, the Sino-Thai military hero and future king of Siam who had himself escaped from Ayutthaya to Siam's eastern seaboard, neighbouring Cambodia, convinced some of those refugees to join his army in counter-attacking the Burmese and resurrecting the Siamese kingdom. At his new capital of Thonburi, King Taksin rewarded "the Portuguese who had fought for him" with a favourably situated settlement site a short distance downriver from the walled citadel and Grand Palace, directly alongside the old Chinese trading settlement of Kudi Chin (Map 2.3; Mendonça e Cunha 1976, p. 143). In recognition of their loyalty, they were awarded privileged positions in the Royal Pages Department (*krom mahatlek*) and Royal Bodyguard (*krom thahan raksa phra ong*) (Manich 1972, pp. 333, 340).

Within a year of the kingdom's revival under King Taksin two French priests, Bishop Lebon and Monsigneur Coudé (alternatively Corré, Cordé, or Condé), attached to the Missions Étrangères, arrived to minister to Thonburi's small Portuguese community. They were joined in 1770 by a third French priest, Msgr. Garnault. That year they led the community in building a little thatch-roofed church, Santa Cruz, by which name the parish came to be known. However, as religious leaders of the Portuguese community

MAP 2.3
Thonburi and Bangkok: Portuguese settlements and related sites, post-1782

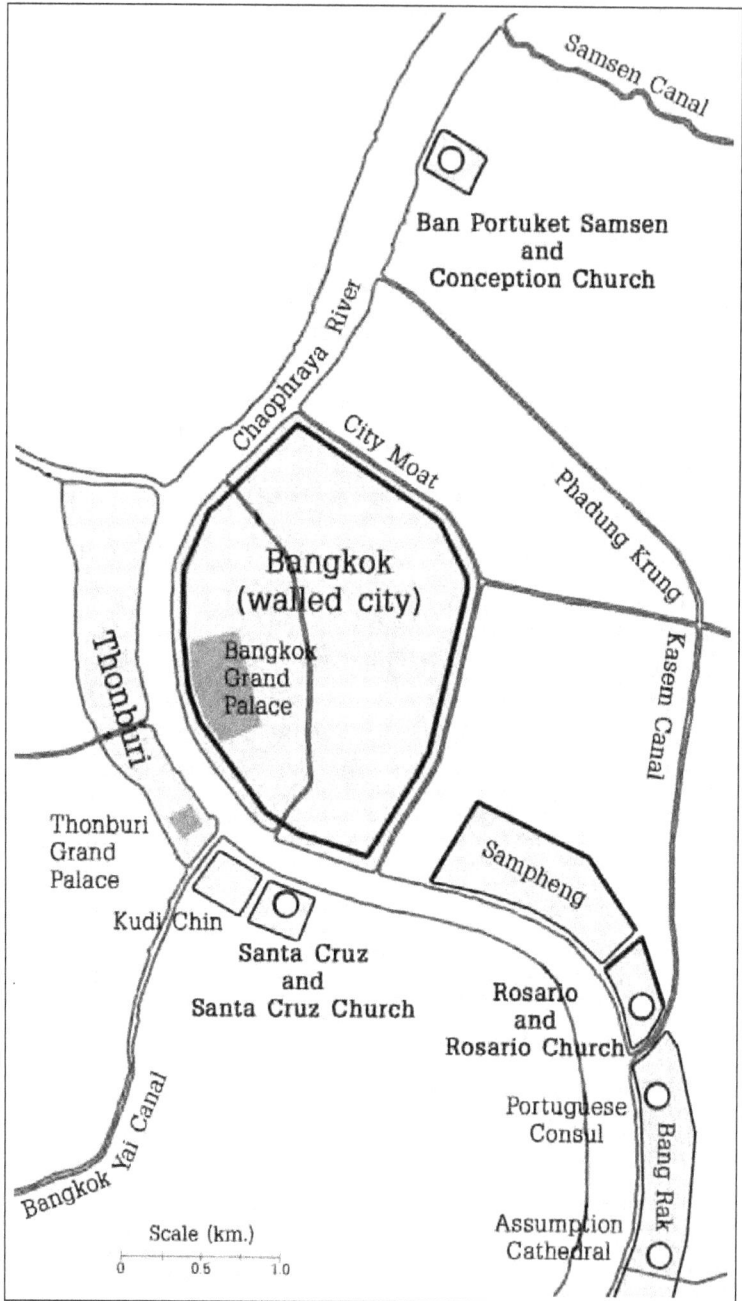

at Santa Cruz those French clerics did not fit well. Their Portuguese and Thai language fluency was weak, their acquaintance with Portuguese custom was limited, their liturgical conventions differed from the locally preferred forms, and their airs of cosmopolitan superiority were deeply resented. The Portuguese community chafed under their officious authority; and it long remembered the strained attitude of their narrow-minded French pastors to the prospect of a return of their Portuguese counterparts.

In 1769, a Portuguese Dominican friar, Fr. Gore, who had fled with the Portuguese refugees from Ayutthaya to Cambodia, arrived at Thonburi with a party of those returning exiles. He and his flock were not well received by the resident French priests. In rejoinder, the "Cambodian" households departed with him to establish a new parish as Ton Samrong (later known as Rosario, and then Talat Noi) (Map 2.3), a vacant site along the east bank of the river over two kilometres downstream. They took with them their most treasured possessions, two holy icons carved of wood, the "Mother of the Holy Rosary" and the "Corpse of the Lord Jesus", both of which, it is said, had been saved from the flames of Ayutthaya. They built for the safekeeping of those treasures, at great expense for the impoverished community, a plastered brick sacristy including a prayer chamber and caretaker-priest's bedroom. Following the death of Fr. Gore in 1773 they returned, begrudgingly, to attend weekly mass at Santa Cruz (Joseph 1997, pp. 10–18).

A crisis in the Portuguese community's relations with the Thai state sprang up in 1775 when three members of the Santa Cruz community serving as senior officials in the Thonburi government refused to partake of the royal "water of allegiance" ceremony used to pledge fealty to the king. Their refusal was instigated by Bishop Lebon, who considered this a pagan practice, apparently because of its unseemly similarities to the use of holy water in Catholic communion. King Taksin was deeply offended by this serious snub of royal ritual and had the three officials imprisoned until they recanted two months later, whereas the unrepentant priests remained in shackles for nearly a year (Pallegoix 2000, pp. 387–90; Terwiel 2005, pp. 51–53).

In 1779, Bishop Lebon and Msgrs. Coudé and Garnault were collectively deported from Siam, the victims of their own narrow-minded intolerance of "heathen practices" and their obstinate inflexibility in the face of King Taksin's increasingly volatile temperament. After the death of Lebon (at Goa) and the dynastic turnover of 1782, Coudé returned to Phuket, where he served as bishop until his death in 1785. Garnault managed to return to Bangkok (from Kedah), was elevated to bishop in 1787, and stayed on until his death in 1811 (Pallegoix 2000, pp. 392–93). In his footsteps followed an uninterrupted sequence of French bishops at Bangkok up to 1965, when the Vatican finally acceded to the installation of Thailand's first Thai bishop (Assumption 1995).

In the disturbances at Thonburi leading to the dynastic overthrow of 1782, the rebel forces besieged Thonburi's Grand Palace only to be stopped by the concentrated cannon and musketry fire of the Royal Guard of perhaps a hundred men, led by thirty-six Portuguese gunners (Pallegoix 2000, pp. 393–94). However, the Portuguese were eventually forced to abandon their posts and rush off to Santa Cruz to protect their families when the rebels threatened their settlement. "[Their precipitous return to Santa Cruz] did not prevent the camp of the Christians from being looted …. The church was completely stripped; everything [the rebels] could find there was taken away…. Only a few images and the stripped building were left. Thus [was] the loyalty of the Christians toward the King …, rewarded" (Pallegoix 2000, p. 394). That event was crucial in the history of Siam, as the loss of Taksin's Portuguese bodyguard left the Grand Palace virtually defenceless, leading directly to the king's abdication to the rebel forces, and then the rebels' overthrow by the Chakri coup. With that incident the traditional Portuguese role in the Royal Guard and Royal Pages Department came to an abrupt end, though the skilled Portuguese gunners were eventually reinstated by the Chakri kings to play an important role in the Bangkok regime's artillery corps.

FROM INTEGRATION TO ASSIMILATION

Portuguese Consuls

The years of Siam's recovery from the fall of Ayutthaya coincided with a period of exceptional political turmoil in the Western world — the American War of Independence, the French Revolution, the Napoleonic Wars, and more. Those preoccupations turned Western attention away from the East. Nevertheless, though the outposts of Portuguese empire had fallen into decline, Portugal sought to revive its diplomatic relations with Siam. A Portuguese envoy arrived at Bangkok from Macao in 1786, bearing a royal letter from Lisbon. That was Siam's first formal contact with a Western power since well before 1767 (Thailand, Department of Fine Arts 1963, pp. 2–9, 211–20). In response to that missive King Rama I, recalling past Siamese-Portuguese relations, sent a letter stating: "The King will not in future cause Your Majesty the inconvenience of sending troops and ammunition [in response to our overtures], but requests that orders be given to the

Government of Goa to send three thousand muskets during 1787. Should Your Majesty's subjects wish to establish a factory [i.e., a trading post], the King is willing to grant land for this purpose …." (Mendonça e Cunha 1971, p. 143; Silva 1997, vol. 2, p. 141, quoted in translation). Apparently, nothing came of that initiative, as in 1816 a letter was sent from Macao stating that orders had been received from Portugal "to endeavour to renew the old relations between Macao and Siam. [Such a letter had already been sent] in 1811, but unfortunately the ship that was bound for Siam had been lost and no one had been saved" (Silva Rego 1982, p. 15).

In response to the 1816 letter, a Thai official was sent to Macao in 1818, and that led to the arrival of a Portuguese mission headed by Carlos Manuel de Silviera at Bangkok in 1820, carrying a draft treaty aimed at restoring formal diplomatic and commercial relations between the two kingdoms. The treaty was duly negotiated and adopted, and in confirmation Siam ceded to Portugal a plot of land for the proposed "factory" and residence of the Portuguese consul. The plot was situated well downstream from the walled capital, directly below the Portuguese parish of Rosario (Map 2.3); it was 100 metres deep and stretched 144 metres along the riverfront, with two landings. Accompanied by a small staff and garrison reporting to Macao, de Silviera took up residence there in 1821. He was awarded the rank and title of Luang Aphai Wanit in the Siamese nobility — *wanit* (an antique rendering of *phanit*, or "commerce") referring discreetly to his role as arms trafficker (Silva Rego 1982, pp. 15–17; Mendonça e Cunha 1976, pp. 145–47; Silva 1997, vol. 3, pp. 41–42; Thipakorawong 2005, pp. 83–84).

The arms sold to Siam by de Silviera on behalf of the authorities at Macao were used to strengthen the defences at Paknam (at the mouth of the Chaophraya River) and other fortified positions against a threatened Burmese invasion. However, the consul's further efforts to develop Portuguese state trade with Siam did not succeed, as no further officially sanctioned Portuguese vessels visited Bangkok during the 1820s after the initial arrival of arms, though some private, illicit trade between Bangkok and Macao did develop, principally in munitions and rice carried on Chinese junks, while de Silviera was left high and dry. In his lonely vigil, de Silviera in 1828 befriended Carl Gutzlaff and Jacob Tomlin and their wives, the first Protestant missionaries to arrive at Bangkok. He offered them guest residential quarters at the rear of the consular compound, an arrangement later extended on a rental basis. With the arrival of additional missionaries, that presence was in later years expanded into Siam's first Baptist mission. In 1829 de Silviera finally departed Bangkok, having served as the first recorded Western resident at Bangkok, his consulate being the only one established at Bangkok prior to the Fourth Reign (1851–1868).

Following closely on the heels of that initial Portuguese diplomatic foray, the governor-general of British India in 1821 sent John Crawfurd to negotiate formal trade relations with Siam. Crawfurd records that he was met by a Portuguese interpreter upon his arrival at Paknam, and then by the harbour master, whom he referred to as a "native Christian". He later met with another local Christian, Pascal Ribiero de Alvergarais — particularly well educated, as he could converse in Thai, Khmer, Portuguese, and Latin — who was said to hold "a high title, and a post of considerable importance" in the Siamese government (Crawfurd 1967, pp. 72, 83, 179). Crawfurd was informed that Bangkok's population of Portuguese descent was 800 and that Siam's total Portuguese population amounted to around 2,000 (Crawfurd 1967, pp. 451–52). A physician accompanying the Crawfurd mission estimated that some 200–300 of the kingdom's Christians (presumably Portuguese mestizos all) lived at the eastern seaboard port of Chanthaburi, which boasted its own church (Finlayson 1988, pp. 255–58).

Following the departure of Portugal's first consul at Bangkok, his post was briefly downgraded to "political and commercial agent". In 1832 it was returned to its former status, and a succession of nine consuls followed through the end of the Fifth Reign (1910), interspersed with several periods of vacancy during which the post was temporarily filled by local merchants serving as honorary consuls. In the 1870s the consulate was rebuilt, but not to everyone's satisfaction, and by 1902 it had become so badly neglected that "the land had been divided into four parts, three of which were rented out" (Morbey 2006, pp. 51–54; Silva Rego 1982, p. 22). During the Sixth Reign (1910–1925), Macao appears to have decided to strengthen its presence at Bangkok, as the post was in that reign finally upgraded to ambassadorial level.

A new treaty of trade and friendship was promulgated by Lisbon and Bangkok in 1859 as one in the series of standardized compacts concluded between Siam and the Western powers in the wake of the pathbreaking Bowring Treaty of 1855 (Silva Rego 1982, pp. 19–21). Of particular interest was its extraterritoriality provision, giving Portugal jurisdiction over all Portuguese subjects or *protegés* in Siam, a diplomatic category extending beyond citizens, referring principally to locally born descendants of Portuguese nationals. Exempt from prosecution under Siamese law, local Portuguese subjects, identifiable primarily on the basis of their families' vital records maintained at their churches, found themselves in an advantageous position. Most importantly, Portuguese subject status exempted them from the annual labour conscription (*corvée*) under the formal Thai patron-client (*nai-phrai*) system. Furthermore, as Bangkok's principal importers of wines and other spirits, the merchants under Portuguese protection were long able to circumvent Siamese efforts to regulate the trade in alcoholic beverages.

In the 1860s, the United States consul, James M. Hood (at Bangkok 1865–1868), innovated the sale of "protection papers" extending the privilege of extraterritorial status to "eligible" (that is, willing-to-pay) non-Thai Asian residents in Siam. That convenient American entitlement was especially sought after by the local Chinese, as China had not entered into a treaty relationship with Siam, and thus its citizens in Siam had no extraterritorial rights. Hood was soon recalled by his government for his gross misuse of his consular powers for personal profit in issuing those fraudulent certificates of United States subject status, but the idea had caught hold, and the Portuguese consul, among others, took to selling protection papers to local (mainly Chinese) residents seeking the advantages of tax exemption, immunity from police harassment, privileged standing in the law courts, etc. (Silva Rego 1982, pp. 20–21, 22; Hong 2003). For instance, Chinese-owned pawnshops, in acquiring Portuguese protection, managed to frustrate the Siamese government's efforts to control their nefarious dealings in stolen property (Tomosugi 1993, pp. 123–31). One favoured means whereby applicants for diplomatic protection secured the Portuguese consul's sympathetic consideration was for them to convert to Catholicism, which appears to have contributed to the growing Chinese element in the congregation affiliated with the Holy Rosary Church (later rebuilt and renamed Calvary Church), located conveniently near Sampheng, Bangkok's main Chinese settlement (Map 2.3). Only in 1925 were Portuguese extraterritoriality privileges finally ended with a new treaty (Silva Rego 1982, pp. 22–23).

Parishes and Churches

Churches historically defined Siam's Portuguese settlements. Their crucifix-topped steeples stood out against the brilliant tropical skyline to announce that there their congregations could secure communal shelter, comfort, and security. Initially located only at Ayutthaya, churches were built by the Catholic missionaries over the centuries at a number of provincial capitals, from Phuket and Songkhla in the south to Chanthaburi in the east and Phisanulok and Chiangmai in the north, though the congregations were invariably very small. By sheer coincidence, Bangkok at an early date came to replicate Ayutthaya in its three Portuguese parishes bordering the river, each boasting its own church — Immaculate Conception, Santa Cruz, Holy Rosary — with a fourth, French-founded church (later upgraded to a cathedral) — Assumption — situated well away at the western anchorage at Bang Rak (Map 2.3). A fifth church, St. Francis Xavier, added in the 1850s to accommodate a newly arrived Vietnamese community, will be disregarded here (see, however, Chapter 7, subsection on "Ban Yuan (Samsen)"). But unlike Ayutthaya, where the three Portuguese churches and parishes stood near enough to one another for their separate parishes to coalesce into a single Portuguese settlement, the churches at Bangkok were separated by kilometres distance, creating three distinct Portuguese enclaves. Today they continue to be referred to as "Portuguese" neighbourhoods though it would be more appropriate to speak of them as peopled by "Thai Catholics of Portuguese descent".

(a) *Ban Portuket (Samsen)*
The first Portuguese parish in the vicinity of present-day Bangkok was founded during the seventeenth-century reign of King Narai by a troublesome faction that had been expelled from the Portuguese settlement at Ayutthaya for reasons unknown. They were assigned a new settlement site along the Chaophraya River at Samsen, some five kilometres north of the Thonburi guardpost. The site's relatively high ground — in the Chaophraya delta a metre in altitude can make a world of difference — today still avoids much of the annual flooding for which Bangkok is notorious. There, in 1673, they built the Church of the Immaculate Conception, served by a Dominican friar. How that small community survived over the following generations, and particularly how it outlived the Burmese depredations of the 1760s, is not recorded. Whatever its original population, the Portuguese parish at Samsen has scarcely grown over the more than three centuries of its existence, as it had reached only 900 by the mid-nineteenth century (Pallegoix 2000, p. 405) and today is said by the resident pastor to be a mere 500–600 strong.

At the start of the First Reign, in the immediate aftermath of a Siamese invasion of Cambodia (1781/82), a group of 400–500 Christian "Khmer" — most of them actually Portuguese refugees who had fled to Cambodia from Ayutthaya in 1767 — arrived at Bangkok, accompanying the several thousand Khmer war prisoners brought back from the Thai military campaign. They were assigned to repopulate Ban Portuket (Samsen), largely deserted since the Burmese upheaval of 1766 (Thipakorawong 2009a, p. 37). The village church received their holy icon (formerly at Ayutthaya), the delicately carved, crowned "Santa Maria de Mendese", which continues

to grace the Conception Church chapel today. The small settlement was
strung out along the riverfront, with the church and cemetery to the rear.
The upstream stretch contained the "Khmer" community, most of whom
were market gardeners and livestock raisers (chickens, ducks, pigs, some
milch cows). The southern section housed the old village families, many
holding government posts, including officer rank in the royal artillery. The
village head during the early Bangkok era — possibly serving as "capitan" of
Bangkok's entire Portuguese community — was typically an artillery officer
carrying the rank and title of Phraya Wiset Songkhram Pakdi; successive
holders of that office founded the Wisetrak and Wongpakdi lineages.

Early in the Bangkok era, the Dominican friars serving at the Church
of the Immaculate Conception were replaced (with much difficulty) by
French priests of the Missions Étrangères. Msgr. Jean-Baptiste Pallegoix,
the best-known of that series of French pastors, served there from 1830 to
1862. In 1834 he had a new church building erected to replace the former,
dilapidated edifice. The rebuilt structure still exists — a small, low-roofed
brick and mortar chamber situated behind the present-day impressive church
building, enhanced by a bell tower added in 1883. When Msgr. Pallegoix
was promoted to bishop of Bangkok in 1838, he created a stir by refusing
to move from Ban Portuket to the bishop's residence at the Assumption
Cathedral. That act of humility exemplified his remarkable character,
which helps explain why he was befriended by Prince Mongkut (the later
King Rama IV) during the prince's 1829–1837 residence as a monk at Wat
Samorai, situated directly alongside Ban Portuket. In affirmation of that
friendship, King Mongkut personally attended the bishop's funeral in 1862.

(b) Santa Cruz

The largest of Bangkok's Portuguese parishes is clustered around the Santa
Cruz Church, along the west bank of the river less than half a kilometre
downstream from the old Thonburi citadel. The village is popularly, though
incorrectly, referred to as Kudi Chin, the name of an old Hokkien Chinese
settlement directly upstream. According to the village priest, the population
of Santa Cruz today stands at 1,550, a doubling of its size from the mid-
nineteenth century (Pallegoix 2000, p. 405). The parish was founded in
1768 by no more than 400–500 Ayutthaya survivors. That population was
increased by a contingent of several hundred "Khmer" refugees (Ayutthaya
Portuguese who had initially fled to Cambodia) shortly thereafter and
then was reduced by perhaps a third when that dissident faction split off
in 1772 to form a new parish downstream at Ton Samrong (later known
as Rosario). Despite that disruption, Santa Cruz remained Siam's premier

Portuguese parish throughout the Bangkok era (Francis 1999, pp. 9–22). Until the founding of the Assumption Cathedral far downstream in 1821, Santa Cruz served as the residence of Siam's Catholic bishop (Assumption 1995). An unbroken sequence of French priests officiated at the Santa Cruz Church until 1942, when the first Thai priest was installed; since then all the officiating priests at Santa Cruz have been Thai.

"The land the King gave these Christians was formerly considerable, but the river undermined it every year" (Pallegoix 2000, p. 407). That increased the residential crowding along the riverside, with the community's kitchen gardens, fruit orchards, and graveyard pressing from behind. Succumbing to one of the periodic scourges that afflicted bamboo-and-attap dwellings, the entire settlement, church and all, burned down in 1833. The rebuilt church was inaugurated in 1845. As of 1852 it was described as a fine brick-built sanctum that had replaced the former "low and swampy shed where the altar had become a shelter for snakes" (Pallegoix 2000, p. 407). It was rebuilt again, along more elegant European lines, in 1913–1916. The architectural style and artistic motifs of the still-standing structure, including the central dome and interior frescos, suggest a miniature, much-simplified version of the main throne hall of Bangkok's Dusit Palace, built around the same time. Apparently, the team of Italian artisans recruited by King Chulalongkorn (r. 1868–1910) for the construction of that palace volunteered their services as fellow Catholics for this project (Francis 1999, pp. 13–14).

Over the course of the nineteenth century, a number of the community's residents pursued careers as minor officials in the Ministry of Trade and Foreign Affairs; others entered the import-export trades or engaged in the mechanical arts as gunsmiths, nautical engineers, watchmakers, architects, and the like. In addition to arms manufacture, arms dealing via Macao (in close concert with the Portuguese consul) appears to have been a lucrative pursuit for the merchants of Santa Cruz. During the 1830s and 1840s the Siamese government, much absorbed in its military campaigns against Vietnam to the east and Patani to the south, actively sought arms. Robert Hunter, a Singapore-based British trader who had received permission to establish a residence along the river directly adjacent to Santa Cruz, collaborated with a Santa Cruz-based arms dealer known simply as Joseph. Hunter did much business with the court and was awarded the title of Luang Awut Wiset Prathet Phanit (*awut* referring to his association with arms, *phanit* suggesting his commercial role). In 1844, Hunter was expelled from Siam for opium smuggling and other transgressions, leaving Joseph to his own devices (Moore 1914–1915). He seems to have made his way successfully, however, as in 1851 Siam's main arms trafficker was the Santa

Cruz firm of Messrs Joaquin and Joseph, and in 1855 Joseph was called on to serve as the principal interpreter at the Bowring negotiations (Battye 1974, pp. 56, 96).

Robert Hunter had another important association with Santa Cruz. In 1825 he married Angelina Sap, a descendant of Constance Phaulkon (1647–1688), a seventeenth-century political luminary at Ayutthaya, and Marie Pinar de Guimar, scion of a leading family of Ayutthaya's Portuguese community. Phaulkon had arrived at Siam in 1675 as a Greek adventurer in British employ and despite his *farang* origins had risen to ministerial rank in the Siamese administration before suffering execution in the dynastic overthrow of 1688. Some years later his widow found service in the royal kitchens as matron in charge of sweets and fruits, and sporadic information on her line of descent remains on record (Turpin 1997, p. 98; Hudson 1983). Hunter thus married into the very heart of Siam's Portuguese community. And carrying that tradition further, Robert Jr., the son of Robert Hunter and Angelina Sap, around 1844 married a daughter of one of Santa Cruz's leading residents, Pascal Ribiero de Alvergarais.

Robert Hunter, Jr. (c.1826–1865), as a standing member of the Santa Cruz community, was sent to Great Britain for his education; upon return he was appointed secretary and interpreter to Chaophraya Si Suriyawong, minister of military affairs (*kalahom*). In that capacity, he served as a liaison officer in the hosting of the Bowring mission of 1855. Following promulgation of the Bowring Treaty that year he was appointed Bangkok's harbour master, with the rank and title of Luang Sura Sakon. His residence stood in front of his mother's ancestral home along the Santa Cruz waterfront, a short walk upstream from his father's former domicile, which had been converted into the State Guest House for visiting embassies. His children carried on the family tradition in Siamese government service.

Yet another well-remembered nineteenth-century personality of Santa Cruz's Portuguese community was Francis Chit (or Chitrakhan) (1830–1891). He was a lifelong congregant of the Santa Cruz Church, with his home standing along the riverbank near the church compound. As a young man he helped introduce to Siam the latest techniques of photography and was recruited as official court photographer by King Rama IV (r. 1851–1868). In that capacity, he received the rank and title of Luang Akhani Narimit. Beyond his official duties, he set up a photography shop in 1863 in a rafthouse on the river in front of his Santa Cruz residence. In the 1880s he relocated his shop to a rowhouse along Bangkok's fashionable New Road near the Phraya Si intersection, becoming the city's first studio photographer. Among his other business ventures he introduced Bangkok's first gas works, located at the Sao Ching Cha marketplace, founded in time to illuminate the coronation of King Rama V in 1872.

(c) *Rosario, or Talat Noi*

The dissident faction of several hundred "Khmer Christians" that separated from Santa Cruz in 1772 established a new settlement on the opposite riverbank several kilometres downstream, at Ton Samrong. Initially, that settlement came to be referred to as Rosario, after the name of its church; in the twentieth century it merged into the larger neighbourhood known as Talat Noi (the Small Market) in contradistinction to Sampheng, the neighbouring Chinatown, which was sometimes called Talat Yai (the Large Market). The Holy Rosary Church (Rosario) was not built until 1787, after the services of Francisco de Chagas, a Dominican friar, had been secured from Goa through the good offices of the governor of Macao (Mendonça e Cunha 1976, p. 143). The original congregation (excluding non-communicants) is said to have numbered only 137; by the mid-nineteenth century it had grown to 350, and as of 1901 the number had reached 700–800 (Pallegoix 2000, p. 405; Joseph 1997, p. 24). But the total population may have been much larger, as the local community was said to have included a number of recusants. The admixture of many Chinese congregants over the subsequent century makes later estimates irrelevant to any assessment of Talat Noi's Portuguese population.

The original church at Rosario was an attap-roofed wooden structure raised on pilings to withstand the annual flood. It consisted of a meeting hall and sacristy backed by a small dormitory for the resident cleric, with the communal cemetery behind. A wooden icon rescued from Ayutthaya, "Mother of the Holy Rosary", the church's namesake, was installed as the chapel's centrepiece, and its companion piece, the "Corpse of the Lord Jesus", was stored in a cabinet in the sacristy, to be taken out for procession once a year on Good Friday. As the parish had been established without a resident cleric, a French priest from Santa Cruz occasionally visited to say mass; in 1822 one of those French priests was reluctantly accepted as Portuguese Rosario's first resident pastor. Under his initiative, the church was rebuilt in 1838, and again in 1852. Yet another reconstruction was initiated in 1891. Upon completion in 1897, the enlarged, Gothic-style edifice was renamed the Calvary Church (known locally as Wat Kalawa). A convent and convent school were built alongside at around the same time (Joseph 1997, pp. 18–24).

The community's economic interests from the outset focused on the nautical trades, including ship repair, the forging and casting of ships' iron fittings, sail-making, rope-making, mechanical maintenance, and ships' chandlering. Those specialties evolved rapidly with the technological revolution to maritime steam and iron hull transport. With Siam's foreign trade boom of the second half of the nineteenth century, the iron foundries along the Rosario waterfront profited greatly from the bustling Western river-port directly downstream at Bang Rak. In view of the many workshops lining the path paralleling the shoreline leading upstream from Rosario, Cooking Pan Lane (*trok rong kratha* — referring to the Chinese-style iron cooking pans, *kratha* or *wok*, that were produced for export in the lane's many small forges), visiting British sailors in the nineteenth century came to refer to the area as "Vulcan's Kitchen".

Unlike Bangkok's other, inward-looking Portuguese communities, Rosario became caught up in the city's economic boom, surrounded by such major firms as A. Markwald and Co. (1858–1917), a German agency house, rice miller, and petroleum importer; the Bangkok Manufacturing Co. (founded 1901), an American- and British-owned producer of ice, soda water, and cold storage services; the Nai Lert Co. bus terminal (founded 1907), providing horse-drawn and later motorized bus service across Bangkok; Kiam Hao Heng and Co., one of Bangkok's main department stores in the early twentieth century; and the Siam Commercial Bank branch office at Talat Noi (established 1912). On the downriver side, across the Phadung Krung Kasem Canal, lay the original Customs House (1856–1884) and Portuguese Consulate, and on the upriver side were located the head offices of the Public Works Department (from around 1888) and Harbor Department (from 1892). Furthermore, the neighbourhood was administratively integrated into Sampheng, Bangkok's Chinatown, upon the establishment of the Samphanthawong District (1915), and with major improvements in land transport the influx of Chinese shophouses from Sampheng accelerated. All those developments led to the progressive dilution of the neighbourhood's Portuguese character, making Talat Noi today the most cosmopolitan of Bangkok's old Portuguese settlements.

Rosario's integration into Bangkok's increasingly commercial economy under the free trade regime introduced in the mid-nineteenth century is illustrated by the careers of several of its leading citizens. One was Luiz Maria Xavier (1840–c.1910). Of full Portuguese descent, he received the rank and title of Khun Phasa Pariwat as an interpreter serving with the Harbor Department from the 1860s. In the 1880s he established the Louis Xavier Rice Mills, with his main mill situated adjacent to his residence along the Phadung Krung Kasem Canal, within 300 metres of the Holy Rosary Church (Wright and Breakspear 1908, pp. 152, 153). His son, Celestino W. Xavier, was educated in England and then served as Chargé d'Affaires with the Thai legation at Paris. After his return to Bangkok around 1890, he served as under-secretary of state (equivalent to deputy minister) of foreign affairs with the rank and title of Phraya Phiphat Kosa, supervising the Harbor Department. He was one of the four senior officials who collaborated in 1906 in building Si Phraya Road, a major Bangkok thoroughfare running from the river inland past his family residence and rice mill. He was held in such respect that for some time during the Sixth Reign (1910–1925) he was called upon to serve as honorary consul for Portugal.

A similar case was that of F.V. de Jesus. Born in Bangkok in 1864 and heir to a well-to-do Rosario family, he was educated in Singapore. Upon his return to Bangkok in 1879 he joined Grassi Brothers, a leading construction firm later absorbed into the East Asiatic Company, one of Bangkok's foremost agency houses. In 1897, he was appointed manager of the firm's Wat Phraya Krai sawmill along the Yan Nawa riverfront (see Chapter 5, "Site 18, Bang Uthit"). In 1906 he accepted an offer from Chaophraya Surasak Montri, former chief of the Siamese army and minister of agriculture, to manage the Sriracha Company, a logging enterprise along the eastern seaboard. He joined the firm's board of directors in 1908 and eventually retired a wealthy man (Wright and Breakspear 1908, p. 179). These examples speak to the close participation of Talat Noi's Portuguese community in Siam's economic boom and its progressive integration into the larger Thai world.

Cultural Assimilation

Ethnicity is an elusive concept, primarily because its parameters are ultimately defined by the subject population itself. Thus, Bangkok's Portuguese community remained "Portuguese" for centuries despite its progressive racial hybridization through local intermarriage, cultural integration through linguistic change, and political affiliation through service to the Siamese state. As one of Bangkok's smallest and most distinctive ethnic minorities, the Portuguese historically sought strenuously to maintain their ethnic integrity through such means as clearly delineated communal boundaries, endogamous marriage, hereditary vocations, and strict adherence to Roman Catholic traditions. However, the most powerful instrument of ethnic identification, adherence to a distinct language or dialect, faded away long ago; by the late nineteenth century Portuguese language fluency had virtually vanished from the Siamese scene. Representative of the general situation, though distant from Bangkok, it could be said in the early twentieth century that "[there] is still a colony of [Portuguese] descendants, with high-sounding names they cannot pronounce, round the Catholic church at Mergui [, along the Andaman coast]" (Harvey 1925, p. 202).

A century ago Bangkok's Portuguese neighbourhoods resembled little closed societies, ever suspicious of outsiders. With few exceptions, their residents were members of the local church congregation and adhered faithfully to Roman Catholic ritual and doctrine. The households maintained intimate relations with one another, and in fact virtually all of them were close kinsmen through their insistence on endogamous Catholic marriage. Conformity to communal norms and standards was resolutely enforced through peer pressure and the invocation of religious dogma. Each parish lived in the shadow of its church and under the spiritual aegis of its resident pastor, participating in an endless cycle of worship and ritual. The children received a rigorous religious education at the parish school. Most of the men pursued their artisans' trades from their homes. Many of the women produced their popular sweets, featuring sugared egg-yolk custards and pastries, for sale in the local marketplace. Their one sin — if it could be called that — was low-stakes gambling, a pastime of card-playing and dicing that remained well controlled by communal proscriptions against excess (Francis 1999, pp. 18–19).

Other than their conspicuous church facades, Bangkok's Portuguese settlements were scarcely distinguishable from the many Thai villages lining the riverbank. Careful observation revealed, however, that their attap-roofed, bamboo- or plank-walled dwellings were set directly on the ground, some with slight clearance, but none in the eminently practical, flood-resistant Thai style atop stilts. Furthermore, the women and girls differed in their looks from the neighbouring Thai by letting their hair grow long, preferring "Western" dress (fully covering the upper torso), and generally avoiding betel chewing (and thus blackened teeth). The casual visitor would also note that they bore common Christian names — José, Domingo, Jaime, Manuel; Maria, Rosa, Anna, Marta — and that many retained Portuguese surnames — Gomes, Ribeiro, da Cruz, Fonseco, Diaz, Rodrigues, de Paiva, Lopes, de Souza. Several members of the present-day Bangkok elite have sought to revive that remembrance of their Portuguese ancestry. For instance, Pathorn Srikaranonda, a well-known concert artist, appends his Portuguese lineage name of "de Sequeira" to his signature though that surname was long ago Thai-ized as "Srikara". Thus, a lingering pride of Portuguese ancestry can be glimpsed.

Modern Thai cuisine also contains vestiges of the Portuguese past. It was the Iberian voyagers who brought to Siam such New World crops as potatoes (known as *man farang*, or "Western tubers"), maize, cassava, tomatoes, peanuts, and chili pepper, all staples of the modern Thai diet. They also introduced tobacco and such popular snacks as candied egg-yolk (*foi thong, thong yip*, and *thong yot*), egg custard (*sangkhaya*), sponge cake (*khanom farang*), fried pork skin (*nang mu krop*), as well as bread (*khanom pang*), and also possibly, according to a recent Portuguese ambassador, such dishes as curry puffs, stews, and stuffed omelets (*khai yat sai*) containing beef tongue, ox tail, pigs' trotters, tripe, and the like. It is further speculated by a Ban Portuket matron that roast suckling pig (*mu han*), today prepared in the Chinese style by splitting the carcass and spitting it over a grill, is a refinement of the Portuguese tradition of roasting whole skewered pig over a charcoal pit.

Roman Catholicism has remained an indissociable element of Siamese Portuguese culture over the five centuries of that culture's presence in Siam. Early on, the Portuguese missionaries gave way to the French, and throughout much of the Bangkok era it was the Paris-based Missions Étrangères that continued to control the Siamese pastorate, with French-speaking clerics officiating in church and school. As a compromise, Thai came into use as their language of convenience, leaving Portuguese (and Latin) by the wayside. French priests served as parish heads up to the Second World War period. It was not until after the Second Vatican Council (1962–1965) that the first Thai bishop at Bangkok, Fr. John Nittayo, was appointed after several centuries of French prelates. Under that sort of ecclesiastical colonialism, the Church consistently emphasized a generic form of Euro-centric Catholicism rather than promoting and protecting any specific ethnicity. Today, with nearly all priests coming from the local population and with the Portuguese tongue no longer in use, masses are conducted in Thai. The Portuguese heritage has slackened in the face of that unrelenting pressure.

Under the continuing emphasis on Roman Catholicism, Bangkok's so-called Portuguese community — "so-called" because its self-recognition of its Portuguese roots, as distinct from its Catholicism, continues to fade — has struggled in recent decades to maintain its "critical mass", the minimum population required to sustain an essentially endogamous population. The loss of congregants through conversion to Buddhism, primarily through occasional instances of intermarriage with members of the surrounding Buddhist populace, is a topic not gladly delved into by local informants. But it is clearly a significant issue, as the Portuguese community has barely grown over the course of the Bangkok era, in striking contrast with the rapid growth of the population at large. Here, reliance on endogamy may well have proved counter-productive as a critical means of ensuring ethnic survival and well-being in a plural society.

Out-migration from the fast-fading Portuguese community has also been motivated by the progressive commercialization and modernization of the Thai economy. Over the course of the twentieth century a number of households migrated from the old Portuguese parishes to the commercial districts of Bang Rak and Yan Nawa, and further afield, to find work with Western firms as clerks and compradors, technicians and executives, using their parish school education, vocational and linguistic skills, and Christian connections to secure preferred positions. Their move from the traditional home-based vocations to salaried employment in centrally located offices and factories promoted their social secularization. It accelerated the Thai-ification process from ethnic *integration* — the maintenance of close cross-cultural working relationships — to cultural *assimilation* — the effective abandonment of distinctive convictions and practices in favour of the prevailing national lifestyle. Many of them have melted into the cosmopolitan scene, having fully crossed the ethnic divide from "Portuguese" to "Thai of Portuguese descent" and finally "Thai Christians" or simply secular "Thai".

3

Safe Haven: Mon Refugees

OLD MON AND NEW

Over the course of the past millennium, a succession of Mon (or Raman) migrations crossed the Tenasserim divide from their Irrawaddy delta heartland in present-day Burma to settle in Siam's Chaophraya watershed. The earliest known instance of such migration created the fabled Mon kingdom of Dvaravati, centred along what centuries later came to be the western rim of the Thai kingdom of Ayutthaya (Dhida 1999). Each new migration encountered earlier well-established Mon communities at their journey's end. In many cases the encounter raised tensions between the old and new settler groups, and in each case the newly arrived groups, or "New Mon", became, in due course, established communities, or "Old Mon", who were to face yet newer bands of Mon immigrants in their turn. The distinction between Old and New Mon thus historically presented a "moving target" in the history of Mon migration into the Chaophraya watershed and their interaction with Thai civilization.

Ramanya Desa (Land of the Mon) is remembered as one of the great early civilizations of Southeast Asia. At its height, the configuration of Mon states collectively termed Ramanya Desa reached from the Irrawaddy basin and Andaman littoral over the Tenasserim hills across the Chaophraya watershed, from the Bay of Bengal to the Gulf of Siam. Over a millennium ago the Mon people adopted Theravada Buddhism as the cultural foundation of their vibrant civilization. Having absorbed and adapted much of their lifestyle from South Asia, the Mon in turn contributed greatly to the cultural evolution of their Southeast Asian neighbours, including the Khmer, Thai, Lao, and Burmans. But the halcyon days of Mon hegemony withered away many centuries ago under the mounting pressure of Thai, Shan, and Burman

southward expansion, leaving a reduced Mon empire long known to the
Thai as Hongsawadi (Mon: Haṃsavati; Burmese: Bago; English: Pegu).
Subsequent centuries of Burmese depredations upon the Mon heartland
radiating from Pegu to Yangon (English: Rangoon), Satem (Syriam), Sutham
(Thaton), Molamloeng (Moulmein), Maotama (Martaban), Tawai (Tavoy),
and Tanao-si (Tenasserim) left a much-diminished culture zone (Dhida
1999; South 2003, pp. 49–77).

From the mid-sixteenth century onward, unremitting Burmese
oppression of Hongsawadi and its dependencies induced a persistent
trickle of Mon households and villages, punctuated by a succession of
larger Mon flights, across the Tenasserim hills to the safe haven offered by
Siam. Some nine major Mon migrations — the precise number varies in
different sources — are said to have crossed into Thai territory: six during
the Ayutthaya era from the mid-1500s to around 1760; one during the
Thonburi period; and two during the first two reigns of the Bangkok era
(Halliday 1913; Suporn 1998, pp. 43–74; South 2003, pp. 81–83). Perhaps
somewhat too ingenuously, it has been suggested that "The Thai kings
always greeted these refugees with good will, using them as colonies for
the population of territory (granting land to the exiles) or making allies of
princes who were on the run and using them against the Burmese" (Guillon
1999, p. 194). Similarly, and similarly oversimplified:

> It was by force of circumstances that the Mon were controlled by the
> Burmese, and the Mon had an abiding desire to free themselves from
> the Burmese yoke. As long as they could not free themselves, they were
> obliged to let the Burmese use them in every battle against the Thai.
> The more hardships and deaths they suffered, the more they longed to
> be free of the Burmese yoke.... As a result, a voluntary linkage between
> the Thai kingdom and the Mon region ... came into existence, since the
> Mon immigrants urged their countrymen who were still living in Mon
> territory to follow them and seek protection under the Thai (Damrong
> 2008, pp. 90–91).

Those retrospective glosses fail to consider, among other matters, the many
peaceful Mon villages involuntarily swept up and carried off during the
repeated Thai military incursions and slave raids across the Tenasserim
divide. As an astute seventeenth-century Western ambassador observed:
"[The Siamese busy] themselves only in making slaves. If the Peguins [i.e.,
Mon], for example, do on one side invade the lands of Siam, the Siameses
[sic] will at another place enter the Lands of Pegu, and both Parties will
carry away whole Villages into Captivity" (de La Loubère 1969, p. 90).

The many bands of Mon refugees arriving in Siam during the late Ayutthaya period (1590–1767) received settlement tracts scattered about Siam's western hills, western seaboard, and central plain, with their more privileged numbers settling at the capital and its environs. A large refugee contingent arriving in 1663, for instance, was "given lands to build houses in a place called Sam Khok between the … capital city and … Nonthaburi, near the monastery of Tongpu [northeast of the capital,] and along the canal of Khucham on the outskirts [south] of the capital city" (Damrong 2001, p. 230). As a welcome addition to Siam's perennially inadequate manpower base, the Mon immigrants received fertile rice-paddy and fruit-gardening tracts on the understanding that they would stand ever ready to provide military support to the Siamese state. The Mon asylum seekers proved to be loyal and trustworthy subjects under royal patronage (Ong 2007, p. 4). Serving in their own military regiments led by their own officers, they gained an enviable reputation as valiant warriors and faithful guardians of Siam's western frontier. Their chiefs were awarded ranks and titles in the Siamese nobility, some reaching ministerial rank, with their commander-in-chief carrying the honorific military title of Chakri Mon. Unlike the recurrent strife between the Thai and their other Southeast Asian neighbours, there is no evidence of any significant antipathy between them and the immigrant Mon — despite the fact that Mon troops and Mon officers participated in many of the intermittent Burmese incursions into Siamese territory.

Though the culture that the Mon brought with them to Siam boasted a number of distinctive features (Chuan 1994), it was in its elemental form quite compatible with its Thai counterpart (Halliday 1922; Foster 1973, p. 206). That compatibility was nurtured by centuries of two-way social intercourse and acculturation, to which was added the two peoples' shared suffering at the hands of their common Burmese adversary. Perhaps the most deep-rooted cultural difference was linguistic. Distinctions of a somewhat less elemental order included the Mon preference for living in separate villages from their Thai neighbours and maintaining their separate village-centric society (closely associated with norms of Mon endogamy); practice of a reputedly purer, or more orthodox, version of Theravada Buddhist ritual; lingering customs of spirit worship and kindred totemism; distinguishing nuances of art and artisanship, dress, diet, and the like; and preservation of their sense of unique origin and political heritage (Smithies 1972; Foster 1973). All of that was offset by such shared Mon-Thai social institutions as bilateral kinship, matrilocal residence, polygynous marriage, Theravada Buddhist monasticism, village sodality, and patronage networking, as well as a subsistence economy based on wet-rice cultivation. In fact, Thai-Mon ethnic affinities were sufficiently close that intermarriage of Mon women into the Thai aristocracy appears to have been commonplace (despite Mon protestations of ethnic endogamy). The esteem with which the Mon were regarded by the Thai is often attributed to their historically civilizing role, particularly as the fabled transmitters of Theravada Buddhism to mainland Southeast Asia. Still today, "to be Mon in Thailand is considered rather high class" (South 2003, p. 29).

* * *

In broad perspective, the Mon of ancient Ramanya Desa who settled the Chaophraya basin a millennium ago and who over subsequent centuries merged into the Thai cultural mainstream are sometimes termed Old Mon, as distinct from the New Mon migrations that accompanied the progressive disintegration of Hongsawadi from the mid-sixteenth to early nineteenth centuries. That distinction between Old and New Mon, marking the epochal divide between Southeast Asian antiquity and the more recent past, is so self-evident as scarcely to require these differentiating terms. More narrowly, and certainly more incisively, the Old-Mon/New-Mon distinction is often applied to the contrast between the immigrants of the Ayutthaya era and those who arrived following the revival of the Siamese kingdom under the Thonburi and early Bangkok regimes. That distinction was well recognized by the Thai and Mon themselves, with the Old Mon survivors of Ayutthaya systematically receiving precedence and preference in rank, title, and function during the Thonburi reign. It was vividly highlighted during the dynastic turnover of 1782 with the leadership conflict between Ayutthaya's Mon survivors (headed by Phraya Ramanwong) and the more recent, Thonburi-period immigrants (led by Phraya Cheng). Lastly, the repeated incidence of Old-Mon/New-Mon frictions can be seen also as distinguishing between the Mon of the period of migrations, lasting into the Second Reign, and those of later generations of the Bangkok era who, through quickening assimilation, came eventually to be known as "Thai of Mon descent". In sum, the Old-Mon/New-Mon distinction speaks of a series of instances of intra-Mon frictions, tensions, and conflicts in Thai history: first, the epochal series of cultural reconfigurations in Mon-Thai relations across the Tenasserim watershed dating back many centuries and culminating in the late Ayutthaya period; secondly, the Mon role in the pair of successive Thai dynastic transitions involving the consecutive relocations of the capital of Siam from Ayutthaya to Thonburi and then from Thonburi to Bangkok in the late eighteenth century; and thirdly, the dramatic inter-generational Thai-ification of immigrant Mon ideology and attitude marking the unprecedented political, economic, and social changes of the late nineteenth century. Thus, the distinction between Old and New Mon in Thai history is a historically shifting study in cultural relativity residing, ultimately, in the evolving identity of Mon ethnicity itself. Within the historical context highlighted in this chapter, the New/Old Mon distinction that emerged in the Thonburi period proved particularly significant.

Mon Communities at Ayutthaya and Thonburi

Ayutthaya

Relations between the Mon and Burmese crossed a historic divide in the sixteenth century. Around 1540, Tabinshweti, the Burmese ruler of Toungoo, conquered the Mon homeland and made Hongsawadi his new capital, ending centuries of Mon independence (Harvey 1925, pp. 153–62). That watershed was succeeded by repeated cycles of Mon insurrection and Burmese repression, radiating across frontiers to foment chronic confrontation between the Burmese and the Thai. Under the grievous conditions imposed by recurring waves of Burmese expansionism, Mon migrations eastward, crossing the frontier to Thai sanctuary, flared repeatedly: in the wake of the Burmese capture of Pegu and Martaban (1539 and 1541, respectively); accompanying the flight of Siam's Prince Naresuan from Pegu (1584) and again following his military campaigns against Pegu and Toungoo (1595 and 1600); in the aftermath of Burmese reprisals against Mon peasant insurrections (around 1628, and again in 1661–1662); in reaction against yet another Burmese subjugation of the Mon homeland (1755–1757); and again, following the suppression of a Mon insurrection along the Andaman coast (1763).

The immigrants constituted a broad cross-section of Mon society: nobles and their retinues chafed raw under demeaning subordination to their Burmese overlords; farming households whose adult males faced recurring Burmese conscription under slave-like conditions, leaving their dependants in dire straits; and monks who, as the designated conservators of Mon culture, repeatedly found themselves a prime target of Burmese repression. The arriving contingents were settled in concentric zones of habitation radiating from Ayutthaya in rough accord with their status and power. Most found hospitable shelter in the Meklong River basin, reaching from the Kanchanaburi frontier down to the Gulf of Siam (Sisak 2004, pp. 51–57). Others, including those who had been brought to Siam as war captives — perhaps not all that unwillingly, given their oppression under Burmese rule — settled the less fertile littoral (Sisak 2000, pp. 44–46). The smaller, elite battalions that accompanied their leaders to the capital were allotted the Sam Khok (Three Knolls) wet-rice tracts reaching from the Kret Yai Canal (Large Bypass Canal) to the Kret Noi Canal (Small Bypass Canal) along the lower Chaophraya River, as well as the productive Thung Pho Sam Ton (Three Fig Trees Tract) and adjacent areas along the Pho Sam Ton and Lopburi Rivers, in the more immediate vicinity of the capital (Map 3.1). The chiefs and their senior officers were provided residential sites within the walled capital itself.

The first clearly documented Mon flight to Siamese sanctuary, accompanying the return of Prince Naresuan and more than 10,000 Thai who had previously been carried off from Siam as Burmese war captives, arrived at Ayutthaya in 1584/85 (Cushman 2000, pp. 88–90; Damrong 2008, pp. 38–39). The refugees' favourable reception set the tone for the migrations that followed. With the installation of Naresuan as viceroy (*uparat*) at Ayutthaya's recently built Front Palace, defending the city wall at its most vulnerable point, the Mon leaders Phraya Kiat and Phraya Ram with their personal retinues were settled alongside. There they established Ban Khamin (a village name probably of much later origin) and founded Wat Khun Saen, popularly known as Wat Chao Mon (Temple of Mon Princes). Their spiritual leader was installed as abbot at Wat Mahathat, one of Ayutthaya's most distinguished royal temples, with the exalted title of Somdet Ariyawong, serving as patriarch of a specially created Mon monastic order (*ramanya nikai*) within Siam's monastic brotherhood. His devout followers settled directly alongside and founded there a smaller Mon temple, Wat Nok (Cushman 2000, pp. 89–90; Damrong 2008, pp. 39–41). The main supporting body of Mon troops and their dependants was settled some thirty kilometres downriver, at Sam Khok. In addition, captive-peasant village contingents swept up along Naresuan's marches through the Mon country were settled at a greater distance from the Siamese capital, under close watch. Following Naresuan's elevation to king and his invasion of the Mon country a decade later, further substantial numbers of fugitives and captives were carried off to Siam from Tenasserim and Tavoy (Cushman 2000, pp. 89–90, 136). That process of Mon migration, both voluntary and forced, repeated itself spasmodically over the subsequent century-and-a-half of Ayutthaya's hegemony.

Mon refugee arrivals accelerated in the closing decades of the Ayutthaya era. Many of the newcomers, as earlier stated, were provided with land in the Pho Sam Ton wet-rice tract a few kilometres upstream from the walled

MAP 3.1
Ayutthaya: Mon settlements and related sites, pre-1767

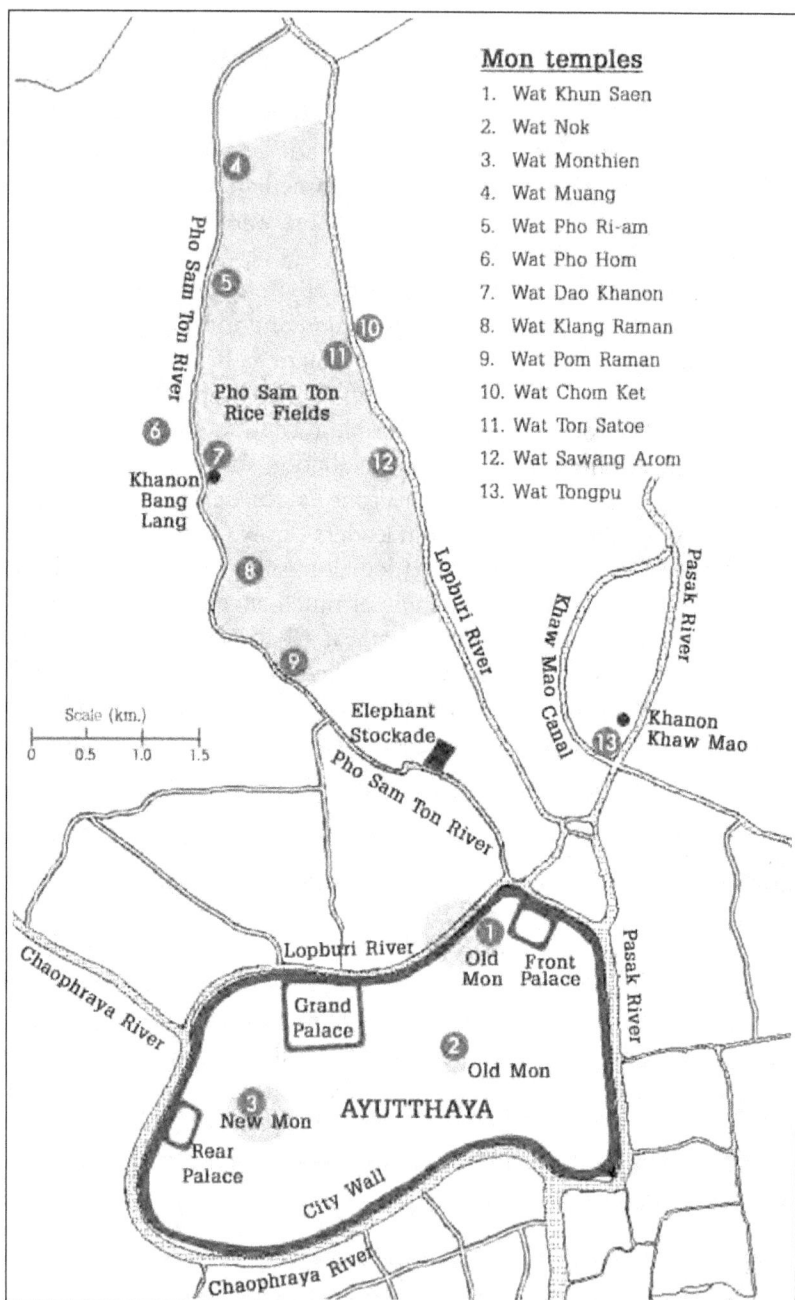

Mon temples

1. Wat Khun Saen
2. Wat Nok
3. Wat Monthien
4. Wat Muang
5. Wat Pho Ri-am
6. Wat Pho Hom
7. Wat Dao Khanon
8. Wat Klang Raman
9. Wat Pom Raman
10. Wat Chom Ket
11. Wat Ton Satoe
12. Wat Sawang Arom
13. Wat Tongpu

Pho Sam Ton River

Pho Sam Ton
Rice Fields

Khanon
Bang
Lang

Lopburi River

Khaw Mao Canal

Pasak River

Scale (km.)

0   0.5   1.0   1.5

Elephant
Stockade

Khanon
Khaw Mao

Pho Sam Ton River

Chaophraya River

Lopburi River

Old
Mon

Front
Palace

Grand
Palace

Old Mon

Pasak River

New Mon

AYUTTHAYA

Rear
Palace

City Wall

Chaophraya River

city (Map 3.1). Under the direction of Ayutthaya's Mon nobility, those communities were assigned the task of defending the major northern routes of approach to the capital. The most important of the Mon strongpoints was the military guard post (*dan*) and transit tax station (*khanon*) at the riverside village of Bang Lang and its temple, Wat Dao Khanong (a corruption of *dan khanon*). A parallel guard post and transit tax station was situated along the Pasak River at the confluence of the Khaw Mao Canal (Deep-Fried Coconut-Batter Bananas Canal — referring to a popular Mon delicacy). And yet another was set up some ten kilometres downriver from Ayutthaya at Ban Tanao-si (San 2000, pp. 61, 62). The close association between many of Siam's Mon immigrant settlements and the various guard posts placed at strategic points along the main access routes to Ayutthaya provides compelling circumstantial evidence that Mon officers and their troops were relied on to keep watch over the approaches to the capital, just as other Mon military units patrolled Siam's western borderlands. Mon military units also served in the Royal Elephantry Department (*krom khochaban*), capturing, domesticating, and training war elephants at the royal elephant stockade located alongside the Pho Sam Ton fields and at the royal elephant stables within the Ayutthaya city wall not far from Ban Khamin, as well as manning the army's elephant corps in war (Varah 2004, pp. 156–59).

With the repeated Burmese subjugation of Hongsawadi and its dependencies, the Andaman lowlands were gradually depopulated while the size and number of Mon refugee settlements around Ayutthaya continued to increase. During the course of a particularly ferocious Burmese suppression of the Mon homeland in the 1750s, Ma Pu — a Mon chief of unknown rank and title, possibly the governor of Yangon — fled with a sizeable contingent of partisans to Siamese sanctuary. Those "New Mon" were welcomed at Ayutthaya, where Ma Pu's peasant followers joined the many "Old Mon" refugees already settled at Sam Khok, with his regular troops being accommodated in the Pho Sam Ton tract (Cushman 2000, p. 446). Ma Pu was awarded the Siamese rank and title of Phraya Noradecha, and he and his personal retinue were provided with residential quarters within the walled city in the vicinity of Wat Monthien, near the Rear Palace, at a considerable distance from the Old Mon settlement alongside the Front Palace. His son, Ma Dot, received the rank and title of Luang Bamroe Pakdi, eventually rising to the rank of *phraya*. In the throes of Ayutthaya's final agony, the chief of Siam's Mon military, Phraya Ram Chaturong (Chuan), died. In the chaotic closing months of the city's siege, he was apparently replaced by Phraya Bamroe Pakdi (Ma Dot), who also inherited his title. The newly appointed Phraya Ram Chaturong (Ma Dot) and those of his followers who managed to survive the Burmese slaughter at Ayutthaya were among the first refugees to join King Taksin at Thonburi in 1767/68.

Thonburi

In contrast to the fertile plains surrounding Ayutthaya, the lower delta, stretching from Thonburi to the sea, was in the sixteenth century a vast brackish swamp thickly jungled with mangrove stands, nipa palm thickets, and scrub-covered tidal flats threaded with meandering tidal streams, sparsely populated by isolated hamlets of foragers and fisherfolk (Tanabe 1978, pp. 40–52; Sisak 2000, pp. 37–51). Far removed from the wet-rice farmlands of the upper delta, the lower delta was not a preferred Mon habitat. From the seventeenth century, however, as the annual inundation of river-borne silt gradually elevated the terrain, the downstream delta came to be colonized by Mon war captives who were assigned to strategic riverside villages standing sentry along the kingdom's maritime fringe; many old Mon village temples, abandoned or rebuilt, continue to line the downstream river today in affirmation of that history. The fortified way station at Thonburi became the natural nerve centre of that downriver waterways-threaded hinterland (Map 3.2).

Thonburi itself had initially served as a minor provincial trading post before graduating to a more prominent role as principal guardian gateway of maritime access to Ayutthaya. There, all arriving vessels were required to anchor for merchandise inspection, toll payment, and off-loading of their guns before proceeding on upstream to capital. Thonburi's defensive role was reinforced during the reign of King Narai (r. 1656–1688) with Western-style fortifications built under the direction of French engineers (Cushman 2000, pp. 307–308; Suchit 2005, pp. 46–50). Mon captives who had been carried off from the Andaman borderlands in 1595 following Naresuan's ultimately unsuccessful campaign against Burmese-held Hongsawadi may have been among the first settlers assigned to man the Thonburi guard post. It is said that they were provided with land in the neighbourhood of what is today Thonburi's Mon Canal, far downriver from Ayutthaya, as Naresuan "distrusted them very much at first" (Halliday 1913, p. 14). That may well have been the origin of the Mon settlement situated directly behind the old Thonburi fort and still in evidence there today, though it may also refer to the better-known Mon village of Bang Yi-roea Mon.

(a) *Bang Yi-roea Mon (Mon Boat Village)*

The evidence of a Mon presence in the immediate Thonburi vicinity dating back to the Ayutthaya era consists almost entirely of the area's

MAP 3.2
Major waterways and Mon population centres of the Chaophraya Delta

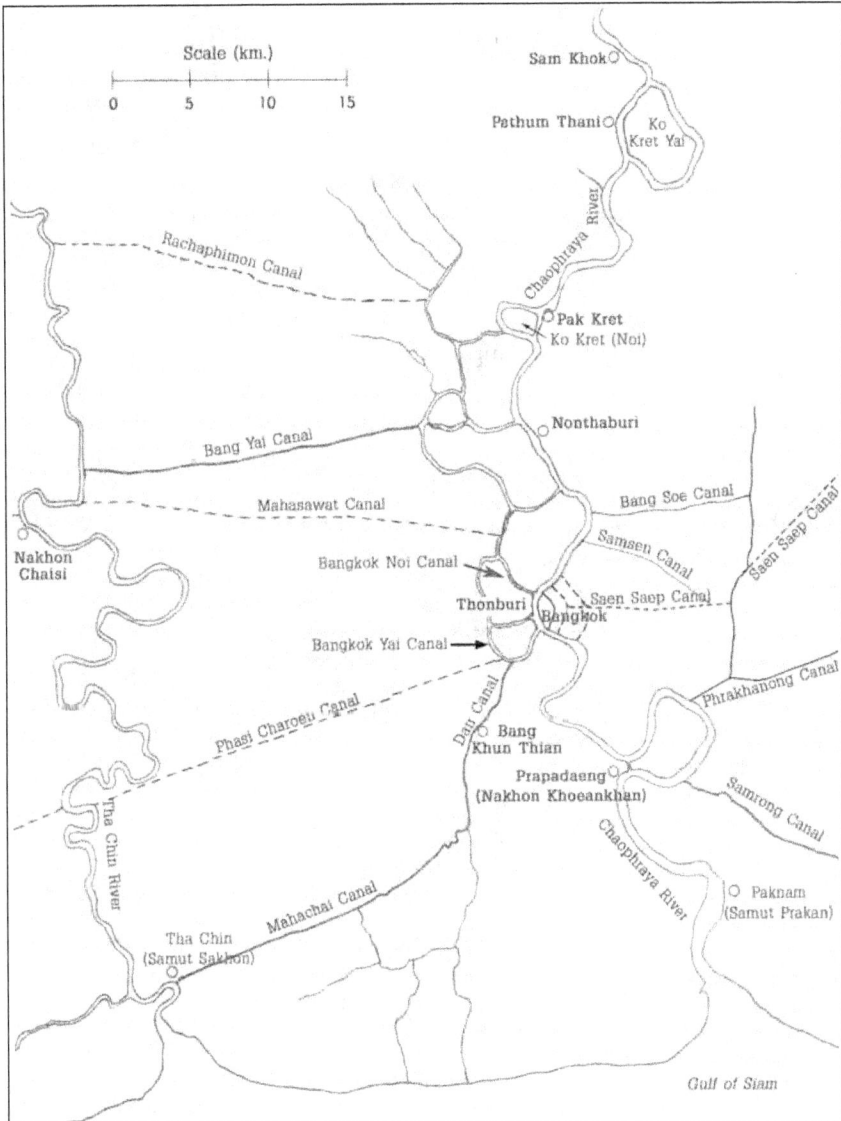

Legend

⌒⌒ = Major waterways of the Ayutthaya period.

- - - = Major waterways added during the Bangkok period.

○ = Mon population centers.

Source: Waterways based on Tanabe (1978), pp. 46, 55, 61, 62.

several surviving Mon, or formerly Mon, monastery-temples. The antiquity and original ethnic affiliation of ancient Thai temples — and thus their supporting communities — can often be ascertained from their names, architectural elements and artistic motifs, and recorded histories (N. na Paknam 1999, pp. 75–92, 107–11, 163–92); that is no less the case for Mon temples. On those grounds, a number of present-day temples in the Thonburi vicinity can be said to date back to Mon settlements of the Ayutthaya era: among others, Wat Lingkop (today Wat Bowon Mongkhon) and Wat Samorai (today Wat Rachathiwat) on opposite shores of the river several kilometres upstream from the Thonburi fort; Wat Bang Yi-roea Noea (today Wat Rachakhroe) and Wat Bang Yi-roea Tai (today Wat Intharam) a few kilometres west of the river along the Bangkok Yai Canal; Wat Klang (today Wat Nak Klang) behind the Thonburi fort; and Wat Khok Kraboe (today Wat Yannawa) on the opposite river shoreline about four kilometres downstream (Map 3.3 shows some of those sites). Each was an integral and indispensable feature of the larger Mon presence, associated in a complex ritual relationship with its own lay community featuring an ongoing exchange of subsistence in return for pastoral and social services (Bunnag 1973, pp. 51–85).

Bang Yi-roea Mon was one of the most vibrant of those old communities. It nestled along the southern bank of the Bangkok Yai Canal not far from its confluence with the Dan Canal (Guardpost Canal, later known as the Bang Khun Thian Canal or Bang Luang Noi Canal), a major transverse waterway linking Ayutthaya with Siam's Mon-populated western seaboard provinces. The original excavation dates of the Dan Canal and its westward extension, the Mahachai Canal (Map 3.2), are unknown, but it is recorded that the entire 30-kilometre route was widened in 1704–1705 by a force of some 60,000 impressed labourers, surely including large numbers of Mon conscripts (Tanabe 1978, p. 46; Cushman 2000, pp. 394, 405, 407). The still recognizably Mon district of Bang Khun Thian in the southwestern Bangkok suburbs, marked by the three old Mon temples of Wat Takam, Wat Hu Kraboe, and Wat Bang Kradi, apparently dates from that time. Bang Yi-roea Mon served as a way-station for long-distance transport between Ayutthaya and the western borderlands and was closely associated with the nearby guardpost that gave the Dan Canal its name. Its two temples gained lasting renown. Wat Bang Yi-roea Noea (the Upstream Temple) is remembered — on a plaque still standing at a prominent spot on the temple grounds — as the cremation site of Phraya Phichai Dap Hak (Thong-di), a Mon hero of the Thonburi period executed in the dynastic turnover of 1782 as a Taksin partisan. It was rebuilt during the First Reign by Chaophraya

MAP 3.3
Thonburi: Mon settlements and related sites, 1767–1782

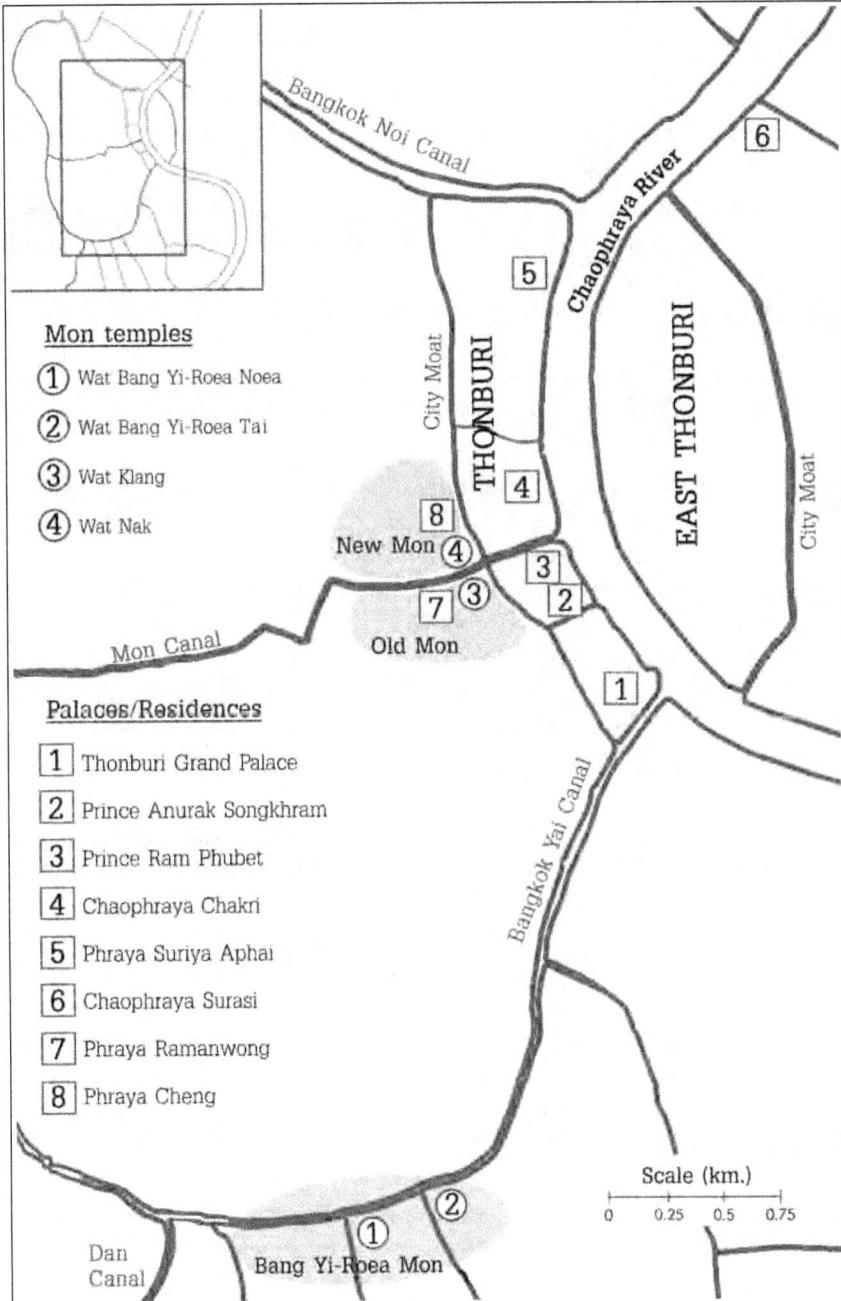

Mon temples

1. Wat Bang Yi-Roea Noea
2. Wat Bang Yi-Roea Tai
3. Wat Klang
4. Wat Nak

Palaces/Residences

1 Thonburi Grand Palace
2 Prince Anurak Songkhram
3 Prince Ram Phubet
4 Chaophraya Chakri
5 Phraya Suriya Aphai
6 Chaophraya Surasi
7 Phraya Ramanwong
8 Phraya Cheng

Phra Khlang (Hon, or Hon-thong), himself a distinguished Mon-affiliated noble, and was rebuilt again in the Third Reign by his grandson, Prince Dechadison (Mang). Wat Bang Yi-roea Tai (the Downstream Temple) served as the cremation site for a number of important personages of Mon ancestry or affiliation during the Thonburi period, among them Princess-Mother Thepamat (Nok-iang, mother of King Taksin, died 1775); Prince Inthara Phithak (died 1776); and Chaochom Chim Yai (died 1779, in childbirth), daughter of Chaophraya Chakri (Thong-duang) and a consort of King Taksin. It was rebuilt in the Third Reign by Phraya Si Sahathep (Thong-pheng), a well-known Mon nobleman. During the Fifth Reign, the extension of Taechiu Chinese settlement along the west bank of the Chaophraya River, hiving off from Sampheng, Bangkok's Chinatown, transformed this Mon village to a Chinese commercial outpost known as Talat Phlu (Betel Leaf Marketplace), featuring a regular ferry service to the Sampheng docks. With that influx, the distinctly Mon character of the area withered away.

(b) *Ban Mon (the [Old] Mon Village)*

As the senior Mon survivor of the Ayutthaya disaster serving King Taksin at Thonburi, Luang Bamroe Pakdi (Ma Dot) was appointed chief of Siam's Mon military, with the newly coined rank and title of Phraya Ramanwong (Van Roy 2010a, pp. 209–10). In that capacity, he commanded all Mon troops at the capital, including the Mon elements of the royal guard. From the outset, the royal patronage extended to the Mon refugee community was symbiotic in intent and effect. So long as the Burmese remained a threat, the Mon militia (*asa mon*) comprised an essential element of Siam's security apparatus. The relatively professional, full-time military role of those elite troops was indicated in their elevated status, as distinct from the indifferently trained, inadequately equipped, seasonal conscripts who formed the bulk of the army (Suporn 1998, pp. 119–25). In the Bangkok era, that system was formalized into a group of ethnically specialized military detachments, including the Department of Mon Militia (*krom asa mon*), assigned principally to patrol Siam's western frontier; the Department of Vietnamese Militia (*krom asa yuan*), a body of Vietnamese war prisoners skilled in artillery; and the Department of Cham Militia (*krom asa cham*), consisting of Cambodian Cham troops assigned primarily to the eastern frontier, only to be dissolved with the stabilization of Siam's borders and the reform of the military along Western lines over the course of the Fifth Reign (Battye 1974, pp. 209–59, 397–492). Whether the Mon Militia Department and its specialized function dated from before the Bangkok period is unclear, but it certainly fit closely with King Taksin's aggressive military strategy. His innovative policy of dispersing his forces to the frontier provinces while leaving the centre lightly defended was a brilliant reversal of the static, siege mentality that had preoccupied the Thai throughout the Ayutthaya era. But that strategy ultimately undid him in 1782 when his limited troop strength at Thonburi proved inadequate to contain mutiny and revolt.

King Taksin provided Phraya Ramanwong and his retainers the site of an old, abandoned village a five-minute march west from the Thonburi Grand Palace, backing the Thonburi City Moat and bordering the Mon Canal (Map 3.3; Sansani 1994, p. 182; Parate 2008, p. 97). The Mon Canal served as that community's "front doorstep" and primary means of access to the river, which accounts for its name. However, no evidence, physical or documentary, has survived to suggest the canal's date of origin. Its earliest mention appears in a Burmese espionage map of the late 1770s (Surin 2002). The canal was likely enlarged around that time from a minor drainage sluice to a substantial waterway, after the Burmese threat had receded and the local populace could be redeployed for such a labour-intensive public works project. The village clustered around Wat Klang (today Wat Nak Klang), a temple dating from the Ayutthaya era which, like many temples along the Burmese line of march to Ayutthaya, had been abandoned in 1766/67. The temple was re-established soon after Taksin designated Thonburi the new capital, with the installation of Phra Thammachedi, an eminent Thai — not Mon — monk, as its abbot. The arrival of Phraya Ramanwong and his followers soon thereafter created a problem, as the Mon settlers required a temple affiliated with the Raman order — practising Mon Buddhist ritual, speaking the Mon vernacular, sustaining Mon culture — which required a Mon abbot. So, in 1770 or shortly thereafter Phra Thammachedi was dispatched to Phisanulok to help restore the northern monastic order to Buddhist orthodoxy in the wake of the heretical teachings of Chao Phra Fang, the recently executed leader of a powerful regional insurgency. In his absence, a Mon monk, Phra Khru Thep-sithithep-thibodi, was appointed as his replacement. Unpleasantries were avoided upon Phra Thammachedi's return to Thonburi in 1780 with his installation as abbot of Wat Photharam (commonly referred to as Wat Pho, later renamed Wat Phra Chetuphon) and promotion to the senior ecclesiastical title of Phra Phimontham (Wat Nak Klang 1997, pp. 53–54). By such means, Ban Mon established a firm Mon ethnic presence at Thonburi, a presence that remains on site today, though much attenuated with a persistent influx of suburban Chinese households.

(c) *Ban Mon Mai (the New Mon Village)*
Continued Burmese oppression of the Mon people through enslavement, confiscatory taxation, forced acculturation, and brutal punishment inspired

yet another popular uprising in the Burmese-occupied Mon principalities in the 1770s. Led by Phraya Cheng, a Mon chieftain serving as governor of Burmese-controlled Troen (Ataran) in the Tenasserim hills, the rebels attacked Burmese-held Martaban. The insurrection ultimately failed and resulted in a 1774/75 flight of perhaps 10,000 Mon refugees, some 3,000 of them headed by Phraya Cheng himself, over the Tenasserim divide into Siamese sanctuary (Damrong 1939, pp. 1–5; Van Roy 2010a, pp. 213–14). That sizeable body of seasoned warriors was received by King Taksin as a welcome addition to Siam's depleted manpower base.

Most of those new arrivals were settled along the Chaophraya River upstream from Thonburi, from Pak Kret to Sam Khok (Map 3.2), while Phraya Cheng and his personal entourage were provided a residential site along the outer bank of the western Thonburi City Moat, at Wat Nak (today Wat Phraya Tham), directly across the Mon Canal from Phraya Ramanwong and the existing Mon settlement at Wat Klang (Map 3.3; Sansani 1994, p. 184). The establishment of that New Mon stronghold realigned Thonburi's factional politics, as Phraya Ramanwong and Phraya Cheng soon came into conflict over issues of protocol and power. While Phraya Ramanwong was senior in age, rank, and title at Thonburi, Phraya Cheng claimed precedence on grounds of descent from Banya Dala, the last independent Mon ruler of Hongsawadi; furthermore, he had the allegiance of a formidable fighting force (Sujaritlak 1983, p. 47; Nidhi 1996, pp. 497–99). The installation of their respective residential compounds and retinues confronting one another across the Mon Canal surely contributed to that revival of the tradition of Old-Mon/New-Mon tensions. Phraya Cheng's and Phraya Ramanwong's residences outside the walled city were paired with the residences of their respective patrons within the city wall. Phraya Cheng's compound stood directly across the city wall and moat from that of Chaophraya Chakri (Thong-duang), which overlooked the river north of the Mon Canal. Similarly, Phraya Ramanwong's compound was situated outside the city wall and moat behind the Outer Palace (Wang Nok), the riverside residence of Prince Anurak Songkhram (Chao Ramlak, one of several "nephews" — probably fictive kinsmen formerly associated with the Ayutthaya royal family — serving as senior military aides to King Taksin). Another such royal "nephew" was Prince Ram Phubet (Bunchan), a skilled military commander whose palace stood directly alongside that of Prince Anurak.

The enmity between Thonburi's Old and New Mon leaders erupted in armed combat in March 1782, during the course of a rebellion against the purported maladministration of the Taksin regime. The shifting factional alignments in that political crisis remain murky, but the essential participants

formed a triangular face-off between the "rebels" (led by Phraya San), the
"royalists" (headed by Prince Anurak Songkhram and Phraya Ramanwong),
and the "opportunists" (commanded by Chaophraya Chakri and Chaophraya
Surasi, off campaigning in Cambodia but represented at Thonburi by their
nephew, Phraya Suriya Aphai). In that confrontation, Phraya Ramanwong
appears to have remained steadfastly loyal to King Taksin, Prince Anurak
Songkhram evidently defected to Phraya San, and Phraya Cheng aligned
himself with the forces of Phraya Suriya Aphai (Nidhi 1996, p. 499). That
interpretation carries the conjectures, first, that Prince Anurak, recognizing
the untenable position of the royal faction absent King Taksin's charismatic
leadership, crossed over to the rebel side in expectation that he would be
installed as the next king and, second, that Phraya Ramanwong, unaware
of those intrigues, was misled by Prince Anurak into entering battle against
Phraya Suriya Aphai on behalf of the rebels. An apocryphal tale has it that
at the critical moment, with the troops of Phraya Suriya Aphai about to be
overrun by the combined rebel and royalist forces, an urgent appeal by Siri
Rochana (Rocha, or Rot), wife of the absent Chaophraya Surasi, to Phraya
Cheng convinced him to mobilize his troops in support of the beleaguered
Chakri forces. Only Phraya Cheng's pre-existing enmity against Phraya
Ramanwong, as well as his factional leanings and personal association
with Chaophraya Surasi, can effectively explain that dramatic decision
(Nidhi 1996, pp. 551–52, citing Historical Publications Committee 1971,
p. 97). Ultimately, the victory of the Chakri faction proved fatal for Phraya
Ramanwong (as well as Taksin's royal "nephews", Princes Anurak and Kam
Phubet), whereas Phraya Cheng was rewarded with elevation to chief of
Siam's Mon military forces (Damrong 1937, p. 94; Thipakorawong 2009a,
p. 15). The divergent destinies of Phraya Ramanwong and Phraya Cheng
profoundly influenced the subsequent history of Siam's Mon leadership.

MON SETTLEMENTS AT OLD BANGKOK

Perhaps because the Chakri kings boasted Mon ancestry, and certainly
because Thonburi's Mon community played a vital role in the coup that
brought the Chakri dynasty to power, several Mon lineages attained
prominent positions among the nobility of the early Bangkok period. With
Burma remaining a threat at least until the mid-1820s, the Mon military
contingents along the western frontier continued to be relied on. Hence,
for much of the nineteenth century "being Mon" entailed a continuing
claim on the patronage of the Mon elite, and a claim on employment in the
traditional Mon military establishment. That congeries of circumstances

was well reflected in the Mon settlements scattered across Old Bangkok's cityscape.

The Bangkok Side

(a) *Ban Phra Athit*

In the aftermath of the Chakri coup of 1782, the friendship between Phraya Cheng and the leaders of the new regime matured into a formal patron–client relationship whereby Phraya Cheng was awarded the new title of Phraya Mahayotha and elevated to commander of Siam's Mon militias, under the direct supervision of Prince Surasinghanat (Bunma), the First-Reign viceroy. Cheng and his retinue were then relocated from Ban Mon Mai, their former settlement along the Thonburi outskirts, to a prestigious Bangkok riverfront tract that came to be known as Ban Phra Athit (Sun Village, named after the nearby Front Palace bastion, Pom Phra Athit), in the shadow of the viceroy's Front Palace stronghold (Map 3.4). Several years later the relationship between the Front Palace and the New Mon leadership was further solidified by the elevation of Phraya Mahayotha to ministerial rank (*chaophraya*) and, some years thereafter, by the marriage of one of his granddaughters, Chamot, to Prince Bua, a son of the viceroy, producing the Pathomsing royal lineage. The viceroy further extended his patronage of the Mon community with the construction of a royal temple, Wat Chana Songkhram, to serve the recently established Ban Phra Athit.

Among his services during the Second Reign, Chaophraya Mahayotha (Cheng) assisted the viceroy in 1823 in upgrading the downstream outpost of Prapadaeng to a well-fortified military redoubt. Its ramparts featured three cannon-armed bastions on the east bank and five on the west. A Mon garrison of 300 troops, with their households totalling over 1,000 persons, was installed there. The fort's name was glorified to Nakhon Khoeankhan (Great Barrier City), and Chaophraya Mahayotha's second son, Tho-ma, was appointed governor. An unbroken succession of eight direct descendants of Chaophraya Mahayotha served as governors of Nakhon Khoeankhan to its military dismantling and downgrading to civilian status in the Sixth Reign, a century later (Sujaritlak 1983, p. 60). In the 1920s the old, abandoned fortifications and military billets were converted to a leprosarium. The town of Prapadaeng lingers on today as a repository of Mon culture and ethnic pride.

The river frontage of Bangkok's New Mon settlement at Ban Phra Athit stretched a half kilometre north from the mouth of the Inner City Moat (that segment called the Rong Mai Canal) to the mouth of the new City

MAP 3.4
Bangkok: Mon settlements and related sites, pre-1910

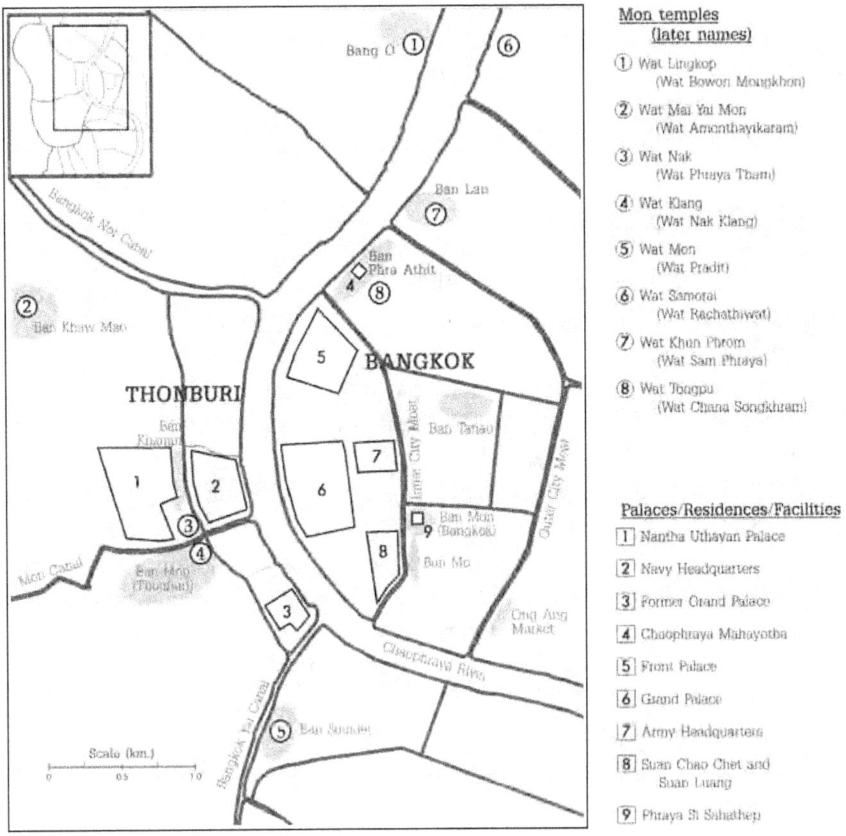
Bang O
Ban Lan
Bangkok Noi Canal
Ban Phra Athit
Ban Khaw Mao
BANGKOK
THONBURI
Ban Tanao
Inner City Moat
Outer City Moat
Ban Mon (Bangkok)
Ban Mo
Ban Mon (Thonburi)
Mon Canal
Ong Ang Market
Chaophraya River
Bangkok Yai Canal
Scale (km.)
0
0.5
1.0
Mon temples
(later names)
① Wat Lingkop
(Wat Bowon Mongkhon)
② Wat Mai Yai Mon
(Wat Amonthayikaram)
③ Wat Nak
(Wat Phraya Tham)
④ Wat Klang
(Wat Nak Klang)
⑤ Wat Mon
(Wat Pradit)
⑥ Wat Samorai
(Wat Rachathiwat)
⑦ Wat Khun Phrom
(Wat Sam Phraya)
⑧ Wat Tongpu
(Wat Chana Songkhram)
Palaces/Residences/Facilities
1 Nantha Uthayan Palace
2 Navy Headquarters
3 Former Grand Palace
4 Chaophraya Mahayotha
5 Front Palace
6 Grand Palace
7 Army Headquarters
8 Suan Chao Chet and
Suan Luang
9 Phraya Si Sahathep

Moat (that segment known as the Banglamphu Canal). Prevented by the city wall from extending more than 50–70 metres inland from the river shore, the settlement spread into the river itself, with the shoreline becoming crowded with double- and triple-moored lines of Mon rafthouses. At the centre of that riverfront tract, backed by the city wall, stood the residence of Chaophraya Mahayotha (Cheng), later inherited and repeatedly rebuilt by a succession of his male heirs (the Kochaseni lineage): Chaophraya Mahayotha (Tho-ria), Phraya Damrong Rachapholakhan (Chui), Prince Naret Worarit (Krisada Phinihan), and in the twentieth century Prince Charunsak Kridakan. Round about were clustered the dwellings of their adult sons and other kin, along with those of their senior lieutenants.

Upon the introduction of formal land title registration in the 1890s, Prince Naret received the king's permission to obtain title deeds for the entire 26,000-square-metre riverside tract. Thus, when the property was transferred to the Crown Property Office (*phra khlang khang thi*) a year after Naret's death in 1925, his son Prince Charunsak received generous compensation on behalf of the family (Sujaritlak 1983, pp. 26–32).

Directly behind the riverside settlement, within the city wall, the newly arrived Mon community in the 1780s established a Raman (i.e., Mon) temple, Wat Tongpu, on the grounds of an old, abandoned Thai village temple, Wat Klang Na (Temple Amidst the Rice Fields) (see Chapter 7, subsection on "Ban Klang Na"). About a decade later, in his role as royal patron of the Mon nobility, the First-Reign viceroy sponsored the reconstruction of Wat Tongpu on an expanded scale as Wat Chana Songkhram (Temple of Victory in War) in honour of the Mon participation in Siam's recent triumphs over the Burmese. It became the heart of Siam's Raman monastic order with the installation there of Phra Maha Sumethachan as administrative head of the order's central region. At the same time, Phra Sumetha-noi, abbot of Wat Racha Khroe, was appointed to head the sect's southern administration, and Phra Traisonthai, abbot of Wat Intharam, was designated to head the northern administration (Suporn 1998, p. 188). Successive abbots of Wat Chana Songkhram, invariably carrying the title of Phra Sumethachan, continued to serve as the Raman order's patriarch to the close of the nineteenth century.

Confined to the shoreline fronting the city wall, and with the city's inner and outer moats blocking its extension at either end, the Mon settlement at Ban Phra Athit soon became overcrowded. Thus, the small cross-river village of Bang O, with its own Mon temple, Wat Lingkop, grew into a satellite settlement of Ban Phra Athit. Prince Senanurak (Chui), the Second-Reign viceroy, demonstrated his continued patronage of the New Mon nobility by sponsoring the reconstruction of that temple, upgrading it to royal status, and renaming it Wat Bowon Mongkhon (Temple of Viceregal Good Fortune). Ancient Thai custom prohibited all cremations within the walled city other than those of the most senior royalty. Standing within the Bangkok city wall, the Mon spiritual centre of Wat Chana Songkhram was thus prevented from carrying out that most important rite of passage for the Ban Phra Athit nobility. The establishment of Wat Bowon Mongkhon served specifically as an act of royal patronage according appropriate dignity to the cremations of Bangkok's Mon elite. It was possibly as a visitor to Wat Bowon Mongkhon, reportedly in 1825 (though possibly a year or so later), that Prince Mongkut was inspired by the abbot, Phra Sumethamuni,

to "purify" the Thai monkhood through the adoption of traditional Mon
monastic practice — and thus to found the Thammayut order (Reynolds
1972, p. 80).

(b) Ban Phraya Si

Under Thai law, the penalty for rebellion was execution accompanied (for
the family's collective punishment) by the loss of rank and title plus the
forfeiture of all privileges and property amassed over the course of the
perpetrator's lifetime. The execution of Phraya Ramanwong (Ma Dot)
and his lieutenants in 1782 thus left their surviving families destitute. In
his continuing effort to demonstrate his benevolence as a righteous ruler
(and to stave off possibilities of further rebellion), King Rama I restored
the survivors to a position of dignity. The newly laid-out walled city of
Ratanakosin needed population — royalty in the citadel (between the Inner
City Moat and the river) and nobility in the outer precincts (between the
inner and outer moats). Among the many households "invited" to move to
the new noble quarter were the residual leadership of Thonburi's Old Mon
community. They were provided with a residential site along the outer bank
of the Inner City Moat, well separated from the New Mon settlement at
Ban Phra Athit. In contrast to the conjunction of Ban Phra Athit with the
Front Palace, the newly established Old Mon village was situated within the
city's southern sector, under the jurisdiction of the Grand Palace. The site
was initially called simply Ban Mon, but some four decades later it came
to be known as Ban Phraya Si (Map 3.4).

Leadership of the surviving Old Mon nobility devolved upon Phraya
Nakhon In (Ma Khon), Phraya Ramanwong's senior son-in-law. He served
as commander of the Swords-in-Both-Hands Regiment (*kong dap song
moe*), one of the five Mon military contingents guarding Siam's western
frontier. At Thonburi he had resided in his father-in-law's compound, but
he escaped punishment in the revolution's aftermath, apparently due to his
absence from Thonburi on military duty. Upon his return to the capital and
formal submission to the newly installed Chakri regime, he was ordered
to relocate with his family to the Bangkok-side residential site (Phusadi
2002, vol. 1, p. 37). His eldest grandson, Thong-pheng (Phraya Si Sahathep,
forebear of the Siphen lineage), in due course became the family head and
inherited that residential site, which came to carry his titular name as Ban
Phraya Si (Sansani 1994, p. 183; Parate 2008, pp. 97, 99; Van Roy 2010*a*,
pp. 210–11). Thong-pheng married a niece of Riam (ultimately elevated
to Princess-Mother Si Sulalai), a consort of King Rama II who bore Prince

Chesada Bodin (Thap), the later King Rama III. Through that fortuitous royal connection, Thong-pheng was appointed to a position in the Ministry of Civil Affairs (*krom mahadthai*) that gave him control of upcountry teak concessions and the lucrative teak timber tax farm (Sujaritlak 1983, p. 66). The continuing influential positions held in that ministry by several generations of his descendants — including his son Phoeng, who inherited his title and whose children were the first generation of the lineage to use the Siphen surname — ensured them a lucrative role in the administration of Siam's teak industry well into the twentieth century.

Among the public works projects that Phraya Si Sahathep (Thong-pheng) directed on behalf of King Rama III was the construction of Saphan Mon (the Mon Bridge), a substantial structure consisting of teak foundation timbers and teak plank flooring supported by masonry buttresses spanning the Inner City Moat alongside his residence (Sirichai 1977, pp. 31, 141). It was built to replace a nondescript pedestrian crossing that had lasted from its construction in the First Reign until its destruction in a great fire in 1831. Phraya Si Sahathep's compound and a broad surrounding swath of hundreds of commoners' dwellings as well as several nearby princes' palaces were consumed in that wildfire. The King expressed his sympathy with the people's suffering by extending the settlement area for the dispossessed community and awarding additional land for Phraya Si's rebuilt compound (Thipakorawong 1995, p. 45; Phusadi 2002, vol. 1, pp. 37–38). The enlarged compound of 12,000 square metres came to contain Phraya Si Sahathep's own residence plus about twenty homes of his kin and subordinates. Beyond that spread the humbler dwellings of his lesser retainers, clustered along the outer bank of the Inner City Moat and on houseboats moored to the shore. That extension of Ban Phraya Si later came to be known as Ban Mo (Pottery Village). The construction of Charoen Krung Road in 1862/63, followed by Foeang Nakhon Road in 1863/64, created an intersection abutting Ban Phraya Si that came to be known as Si Kak Phraya Si (the Phraya Si Crossroads). Ban Phraya Si occupied the northwestern quadrant of the intersection, reaching some 140 metres from the crossroads to the foot of the Mon Bridge. Over the course of the Fifth Reign, the descendants of Phraya Si Sahathep gradually dispersed to other Bangkok neighbourhoods and upcountry postings, and Ban Phraya Si reverted to the Privy Purse, which built stylish shophouse rows along the intersecting street-fronts. With Siam's turn-of-the-century economic boom, Si Kak Phraya Si became the centre of Bangkok's then most fashionable shopping district.

The Thonburi Side

(a) *Ban Mo and Ban Khamin*

At the entrance to the present-day Thonburi neighbourhood adjoining Wat Nak Klang stands a signboard erected by the Bangkok Municipality proudly proclaiming the community as Ban Mo (Pottery Village), replicating the name of the commercial neighbourhood bordering Bangkok's Inner City Moat alongside Ban Phraya Si. The name refers to a cottage industry to which many Mon households were drawn with Siam's growing commercialization as the nineteenth century wore on (Tomosugi 1993, pp. 137–40; Alisa 1999; Pisarn 2007). Thonburi's Ban Mo stretches across the Mon Canal to fade into Ban Khamin (Map 3.4). That small village, as its name suggests, depended on another Mon cottage industry, the processing and marketing of *khamin*, a fashionable turmeric-based cosmetic not dissimilar to the ubiquitous Burmese face-powder, *thanaka*, produced from an aromatic wood pounded into powder with an admixture of slaked lime for use as a beautifying application (Suchit 2002, pp. 229–33). Those two cottage industries — facial cosmetic and earthenware pottery — represent the variety of occupational expedients to which the remaining Thonburi Mon villagers turned to supplement their subsistence staples of rice and freshwater fishing in the decades following the departure of their noble patrons.

The persisting Old-Mon/New-Mon factional tensions of the early Chakri reigns are reflected in the history of the twin Mon temples — initially known as Wat Klang and Wat Nak — that defined Thonburi's Old and New Mon settlements. To commemorate the former residence of Phraya Cheng at the New Mon village, Wat Nak was rebuilt early in the Second Reign on an enlarged scale, incorporating his former residential compound. Chaophraya Ratana Thibet (Kun), a Chinese tycoon who had maintained close ties with Chaophraya Mahayotha (Cheng) and had married one of his daughters, served as director of that reconstruction project. After his death in 1813 his sons completed the reconstruction project. The temple was renamed Wat Phraya Tham (Temple Built by Phraya) in their honour and was raised to royal status in the Third Reign. Phra Nikrom-muni (Benchawan), a junior son of Chaophraya Ratana Thibet, was installed as the temple's abbot (Wat Phraya Tham 2007, pp. iv, x).

At the same time, the descendants of Phraya Ramanwong, wishing to commemorate discreetly their unjustly defamed ancestor, sought royal permission to establish a small temple on the site of his former Thonburi residence. Thus, in the Second Reign, Wat Noi came to be situated directly behind Wat Klang. In the Third Reign, the two adjoining temples of Wat

Noi (now renamed Wat Nak) and Wat Klang were merged and upgraded
by Phraya Si Sahathep. The combined temple was then renamed Wat Nak
Klang and elevated to royal status by King Rama III (Wat Nak Klang 1997,
p. 54). The closely parallel histories of Wat Phraya Tham and Wat Nak
Klang, both founded in the Second Reign to commemorate the residential
sites of the former Old Mon and New Mon leaders and both raised to royal
status in the Third Reign to honor the respective communities, suggests the
lingering Mon factional sensitivities that the successive Thai kings sought
to dampen through such even-handed diplomacy.

(b) *Ban Khaw Mao*

Since the reign of King Taksin, Thonburi's Mon villagers had cleared large
tracts of fertile farmland well into the Thonburi interior for cultivation as
rice fields and fruit orchards. That arrangement was disrupted around 1866,
shortly before the end of the Fourth Reign, by the intrusion of a sprawling
royal retreat, the Nantha Uthayan Palace (Map 3.4). The palace grounds
as laid out by the royal corps of engineers infringed upon a great swath
of the land that had, since the Thonburi period, been held in usufruct by
the Mon community. Invoking the royal right of eminent domain, the
king's factotums simply expropriated what they considered suitable for
the king's pleasure (though the king generously paid an unknown sum
in compensation), ringed it with moats and fencing, and built within its
compass a cluster of luxurious royal bungalows and lush gardens. King
Mongkut died before completion of the palace, and the unfinished project
was then abandoned. His son, King Chulalongkorn, had a number of its
teak residences dismantled for the construction of palaces for his younger
brothers. In 1878, an experimental boys' boarding school, the King's
School (also known as the Suan Anand School), was founded on the
unused property as a royal project, with an American missionary, Samuel
McFarland, serving as director until the school was moved out in 1891.
Following the government reorganization of 1892, the deserted palace
grounds were converted to a training facility for the Mon marines who had
not many years before been transferred to the nearby navy headquarters
from Prapadaeng and Ban Somdet (see below). As a result, Thonburi's Ban
Mo and Ban Khamin neighbourhoods are today heavily Navy-affiliated, and
Wat Nak Klang and Wat Phraya Tham frequently host religious ceremonies
under the sponsorship of senior naval officers.

The Mon villagers who had in the 1860s been evicted from the
Nantha Uthayan Palace site had no recourse but to move to new land
deeper within the Thonburi interior. Their new village, founded in an

isolated Thonburi tract, was named Ban Khaw Mao (reminiscent of the Mon village and transport canal of that name at Ayutthaya). There they carved out new farmlands and built Wat Mai Yai Mon (the Large New Mon Temple, today known as Wat Amon-yikaram). A century and a half later the local community retains no memory — at least so its elders aver — of its unfortunate origins.

(c) *Ban Somdet*

Not long after the start of the Chakri dynasty's Third Reign, the British entered into war against the Burmese. King Rama III decided to exploit the unsettled border situation by having Chaophraya Mahayotha (Thoria) lead a body of Mon troops across the Tenasserim range to "sweep up" (*kwat*) captives (Suporn 1998, p. 74). Some of the Mon captives were posted downstream from Bangkok at Nakhon Khoeankhan (Prapadaeng). Others were settled upriver, at Bang Lamut (today largely obliterated beneath the west-bank approaches to the Rama VI Railway Bridge and Rama VII Highway Bridge). There they founded Wat Bang Lamut (known today as Wat Wimut). In the closing years of the Third Reign a number of the Bang Lamut war captives were conscripted to build and man a new navy shipyard along the Bangkok Yai Canal, under the authority of Chaophraya Prayurawong (Dit), in charge of the Ministry of Military Affairs (*krom kalahom*). In the fields behind, a facility was built to house and train a regiment of Mon marines drawn from Nakhon Khoeankhan and Samut Sakhon. The new settlement site came to be called Ban Somdet, and the conscripts built there a Mon village temple called Wat Pradit (Map 3.4; Sujaritlak 1983, pp. 35–40). The shipyard and marine camp at Ban Somdet were terminated during the Fifth Reign, and their personnel were reassigned to the royal shipyard alongside the new navy headquarters built on the site of Rama I's former residential compound (Phra Niwet Doem) and the marine camp erected in the former Nantha Uthayan Palace grounds. That move greatly bolstered the Mon marine presence at Thonburi's Ban Mo and Ban Khamin.

Some Other Mon Sites

(a) *Ban Lan*

Luang Chat Surenthon (Sawat), a Mon survivor of the fall of Ayutthaya, served the Thonburi regime as a junior officer under Chaophraya Chakri (Thong-duang). His military prowess became known to Chaophraya Surasi (Bunma), who befriended him and became his patron. Through continued valour in war, Sawat was promoted to Phraya Racha Songkhram, and he and his entourage were provided with a riverside residential site directly upstream from Chaophraya Surasi's stronghold at Bang Lamphu (Map 3.4) and the Khmer settlement at Bang Lamphu Bon (see Chapter 7, subsection on "Ban Rong Mai and Bang Lamphu Bon"). In the distribution of royal perquisites, he received the talipot palm leaf (*bai lan*) tax farm. Thus, his settlement came to be called Ban Lan (Talipot Palm Village). The cultivation and harvesting of talipot palms in the Chaophraya delta marshes was a long-established Mon enterprise; Ban Lan served not only as the industry's tax administration centre but contained palm-leaf curing and warehousing facilities. Most of its Mon households were occupied in the labour-intensive manufacture of palm-leaf manuscripts (*khamphi*), ritual fans (*talapat*), woven bags and baskets, thatch, and the like.

Sawat did not have many years to savour his success, as he died before the end of the Taksin reign. Only one of his children, Khun Phrom Raksa (Sat), remained at Ban Lan to continue in his footsteps. When Sat died without progeny, the talipot tax farm passed to another noble, probably a member of the New Mon nobility under the patronage of Chaophraya Mahayotha. Sat's property was inherited by his dispersed siblings, who decided to erect on the site of the now-deserted family compound a temple which they named Wat Khun Phrom in their brother's memory. With those developments the name Ban Lan fell into disuse, to be replaced by Bang Khun Phrom. During the Third Reign, Phraya Racha Suphawadi (Khun-thong), Phraya Rachanikun (Thong-kham), and Phraya Thep Worachun (Thong-ho) — three sons of Phraya Surintharamat (Ma Tho-poen) and Khunying Phawa, Sat's sister — decided to rebuild the temple and present it to King Rama III. The king raised it to royal status and in their honour renamed it Wat Sam Phraya (Temple of the Three Phraya) (Phobun 2003). Over the following several generations, the local Mon population was gradually replaced by a mix of Thai and Lao households, and the temple's monastic affiliation shifted from the Raman order to the Mahanikai.

(b) *Ban Tawai*

"Tavoy is adjacent to the Mon lands north of Tenasserim, but the inhabitants are Tavoyan, who are a separate people [,] a distinct ethnic group who speak a dialect of Burmese" (Damrong 2008, pp. 78, 150 ft. 95). In fact, the people of Tavoy historically defied straightforward ethnic classification; for want of any better alternative, they are listed here as Mon. The First Reign chronicle refers to a 1791 rebellion of Tavoy against the suzerainty of the Burmese, and then to the people's opposition to the opportunistic but ultimately unsuccessful 1793 intervention by the Thai (Thipakorawong 2009a, pp. 140–53). In the aftermath, large numbers of Mon and Burmese rebels as well as many Thai war captives accompanied the retreating Siamese forces on their return to Bangkok. The ousted governor of Tavoy and several hundred of his retainers were among the refugees; upon reaching Bangkok and pledging allegiance to King Rama I, they were temporarily domiciled near Wat Saket, directly east of the newly built Bangkok city wall and moat. Most of the lesser members of the migrant group were assigned to drain the back-swamps of the Khok Kraboe district (later known as Yan Nawa) and settle there as farmers, with the former governor of Tavoy and his entourage eventually joining them there (Thipakorawong 2009a, p. 149). The district of Khok Kraboe was located along the left bank of the river downstream from the Chinese settlement at Sampheng and the western anchorage at Bang Rak. An early twentieth-century observer remarked that "descendants of eighteenth-century Tavoyan immigrants [still] cultivated paddy fields on the east bank of the Chao Phraya River, extending from Bangkok to the Gulf and encompassing much of present-day Samut Prakan Province" (Schmitt 1904, cited in Damrong 2008, p. 150, n. 95). The principal temple in the area, known as Wat Khok Kraboe, was in the Third Reign renamed Wat Yannawa, and the main Tavoy settlement came to be known as Ban Tawai (Tavoy Village). At the heart of the settlement they founded Wat Don Phama and Wat Prok Phama, and further downstream they established several others, including Wat Lum Lakhon (now Wat Lum Charoen Satha) and Wat Mathoeng (later rebuilt as Wat Phraya Krai), all affiliated with the Raman order. During the Third Reign many of the Mon villagers were conscripted to join the Lao war captives serving at the royal shipyards built along that stretch of the river in support of the Siamese war with Annam (see Chapter 4, subsection on "Ban Kruay").

From the Fourth Reign on, the Mon and Lao communities situated directly behind the *farang* maritime transport companies and shipyards of the Yan Nawa district, and within ready walking distance of Bang Rak, came under growing Western influence. By the turn of the century the rising demand for English- and French-speaking local staff in the city's Western firms had prompted the *farang* business community and consulates to sponsor missionary-led Western-language education at the local temple schools.

> The Wat Don Thawai School was … established in 1903 for teaching the Thawai …, Shan and Burmese migrants living in Ban Thawai …. In 1904, the royal temple of Wat Yannawa became the second institution to offer a bilingual … education…. In 1911, Wat Lao School (present name, Suttivararam School) provided trilingual education — French, English

and Thai — for Lao residents in the area. In the 1910s, Wat Prok Temple which was established for serving the Mon, Burmese and Shan migrants also provided bilingual education (Phibul 2015, p. 432, citing Phibul 2013, p. 109 and Wat Yannawa n.d., pp. 28–29).

Rising nationalist sentiment in the 1910s–1920s led the government to tighten its control over the ethnic minorities in the Ban Tawai area by replacing the Mon, Lao, and Shan abbots at Wat Don Tawai, Wat Prok, and Wat Suthi-wararam (Wat Lao) with Thai abbots and instituting the standard Thai curriculum rather than continuing the multilingual, Christian-influenced education and teaching systems previously introduced by Western missionaries. Those changes undermined the ethnic individuality of the local populace and contributed to the formation of a national Thai identity (Phibul 2015, p. 434).

(c) *Ban Tanao*

On the origins of Ban Tanao (Tenasserim Village (Map 3.4)) not a word of documentation has been discovered. The only surviving evidence resides in Tanao Road (formerly Ban Tanao Road), a local street name superimposed upon the northern stretch of Foeang Nakhon Road. Tanao Road crosses the Lot Thepthida Canal (The Wat Thepthida Conduit Canal) to meet Rachadamnoen Avenue at the Khok Wua (Cattle Pens) intersection. Reminiscences by the neighbourhood's elderly residents several decades ago suggest that the early settlers specialized in the production of homespun cloth (Tomosugi 1993, p. 37). All else is surmise. A speculative reconstruction of the settlement's history places its origins in the First Reign, upon Siam's 1793 invasion of the Andaman coastlands (Thipakorawong 2009a, pp. 145–55). Tenasserim had been closely associated with Tavoy in the rebellion against Burmese oppression, and when the Thai withdrew after the expedition to force the Burmese out, its governor and many followers accompanied them back to Bangkok. There, having pledged fealty to King Rama I, their leader was rewarded with a noble rank and title (long lost to memory) and a settlement site within the city wall, alongside the Lot Thepthida Canal near Wat Khok Kraboe (not to be confused with the identically named temple fronting Ban Tawai). Perhaps, in view of the name *kraboe* (water buffalo) associated with the locale, they took up work initially as cattle herders.

The settlement appears to have merged relatively early and easily into the surrounding cityscape. By the 1850s the area was well populated by Thai households in government service. Wat Khok Kraboe was at that time rebuilt under the patronage of Prince Udom Ratanarangsi (Anop) and was renamed Wat Mahan Noparam in his honour. Early in the following decade a roadway — today's Tanao Road — was extended through the neighbourhood to allow vehicular traffic. In 1872, a small Chinese merchant community and shrine, Sanchao Pho Soea, was moved there from its former site near the Brahman temple and ceremonial swing (*sao ching cha*) to make way for the expansion of Bamrung Moeang Road. The construction of Singapore-inspired roadside rowhouses then brought a variety of European and Indian shops catering to the Thai elite. And so the original Mon community dissolved into the surrounding urban scene, leaving only its name in memory.

(d) *Pottery marketplaces*
Historical interest in Siam's Mon population typically focuses on the elite families and fighting forces, but the great majority of Mon households throughout the nineteenth century continued to consist of subsistence farmers, even in the environs of the capital. Increasingly, however, as the market economy penetrated the peasant world, Mon villagers turned to such commercial pursuits as firewood and thatch gathering, charcoal making, salt farming, lime slaking, market gardening, and inland water transport. Particularly profitable was the commercial production of fired brick and earthenware. Brick came into increasing demand with changing architectural technology in the construction boom of the late nineteenth century. In response to the rising demand for construction materials in the economic boom of the time, Thonburi's Mon villagers established a number of brickyards along the Mon Canal upstream from Thonburi's Ban Mo. Their success attracted competition, and so in 1889 they were joined by the Bangkok Brick and Tile Works, located along the Mon Canal near Wat Khrut. The firm was founded by John Clunich, an Englishman who had earlier been recruited as Royal Architect to design and supervise the construction of the Chakri Maha Prasat Throne Hall in Bangkok's Grand Palace. Clunich found dealings with his Western partners burdensome, and out-performing the local Mon brick-makers even more difficult, so the firm was dissolved before 1907, and the Mon were left in control of the industry (Phirasi 2005, pp. 81–107). Along with brick, there arose a market for sand, gravel, and lime (the main ingredients for cement and concrete), which in turn nurtured the development of a Mon bulk transport industry along the Chaophraya River. Several Mon marketplaces and warehousing facilities for those building supplies arose along the Bangkok outskirts. As of the 1970s it could still be said that "a large proportion

of [the] construction materials used in Bangkok arrives in Mon barges" (Foster 1973, p. 205).

Similarly, with increasing consumerism a ready household demand arose for a wide assortment of earthenware jars, bowls, pots, and pans (*tum, mo, ong, ang, khrok*, and others) for water collection, rice storage, cooking, planting, and the like. Under the compulsions generated by Siam's rapidly commercializing economy, a number of Mon households moved from Sam Khok and Pak Kret to Bangkok, where they established marketplaces for their earthenware goods, chief among them Talat Ban Mo (the Pottery Village Marketplace) along the Inner City Moat, Talat Ong Ang (the Pots and Pans Marketplace) along the Ong Ang Canal (the lower stretch of the City Moat), and Talat Nang Loeng (the Martaban Jars Marketplace) at the confluence of the Phadung Krung Kasem Canal and Prem Prachakon Canal. Each of those marketplaces evolved, in due course, into a crowded, raucous, Chinese-dominated commercial neighbourhood, leaving only the old name as a testament to the former Mon presence (Tomosugi 1993, pp. 14–16, 61–64).

THE FADING OF MON ETHNICITY

Few numbers have been cited for the various Mon migrations to Siam, but it can be hazarded that the individual treks rarely exceeded 10,000–20,000 people, with the last and largest (1815) reported to have reached as many as 40,000 (Thipakorawong 2005, p. 58). The uncertainty of the cited numbers is underscored by their rounding to thousands, and often to tens of thousands. It is also unclear whether the numbers cited in specific cases refer specifically to able-bodied men — the decamping warrior contingents — or, alternatively, whether they refer to households rather than individuals. With the migration of 1815, the flow of Mon refugees into Siam ended abruptly, though occasional small contingents of captives continued to arrive for another decade or so. The threat of Burmese incursions into Thai territory ceased altogether as British colonial expansion into Farther India closed the Tenasserim frontier in the 1820s. Thereafter, Siam's Mon population can be estimated to have grown in accord with the "natural" growth rate of pre-industrial populations (in the absence of war, famine, and disease) of 1 per cent or so annually (Harris 2001, pp. 13–38). Adopting a conservative Mon population estimate of 150,000 as of 1820, that growth rate would have resulted in a population of some 350,000 by 1900. Yet, by the turn of the twentieth century, Siam's recorded Mon population had fallen far short of that projection, and that shortfall only increased over the course of that century. It is certainly the fading of Mon ethnic identity, not their physical number, that accounts for that decline.

Nearly a century after the last major Mon in-migration, Siam's first, awkward try at a formal demographic survey — the 1903 census of twelve administrative regions (*monthon*) of Central Siam — showed a total population of 3.3 million, of which the Mon portion was said to be only 29,000, less than 1 per cent (Grabowsky 1996, p. 56; Suporn 1998, p. 101). The 1909 follow-up census of the Bangkok administrative region "did not even recognize the Mon as a separate 'race' [sic]" (Grabowsky 1996, p. 56). A variety of ad hoc estimates of Thailand's Mon-speaking population over the following eight decades suggest that the late twentieth-century total was anywhere between 60,000 and 200,000 (Bauer 1990, p. 24). In substantiation, a meticulous, privately organized Mon census of 1969–1972, based on declared descent rather than spoken language, found a mere 94,000 (Sujaritlak 1983, pp. 23–24; Bauer 1990, pp. 24, 26).

Other than outright undercounting, and in the absence of demographic catastrophes, the growing gap between Siam's expected and actual Mon population since the end of the era of migrations can only be attributed to a wholesale Mon assimilation into the Thai ethnic mainstream. In that perspective, the Mon in Thailand today clearly represent an endangered cultural species, virtually extinct in the metropolitan center where, at most, their descendants consider themselves "Thai of Mon ancestry", with the ethnic survivors clustered predominantly in scattered provincial pockets.

The integrative effects of commercialization, requiring intensive cross-cultural exposure by all participants involved in all aspects of the spreading market system, had a corrosive effect on Mon ethnicity throughout Siam. In addition, the convergence of several other forces working in Bangkok and its immediate environs accelerated Mon assimilation into the emerging Thai nation-state over the course of the Fifth Reign. Foremost among them were the centralization of the kingdom's military command structure at Bangkok, the professionalization of the Bangkok metropolitan police force, the conversion of Bangkok's Mon temples to the Thai monastic orders, and the decline in royal patronage of Bangkok's Mon elite. The implications of each of those four factors for Bangkok's Mon community are briefly reviewed below.

First, the growing threat of Western colonialism during the Fifth Reign motivated, among much else, a progressive reorganization of Siam's military bureaucracy, featuring an increasingly centralized command structure that culminated in the 1887 formation of the War Office (*krom yuthanathikan*) (Thailand, Department of the Army 2004, pp. 80–115;

Battye 1974, pp. 271–83). The key components of the consolidated military command, split between the army and navy, were situated axially east and west of Bangkok's Grand Palace (Map 3.4). The army was provided with an imposing headquarters, cadet school, and officers' billets along the Parade Ground (*sanam chai*) fronting the eastern wall of the Grand Palace, with the royal bodyguard plus infantry and cavalry barracks and stables alongside at the Royal Gardens (*suan chao chet* and *suan luang*). At the same time, an equally handsome navy headquarters, cadet school, shipyard, arsenal, and officers' billets were established along the Thonburi riverfront at the Former Royal Residence (*phra niwet doem*) directly across the river from the Grand Palace, with sailors' and marines' barracks directly behind at the former Nantha Uthayan Palace (now known as *suan anan*). Among the multi-ethnic forces assigned to staff those new army and navy facilities were upwards of 5,000 Mon officers and enlisted men from the dormant western frontier regiments and the naval bases at Ban Somdet and Prapadaeng. The Mon troops were thrust into a radically new, cosmopolitan social environment requiring constant interaction at close quarters with their Thai infantry compeers and Thai officer corps who were themselves struggling to adjust to the new Western-influenced norms of military conduct. A congeries of unremitting pressures for social conformity — shared residential facilities (barracks life for the enlisted men), strict discipline within a rigid military hierarchy, mandatory communication in the Thai language, attendance at an interminable series of ceremonial events (royal musters, parades, processions, receptions, regattas, sermons and recitations, cremations, and the like), and appropriate conduct for advancement within the military bureaucracy — combined to impel rapid acculturation (Battye 1974, pp. 291–303).

Second, during the Fourth and Fifth Reigns the long-established system of Mon police patrol units (*kong trawen*) — conducting both land and water surveillance of the metropolitan precincts under the aegis of the Ministry of the Capital (*krom nakhonban*) headed by a series of ministers invariably titled Chaophraya Yomarat, a number of them Mon — gradually evolved into a professional police force. That system had never been known for its effectiveness; its professionalization aimed to remedy its weaknesses. In a preliminary departure from the Mon grip on the capital's weak security apparatus, a British police superintendent, Captain S.J.B. Ames (Luang Rathaya Thiban), was recruited from Singapore during the Fourth Reign to direct a small body of South Asian patrolmen (*kong polit*) in suppressing crime and violence in the Chinese and Western city precincts (Battye 1974, p. 93; also see Chapter 7, subsection on "The Bangkok Police

Constabulary"). That prototype was then applied in the Fifth Reign to the reformation of the ad hoc patrol system into a full-fledged municipal police force. Prince Naret Worarit — himself a royal descendant of Chaophraya Mahayotha through his mother, Chaochom Manda Sonklin, a consort of King Rama IV and royal patron of Siam's Mon community — served from 1886 to 1889 as a member of the select committee established to reorganize the Ministry of the Capital, and he then headed the reformed ministry from 1889 to 1907. Initially, Naret built up the strength of the Metropolitan Police Department (*krom kong trawen*) by negotiating the transfer of Mon troops from Bangkok's army and navy bases as well as the remaining Mon marines from Nakhon Khoeankhan. By April 1893, over 3,000 men had been reassigned from those military facilities and another 900 were awaiting transfer, though this was still considered inadequate in view of the incessant calls for a substantial police presence at royal ceremonial functions (Suporn 1998, pp. 128–31, 139). Further to generating adequate manpower, King Chulalongkorn sought also to replace the patrol system's traditional patronage network with performance-based advancement. To that end, the ethnic solidarity of the Mon police force was gradually shredded with the imposition of performance standards as a basis for promotion, the enlistment of increasing numbers of ethnic Thai recruits, the dispersal of the Mon patrolmen among a number of precincts (each with its own, multi-ethnic police stations and police barracks, as well as its own multi-ethnic clientele), and finally the replacement of Naret himself by Pan Sukhum in 1907 (later promoted to Chaophraya Yomarat), a Thai bureaucrat entirely uninterested in Mon status sensitivities.

Third, the Raman monastic order fell into decline during the closing decades of the nineteenth century, making it increasingly acceptable and convenient for young Mon men to consider ordination in one of the two Thai monastic orders (Mahanikai and Thammayut) or skip that traditional male rite-of-passage entirely. Contributing to that process was dissension within the Raman monastic community. During the 1890s, Phra Sumethachan (Si), abbot of Bangkok's Wat Chana Songkhram and patriarch of the Raman order, became embroiled in a scandal over alleged abuse of authority (Sujaritlak 1983, pp. 117–19). A draconian solution to that problem was arrived at in an 1895 decision to merge many of the kingdom's Raman temples into the Thammayut order, followed by the Sangha Act of 1902, which reorganized Siam's monastic bureaucracy along narrowly circumscribed lines that pointedly omitted reference to the Raman order (Suchaw 2001, pp. 173–77). The Raman order was thereby effectively dissolved as a separate administrative entity (Suporn 1998,

p. 195; Bunchuay 1979, pp. 121–24), and all of Bangkok's Mon monks were required to adjust their daily practice, ritual, dress, and language accordingly. Senior Mon monks were systematically replaced by young Thai monks in Bangkok's former Raman-order temples, and so Mon speaking and reading skills as well as Mon temple ritual fell into obsolescence (Sujaritlak 1983, p. 121; Suporn 1998, pp. 185–97). That monastic Thai-ification process restricted subsequent generations of Bangkok's Mon youth to a Thai education. Bereft of that element of their cultural heritage, many Mon households moved out of Bangkok to the peripheral, more conservative Mon communities — some downstream to Prapadaeng and Bang Khun Thian and many more upstream to Nonthaburi, Pak Kret, and Pathum Thani — leaving those who stayed behind all the more exposed to the forces of acculturation. Wat Chana Songkhram, the spiritual centre of Bangkok's Mon community, faded from prominence in the process. In the absence of its former elite patronage, its facilities deteriorated, until its gradual revival as a popular Mahanikai temple in the closing decades of the twentieth century (Matichon 2005).

Cross-cutting each of the aforementioned factors, the administrative reforms of the Fifth Reign led to a withering away of the system of royal patronage that had provided the Mon nobility with a privileged place in Siam since the late sixteenth century. In the traditional Siamese patrimonial state, formal royal-noble patron-client bonds had been a hallmark of the political system (Mead 2004, p. 13). The Mon nobility, and through it the Mon commons, had received valuable perquisites from their royal sponsors for their steadfast military service. Phraya Cheng and subsequent generations of his entourage at Ban Phra Athit, in particular, had benefitted greatly, initially in return for the support they had extended during the Chakri coup of 1782 and subsequently for their military and related services under the patronage of the successive Chakri-dynasty viceroys. Following pacification of the volatile western frontier, however, the value of the Mon military contribution fell into decline, and with it the Mon nobility began to slip from royal favour. The death of the Fifth Reign viceroy in 1885 and the dissolution of his office soon thereafter further disrupted the Mon patronage position. In the aftermath, Prince Naret, as both royal patron of the Mon nobility and proponent of the emerging meritocracy, found himself in the uncomfortable position of straddling the inter-generational divide. Shunted aside from royal favour under Naret's ambivalent patronage, Bangkok's Mon nobility and their retinues adjusted by dispersing to new opportunities, and both the Old Mon neighbourhood at Ban Phraya Si and the New Mon at Ban Phra Athit were absorbed into the amorphous urban maelstrom. Bangkok's Mon elite were thus gradually shorn of their privileged position and scattered as the old formal royal-noble patronage relationships were progressively attenuated and eventually superseded, to survive only as a network of informal noble-commoner patron-client links in the peripheral Mon settlements.

In conclusion, unremitting pressures favouring acculturation over the course of the late nineteenth century and the subsequent decades — closely identified with eased strictures against cross-cultural marriage, at least within the Bangkok metropolitan area — diffused "Mon" identity to self-representation as "Thai of Mon descent". In the process, lingering Old-Mon/New-Mon distinctions slipped into oblivion. And so, Bangkok's Mon population was gradually absorbed into the Thai mainstream, until over the course of the twentieth century its former ethnic identity became a fast-receding memory — reminiscent of the fabled fate of ancient Ramanya Desa and Dvaravati. The decline of abiding Mon customs and festivals to the self-demeaning status of tourist attractions at the peripheral Mon settlements, recurrent nostalgic reviews and revivals of obsolete Mon folkways, and the occasional literary *cri de coeur* on the resilience of Mon culture in the face of the encroaching Thai nation-state speak eloquently of that waning. "It would scarcely be an exaggeration, then, to say that Mon society and culture have disappeared in many areas and are highly attenuated in others" (Foster 1973, p. 220). That end is nowhere more evident than in and around the present-day Bangkok metropolis.

4

Under Duress: Lao War Captives

OF LOVE AND LOATHING

Relations between Siam and the Lao states of the Mekong watershed soured during the Thonburi period (1767–1782). Whether that was primarily due to the dynamics of Burmese influence in the Lao country, the newly found might and exuberant expansionism of the Thonburi regime, or personal animosities between Thonburi's King Taksin and King Si Bunyasan of Vientiane remains a moot point. What is beyond dispute, however, is the political decline of the Lao states following the 1707 fragmentation of the kingdom of Lan Chang into the rival states of Luang Prabang, Vientiane, and Champasak, which deeply affected the capacity of the Lao to withstand pressure from their Siamese, Burmese, and Vietnamese neighbours. The result was a process of growing humiliation for the Lao at the hands of their Thai ethnic cousins (Wyatt 1994*b*). A respected pair of Lao scholars has succinctly expressed the lingering sentiments as a "Lao-Thai saga of love and loathing" (Mayoury and Pheuiphanh 1994, p. vii).

The roiling tensions between Thonburi and the Lao states led, in 1778–1779, to a powerful Thai military campaign against the Mekong riparian states, culminating in the conquest of the Lao capital of Vientiane and the capture and transport to Thai territory of large numbers of war prisoners (*chaloei soek*), including many members of the Vientiane royal family and its entourage. Si Bunyasan and several of his sons managed to escape the besieged capital into Vietnamese sanctuary. But his eldest son and viceroy (the *uparat*, nearly always the king's senior son or younger brother), Nanthasen, and other members of the royal family were caught and carried off to Siam along with masses of war captives and other booty, including the Phra Kaew and Phra Bang Buddha images, the chief palladia of the ancient Lao kingdom of Lan Chang. That conquest of Vientiane and its subordinate principalities marked a historic transition of the Lao states from political independence to tributary status to Siam, immortalized, to the lasting chagrin of the Lao, by the installation of the Phra Kaew Buddha image at Thonburi, Siam's spiritual centre.

The 1779 debacle set off a series of forced migrations from the Lao states to Siamese territory stretching well into the nineteenth century (the Thonburi-Bangkok dynastic transition, from the Lao point of view, being an inconsequential episode in that essentially seamless process). Those early decades of Lao political disruption saw tens of thousands of captives marched off to Saraburi, and from that staging point further afield — to Phetburi, Ratburi, and Nakhon Chaisi in the southwest and to Prachinburi and Chanthaburi in the southeast. Over the following century, several further forced migrations moved the bulk of the Lao population south from the Mekong watershed onto the Khorat plateau. The most dramatic march followed the crushing defeat of the Lao rebellion of 1827–1828. "The massive deportation in the wake of 1827 resulted in a five-fold disparity between the population of Laos and Thailand's Northeast (Isan)" (Mayoury and Pheuiphanh 1998, p. 61, ft. 100). The magnitude of that displacement, it has been claimed, ranged from 100,000 people to more than 300,000 (Mayoury and Pheuiphanh 1998, p. 49, n. 100). A third, lesser wave followed the Thai response to the Ho (southern Chinese bandits) incursions into the Lao states in the 1870s. It resulted in the relocation to Thai territory of captive contingents of several Lao cultural minorities, including Lao Phuan and Song Dam war captives from the Xieng Khouang Plateau and neighbouring uplands bordering Vietnamese territory (Snit and Breazeale 1988, p. 31).

The series of forced Lao migrations and resettlement programmes into Thai servitude caused "profound human suffering" (Snit and Breazeale 1988, p. 29), though it may be something of an exaggeration to state that "Fully two-thirds died during their journey to Siam" (Mayoury and Pheuiphanh 1998, p. 42). While the three eighteenth–nineteenth century Lao migrations extensively depopulated and impoverished the left bank of the Mekong, they transformed the demographic face of Siam and contributed immeasurably to its development. In each case, those who were "swept up" (kwat) and carried off into Siamese captivity consisted of three groups. The largest group comprised common folk, who were settled as virtual serfs in underpopulated provinces and districts, ever available as war slaves (that chaloei) to serve the Thai elite well beyond the limits of the labour conscription (corvée) that was annually imposed on the kingdom's freemen (*phrai*) (Ishii 1986*b*, pp. 173–74; Chatchai 1982; Turton 1980, pp. 254–57). "Captives" (*chaloei*) and "slaves" (*that*) here become virtually interchangeable terms. And thus, "the common stereotype that Lao ancestry is considered low class and shameful" (McDaniel 2011, p. 39).

The other two groups of war captives — aristocrats and artisans — were far smaller in number and were accorded far better treatment. Both those groups were settled in close proximity to the Thai capital and placed under the protection of the Thai king (at the Grand Palace) and his viceroy (at the Front Palace). The Lao aristocracy at Bangkok were held hostage to the fidelity of their close kin who had been permitted to retain their positions as vassal rulers and ranking officials of the respective Lao principalities. They also played a useful role as intermediaries between the Thai provincial administration and the Lao communities dispersed about Siam. Similarly, the captive Lao craftsmen were valued for their contribution to the skills base of the Royal Artisans' Departments (*krom chang sip mu*) serving the courts of both the Thai king and his viceroy, in particular gold- and silversmiths, bronze-casters, woodworkers, and architects and civil engineers. The Lao were also esteemed for their court dancers and musicians as well as for the spiritual eminence of their forest monk (*aranyawasi*) tradition.

Under traditional Siamese legal precepts, all those captive people were considered royal or state slaves (*that luang, kha luang*). As property of the king, their legal status was, in effect, extra-legal. Unlike debt slaves, they were relegated to perpetual bondage (Ishii 1986*b*, pp. 173–74). The Thai legal code of 1805 referred to the price at which war captives could presumably free themselves, but it was set at a rate that was effectively impossible to meet (Chatchai 1982, p. 39). Even in cases where slaves were awarded by the king to his loyal subordinates, it was understood that they would in due course revert to the Crown. Because of the status of war slaves as royal property, the series of decrees issued during the Fifth Reign to free the kingdom's slaves did not clarify the anomalous position of those who had been acquired by capture (permanent or hereditary slaves) but dealt instead with the problem of debt slavery (redeemable slaves or indentured bondsmen). The first of those acts, promulgated in 1874, identified seven classes of slaves: debt-slaves, the offspring of debt-slaves, children sold into slavery by their parents, slaves sold by their owners, those who entered into slavery to escape debt or other trouble, those who entered slavery to escape famine, those captured in war. But implementation of that and subsequent acts does not appear to have taken war captives into specific account (Chatchai 1982, pp. 202ff).

Relatively little is known of the nineteenth century presence of Lao war captives at Bangkok for several reasons. First, communities of inferior status in the social hierarchy did not warrant documentary attention in the Thai court archives (*chotmaihet*) or annals (*phongsawadan*). Second, the forced residency of Lao aristocrats as war captives at the Thai capital carried a stigma among the Lao themselves, which did not favour close documentation or long memories. An exception is *Nirat wang bang yi-khan* (Elegy on the Bang Yi-khan Palace Community), a personal poetic lament composed by Khun Phum, a lesser member of Bangkok's mid-nineteenth-century Lao exile aristocracy (Phum 1922). Third, the records of the Front Palace, which had special responsibility for the Lao captives, did not long survive the late nineteenth century abolition of the viceroyalty. Lastly, the gradual easing of the "slave" status of particular ethnic groups was deliberately kept off-the-record to avoid invidious comparisons and unrest in other, less favoured ethnic communities, and to forestall diplomatic unpleasantries with the Western powers. But enough information has filtered through, much of it from temple records and some of it circumstantial, to permit a brief review of the histories of several of Bangkok's Lao communities: two (Bang Yi-khan and Bang Khun Phrom) upstream from the walled city; two (Bang Sai Kai and Ban Kruay) downstream; and three (Ban Lao Phuan, Ban Kraba, and Ban Ti Thong) within the walled city itself.

UPSTREAM: THE LAO ARISTOCRACY

One of the many striking parallels between the Siamese and Lao political systems to the end of the Vientiane dynasty in 1828 was the administrative role assigned to the viceroy (*uparat*). The viceroy of Vientiane was assigned responsibility for oversight of the subject principalities to the north, including Chiang Khwang (the Lao Xieng Khouang) and Sip Song Chu Tai (the Lao Sib Song Chau Tai), home of the Phuan and Song Dam ethnic groups. Correspondingly, the king of Siam traditionally accorded his viceroy special authority over the northern territories of Lan Na and Lan Chang. That explains why at Bangkok both the Lao royal compound at Bang Yi-khan and the cross-river Lao Phuan settlement at Bang Khun Phrom were located just north of the walled city, a short distance from the Front Palace, the viceroy's stronghold. Similarly, the residences that the Chiangmai (Lan Na) "Lao" aristocracy maintained for their obligatory periodic ceremonial visits to Bangkok were situated first along the river directly upstream from the Front Palace and later further north at the mouth of the Samsen Canal (see Chapter 7, subsection on "Ban Phayap"). Maintaining that tradition despite the abolition of the viceroy's mandate, a mansion was built in the early 1890s for Chao Intha Wichayanon, the chief of Chiangmai, along the riverbank at Bangkok Noi, directly across from the defunct Front Palace (see Chapter 7, subsection on "The Front Palace Guest House").

Wang Lao/Bang Yi-khan

The Lao royal captives of the 1779 conquest of Vientiane — headed by Si Bunyasan's eldest son, Nanthasen, his eldest daughter, Khiawkhom, and a younger son, Anuwong — arrived at Thonburi around 1780. They were settled along the right bank of the Chaophraya River about a kilometre upstream from the Thonburi citadel, at Bang Yi-khan (Map 4.1), under close oversight from the nearby military cantonment of the conquering general, Chaophraya Surasi (Bunma, later elevated to Prince Surasinghanat, the First-Reign viceroy), situated directly across the river at Bang Lamphu. Nanthasen did not stay long at Bang Yi-khan. Upon Si Bunyasen's death in 1781, he was appointed vassal king of Vientiane and immediately returned home to take up his post. Upon his arrival at Vientiane in 1782 his brothers Inthawong (the new viceroy) and Phromwong were dispatched to join Anuwong at Bangkok as royal hostages. For that and several subsequent reigns, Wang Lao (the Lao Palace), the royal compound at Bang Yi-khan housing, over the course of time, many hundreds of Lao aristocrats and their retainers in a cluster of well-built teak "palaces" surrounded by their lesser followers' rudimentary dwellings, remained the Bangkok residence of Vientiane's royal hostages (S. Plainoi 2002, p. 101).

Inthawong, accompanied by Phromwong, arrived at Bangkok in 1783. When, after the death of King Nanthasen, Inthawong succeeded to the throne of Vientiane in 1797, Anuwong was appointed his viceroy. And then, when King Inthawong died in 1804, Anuwong succeeded him. Thus, three sons of Si Bunyasan, in turn, served as viceroy of Vientiane and then, in rapid succession, succeeded to the throne. In each instance, the Lao viceroy spent much of his time at Bang Yi-khan representing the interests of Vientiane at the court of Bangkok. That tradition continued with the appointment of Anuwong's son Khli as viceroy in 1804. However, when Anuwong started plotting rebellion against Rama III around 1825, Khli quietly withdrew from the viceroyalty and was replaced by Anuwong's half-brother Tissa.

The Thai-Lao war of 1827–1828 — often referred to as the Chao Anu Rebellion — was lost by Anuwong, with tragic consequences. Not only was Vientiane looted and razed to the ground but tens of thousands of Lao peasants were brutally removed from their homeland and forcibly resettled as war captives in the Thai provinces. The deposed King Anuwong and many

TABLE 4.1
Vientiane Royal Family Genealogy
(Major personalities only)

Si Bunyasan
(Fifth reign of the dynasty)
(r.1751–1779, d.1781)

Khiawkhom

Nanthasen	Inthawong	Phromwong	Anuwong	Tissa
(Uparat,...–1781)	(Uparat, 1782–1795)		(Uparat, 1795–1804)	(Uparat, 1825?–1827)
(r.1781–1794)	(r.1795–1804)		(r.1804–1827)	

Thongsuk
(Rama I consort)

CF Kunthon Thipayawadi
(Rama II queen)

CP Aphon
CF KPY Bamrap Porapak
CF Piu

Po (Suthisan)
Ngao (Rachawong)
Yo (Rachabut)
Khli (Uparat, 1804–1825?)
Prathum (Rama I consort)
Chan (Rama III consort)
Noi (Rama III consort)

.........= ....*Thonkaew*

Duangkham
(Rama IV consort)

POC Nari Ratana
POC Pradit Nari

Notes: CF = Chao Fa – queen's offspring
POC = Phra Ong Chao – consort's offspring
KPY = Krom Phraya – senior prescriptive ranks
Uparat, Rachawong, Rachabut, and Suthisan = Lao royal ranks and titles (listed in order of seniority).
Italicized names = females

Sources: Pramuan 1939, pp. 74–80; Department of Fine Arts 2002, pp. 219–75.

MAP 4.1
Lao upstream: Bang Khun Phrom, Bang Yi-khan
(late 19th–20th centuries)

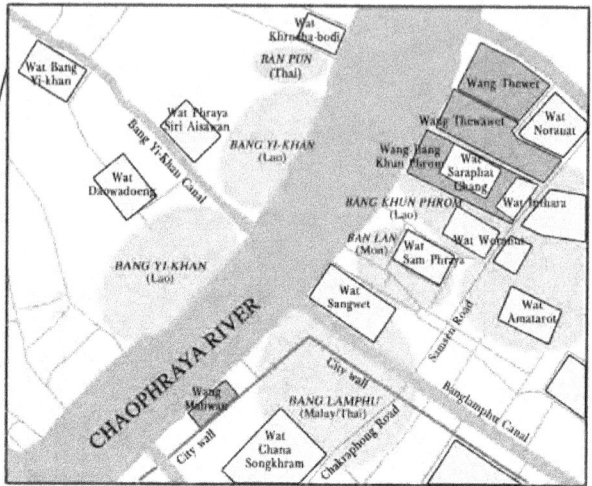

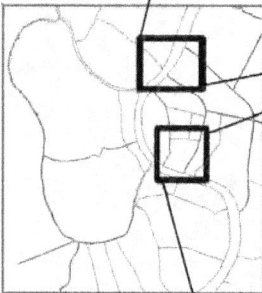

MAP 4.2
City Lao: Ban Mo,
Ban Kraba,
Ban Ti Thong
(late 19th–20th
centuries)

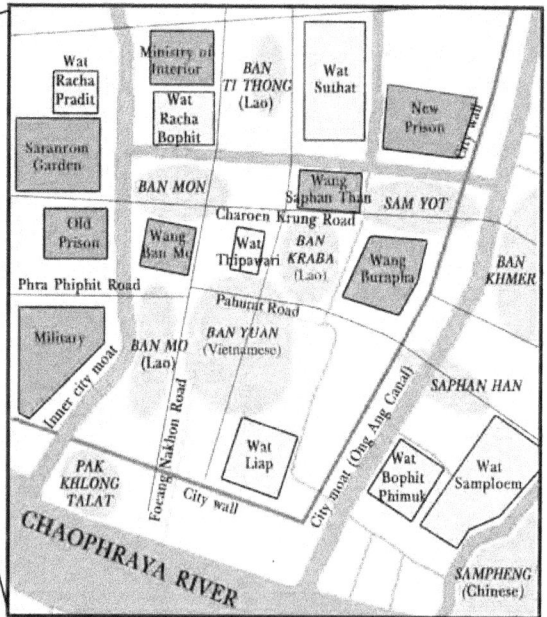

members of his household, including a number of his wives and twenty-three of his children, were caged and executed at Bangkok. Included in the booty brought to Bangkok in 1828 was the Phra Bang (or Prabang) Buddha image, which had been returned to Vientiane in 1782 upon the elevation of Nanthasen. Rubbing salt into the Lao wounds, Rama III had the Phra Bang image installed in a special pavilion at Wat Samploem (Wat Chakrawat), adjacent to the site of Anuwong's execution. (Among his efforts to redress the excesses of the Third Reign, Rama IV in 1867 returned the palladium, this time to Luang Prabang, as Vientiane had been utterly destroyed.) Tissa, Anuwong's half-brother and viceroy, responsible for the eastern flank of the Lao military campaign, opted at the last moment to defect to the Thai cause. His desertion left Anuwong at a fatal disadvantage at the decisive battles of Sompoi and Khaosan (in present-day Northeast Thailand not far distant from Nongkhai). For his loyalty to the Siamese throne, Tissa was designated chief Lao representative at Bangkok, though he was despised by his own people and largely written out of history. He was eventually awarded the Bangkok spirits monopoly (*akon sura*); a consortium of Chinese investors who contracted the business end of his monopoly eventually established a distillery along the river at Bang Yi-khan, on the former site of Wang Lao (Pramuan 1939, p. 78). (The site is today occupied by the Rama VIII Park and Princess Kalayani Music Conservatory.)

Many of the leading figures of the royal Lao settlement at Bang Yi-khan were disposed of in the spate of executions that followed the 1828 fall of Vientiane. Of the survivors of that royal culling, a number of the daughters of Bang Yi-khan were absorbed into the Thai aristocracy as wives and consorts. Many of the surviving sons found their way into government service in the Fourth and Fifth Reigns, and some were appointed as provincial governors and lesser officials in the Thai Northeast. With that, the royal Lao compound at Bang Yi-Khan fell into terminal decline. Among the dispersed survivors stemming from Siam's captive Vientiane dynasty today are the Chaliwan, Chanthanakon, and Sithisaributl lineages (Pramuan 1939, pp. 78–80), but no Lao remnants are evident any longer at Bang Yi-khan.

The Bang Yi-khan royal community maintained a strong presence at the Siamese court over the course of the nineteenth century through a series of remarkable women. King Si Bunyasan's eldest daughter, Princess Khiawkhom, had been a cause of dissension between Vientiane and Siam when negotiations concerning an inter-dynastic marriage in 1771 and again in 1775 bogged down (Wyatt 1994b, pp. 187, 190–91). In the 1779 conquest of Vientiane, she was among the royal family members captured and transported to Bangkok. She was installed in the Grand Palace Women's

Quarters during the First Reign, but there is no indication that any amorous relationship ever developed between her and Rama I. Another member of the Lao royal family, Princess Thongsuk, daughter of King Inthawong, did bear a child by Rama I. In recognition of her dual royal lineage, her daughter, Princess Kunthon Thipayawadi, was raised to the rank of celestial princess (*chao fa*). She had the further distinction of being raised to a queen of Rama II (her half-brother) and bore four children, of whom Prince Bamrap Porapak (Klang), popularly known as Prince Maha Mala and forebear of the Malakul lineage, later played an important role as royal patron of the Lao communities at Bangkok and Saraburi.

In addition to those political alliances, Rama I succumbed to a romance with Khamwaen (commonly referred to as Chaochom Waen), the daughter of a Lao nobleman and herself a lady-in-waiting to Princess Khiawkhom. Despite her relatively low status within the Lao ruling elite, the king raised her to First-Class Royal Consort (*chaochom chan ek*). She came to wield great influence as a confidante of the king and capable representative of the Lao cause. None of the other Lao royal and noble women taken into the palace in that or subsequent reigns ever managed to equal her achievement. Nevertheless, Waen did suffer one great disappointment in failing to bear a child. She sought to overcome that misfortune through numerous meritorious acts (Sansani 2007, pp. 3–10), including the founding of two important Lao temples at Bangkok (one, Wat Dawadoeng, at Bang Yi-khan, discussed below; the other, Wat Sangkhrachai, near Bang Sai Kai, to be discussed at a later point in this chapter).

In the later years of the First Reign she founded Wat Khrua In, situated along a branch of the Bang Yi-khan Canal in the orchards behind the Wang Lao riverside settlement. The temple was named after Phra Achan In, a renowned Lao meditation practitioner who was installed as its first abbot. After an auspicious beginning, the temple was expanded and upgraded in the Second Reign by Princess Kunthon Thipayawadi and was renamed Wat Dawadoeng-sawan (Tavatimsa Heaven, Indra's abode, from which the Buddha is said to have descended to earth by ladder). Late in the Third Reign it was rebuilt on an expanded scale and formally raised to royal status (entailing regular royal financial support) as Wat Dawadoeng-saram (the suffix, *aram*, identifying it as a royal temple); perhaps Rama III was seeking atonement for the brutality of his earlier conquest of Vientiane. But with the decline of the local Lao royal community, the temple gradually fell out of favour. By the later years of the Fifth Reign it had been abandoned by all its resident monks but the abbot (Wat Dawadoeng 2004, pp. 54–58). Meager local support during the Sixth and Seventh Reigns proved barely sufficient to keep the temple afloat. Today, with the re-emergence of Bang Yi-khan as a suburban Bangkok neighbourhood following the construction of the nearby cross-river Rama VIII Bridge, the temple has been comprehensively rehabilitated.

Bang Lao Phuan/Bang Khun Phrom

Under the vigorous rule of Siam's obedient vassal, Nanthasen, resurgent Vientiane in 1786 and again in 1794 invaded Chiang Khwang, capital of the recalcitrant Phuan state in the northeastern Lao uplands. Thousands of Lao Phuan captives were carried off as tribute to Rama I and settled at scattered sites in the Siamese hinterlands (Bang-on 1998, pp. 40–42; Breazeale 2002, p. 265). Several contingents of war captives with carpentry skills were sent on to Bangkok around 1789 and were settled upstream from the walled city, directly across the river from Bang Yi-khan, at a site that came to be called Ban Lao Phuan (and later Bang Khun Phrom) (Map 4.1). There they were set to work fashioning pirogues (*roea phai*), massive hollowed-out logs fashioned into fresh-water naval craft, the lesser cousins of the magnificent royal barges for which Thailand is renowned today. At the mouth of the minor canal flowing through their settlement they dug a boat basin (*khung*) for mooring and turning their boats. (That former boat basin is today buried beneath a massive annex to the Bank of Thailand.) Inthawong, at that time Vientiane's viceroy and the ranking member of Bangkok's Lao royal establishment, assumed the role of patron to Ban Lao Phuan. The community's later name, Bang Khun Phrom, probably arises from Khun Phrom Raksa (Sat), a Mon minion of the First Reign viceroy and nearby resident whose patronage of the local population was long remembered (see Chapter 3, subsection on "Ban Lan"); alternatively, it has been thought to derive from Phromwong, younger brother of Nanthasen and Inthawong, a resident of the area who has left no other trace.

A cluster of temples marks the original site of the Lao Phuan settlement, including Wat Woramat (rebuilt and renamed Wat Mai Amatarot), Wat Woranut (today Wat Iam Woranut), and Wat Intharam (today Wat Inthara Wihan, popularly referred to as Wat In). Of particular interest is Wat In, which had originally been founded by Chinese settlers during the Ayuthaya era, around 1752, as Wat Rai Prik (Temple in the Pepper Fields) and had apparently been abandoned upon the collapse of Ayutthaya. The Lao Phuan captives revived the dilapidated temple for their own use. As overseer of the Phuan community during his tenure as Lao viceroy residing at Bang Yi-khan, Inthawong sponsored the temple's reconstruction and appointed a renowned Lao meditation master to serve as its first abbot. Upon Inthawong's installation as ruler of Vientiane the temple was reconsecrated as Wat Intharam in his honour (O'Connor 1978, p. 124; Wat Inthara Wihan 1994, pp. 25, 87–88). Its Lao royal sponsorship was reflected in the incorporation of the honorific suffix, *aram*, in its name. That the Siamese Crown, too, patronized the temple is affirmed by the order of Rama II in 1817 including Wat In among the thirty-three royal temples of Bangkok to receive lanterns and lantern posts as a meritorious offering (Wat Inthara Wihan 2001, pp. 44–46). However, in the wake of the 1827–1828 Lao rebellion and the subsequent loss of royal patronage, the temple fell upon hard times.

In place of their former royal patronage, Wat In and the surrounding Lao community found a powerful benefactor in a famed charismatic monk, Somdet Phra Phuthachan (To Phromrangsi 1787–1871) (Thipakosa 1985; McDaniel 2011). With his mother, though apparently fatherless, he had been an early resident at the Lao Phuan settlement of Bang Khun Phrom and thus was probably of Phuan ancestry himself. In his youth he had studied at Wat In as a disciple of its first abbot, and he had gone on to monastic ordination and advanced meditation studies with other masters, gaining such esteem that he was eventually appointed abbot of Wat Rakhang Khositaram, one of Bangkok's most prestigious temples, located at the centre of Thonburi directly across the river from the Grand Palace. Despite his highly successful clerical career, he maintained lifelong contact with Bang Khun Phrom and Wat In. In 1867, at the advanced age of 80, he decided to commemorate his origins with the construction at Wat In of a gigantic standing Buddha image (32 metres tall, not completed until 1926), murals on the ordination hall walls depicting his biography, a magic well dispensing holy water, and a shrine memorializing his parents (Wat Inthara Wihan 1994, pp. 40–43). His sponsorship of the temple's revival is today well remembered, though the community's memory of its Lao Phuan ancestry has faded.

Another temple associated with the nineteenth-century Lao Phuan settlement was Wat Saraphat Chang (Temple of Various Artisans). After Champasak (southern Laos) was taken by the Thai in 1827, its ruler, Prince Yo, a faithful son of the rebellious King Anuwong, was dethroned and a new ruler, more trusted by Bangkok, was installed. "Yo, his family, his goldsmiths, and blacksmiths were conducted to Bangkok" (Mayoury and Pheuiphanh 1998, p. 221). Yo and his family were disposed of, but his captive artisans were settled alongside Bang Khun Phrom to serve the Crown. There they built Wat Saraphat Chang, which after more than five decades in support of its little Champasak Lao community fell into decline and was abandoned

during the course of the Fifth Reign. The site was razed in the early 1900s
and incorporated into a palace (Bang Khun Phrom Palace) built for Prince
Nakhon Sawan (Boriphat), a senior son of King Chulalongkorn, leaving
no trace of its earlier presence. The riverside tract stretching from Prince
Boriphat's palace upstream to the mouth of the Phadung Krung Kasem
Canal gradually came to take on a royal character (Map 4.1). In 1895,
the Thewet Palace, residence of Prince Chanthaburi Narinat (Kitiyakon),
was built at the mouth of the canal, and in 1918 the Thewawet Palace,
awarded by King Wachirawut to Prince Thewawong Waropakan (Thewan
Uthaiwong), was installed between the Thewet Palace and Bang Khun
Phrom Palace, completing the transformation of the riverfront tract from
a Lao commoners' community to an aristocratic Thai neighbourhood that
came to be known as Thewet.

In 1898, Bang Khun Phrom was bisected with the construction of a
major new thoroughfare, Samsen Road, running north from the walled city
(Map 4.1). Samsen Road was initially planned as a majestic royal passage
from the Grand Palace to the Suan Dusit district, where a great new royal
palace complex was to be laid out for Rama V. That plan was soon revised
with the construction of the far grander Rachadamnoen Avenue, but Samsen
Road remained an important route, opening Bangkok's northern suburbs
to vehicular traffic. As a straight, broad, paved thoroughfare intended for
royal use, the right-of-way of Samsen Road required the severe truncating
of Wat Woranut. That moved the centre of local community life fully to
Wat In, which had formerly stood at the settlement's periphery as a socially
distant meditation retreat.

The Bang Khun Phrom Palace was planned around the same time
as the construction of Samsen Road. Its layout directly across Samsen
Road from Wat In required the acquisition of two parcels of temple land
— the site of the abandoned Wat Saraphat Chang and the strip cut off
from the rear of Wat In by the construction of Samsen Road. Ancient
tradition, however, decreed the sacrosanct status of monastic land. Years of
negotiation between the Privy Purse and the ecclesiastical authorities were
required to resolve the issue, until in 1904 it was agreed that an 80-acre
plot of crown property at Minburi, a district well northeast of Bangkok
populated by many Lao (and even more Muslim) villages, would be ceded
to Wat In in exchange for the Wat Saraphat Chang site. In addition, it
took until 1914 to transfer possession of the narrow Wat In temple strip
along the west side of Samsen Road in exchange for the then-substantial
sum of 9,590 baht (Wat Inthara Wihan 1994, pp. 192–206). That royal
project and its spin-offs succeeded in removing the local Lao community

from its former river frontage. As for the riverside aristocracy, the Bang Khun Phrom Palace was in 1933, a year after the People's Revolution, converted to the Army Headquarters and then, in 1946, to the Bank of Thailand headquarters, which continues to occupy the site today. With those intrusions along the Thewet riverbank, the Lao Phuan community was pressed ever further inland, a relocation process that marked the community's long-term decline.

In the Sixth Reign, the name of Wat Intharam was changed to Wat Inthara Wihan to eliminate confusion with Thonburi's venerable Mon temple of the same name located along the Bangkok Yai Canal. With that name change, Wat In's association with Vientiane's King Inthawong was attenuated, and any lingering association of the temple with Thai royal patronage (including the prestigious suffix, *aram*) was eliminated. That change had little local significance, however, as the temple had long been popularly known as Wat Bang Khun Phrom Nai — as distinct from Wat Bang Khun Phrom Nok, or Wat Mai Amatarot. Only in recent decades has it become common practice once again to refer to the temple as Wat In.

DOWNSTREAM: THE KING'S CONSCRIPTS

While Bangkok's upstream communities were assigned to the oversight of the Front Palace, the bulk of the walled city and the districts downstream were retained under the direct supervision of the Grand Palace. Thus, the contingents of Lao war captives brought to Bangkok to serve the respective courts occupied separate zones of habitation. For the construction of the new capital of Ratanakosin in 1783/84, the king is said to have conscripted 10,000 Cambodians — probably an exaggeration — to dig a new City Moat (*khu moeang*) and several related canals (see Chapter 7, section on "Ban Khamen"). In addition, he mobilized 5,000 Lao from the principalities along the west bank of the Mekong River to erect the city wall and its bastions as well as the main lineaments of the Grand Palace and Front Palace (Thipakorawong 2009a, pp. 59–60). Both contingents were drawn from the captive populations that had been carried off to Siam in the wake of the Vientiane campaign of 1778–1779 and the Cambodian campaign of 1781–1782. The Cambodian conscripts were settled directly outside the eastern city wall and moat, in the marshy terrain between Wat Samploem and Wat Saket later known as Ban Khamen (or Ban Khmer). The Lao conscripts were consigned to an undeveloped tract across the river, along the outer bank of the Bangkok Yai Canal (otherwise known as the Bang Luang Canal) west of Thonburi.

Bang Sai Kai

The king's Lao conscripts were settled at the confluence of Thonburi's Bang
Luang Canal and Bang Sai Kai Canal to serve as hard-used manual labour
in the construction of the new city. In addition to the city wall and bastions,
they probably helped build Wat Phra Chetuphon and Wat Mahathat, and
they may have dug the Khanon Canal (later renamed the Talat Somdet
Canal) and the San Canal, both on the Thonburi side of the river not
far distant from their settlement. They may also have participated in the
Second Reign project to extend the rear wall and reposition the bastions
of the Grand Palace.

The settlement at the Bang Luang Canal/Bang Sai Kai Canal juncture
(Map 4.3) was originally known as Ban Lao, or Ban Lao Siphum, after Khun
Siphum, its headman. Many decades later, after most of the Lao had moved
elsewhere, the village name was revised to Bang Sai Kai, merging with a
neighbouring Thai peasant village of that name. Alongside the community,
the settlers dug the Lat Ban Lao Siphum Canal, a shortcut canal reaching to
the older Wat Hiran Ruchi Canal downstream. An adjoining waterway, the
Suan Lao Canal, took its name from the sprawling fruit orchards (*suan*) that
the Lao planted behind their settlement. They also built a village temple,
Wat Ban Lao, which was eventually renamed Wat Bang Sai Kai (S. Plainoi
2002, p. 102; Wat Bang Sai Kai n.d., pp. 2–3).

Local legend has it that the construction of Wat Bang Sai Kai was
initially sponsored by the Lao princes Nanthasen and Inthawong but that
those princely brothers then abandoned the project after a falling-out.
Actually, Nanthasen had departed to accept the throne of Vientiane before
the settlement was founded. It appears, therefore, that Inthawong alone was
the original sponsor while serving as the Lao hostage viceroy at Bangkok,
and that he abandoned the project to build Wat Intharam at Bang Khun
Phrom following the 1789 arrival of the Lao Phuan. It is said that a pious
Sino-Thai tradeswoman, Yai Choen, was then prevailed upon to sponsor
the completion of the temple (Wat Bang Sai Kai n.d., p. 3).

Directly across the Bang Luang Canal from Bang Sai Kai, Chaochom
Waen during the First Reign sponsored the reconstruction of an old temple
later renamed Wat Sangkhrachai. The parallels between that merit-making
project and Waen's sponsorship of Wat Dawadoeng at Bang Yi-khan are
self-evident. The original temple, name unknown, dates to the closing years
of the Ayutthaya period but apparently remained incomplete into the first
Chakri reign. Rama I joined Waen in sponsoring the construction of the

MAP 4.3
Lao downstream: Bang Sai Kai
(19th century)

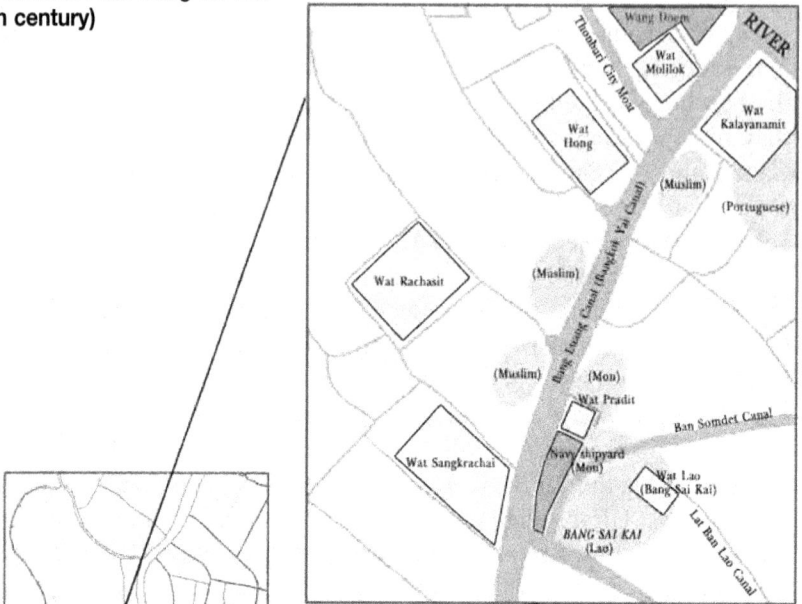

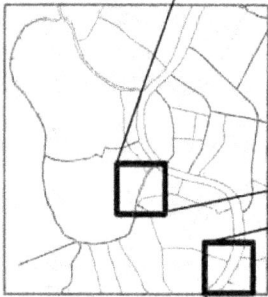

MAP 4.4
Lao downstream: Ban Kruay
(Late 19th century)

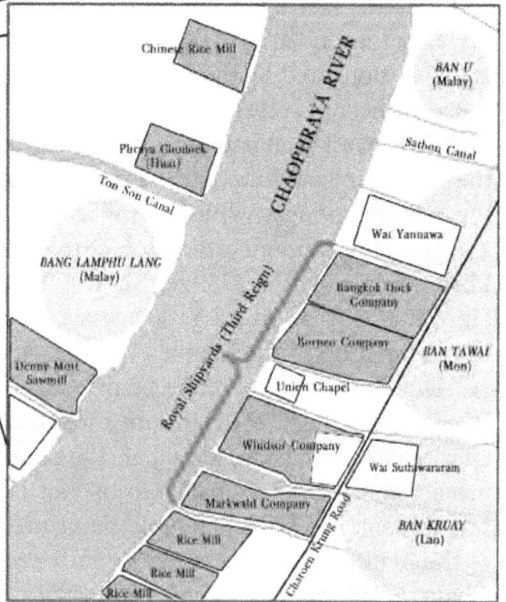

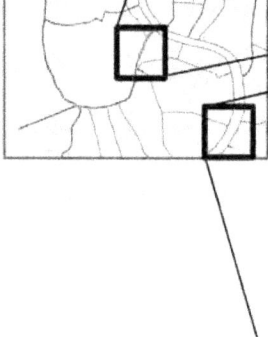

ordination hall. In digging the structure's foundation, the builders unearthed a conch (*sang[kh]*) and a small gilded-bronze image of Phra Kachai (or Phra Sangkachai, a revered disciple of the Buddha himself destined for future reincarnation as a Buddha). The king then formally established the temple as Wat Sangkachai (Sang[kh]-kachai, later revised to Sangkhrachai). Waen retained a close association with the temple, sponsoring the renovation of its ordination hall during the Second Reign. Following her death shortly thereafter and the bequest of her estate to Princess Kunthon Thipayawadi, a garden tract she owned directly alongside was donated to the temple in her memory (Wat Sangkhrachai 1990, pp. 1–8; Thailand, Royal Institute 2007, pp. 3–5).

As will be seen below, Bang Sai Kai lost the bulk of its Lao population around 1828–1830 upon the decision of Rama III to establish royal shipyards along the river at Yan Nawa and provide them with a labour force of Lao war captives. In the wake of the removal of most of the Lao captives to Yan Nawa, Bang Sai Kai reverted to the inconsequential Thai peasant village that it had formerly been, its Lao temple fell into disrepair, and its surroundings are said to have gradually declined into a trackless jungle inhabited by giant trees and poisonous snakes (Wat Bang Sai Kai n.d., pp. 3–4).

A decade later, toward the end of the Third Reign, the area encountered a sudden revival upon the decision of Chamoen Waiworanat (Chuang Bunnag), a leading military officer destined to rise to minister of military affairs (*kalahom*) as Chaophraya Si Suriyawong, to establish a navy shipyard along the Bang Luang Canal, directly across from Wat Sangkhrachai, on the site of the former Lao settlement (Thipakorawong 1995, p. 38). At the new shipyard, Chaophraya Si Suriyawong directed the construction and outfitting of some of Siam's first small steamboats, which he placed at the disposal of Rama IV. To man the new facility, a body of Mon war captives was brought from Bang Lamut, upriver near the present Rama VI Railway Bridge. They established a permanent community neighbouring the shipyard and built there a Mon temple, Wat Pradit. The neighbouring Ban Somdet Canal was rechannelled from the Bang Luang Canal to discharge into the Bang Sai Kai Canal. That altered course demarcated the shipyard and Mon settlement from the Bunnag family estates that were introduced into the area in the Fourth and Fifth Reigns (Piyanat 1999, p. 348).

The tract across the Ban Somdet Canal from the naval shipyard, containing Wat Bang Sai Kai and remnants of the former Lao community as well as a cluster of noblemen's mansions, was gradually repopulated over the course of the Fifth Reign by Thai and Chinese market gardeners as the Bangkok metropolis prospered and expanded. The formerly Lao village of

Bang Sai Kai and its temple revived, but under a new Thai-Chinese ethnic label. In 1890 the consecrated area of Wat Bang Sai Kai was clarified and confirmed by the local authorities. With the monastic administrative reforms of the 1890s and the Sangha Act of 1902, the religious facility was formally upgraded from an unregistered monastery (*samnak song*) to an officially recognized temple (*aram*, a term no longer restricted only to royal temples) designated as a legitimate venue for the ordination of monks (Wat Bang Sai Kai n.d., pp. 5–6; Ishii 1986*a*, pp. 69–70). A shadow of the former Lao presence at Bang Sai Kai lingers on today in folk memories of the community's past and in the continuing local handicraft industry of Lao musical instrument production (Phromphong 2004, pp. 45–57).

Ban Kruay

In 1769, King Taskin led a naval expedition to the South against Nakhon Si Thammarat, which had been a tributary state (*prathet rat*) of Ayutthaya but had claimed independence after the fall of the Siamese kingdom. The ruler of that fiefdom, Chao Nakhon (Nu), and his family were carried off to Thonburi. In 1776, the court favourite who had been installed by King Taksin as vassal ruler of the conquered state died, and Nu was then permitted to return home and resume his reign, now as governor, having provided Taksin with three of his daughters as consorts — and, in effect, hostages.

During their seven-year exile at Thonburi, Chao Nakhon (Nu) and his household were initially placed under virtual house arrest within the city wall. After about two years they were allowed to establish an independent residential compound on an 80-acre tract some four kilometres downstream from the walled city, along the left bank of the river neighbouring Ban Tawai, at the mouth of the Kruay Canal (*kruay* translates as "funnel" and apparently refers here to the gaping mouth and fine anchorage of the canal passing alongside the residential tract). Near his residence at that location, now known as Ban Kruay (Map 4.4), Chao Nakhon received royal permission to found a riverside temple. It was built in 1771–1772 as one of his first projects after moving to the downriver tract; no record of its name survives (Suthiwarapiwat 2006, p. 11). Over the ensuing decades the compound at the Kruay Canal remained a minor presence along the lower reaches of the Chaophraya River, serving as the Bangkok quarters of the Nakhon Si Thammarat ruling elite during their frequent tributary visits to the capital.

In 1833, Siam mounted the first of a series of attacks on Vietnamese territory with the dispatch of a 10,000-man naval flotilla against Hatien and Saigon. Preparations for that expedition began in 1828 with the requisitioning and refitting of a flotilla of Chinese junks to serve as troop carriers and the construction of a squadron of marine barges to ensure adequate food and munitions. That preparatory work was conducted in secrecy under the supervision of Chaophraya Prayurawong (Dit Bunnag), minister of finance and foreign affairs (*phra khlang*, also acting as minister of military affairs), in cooperation with Chao Nakhon (Noi, son and successor to Nu). The work was carried out along the shoreline fronting the Chao Nakhon residential compound, a river stretch that came to be known as Yan Nawa (Maritime District) (Thipakorawong 1995, pp. 37–38). To man the sawmills and shipyards at Yan Nawa, Rama III ordered the resettlement of the able-bodied Lao war captives from Bang Sai Kai. They established their new community at Ban Kruay and adopted the local temple for their own use, leading to its vernacular renaming as Wat Lao, reminiscent of the Wat Lao that they had left behind at Bang Sai Kai.

Writing of his arrival at Bangkok in 1840, a British mariner recalled some years later that the royal dockyards were situated three miles below the walled city, downriver from the Roman Catholic Mission (today known as Assumption Cathedral):

> Here those splendid ships which compose the King of Siam's navy, and which would do credit to any nation, were constructed, under the immediate supervision of an English shipwright; and here vessels of any other nation, that may have met with damage at sea, are thoroughly, and at a very cheap outlay, repaired. There are also one or two dry docks (Neale 1852, p. 25).

Toward the close of his reign, Rama III commemorated those royal shipyards in his renaming of the nearby temple, Wat Khok Kraboe, as Wat Yannawa. At that temple he erected a large stupa with its base in the shape of a Chinese junk, reminiscent of the fleets that he had built there for the Vietnam wars. The continuing presence of the Lao shipwrights' community at Yan Nawa is referred to in a *fin-de-siècle* Bangkok memoire that recalls with nostalgia Wat Lao and the Lao immigrants who settled the area during the Third Reign (Sthirakoses 1992, pp. 26, 27).

In 1864, Rama IV decided to build a downriver extension of the city's first major thoroughfare, Charoen Krung Road. It stretched southward parallel with the river, passing directly behind the old royal shipyards and sawmills at Yan Nawa (Map 4.4). The right-of-way ran through the midst of Wat Lao, leaving the temple severely truncated (Suthiwarapiwat 2006, pp. 1–2). No longer interested in maintaining the old royal shipyards, the king decided to rent the riverside property to commercial interests. The first leaseholder was Captain John Bush, a British seafarer who later served as Bangkok Harbormaster with the title Luang (later raised to Phraya) Wisut Sakhondit. His firm, the Bangkok Dock Company, located adjacent to Wat Yannawa, survives to this day. Additional parcels of the Yan Nawa waterfront were later leased to a line of Western agency houses — Markwald and Company (German), Windsor Rose and Company (German/British), and the Borneo Company (British) — which established their docks and warehouses there, eventually controlling a substantial portion of Siam's rice export trade and passenger liner transport (Wilson 1978, pp. 247–50, 254). Rama IV also donated a plot of Yan Nawa waterfront land to the British community for the erection of their church, known as the Union Chapel for its non-denominational policy. (It moved in 1903 to Convent Road at the corner of Sathon Road and was renamed Christ Church.) Many of the Lao of Ban Kruay, freed by Rama V from their bondage as war captives, found employment as stevedores and warehousemen with the Western firms; however, none are known to have converted to their European masters' religion.

In 1881, Khunying Suthi, wife of Chaophraya Wichiankiri (Men na Songkhla, sixth hereditary governor of Songkhla Province) and a descendant of Chao Nakhon (Noi), rebuilt the badly dilapidated Wat Lao, and Rama V upgraded its name to Wat Suthi-wararam in recognition of its benefactor. Less than two decades later, the temple was again in need of repair, and Pan Wacharaphai, daughter of Chaophraya Wichiankiri and Khunying Suthi, rebuilt the entire temple in memory of her parents. The rear of the Windsor Rose property, cut off from the temple a generation earlier for the construction of Charoen Krung Road, was reacquired by the temple in 1911 to build the Suthi-wararam School, again under the patronage of the descendants of Chao Nakhon (Noi) (Suthiwarapiwat 2006, pp. 2–3). Upon Siam's entry into the First World War on the side of the Allies in 1917, the docks, warehouses, inventories, and ships of the German firms Windsor Rose and A. Markwald were confiscated as war booty. The leased Yan Nawa riverside property also reverted to the Crown. With those newly acquired assets, the government established the Siam Steamship Company (later reorganized as the Siam Maritime Navigation Company), operating out of the former German facilities (Greene 1999, pp. 105–109, 136). In the years following the 1932 People's Revolution, the waterfront where the German firms had formerly stood was converted to the state-run Fish Marketing Organization, Bangkok Fish Market, Cold Storage Organization, and Fisheries Technical Development Department, and the area came to be known as Saphan Pla (Fish Bridge). The area's distinctive Lao ethnic presence had dissipated.

IN THE CITY: ROYAL RETAINERS AND CRAFTSMEN

Within the walled city in the early Ratanakosin period residence was, with few exceptions, restricted to the Thai ruling elite. Pragmatic considerations allowed several small minority settlements — a hamlet of Indian Hindu priests alongside the Brahman shrine (today known as Thewa Sathan Bot Phram) and ceremonial swing near Wat Suthat; a community of Vietnamese artisans along Ban Mo Road skilled in glass-making, niello-ware, and gem-setting; a Mon village of cotton-goods weavers along Tanao Road; a settlement of Malay goldsmiths at the city's northern tip — were established early on to ensure the ready delivery of crucial services to the capital's inner cluster of royal and noble households. One of those service centres was a settlement of impoverished Lao war captives that provided menial labour to the royal palaces. In later decades, as residential restrictions were eased, additional minority neighbourhoods emerged in the *intramuros* district that came to be called the "City". Among those commercial invaders were several clusters of Lao commercial artisans catering to the rising consumer demands of the government bureaucracy, represented by the staffs of the assorted ministries gathered within easy walking distance of the Grand Palace.

Ban Lao Phuan Nai

In 1818, Rama II decided to build an elaborate pleasure garden, Suan Khwa (Garden of the Right), in the Grand Palace. Prince Anuwong, then the viceroy of Vientiane representing his vassal kingdom's interests at Bangkok, offered the services of a contingent of Lao Phuan labourers to dig the garden's elaborate arrangement of ponds and islets (Khaisaeng 1996, pp. 107–23; S. Plainoi 2002, p. 102). For that task, it appears that he recruited a sizeable group of settlers from Bang Khun Phrom. The death of Prince Senanurak, the viceroy of Rama II, only a year before had left Anuwong freer than he otherwise might have been to reassign such a number of his subjects to the king's service. To allow ready access to the construction site, the workers were provided temporary quarters within the walled city, along the outer bank of the Inner City Moat, adjacent to the old Vietnamese settlement of Ban Yuan at the mouth of the Market Canal (Map 4.2). Following the death of Rama II and installation of Rama III, Anuwong, now king of Vientiane, appealed for the repatriation of those long-suffering war captives — along with the many other Lao captives being held at Bangkok and Saraburi — but

his plea fell on deaf ears. Rama III's intransigence apparently contributed
to Anuwong's fateful decision to initiate the Thai-Lao war of 1827–1828. In
the aftermath of the Lao defeat, that same contingent of war captives may
have been called on to carry out the demolition of Suan Khwa, ordered
by Rama III to obliterate that unsavoury reminder of Anuwong's former
connection with the Grand Palace.

The royal chronicle of the Third Reign, much preoccupied with the
relentlessly troubled Thai-Lao relations of the time, refers to this Lao
settlement in passing:

> [One early afternoon in mid-1831] a fire broke out within the walled city.
> It spread from the Drum Tower to the elephant bridge at Ban Mo. The
> fire spread to both sides of the [Inner City Moat], reaching the residence
> of Phraya Si Sahathep and extending along both banks of the canal up
> to the bridge at Ban Mon, because that area contained the huts of Ban
> Lao Phuan Nai (the Inner Lao Phuan Village), which were dry as tinder.
> The fire burned down a number of princes' palaces [on the citadel side
> of the moat] and nobles' residences [on the City side of the moat]. Many
> people died in the fire (Thipakorawong 1995, p. 45).

That unusually vivid description of a disaster within the walled city places
the location of Ban Lao Phuan Nai along the outer bank of the Inner City
Moat, next to the old Mon community. Evidently, the Lao Phuan had
established their settlement directly alongside Ban Mo (Potters' Village),
an adjunct to Ban Mon, the residential site of Phraya Si Sahathep and his
entourage (Phromphong 2004, pp. 84–86). That Mon village name was
eventually extended to incorporate the Lao village locale as well.

The devastating fire of 1831 destroyed the palace of Prince Phithak
Thewet (Kunchon), directly across the Inner City Moat from Ban Mo, and
he subsequently built a new palace (later called Wang Ban Mo) on the site
of the burned-down Lao village, forcing the Lao to rebuild their hovels
southward, toward Pak Khlong Talat (the downstream mouth of the Inner
City Moat). Prince Phithak was royal overseer of the army's Elephantry
Department (*krom khochaban*), its stables located in the royal gardens (*suan
chao chet* and *suan luang*) across the moat from the Lao Phuan village. It is
likely that the Lao war slaves served the royal elephants under his charge,
doling out their enormous quantities of feed, mucking out their stables,
giving them their daily riverside bath. The village was too poor to establish
its own temple; instead, the Lao erected several worship pavilions (*sala
rongtham*) along the path that would several decades later be expanded
into Foeang Nakhon Road which monks from such nearby temples as Wat

Rachaburana and Wat Suthat visited to conduct prayer sessions and other communal rituals (Tomosugi 1993, p. 40).

The royal slaves at Ban Lao Phuan Nai were later assigned to serve the Department of Female Guardians (*krom khlon*), an agency of the Ministry of the Royal Household (*krom wang* — *krom* referring ambiguously to both "department" and "ministry") run by senior ladies of the Grand Palace women's quarters (*fai nai* or *khang nai*). Under their charge, the Lao slaves were assigned to such menial duties as sluicing the latrines and drains in the densely populated Grand Palace women's quarters. In the closing decades of the Fifth Reign, the Ministry of the Royal Household upgraded its sanitary infrastructure, allowing it to dispense with its reliance on slave labour and consequently leaving the Lao Phuan to fend for themselves. Then, around 1900, the king decided to refurbish their neighbourhood edging the Inner City Moat, with the Privy Purse erecting lines of handsome shophouses along both sides of Foeang Nakhon Road, transforming it into a fashionable shopping street. To make way for that redevelopment project the Lao Phuan were evicted from the area.

Ban Kraba

The evicted Lao community was provided a new settlement site nearby, in a tract of reclaimed inner-city wasteland behind Wang Burapha, the palace of Prince Phanuphan Wongworadet (Phanurangsi) (Map 4.2). There the village replicated its former squalor (Bang-on 1998, p. 41). The neighbourhood came to be known as Ban Kraba, in recognition of its primary industry, the production of household wickerware, including various sorts of lidded and unlidded baskets and trays (*kraba*) (Sthirakoses 2002, pp. 24–25; Phromphong 2004, pp. 105–106). They also specialized in the raising of mosquito larvae (*luk nam*), sold as fish food to devotees of the popular gamblers' hobby of fighting fish (*pla kat*), and charcoal retailing. The nearby Pratu Sam Yot (Three Spires City Gate) and Saphan Than (Charcoal Bridge) neighbourhoods, Bangkok's premier entertainment centre of the time, provided them with additional work as snack vendors, lottery touts, and less reputable employments (Sthirakoses 1992, pp. 160–61; Tomosugi 1993, pp. 42–43). The area was upgraded in the first decade of the twentieth century with the creation of Sanam Nam Choet (Potable Water Field), featuring Bangkok's first government-sponsored artesian well, which emptied into a large tank that provided drinking water for the surrounding neighbourhood. The field was rimmed by tenements providing upgraded, relatively hygienic, fire-resistant habitation for the local community. Later, in the Seventh Reign, the area was further improved with the construction of the Chaloem Krung Theater, Bangkok's foremost cinema of the day, and the establishment of the Bampenbun Market, a favoured haunt of the city's transvestites. Today much of the area is covered by The Old Siam shopping mall.

Ban Ti Thong

Among the variety of Lao artisans carried off to Bangkok over the course of the nineteenth century were a number of goldsmiths. One small group of those sought-after war captives was, in the wake of the Thai-Lao war of 1827–1828, provided to Phraya Si Phiphat (That Bunnag) and settled near his residence along the right bank of the river downstream from Thonburi. There, in the shadow of Wat Anongkaram, the community of Ban Chang Thong (Goldsmiths' Village) made its life over the following decades, practising its craft in the service of the noble households occupying the Khlong San district. By the turn of the twentieth century, the origins of the village were becoming blurred in folk memory. Reminiscing to her daughter, Princess Kalayani Wathana, about her ancestry, Princess Mother Si Nakharin (Sangwan 1900–95), mother of King Rama IX, recalled that her family had lived in Ban Chang Thong, where her father had been a goldsmith: "Some of my mother's forebears came from Vientiane. My mother said that seemed likely because at home they liked to eat glutinous rice" (Kalayani 1980, pp. 9, 18).

Just as the residents of Ban Lao Phuan were in the closing decade of the nineteenth century released from their servitude in the Grand Palace, the bonds of the artisans of Ban Chang Thong to their Bunnag family masters were also loosened. Some of them responded to their newfound freedom by moving across the river to Ban Ti Thong (Gold Beaters' Village (Map 4.2)), in the midst of the "City", alongside Wat Suthat, drawn by the commercial promise of the nearby Sao Ching Cha market and Bamrung Moeang Road shophouse neighbourhood (Tomosugi 1993, pp. 54–55; Phromphong 2004, pp. 19–24). Lacking the business acumen and capital to strike out on their own, they were hired by local Chinese merchants to produce gold foil by the hammering of gold lumps into wafer-thin sheets and ultimately tissue-thin gold leaf. The finished product met great demand among worshipers as a devotional item, pasted by them to Buddha images and other religious icons as a meritorious act; it was also used in the classic Thai art of gold-on-black lacquerwork (*long rak pit thong*). But gold-beating (*ti thong*) was only one element in the goldsmiths' repertoire of skills; a wide assortment of Lao goldsmithing techniques was on display in the Chinese shophouses along Ti Thong Road, including gold filigree work, ornamental casting and shaping, and niello inlay. Close to the centre of government affairs, with the Ministry of Interior, Ministry of War, and Ministry of the Capital only a few blocks away, Ti Thong Road gained a reputation for police and military insignia and medallions. Nearby, tailor shops competed in catering to the latest fashions in officers' uniforms; down the street were other shops specializing in handguns and munitions. Vestiges of that shopping scene remain today, though memories of the Lao goldbeaters' ever-tapping presence have all but vanished.

In sum, Ban Ti Thong rose with the emergence of Bangkok's middle class of salaried government bureaucrats during the decades spanning the turn of the twentieth century. The Chinese shophouses and Lao goldsmiths of Ti Thong Road exemplified the new commercial fashion of retail shopping, making the previously unattainable affordable through its well-known devices of mass production, mass distribution, and mass consumption. Formerly, the Lao goldsmiths had been captive craftsmen producing luxury items to the individual specifications of their aristocratic masters. Freed from servitude, they became employees turning out standardized products for display to anonymous shoppers. They symbolized Bangkok's social revolution from patrimonial to commercial norms.

FROM WAR SLAVES TO WAGE SLAVES

Beyond the nineteenth-century Lao communities reviewed above, a number of additional settlements of Lao war captives were scattered about Bangkok's outskirts. Among them were Ban Chang Lo (Metal Casters' Village, situated outside the Thonburi moat, behind the Rear Palace), Ban Samsen Nai (along the Samsen Canal centring on Wat Aphai-tharayam), Bang Kapi (on the Saen Saep Canal alongside Wang Sa Pathum and Wat Pathumwanaram), Ban Thai Talat Nang Loeng (along the Phadung Krung Kasem Canal between Wat Somanat and Wat Sunthon Thammathan), and Taling Chan (along the outer bank of the Bangkok Noi Canal near Wat Rachadathithan). Most of the Lao slaves (*kha luang*) relegated to those communities farmed the king's lands along the Bangkok periphery to supply the royal granaries, while some were contributed to royally sponsored temples as temple slaves (*lek wat, kha wat*) in acts of merit. Just like the Bangkok Lao communities reviewed in the preceding sections, the slave status of those peripheral villages withered away during the closing decades of the Fifth Reign. "Quietly and effectively, … with no royal decree to herald the change, an entire generation of state-owned peasants was [during the closing years of the nineteenth century] released from obligations of servitude" (Snit and

Breazeale 1988, p. 129). That liberation from lifetimes of enslavement was accompanied by a wilful fading away of their self-loathed cultural memory of bondage — and with it their Lao ethnic identity.

The proximate cause of the demise of the Lao captives' slave status was a ploy threatened by the French imperialists in the wake of the Thai-French confrontation of 1893. That stratagem sought to apply the extraterritoriality provision contained in the Thai-French trade treaty to claim French sovereignty over Siam's myriad villages of Lao war captives, "many of which were in the suburbs of Bangkok itself" (Snit and Breazeale 1988, p. 129). The Thai authorities were horrified to discover that under the rules of extraterritoriality all of Siam's population of Lao war captives — and their descendants — could potentially be claimed as French subjects. A pragmatic response to that threat was to suppress the ethnic origins of the enslaved Lao communities and treat them as ordinary "Thai citizens":

> The very existence of captive labour villages became an acute embarrassment. It was imperative that their [ethnic] identity be officially suppressed and their [origins] denied. An obvious first step was the abandonment of the 'captive labour' caste designation within the Thai legal system.... A second step was the formulation of a Thai nationality law in order to establish a legal definition for Thai citizens [and include those communities formally within the Siamese legal framework] (Snit and Breazeale 1988, p. 129).

An initial draft of such a law was circulated in 1899, granting citizenship to all those constituting at least the third generation of resident alien status. The final formulation of that law, the Nationality Act of 1913, granted citizenship to all those born in Siam.

The freeing of Siam's war slaves from their servitude to the Crown and its minions created an instant "footloose" population. Among the peasantry, that suited exactly the manpower requirements of the government's land development programmes, such as the Rangsit irrigation scheme that opened up vast swaths of reclaimed land north of Bangkok. The many Lao (and Malay) settlements stretching eastward from Bangkok along the Samsen and Saen Saep Canals exemplified that policy. Along the more immediate urban periphery, many of the Lao of Ban Kruay found work with the Western logging, sawmilling, and trading houses of Yan Nawa and Bang Rak, and others moved further downstream to the burgeoning port area at Bang Ko Laem. Similarly, many of the craftsmen of Bang Khun Phrom, Bang Yi-khan, and other Lao communities formerly associated with the royal artisans' departments found employment with Chinese merchants intent on developing the local market for luxury goods formerly available only to a tiny elite. Others found menial work with the Bangkok Municipality's waterworks, roadways, and public sanitation departments, and with such proto-public enterprises as the Bangkok Tramways Company and Siam Electricity Company, forming an adjunct to the Chinese-dominated labour movement that emerged in the early decades of the twentieth century. The hardships of forced servitude to the favoured few had faded into the past; the rigours of "voluntary" sweatshop labour in the urban marketplace had taken their place. Thus, "while formal slavery may have ended, other forms of dependence ... continued" (Cruikshank 1975, p. 329).

5

Contending Identities:
Muslim Minorities

FROM *KHAEK ISALAM* ...

In former centuries, Siam's Muslim inhabitants may have accounted for well over a tenth of the kingdom's total population, depending on how far down the Malay Peninsula the Siamese realm is calculated to have extended; one knowledgeable Western resident in the mid-nineteenth century reckoned Siam's "Malay" population at one million, about 17 per cent of the kingdom's total estimated population (Pallegoix 2000, p. 2). The kingdom's retracted southern border following the Anglo-Siamese Treaty of 1909 caused its Muslim population to shrink appreciably. As a result, their number is today believed to account for less than a tenth of the total citizenry. In the absence of official census data by religion, a 1988 estimate of the kingdom's Muslim population multiplied the country's total of 2,600 mosques by a rule-of-thumb figure of 2,000 people per mosque to arrive at a national Muslim population of 5.2 million, or around 9 per cent of the kingdom's total citizenry. For the Bangkok Metropolis, the equivalent figures were 155 mosques and 310,000 Muslims, accounting for 6 per cent of the capital's residents (Thailand, Ministry of Culture, Department of Religious Affairs, Muslim Affairs Bureau n.d. (1988?)). Two decades later, those figures had risen to 174 mosques and 348,000 Muslims, or an estimated 6.1 per cent of the capital's total population (Thailand, National Muslim Center, Office of the Islamic Committee of the Bangkok Municipality, n.d. (2011?)).

Among the Thai populace, the Muslim minority has traditionally been referred to collectively — sometimes pejoratively — as *khaek isalam*, literally "Muslim guests" or "strangers" (Scupin 1998, p. 148; Keyes 2008–09, pp. 21, 27; Winyu 2014, pp. 3, 16), a term that carries subtle exclusionary connotations implicit in a sense of Otherness (Thongchai 2000a). Perhaps that Otherness may arise from the fact that the great majority of the kingdom's Muslims have historically been domiciled in the South, with only a secondary presence concentrated in and around Bangkok. It has even been rather fancifully suggested that the name "Bangkok" (originally Ban Kok) may derive from a centuries-old designation, "Ban Khaek" (Bajunid 1992, p. 25), referring to an early intrusion of those Muslim "strangers" into the Thai heartland. Today, in telling confirmation of the distinction between the Muslims of the South and Centre, those of Central Thailand are commonly termed *thai isalam* (Muslim Thai) in contrast to the *musalim malayu* (Malay Muslims) of the South. In secular terms, the "Thai Islam" have accommodated to the dominant Thai cultural ethos far more readily than have the "Malay Muslims" of the South. In that process, their traditional ethnicity has faded, if language facility, dress, residential location, and work preferences can serve as a gauge (Chokchai 2011, pp. 435–38). Nevertheless, they have managed to retain their traditional religious convictions and practices to a remarkable extent. The Muslims of the Centre and those of the South today thus "converge as adherents of the same religion, but diverge when it comes to giving prominence to ethnicity and language over other forms of identity" (Yusuf 2010, p. 43). Trust and empathy within the group, and conversely suspicion and rejection of outsiders, have gravitated from ethnicity to religion.

The Siamese capital's ethnographically complex Muslim landscape had its origins well back in Ayutthaya times (pre-1767). Ayutthaya's diverse Muslim community was long composed of two distinct elements. One — Persian, Arab, Indian — consisted of "sojourners": long-distance voyagers visiting the Thai capital as emissaries and merchants from distant lands. The other — Malay, Cham, Indonesian (itself a term covering a diversity of ethnicities) — comprised "subjects": war captives, mercenaries, and refugees, primarily from nearby lands of Southeast Asia. The former were predominantly of the Shia persuasion; the latter were invariably Sunni. The two groups differed not only in regional origin and religious denomination but also in socio-political status and economic pursuits, and they were accordingly allotted separate settlement sites at Ayutthaya: The South and West Asians "sojourners" were assigned residential quarters within the walled city while the Southeast Asian "subjects" were relegated to the capital's extramural precincts. At Thonburi and then Bangkok following the fall of Ayutthaya the Muslim community came to be distributed in a more restrictive spatial pattern, situated almost entirely outside the walled city.

The Bangkok-Thonburi hub and its deltaic hinterlands — a region today comprising roughly the 1,569 square kilometres Bangkok Metropolis — constituted in the nineteenth century a unique Muslim catchment zone. Yet, it probably never accounted for more than 7 or 8 per cent of the kingdom's total Muslim population. The preponderance of those people are descendants of the Malay war captives who were assigned to the eastern reaches of the Chaophraya Delta during the 1830s. Other, smaller Muslim settlements of varied ethnicity emerged in earlier reigns to ring the royal city. While those dispersed villages were progressively engulfed over the course of the twentieth century by the sprawling density of the city's commercial neighbourhoods, the basic lineaments of the nineteenth-century Muslim settlement pattern continue to be readily observable in the distribution of mosques (*masjid* or *masyid*, or alternatively *surao*; or archaically *kudi*; or for the Shia denomination, *imambara*) across the area.

The histories of each of the six Muslim ethnic groups at the successive Siamese capitals are briefly reviewed below as background to a series of capsule biographies of twenty-six noteworthy Muslim villages of Old Bangkok (1782–1910). The accompanying figures (Map 5.1 and Table 5.1) indicate the locations of those twenty-six settlements and the corresponding village and mosque names as of 1910. The biographies help clarify the historical logic behind the distribution of Old Bangkok's complex landscape of Muslim-affiliated ethnic settlements and the manner in which those settlements have historically interacted with other ethnic groups, particularly the Thai ruling class. Some of the historical lessons evident in the light of later developments are noted in the Conclusion, with the main one being that Old Bangkok's Muslim community can be better appreciated in terms of its ethnic multiplicity than with regard solely to its religious uniformity.

Before moving on to an examination of Bangkok's various Muslim communities, the title phrase "contending identities" requires a brief explanatory comment. The six individual ethnic groups discussed in this chapter historically shared the religion of Islam. The "contentiousness" referred to here embodies a *double entendre* built on that ethnic-religious duality. It refers first to the various points of dissension, or at least disengagement, that were observable among those ethnic groups at Bangkok over the course of the Ratanakosin period (1782–1910), as demonstrated, for instance, by their separate and discrete village sites and mosques, their resolute adherence to different languages and customs, and the infrequency of intermarriage among them. Secondly, it refers to the incongruity, over the post-Ratanakosin generations (1910–present), between their

MAP 5.1
Old Bangkok: Muslim villages, by ethnic group

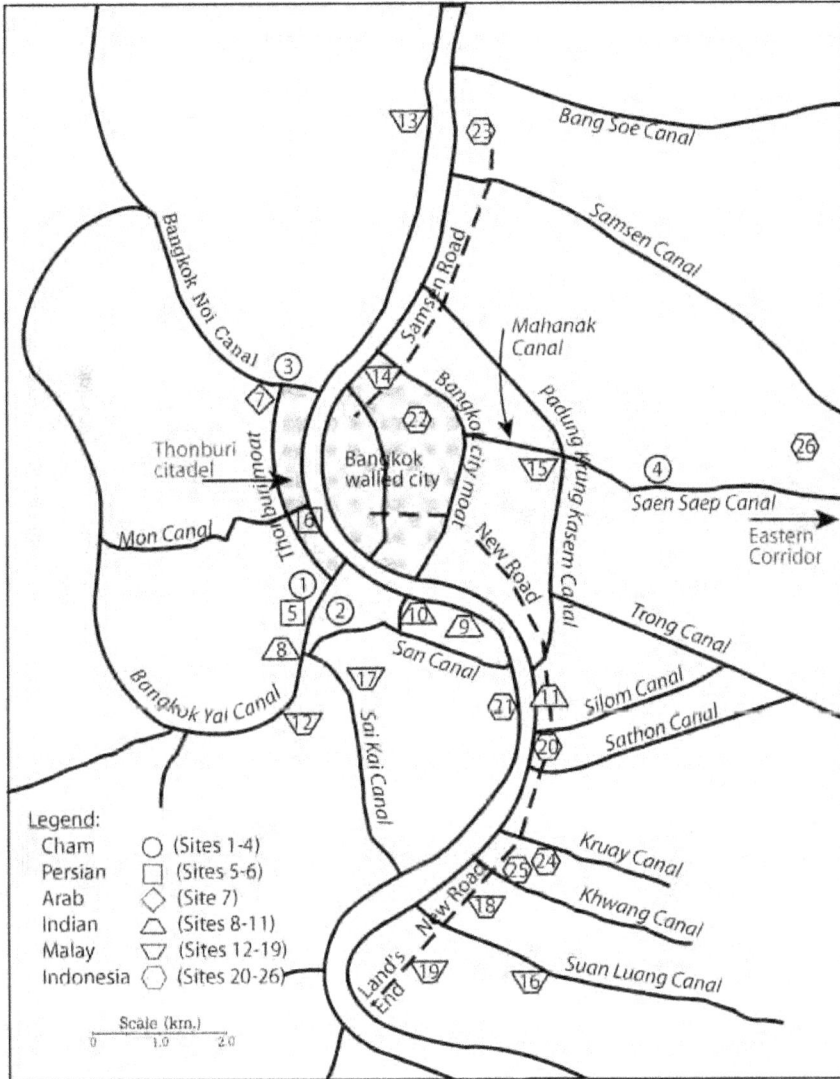

Bang Soe Canal
Samsen Canal
Mahanak Canal
Bangkok Noi Canal
Samsen Road
Bangkok city moat
Padung Krung Kasem Canal
Thonburi citadel
Thonburi moat
Bangkok walled city
Saen Saep Canal
Eastern Corridor
Mon Canal
New Road
Trong Canal
San Canal
Silom Canal
Sathon Canal
Bangkok Yai Canal
Sai Kai Canal
Kruay Canal
Khwang Canal
New Road
Land's End
Suan Luang Canal

Legend:
Cham   ○ (Sites 1-4)
Persian   □ (Sites 5-6)
Arab   ◇ (Site 7)
Indian   △ (Sites 8-11)
Malay   ▽ (Sites 12-19)
Indonesia   ⬡ (Sites 20-26)

Scale (km.)
0   1.0   2.0

Note: The numbered sites and ethnic designations listed here correspond with the 26 villages and mosques listed in Table 5.1.

TABLE 5.1

Muslim villages and mosques of Old Bangkok

Village sites[a]	Traditional village names	Formal mosque names[b]	Ethnic groups
1.	Kudi Yai, Kudi Kao, Ton Son	Ton Son Mosque	Cham
2.	Kudi Mai, Kudi Luang, Kudi Khaw	Kudi Khaw	Cham
3.	Kudi Asa Cham (abandoned, 1910s?)	– (unknown)	Cham
4.	Ban Khaek Khrua, Ban Khrua		
	Ban Khrua Klang	Yami ul-Koiriya Mosque	Cham
	Ban Khrua Nai	Suluk ul-Mattakin Mosque	Cham
	Ban Khrua Nok	Darul Falah Mosque	Cham
5.	Kudi Nok, Kudi Klang, Kudi Charoenphat	*Phadungtham Islam Mosque*	Persian
6.	Kudi Chao Sen	*Kudi Luang Chao Sen* (demolished 1947)	Persian
7.	Ban Khaek Bangkok Noi	Ansarit Sunnah Mosque (destroyed 1945)	Arab
8.	Kudi Nok, Kudi Lang	*Dinfallah Mosque*	Indian
9.	Toek Khaw	*Sefi Mosque*	Indian
10.	Toek Daeng	*Kuwatil Islam Mosque*	Indian
11.	Ban Khaek Bang Rak, Ban Khaek Muang Khae	Harun Mosque	Malay
12.	Ban Suan Phlu	Suan Phlu	Malay
13.	Bang O	Ihachan Mosque	Malay
14.	Bang Lamphu	Chakraphong Mosque	Malay
15.	Ban Tani	Mahanak Mosque	Malay
16.	Ban Suan Luang	al-Athik Mosque	Malay
17.	Ban Khaek Sai Kai, Ban Khaek Ban Somdet	Nurul Mubin Mosque	Malay
18.	Bang Uthit	Bang Uthit Mosque	Malay
19.	Ban Trok Mo	as-Salafiya Mosque	Malay
20.	Ban U	Ban U Mosque	Indonesian
21.	Ban Khaek Lang, Ban Suwanaphum	Suwanaphumi Mosque	Indonesian
22.	Ban Toek Din	Toek Din Mosque	Indonesian
23.	Ban Khaek Kraboe	Nurul Islam Mosque	Indonesian
24.	Ban Kruay, Ban Trok Chan	Darul Abidin Mosque	Indonesian
25.	Ban Khwang	Bayan Mosque	Indonesian
26.	Ban Makkasan	Niamatul Islam Mosque	Indonesian

Notes: a. Village sites follow the numbered site sequence in the text.
b. Mosque names registered with the Thai government (since 1947). Mosques referred to in bold italics denote Shia denomination. All other mosques are Sunni denomination.

waning ethnic pluralism, on the one hand, and their gathering religious
solidarity, on the other. In Islam, as distinct from, say, Buddhism, religious
brotherhood is prescribed as an active duty and thus vies with such other
ethnic considerations as bonds of origin and common descent, language,
and local custom in defining the social group of primary affiliation. In
Bangkok history, that integrative function strengthened over time, and
thus the contending forces of ethnic individuality and religious solidarity
shifted in relative prominence. So, not only did Bangkok's various Muslim
communities contend among themselves in the period before rising
nationalism attenuated their individual ethnicities, but in the subsequent
period they contended collectively to replace their waning ethnic identity
for a rising sense of religious commonality. That theme of dynamic change
within Bangkok's diverse Muslim populace over the more than two centuries
of the city's history underlies much of what follows.

CHAM MILITIAS

The ancient realm of Champa, centred along what is today the central and
southern Vietnamese littoral, was as long as a millennium ago renowned as
one of Southeast Asia's premier maritime powers. During the centuries of
their dominance over the lower Mekong basin the Cham perfected the art
of naval warfare, and that skill was to become one of their defining qualities.
Like many of the seaboard kingdoms of the Southeast Asian archipelago,
they were influenced by a continuing stream of South and West Asian traders
and clerics to abandon their ancestral cults in favour of, first, Hinduism
and, later, Islam. Over the course of the fourteenth-sixteenth centuries
Champa came under unrelenting pressure from the southward-spreading
Vietnamese, compelling a Cham exodus up the Mekong watershed into
Cambodia, with others dispersing across the sea to the Malay Peninsula
and Indonesian islands. Some of those who settled inland were captured
by Siamese raiders as early as the fifteenth century. Others joined Siamese
military campaigns as mercenaries in the early seventeenth century.
They continued to play an important naval role in Siam over the ensuing
generations, extending into the nineteenth century and beyond (Sorayut
2007, pp. 112–13; Scupin 1998, pp. 240–42).

At Ayutthaya, the Cham warriors were provided a settlement site along
the outer bank of the Chaophraya River south of the walled city, bounded
by Khu Cham (the Cham Moat) and Khlong Takhian (the Ironwood Canal).
The Cham militias (*krom asa cham*) gained acclaim for their prowess in
boatbuilding and both freshwater and saltwater naval warfare (Ishii 2012,

pp. 241–42). In ceremonial processions along Ayutthaya's rivers, Cham sailors were accorded the distinction of paddling the royal barges, a function they continued to perform at Bangkok into the twentieth century (Sujaritlak 1983, pp. 95–102). The chief of the Cham community and commander of the Cham militia at Ayutthaya customarily carried the title of Phraya Racha Wangsan (alternatively Bangsan), and that title — plus many others for his subordinates — was reinstated and elaborated in the Bangkok era (Sorayut 2001, pp. 11–25; Ishii 2012, p. 243; Sisak 1996).

Some seventy kilometres down the Chaophraya River from Ayutthaya, at the mouth of the Bangkok Yai Canal, behind the well-fortified Thonburi trade depot and customs station, Siam had since the 1600s posted a Cham military garrison (Cushman 2000, pp. 307–308; Sorayut 2001, pp. 5–8). Over the course of the Burmese invaders' final, fatal strike against Ayutthaya in early 1767, that military outpost was assaulted and destroyed, with its Cham defenders killed, captured, or reduced to headlong flight (Cushman 2000, pp. 496, 498–99; Sorayut 2001, pp. 15–17, 19–20, 28–29). Around the same time, hundreds of Ayutthaya's Muslim households — Persian, Arab, and Malay as well as Cham — anticipating the capital's imminent fall to Burmese assault, outfitted rafthouses on which they stealthily drifted off, bribing the besieging forces along the way to allow their safe passage. Many made their way downstream to Thonburi, where their rafts sheltered beneath the overhanging greenery of the Bangkok Yai Canal. Once the political situation had stabilized following the departure of the Burmese hordes and the investiture of Phraya Taksin as ruler of a reborn Siamese kingdom centred at Thonburi, the Muslim raft dwellers were assigned more permanent village sites ashore, along the new capital's outskirts. The humble beginnings of the Thonburi Reign as a cluster of refugee settlements surrounding King Taksin's nascent citadel marked the start of a remarkable resurrection of the Siamese polity, with the powerful memory of Ayutthaya as its guide. Thonburi's Cham community played no small part in that renaissance by providing naval battalions for Taksin's many military exploits. Later generations of Cham settlers at Bangkok, whether war captives, mercenaries, or asylum seekers, continued to benefit from that legacy.

Site 1: *Kudi Yai (Village on the Bangkok Yai Canal), later Kudi Kao (Old Village), presently Ban Ton Son (Pine Tree Village)* — The Cham presence at Thonburi, dating well back into the Ayutthaya period, centred on a military cantonment situated along the lower reaches of the Bangkok Yai Canal directly behind the fortifications guarding that strategic point on the Chaophraya River. Known as Kudi Yai (after the canal name), that Cham village came to an abrupt end in early 1767 with the destruction of the Thonburi fort at the hands of the Burmese invaders. The site was soon repopulated by Cham survivors of the Ayutthaya holocaust. Over the following years, with the construction of the Thonburi Grand Palace on the site of the former fort, Kudi Yai came to occupy a privileged position, with the Cham reverting to their distinctive naval tradition (Sisak 1996, p. 123; Sorayut 2001, pp. 19–25). In affirmation of that role, Taksin's royal shipyards and barge sheds were established directly across from the Cham settlement, along the outer bank of the Bangkok Yai Canal (that stretch of the waterway now called the Bang Luang Canal, or Great [or Royal] Settlement Canal). In the Third Chakri Reign, however, it was decided to relocate the royal barge sheds to a more prominent site along the opposite shore of the Chaophraya River, at Wat Phra Chetuphon, while the royal shipyards were moved a kilometre up the Bangkok Yai Canal to a new naval base at the confluence of the Sai Kai Canal. Many of the Cham shipwrights and sailors of Kudi Yai followed, and the military importance of the old Cham settlement consequently declined. As if to reassure the Cham villagers of his continued favour, the king extended to them his patronage in the reconstruction of their Kudi Yai mosque, including the gift of a stand of tropical pine trees (*ton son*) to grace its forecourt (Phathara 2007, p. 129). The name of the village and mosque in popular usage was consequently revised to Ton Son, and so it remains to this day, though the pine trees themselves have long since disappeared. Like the settlement's abandonment of its traditional naval function, its changed name has done much to obscure its role in Old Bangkok's history. At the same time, the village has taken on renewed importance in Bangkok's Muslim community through its adherence to the traditional, liberal school of Southeast Asian Muslim thought and practice in the lively local debate over Islamic reform (Winyu 2014, pp. 16–20).

Site 2: *Kudi Mai (New Village), or Kudi Luang (Village on the Bang Luang Canal), later Kudi Khaw (White Mosque Village)* — Some of the Cham refugees who had nestled their rafthouses along the Bang Luang Canal in the wake of Ayutthaya's collapse eventually moved to dryland homesteads on the less crowded canal shoreline opposite Kudi Yai. There they established Kudi Mai (the New Village), leaving Kudi Yai to be redubbed Kudi Kao (the Old Village), and they built there the Bang Luang Mosque, otherwise known as Kudi Luang (Penchan

2008; Saowani 2001, p. 96). At Kudi Mai the Cham settlers found ready employment as shipwrights and sailors at the royal shipyard and barge sheds lining the canal bank. For several generations the village prospered in its naval employment, until the Third Reign removal of the barge sheds to the riverfront at Wat Phra Chetuphon and the shipyard up the Bangkok Yai Canal to the Sai Kai Canal. Thereafter, Kudi Mai, like its cross-canal counterpart Kudi Yai, fell into decline as many of its households moved away and those that remained abandoned their naval calling. Coincident with that cultural dilution, the Bang Luang Mosque was rebuilt in a style emulative of a Thai Buddhist temple, featuring white-plastered brick walls, decorative gables, and tiled roof. In recognition of its gleaming white façade it came to be called Kudi Khaw (the White Mosque), with the village name being revised accordingly. Over the subsequent generations the former close association between Kudi Khaw and Ban Ton Son faded, and today the two much-reduced villages are quite distinct.

Site 3: *Kudi Asa Cham (Cham Militia Village)* — The 1779/80 passage of a Thai army through Cambodia, led by Chaophraya Surasi (Bunma, Siam's future First Reign viceroy), conscripted large numbers of local troops, amounting to around 10,000 men overall, plus foodstocks (Thipakorawong 2009, p. 30). Among those recruits were Cham naval squadrons, several companies of which accompanied the Siamese forces back to Thonburi. After Bunma was installed as Siam's viceroy in 1782, those Cham troops were bivouacked along the Bangkok Noi Canal, directly across the river from the Front Palace, the viceroy's stronghold. There they set up the viceroy's shipyard and barge sheds alongside their cantonment, mirroring the king's Cham naval garrison on the Bang Luang Canal at Kudi Yai (Site 1). The Bangkok Noi Canal settlement endured under the patronage of successive viceroys despite recurrent periods of neglect and attrition during the fallow years between viceroys. Under Phra Pin Klao (Prince Chutamani), the Fourth Reign viceroy, its sailors served on anti-piracy gunboat cruises along Siam's seaboard provinces (Suporn 1998, pp. 134, 136–37). During the Fifth Reign, however, they languished as the viceroy's power waned. The situation came to a head around 1880 with King Chulalongkorn's decision to consolidate the administratively splintered Grand Palace and Front Palace naval forces into a single Royal Navy with its headquarters positioned directly across the river from the Grand Palace. The new facility was formally commissioned in 1883, and with the death of the Fifth Reign viceroy in 1885 and the subsequent abolition of his title and military functions, all the remaining Front Palace naval elements were dissolved, culminating in a fully integrated Royal Navy Department in 1887 (Chaen 1966). With that reorganization, the Cham sailors were transferred from Kudi Asa Cham to the new Royal Navy Headquarters, with some being assigned to the naval fortifications far downstream at Prapadaeng. Remnants of the old Cham settlement along the Bangkok Noi Canal lingered on for several decades into the early twentieth century. Today the site of the former Front Palace naval cantonment, shipyard, and barge sheds is recalled in the shoreline facilities of the Royal Navy Water Procession Transport Department and the neighbouring Royal Barges National Museum, sheltered in the shadow of the Arun-Amarin Bridge crossing the Bangkok Noi Canal.

Site 4: *Ban Khaek Khrua (Muslim Households Village), or simply Ban Khrua* — At the Bangkok end of the Saen Saep Canal, no more than half a kilometre east of its juncture with the Mahanak Canal, was located in the late nineteenth century a group of three linked Cham settlements known collectively as Ban Khaek Khrua — consisting of Ban Khrua Nai (Inner), Klang (Middle), and Nok (Outer) (Aruwan and Baffie 1992; Sorayut 2007, p. 123). The division of that locality into three villages, each with its own mosque and graveyard, suggests separate village origins and establishment dates, with each village initially comprising an independent social unit. The earliest of those villages, Ban Khrua Klang, or Ban Kao (the Old Village), is conventionally believed to have been occupied by Cham war captives carried off from Cambodia by King Rama I around 1782. They were settled along the Nang Hong Canal, a natural eastward extension of the Banglamphu Canal meandering into the Phya Thai scrublands, which they were directed to clear for rice cultivation. They may well have been conscripted in 1783 — before the arrival of the Malay war captives who later populated the area — to help dig the 2.3 kilometre-long segment of the Banglamphu/Nang Hong Canal later named the Mahanak Canal. In 1837 the residual Nang Hong Canal was greatly expanded and extended eastward from its juncture with the Mahanak Canal to become the inner segment of the Saen Saep/Bang Khanak Canal, a major military transport route serving Siam's volatile Cambodian front during the Vietnamese hostilities that preoccupied much of the remainder of the Third Reign. Thus was established Bangkok's so-called "Eastern Corridor", guarded by the Cham militia stationed at Ban Khrua. As the military conflict along the eastern front climaxed in the early 1840s, an additional contingent of Cham war captives was carried off to Bangkok and settled alongside Ban Khrua Kao, to become Ban Khrua Nai. A third contingent arrived subsequently to form the village of Ban Khrua Nok. Those Cham outposts along Bangkok's eastern flank fulfilled military functions quite distinct from those performed by the Grand Palace and Front Palace Cham militias at Kudi Yai (Site 1) and Kudi Asa Cham (Site 3). Over the ensuing decades of uninterrupted peace along Siam's eastern front that community's military tradition lapsed; it was eventually replaced by a commercial specialization in silk weaving for, first, the local luxury market and, later, the burgeoning export and tourist trades.

PERSIAN COURTIERS

Court-sponsored merchant emissaries from the great Muslim emporiums of Persia and India had for centuries been risking the difficult and dangerous but potentially highly lucrative voyage to Siam. During those times, Ayutthaya's commercial and cultural links with the Safavi (Persian) and Mughal (Indian) empires to the west were as celebrated as were those with China and Japan to the east. As royal guests representing powerful overseas interests, the Persian state-traders, in particular, were received with lofty protocol. They brought with them such luxury wares as printed and embroidered textiles, carpets, gemstones, wines, pigments and glazes, and horses, and they returned home with such equally precious goods as ivory, tin, rare woods, aromatics, spices, medicinal herbs, and elephants. The more enterprising among them set up their own docking, warehousing, and processing facilities at Ayutthaya, cultivated advantageous local connections, married local women, entered government service, and rose to high noble rank. Their standing in seventeenth-century Ayutthaya was reflected in their centrally situated settlement, mosque, and graveyard within the city wall. Through their dominance of Ayutthaya's Indian Ocean trade they gained continuing control of the Western Trade Department (*krom tha khwa*), with their chief carrying the rank and title of Phraya Chula Rachamontri (Breazeale 1999, pp. 9–15; Julisphong 2003, pp. 88–108). As that noble represented the commercial interests of Ayutthaya's South and West Asian Muslims at court, it is commonly asserted (in the absence of documentary evidence) that he held titular custody over the kingdom's other Muslim communities as well (Julisphong 2008, pp. 46–47).

To facilitate their long-distance trading ventures, the Persian merchants set up transshipment and production facilities along India's Gujarati and

Malabar Coasts. From there they travelled to Ayutthaya via the Andaman ports of Martaban, Tavoy, Ye, and Mergui (Map 2.1). During the seventeenth and eighteenth centuries several rose to the governorship of first one, then another of those key transit points. The collapse of Persia's Safavi dynasty in the 1730s, followed by Siam's loss of the Andaman ports to Burmese armies during the 1750s and 1760s, had a ruinous impact on the Persian traders' position in Siam. Ayutthaya's fall in 1767 spelled their ultimate commercial collapse. The surviving remnants of Ayutthaya's Persian community were left impoverished and rudderless. Cut off from their ethnic roots, left to their own devices in salvaging what they could of their cultural heritage, aristocratic pedigree, and former wealth, their subsequent generations at Bangkok could best be called "indigenized Persians".

A straggle of Persian survivors of the Ayutthaya catastrophe were among the bevy of refugees who found their way to Thonburi in the wake of Phraya Taksin's liberation of that downriver stronghold. They moored their rafthouses along the Bangkok Yai Canal directly upstream from the Cham community at Kudi Yai (Site 1). In due course, they were absorbed into the new capital's emerging design with the assignment of a dry-land site on which to erect their mosque, graveyard, and residences. Over the course of Taksin's reign, they played no active military role, nor were they able to revive Siam's Indian Ocean trade links. Consequently, in marked contrast to the Cham, they were accorded no great distinction by the warrior king. Their leader, Konkaew, son of Ayutthaya's last Phraya Chula Rachamontri, managed to rise no higher in the nobility than the relatively modest rank of Luang Nawarat until fifteen years into the First Reign, when, through his supporters' intensive lobbying, he was instated as head of the Western Trade Department and awarded his father's former rank and title, with his younger brother, Akayi (or Aga Yi, "Second in Command") succeeding to that position after his death. Bangkok's Persian community thus regained its former administrative command of the Western Trade Department, over which it retained jurisdiction for another century (Julisphong 2003, pp. 88–108).

Site 5: *Kudi Nok (Outer Village), later Kudi Klang (Middle Village), presently Kudi Charoenphat* — Finding little favour with King Taksin due to their lack of military prowess, the Persian asylum seekers at Thonburi bided their time on their rafthouses lining the Bangkok Yai Canal until, most likely soon after the start of the First Reign, they were assigned a dry-land village site upstream from Kudi Yai. Their new village and mosque (or *imambara*, following Shia terminology) at the Thonburi outskirts came to be known as Kudi Nok. There they continued to reside until, around 1797, the Persian community's fortunes were reshaped with the elevation of their leader to the rank, title, and administrative functions of Phraya Chula Rachamontri, accompanied by his relocation to a prominent riverside residence (Site 6) directly across from the Bangkok Grand Palace. Kudi Nok was left under the direction of Aga Yi, who was eventually (after his brother's death) appointed Bangkok's second Phraya Chula Rachamontri. During the Second or early Third Reign, after the establishment of another Shia village (Site 8) further up the Bangkok Yai Canal, Kudi Nok was re-termed Kudi Klang. A century later its name was changed yet again to Kudi Charoenphat, which derives from the name of a major nearby vehicular bridge built in 1913, the first to span the Bangkok Yai Canal.

Site 6: *Kudi Chao Sen (Village of Imam Hussein)* — The dramatic rise in 1797 of Konkaew, the Persian community's leader, to the directorship of the Western Trade Department, carrying the senior rank of *phraya* in the Siamese nobility, was accompanied by the award of a choice residential site along the Thonburi riverbank. Some 400 retainers are said to have accompanied him in founding there the village of Kudi Chao Sen (Imanaga 2000, p. 249). The *imambara* that was built there became the epicentre of Shia worship at Bangkok for the next 150 years. However, the narrowly bounded residential tract necessitated that the village dead would continue to be buried in the Kudi Nok graveyard (Site 5), over a kilometre distant. At Kudi Chao Sen, eight successive direct descendants of Konkaew and his brother, Aga Yi, came to hold the title of Phraya Chula Rachamontri, retaining control of the kingdom's Western Trade Department to its dissolution in the 1890s and exercising titular command over Siam's Muslims to the 1940s (though the last two incumbents carried the reduced rank of *phra*). The community's privileged status entered into irreversible decline in 1892 with the comprehensive government reorganization that eliminated the Western Trade Department. Perhaps in partial atonement for that slight, King Rama V in 1897/98, on the occasion of the settlement's centennial celebrations, sponsored a thorough renovation of its *imambara* and redubbed it Kudi Luang Chao Sen. A generation later, having already lost his noble perquisites with the end of the absolute monarchy in 1932, the Shia leader's role as titular head of the kingdom's Muslim community ended in the turbulent years after the Second World War with the election of a Malay Sunni leader to that position. At the same time (1947), the Kudi Chao Sen village site, including its *imambara*, was dismantled and merged into the neighbouring Royal Navy Headquarters. The residents were relocated to a new village site on Pran-nok Road, along Thonburi's rustic periphery. In memory of its illustrious past, the new settlement and its mosque were named Kudi Luang, with the former *imambara* replaced by a conventional onion-domed mosque.

ARAB VOYAGERS

The commerce-led eastward spread of not only Shia (Persian) but also Sunni (Ottoman and Arab) Islam across Asia intensified over the course of the sixteenth and seventeenth centuries. In that venture, the Arabs generally bypassed the Shia way-stations of the Gujarat region, preferring to round Cape Comorin to India's Coromandel coast before voyaging on to the Southeast Asian trading emporiums. That mutual distancing exemplified the prevailing West Asian imperial hostilities and trade rivalries between Islam's Shia and Sunni denominations. The political-commercial-doctrinal conflict extended to Ayutthaya, where the Arabs were marginalized in the presence of the well-established Persian community (Andaya 1999, p. 136). Lacking the powerful local connections of the Persian traders and bringing cargos often less valuable and varied than those of the well-heeled Persian fleets, the yearly Arab arrival in the wake of the Indian Ocean's western monsoon excited milder levels of interest. Accordingly, the Arabs were left to play a relatively minor role at Ayutthaya. Nothing remains of their modest settlement along the walled city's southern perimeter, established in the shadow of the notable Persian settlement. Nor does any record survive of their trading activities, and virtually nothing of their other interactions with local society. Most likely, they never established much of a permanent presence, most of them undertaking the round-trip journey to Ayutthaya annually or biennially as itinerant merchants.

In the throes of the Ayutthaya catastrophe of 1767 the Arab-Persian, Sunni-Shia rivalry was set aside. A small number of surviving Arab stragglers — recollected by their descendants today as having originated in the Hadramaut (the Yemen-Oman quarter of Arabia facing the Indian Ocean) — joined the conglomeration of Muslim and other asylum seekers drifting downriver to the Thonburi haven. In recognition of the traditional enmity between the Arab and Persian traders, however, King Taksin assigned the Arabs a village site at the far-removed northern end of Thonburi, along the Bangkok Noi Canal, rather than along the more centrally located Bangkok Yai Canal to the south. Unlike the several settlements into which the Shia community eventually divided, the limited number of surviving Arab traders determined that only one Arab village endured at Bangkok.

Site 7: *Ban Khaek Bangkok Noi (Muslim Village on the Bangkok Noi Canal)* — At Thonburi, the Arab refugees from Ayutthaya were granted a residential site along the inner bank of the Bangkok Noi Canal, immediately upstream from the Thonburi city wall and moat (Saowani 2001, p. 97). In its positioning, that settlement twinned with the Cham village at Kudi Yai (Site 1), along the inner bank of the Bangkok Yai Canal just outside the Thonburi city wall and moat. During the First Reign, the small community of dispossessed Arab merchants found a patron in Prince Anurak Thewet (Thong-in), a leading royal trading magnate whose residence, the so-called Rear Palace (Wang Lang), neighboured the Arab village directly across the city moat and wall. In the wake of Thong-in's death in 1806, followed by the deaths of his three senior sons early in the Third Reign, employment opportunities with the Rear Palace trading ventures evaporated, and the Arab village fell into decline. To make ends meet over the ensuing decades, the village turned to a variety of specialized handicrafts, including the weaving of rope, rattan and split-bamboo wares, and sleeping mats, which the village women sold at the popular nearby Bangkok Noi floating market. The Arab community's lifestyle was again disrupted around 1900 with the government's appropriation of much of the village land as part of a large tract to establish the Bangkok terminus of Siam's Southern Railway (Thailand, Royal Railway Department n.d. (1903?)). To make amends for the dispossession of their land and dismantling of their mosque, the king sponsored the construction of a new village mosque directly on the canal bank. However, the diminished village and its rebuilt mosque were again devastated in 1945, this time by Second World War Allied bombing intended for the neighbouring Japanese-occupied Bangkok Noi rail yards. In compensation, the Arab settlement was relocated after the war to the opposite shore of the Bangkok Noi Canal, where its present, imposing Ansarit Sunnah Mosque was built, again under royal patronage. With that record of repeated disaster and destruction, much of the old village history was lost, though the community continues to cling proudly to its Arab heritage and today stands as a leader among Bangkok's reformist Muslims in its advocacy of Arabic Sunni fundamentalism (*wahhabiya*).

Indian Traders

The Indian emporiums of Surat and Ahmedabad for centuries served as the homeports of Gujarati entrepreneurs seeking to extend their business interests to Southeast Asia. Often sharing the risks attendant to their maritime ventures in collaboration with Persian interests, unified with the Persians in their Shia beliefs and practices, melded with them through intermarriage — and thus sometimes spoken of as "Indo-Iranian" — the Gujarati business establishment formed a potent trading connection with Ayutthaya. By the mid-eighteenth century, that Indo-Siamese commercial alignment was coming under rising pressure, not only due to the changing power balance between India's west and east coast business communities with the collapse of Persia's Safavi empire but more immediately from mounting Burmese aggression along Siam's Andaman coast. Well apprised of the approaching Burmese peril, most of the itinerant Indian traders at Ayutthaya and its Andaman ports weighed anchor and sailed off to safer havens in good time. No perceptible Indian element was thus evident in the convergence of Ayutthaya survivors at Thonburi in the early Taksin years, nor was any Indian participation recorded in the recovery of Siam's overseas trade during the first two reigns of the Bangkok period. Only with the pacification of the Indian Ocean transport system after the end of the Napoleonic Wars (1815), the founding of Singapore as a secure maritime entrepôt (1819), the enthronement of Siam's vigorously trade-oriented King Rama III (1824), and the promulgation of the trade-enhancing Bowring Treaty (1855) did a robust Indian mercantile presence reassert itself in Siam. Once the conditions had been laid, the participation of Indian Muslims in Bangkok's expanding economy passed quickly through three expansionary phases.

First Phase: Along the Bang Luang Canal

As of 1844, Bangkok was hosting at least four notable Indian trading ventures, three functioning as branches of Bombay-based "native houses" and the fourth represented by a "native merchant" from Madras (Moore 1914–15, p. 29). The Bombay (Shia) merchants set up shop along the Bang Luang Canal (Site 8), near Bangkok's principal Persian settlement (Site 5). The Madras (Sunni) trader, lacking influential local connections, probably operated directly from his ship or from a rafthouse moored along the riverbank well downstream from the walled city. All the Indian merchants fell under the immediate supervision of the Western Trade Department, administered by Bangkok's locally intermarried and culturally assimilated

Persian-Thai nobility. That ensured a degree of favouritism toward the Gujarati (Shia) trading ventures. In their efforts to gain access to Siam's state-controlled export commodities under favourable terms, they sought the patronage of Phraya Si Phiphat (That), director of the Merchandise Warehouse Department (*krom phra khlang sinkha*) and himself the scion of an Ayutthaya-era Shia lineage (long-since converted to Buddhism). That effort succeeded in the 1840s with the establishment of a cluster of Indian trading ventures along the Khlong San district riverfront in the shadow of That's magnificent estate (Piyanat 1999, pp. 247–48).

The Indian traders initially specialized in the importation of calico and chintz fabrics, with imported gemstones adding a lucrative sideline (Scupin 1998, pp. 243–46; Inthira 2004; Praphatson 2007). Brisk competition in the local luxury textiles market, catering to the discriminating tastes of the Thai aristocracy, soon turned the Indian merchants to the dying, printing, and embroidering of raw imported muslins at their Bangkok facilities. Those textile-processing operations relied on skilled labour, which the merchants acquired through the overseas recruitment of indentured Indian workers, most of whom returned to India upon the termination of their contracts. The transport economics of the long-distance textile trade also required a reciprocal export side. Leather, particularly the delicate and plentiful Siamese deerhide, offered a viable option, though that product involved the odious processing tasks of scraping, tanning, dying, cutting, and drying. With local Thai Buddhist workers refusing to take on those tasks because of religious scruples, the merchants again turned to imported Indian Muslim labour, a procedure that over time discreetly increased the scale of Bangkok's Indian populace.

Site 8: *Kudi Nok (Outer Village), or Kudi Lang (Rear Village)* — Adam Ali, an Indian Shia merchant-adventurer originally from Lucknow, undertook repeated voyages from Surat to Bangkok during the Second and Third Reigns with cargos of high-quality Indian textiles. Through Bangkok's indigenized Persian nobility he gained access to the Thai aristocracy, who frequented his shipboard stores displays with enthusiasm. The profitability of his textile-trading venture convinced him of the value of investing in a permanent Bangkok presence. Permission was eventually received to erect a dock and godowns along the Bang Luang Canal at Thonburi's western outskirts. There, he established a textile dying and printing manufactory staffed by Indian artisans brought in with his annual voyages. The new village and mosque that he founded there for his Indian Shia workforce came to

be known as Kudi Nok (Outer Village, Outer Mosque), leaving the old
Persian village of Kudi Nok (Site 5) to be redubbed Kudi Klang (Middle
Village). His innovative venture, specializing in the local import-export
processing of high-value goods with ethnically compatible skilled labour,
set the standard for Bangkok's later resident Indian merchants. Though
the village has long been absorbed into Thonburi's larger Charoenphat
neighbourhood, the Dinfallah Mosque survives as a remembrance of
those times past.

Second Phase: The Khlong San District

In his capacity as director of the Merchandise Warehouse Department,
administering the royal monopoly trade, Phraya Si Phiphat (That) during
the Third Reign built a line of royal warehouses and docks fronting his
estate along the Khlong San district riverfront. Some of those solid brick
structures were plastered and whitewashed (and thus came to be known as
toek khaw, or "the white brick buildings") while others retained their raw
brick facades (and thus were referred to as *toek daeng*, or "the red brick
buildings"). Late in the Third Reign the royal monopoly trade, based on a
cumbersome system of inventory collection through in-kind tax and tribute
imposition, was abandoned in favour of a major expansion of tax farming,
an income "outsourcing" system under which state revenue gathering was
delegated to Chinese and other trading magnates (Vella 1955*b*, pp. 22–23,
127; Hong 1984, pp. 38–74). As the royal monopoly trade was phased out,
the royal warehouses were emptied of their inventories. Phraya Si Phiphat
then turned to the ingenious expedient of renting the vacant warehouses
to Indian traders, and thereby he was instrumental in the creation of new
Indian merchant settlements (Sites 9 and 10) along the Khlong San district
waterfront.

Site 9: *Toek Khaw (the White Brick Buildings)* — Late in the Third
Reign, several Gujarati Shia merchants received permission to establish
their business premises in the recently vacated government godowns
along the Khlong San district riverfront directly downstream from the
estate of Phraya Si Phiphat. One of the first of those merchants was A.T.E.
Maskati, a textile dealer from Ahmedabad. Earlier in the Third Reign
he had set up a Bangkok branch of his firm at Kudi Klang (Site 5), the
Shia centre along the Bang Luang Canal. Recognizing the favourable
economic prospects augured by the Bowring Treaty, he expanded his
operations in 1856 with a textile dying and printing factory at Toek
Khaw, employing at its peak around 600 Muslim workers (Mani 1993,

p. 913). There he was joined by other recently arrived Indian Shia merchants in building a prayer shelter, eventually rebuilt as the Toek Khaw Mosque, later renamed the Sefi Mosque. They also built there in later years several additional warehouses for expanded inventory storage, factory operations, and workers' quarters. To avoid the language and other cultural difficulties attendant to recruiting local workers for the dyeing of textiles and tanning of leather, they imported much of their own Indian labour force, the origin of the several present-day Shia neighbourhoods lining that riverfront.

Site 10: *Toek Daeng (the Red Brick Buildings)* — In the aftermath of the signing of the Bowring Treaty, this small settlement was developed by a group of newly arrived Gujarati merchants at a prime commercial site on the riverbank less than half a kilometre upstream from Toek Khaw (Saowani 2001, p. 98). It occupied an old line of royal godowns at the mouth of the Khanon Canal (later known as the Talat Somdet Chaophraya Canal), alongside the residential compound of Phraya Si Phiphat (That), who had recently been elevated to Chaophraya Phichaiyat. In 1859, the heirs of the recently deceased Chaophraya Phichaiyat (That) donated to that group of Indian merchants a half-acre plot at that site to build the Toek Daeng Mosque, later renamed the Kuwatil Islam Mosque. The traders at Toek Daeng were led by Ali Asmail Nana, a Shia (Dawoodie Bohra sect) trader from Surat who received the title of Phra Phichet Sanphanit in the Fourth Reign as an interpreter for the Western Trade Department, married a local woman, and speculated in rice and sugar in collaboration with Chaophraya Phichaiyat; under his son, Jusuf Ali Bey Nana, the family firm later transferred its offices cross-river to the Sampheng district's Rachawong Road and prospered in property development.

Third Phase: Cross-river and Downriver

During the boom years bridging the turn of the twentieth century, many of the Indian Shia firms of the Khlong San district relocated their trading headquarters across the river to the Sampheng district's Rachawong neighbourhood, while many of the Indian Sunni firms made a parallel cross-river move to the Bang Rak district. The more enterprising and prosperous among them branched out along such promising lines as commission agents, bankers, insurance brokers, auctioneers, export-goods processors, consumer-goods manufacturers, freight forwarders, shipowners, and property speculators. Despite that climb up Bangkok's commercial ladder, most of them retained their residences and mosques, as well as their principal docking, warehousing, and production facilities, at their established bases along the west bank of the river. Through that spatial buffer, they sought to preserve their families' and communities' cultural integrity and religious orthodoxy in the face of their professional immersion in Bangkok's increasingly cosmopolitan world.

At the same time, the Singapore packet steamer traffic brought in a steady trickle of Indian immigrants — Hindus and Sikhs as well as Muslims — in search of new economic opportunities, many of them accompanied by their dependants. As British subjects, they were (from 1855 to the 1920s) protected by the extraterritoriality provisions of the Bowring Treaty. Their widespread presence is recorded as early as 1883 in the city's first postal register (Thailand, Post and Telegraph Department, 1883; Wilson 1989). Most of them took residence in the Pahurat, Saphan Han, Rachawong, Talat Noi, and Bang Rak commercial neighbourhoods along Charoen Krung Road (more conveniently referred to by its English name, New Road) and also in the less crowded districts along the Sai Kai Canal on the west bank and the newly burgeoning Bang Ko Laem (Peninsular Village) east-bank port district occupying a sharp river bend some ten kilometres downstream from the city centre. There they took up such petty bourgeois trades as stall-keepers and shop-owners, tailors, launderers, syces, butchers, ferrymen, watchmen, postmen, clerks, compradors, and the like. Far outdistanced by Bangkok's fast-growing polyglot population as the twentieth century proceeded, those newly arrived Muslims came to form a relatively inconspicuous element of the city's flourishing and rapidly diversifying mercantile economy.

Site 11: *Ban Khaek Bang Rak (Muslim Village at Bang Rak), also known as Ban Khaek Muang Khae (Muslim Village neighbouring Wat Muang Khae)* — A unique alliance of two intrepid Singapore-based Tamil entrepreneurs — Vaiti Padayatchi and Mhd. Thamby Saibu Maraikayar — played a vital role in stimulating Bangkok's Indian immigration flow following the Bowring Treaty of 1855. Padayatchi, a Hindu import-export trader, and Maraikayar, a Sunni Muslim livestock dealer, entered into a joint venture in the 1860s to raise cattle at Bangkok and export their carcasses to the Singapore market on a regular schedule (Mani 1993, pp. 912–13, 918, 923, 941). To staff that scheme they negotiated an arrangement with the Siamese authorities to bring in a party of Tamil workmen — Hindu cattle herders and drovers to ply their trade in an extensive grazing tract lining the Bang Rak Canal, and Muslim knackers, flensers, butchers, and laders to man the cattle stockyards along the Bang Rak river frontage stretching from Wat Muang Khae to the French legation (Map 7.3). The beef export enterprise, with its Muslim workmen's settlement nestled directly behind the waterfront cattle pens, started up around 1867. However, the incessantly noisome slaughtering operations raised such fierce complaints from the nearby Western legations and business firms that the government was eventually obliged to act. Some time before 1880 the stockyard was condemned, and the workers' quarters were moved back from the riverbank to leave a cleared ships' landing. Soon thereafter there was erected on the vacated site an imposing new Customs House, which opened its doors in 1884. No longer permitted to use the site for beef processing, the Padayatchi-Maraikayar export venture relocated to a new riverfront site near the Muslim village of Ban U (Site 20), half a kilometre downstream; in 1899 the slaughteryard was moved again, this time to Bang Ko Laem, Bangkok's furthest downriver anchorage, at Land's End (Thanon Tok, the lower end of New Road), to be re-established as a government-supervised abattoir from which butchered beef could be shipped directly to Singapore on scheduled steamships or transported daily to downtown Bangkok in refrigerated tram cars. Though some of Bang Rak's Muslim cattlemen accompanied that move, the riverside Tamil village, its graveyard, and its Harun Mosque endured, occupying a prime tract directly behind the new Customs House to become a lasting Bang Rak landmark.

MALAY CAPTIVES

The fiercely independent sultanates bestriding the Malay Peninsula along Siam's southern reaches came under the steadily mounting pressure of Thai expansionism from the seventeenth century onward. They consequently developed an abiding adversarial relationship with the Siamese state. Repeated Thai military expeditions to subjugate the South carried off much booty, including large numbers of war captives, but they failed to coerce the sultanates into lasting submission. Even the Anglo-Siamese Treaty of 1909, which resulted in Siam's formal annexation of Patani (subsequently known as Pattani) while ceding Kedah, Kelantan, Perlis, and Trengganu to Britain, failed to resolve the long-standing Southern political predicament (Ornanong 2012, pp. 58–61). One lasting effect that Siam did achieve over its successive centuries of Southern hegemonism was the recurrent deportation of contingents of Malay aristocrats and artisans to Ayutthaya's and then Bangkok's immediate outskirts, along with the consignment of thousands of Malay peasants to the Centre's deltaic hinterlands, where they tamed the wide-ranging wetlands while eking out a meager subsistence. A reign-by-reign chronology of the sparsely documented history of those forced migrations and their aftermath over the course of the eighteenth–nineteenth centuries is indispensable to an appreciation of the scope and character of Bangkok's evolving Muslim presence.

The Thonburi Reign

During the late Ayutthaya period, thousands of captive Malay households were transported from Patani and the adjacent sultanates fringing the Southern Siamese frontier to the extensive flatlands stretching south and southwest of Ayutthaya, where they were assigned to fill the capital's rice granaries with the yield of their forced labour. Following the depredations and subsequent departure of the Burmese in 1767, some of those households managed to flee back to their ancestral Southern homelands, while others who had managed to evade Burmese capture and deportation resumed their disrupted lives in the vicinity of the old capital. A lesser number accepted King Taksin's invitation to relocate to the newly established royal stronghold at Thonburi, apparently with the promise that they would thereby be relieved of their war slave status. On the evidence of later developments, it is presumed that most of them were assigned to the open tracts stretching eastward from the river up the old Banglamphu Canal into the Thung Kraboe (Buffalo Fields) district. At the start of the First Reign the digging of the Bangkok City Moat (*khu moeang*), which incorporated the lower segment of the Banglamphu Canal, and then the excavation of the Banglamphu Canal's eastward extension, which came to be known as the Mahanak Canal, set the stage for further Malay settlement of that outlying quarter (Sansani 1994, p. 121; Chokchai 2011, p. 414). While nothing remains of the Muslim settlements of Thung Kraboe other than Ban Tani (Site 15), several related Malay villages dating back to the Thonburi Reign survive along other sectors of the Bangkok periphery.

> **Site 12:** *Ban Suan Phlu (Betel-Vine Garden Village)* — In the wake of the Ayutthaya disaster, a small party of uprooted Malay households joined the contingent of Cham and Persian Muslim refugee raft-dwellers moored along the Bangkok Yai Canal under the protection of the Thonburi fortifications. Of low status as (former) war slaves, they were assigned a relatively remote village site some three kilometres up the Bangkok Yai Canal from the Thonburi citadel (Saowani 2001, p. 98), not far from the old Mon settlement of Bang Yi-roea Mon.

There they founded Ban Suan Phlu, cultivating orchards of areca palms and piper-betel vines serving the ubiquitous Siamese betel-chewing market. Nothing further is known of that secluded Malay village until an influx of Chinese market gardeners and traders into the area in the closing decades of the nineteenth century borrowed the village name by titling their canal-side marketplace Talat Phlu (Betel-Vine Market). Not long thereafter the area was further invaded by a railway line running directly past the Malay village and its mosque, linking Bangkok with the western seaboard provinces, with a stop at Talat Phlu. The line started operation in 1904, and following that "opening up" the settlement was enlivened by the addition of a number of Indian Muslim petty traders hived off from the not-far-distant Ban Khaek Ban Somdet locale (Site 17). Despite those evolving demographics and the mounting encroachment of urban infrastructure, commercialization, and ethnic diversity, Ban Suan Phlu today retains a good deal of its old Malay cultural character.

Site 13: *Bang O (Marsh Grass Village)* — This village and its namesake mosque are located on the western riverbank some five kilometres upstream from the Thonburi citadel. Like Ban Suan Phlu (Site 12) and a string of other Malay villages further upstream (beyond the scope of this study), Bang O was reputedly founded by Malay survivors of the destruction of Ayutthaya (Saowani 2001, pp. 96–97). The village leader during the First Reign was raised to Phraya Yotha Samut (Director of Maritime Construction), suggesting his official duties as a senior admiralty functionary, evidently a supplier of ships' timbers and planking for the viceroy's naval base on the Bangkok Noi Canal (Site 3). Like its contemporary counterpart, Ban Suan Phlu, nothing is known of the further history of Bang O until the late nineteenth century, when the village is said to have received an influx of Malays from Songkhla led by Mohammat Phet-thongkham, an enterprising merchant who modernized the settlement's old hand-operated sawmill to steam-power, gained access to an upcountry teak concession, and built a thriving timber export business. As leader of the local community, he sponsored the reconstruction of the Bang O Mosque in 1903. Two decades later, in 1924, the community's economy was disrupted by the construction of a barrage across the Pa Sak (Teak Forest) River that interfered with the rafting of timber downstream to Bangkok, and in 1957 by an additional barrage across the Chaophraya River at Chainat. A subsequent turn to timber and rice exports to the Middle

East brought an influx of Arab influence and with it a surge of Muslim fundamentalism, which remains a conspicuous feature in the village today (Bajunid 1992, p. 45).

The First and Second Reigns

A resurgent Siam bent on replenishing its manpower base in the aftermath of the Ayutthaya disaster turned once again to the South. Demands for the revival of the old tributary relationship with the Malay sultanates were introduced soon after the start of the First Reign but were persistently resisted. Such defiance prompted repeated military campaigns — 1785–1786, 1789–1791, 1808, 1821, 1832, 1838, 1848 — mounted from the Siamese capital and its major Southern surrogates — Nakhon Si Thammarat, Songkhla, Phatthalung — resulting in the recurring transport of convoys of war captives to Bangkok (Thipakorawong 2009b, pp. 92–96, 133–34; Damrong 1993, pp. 2–3; Chokchai 2011, pp. 405–18). The first two of those captive contingents, from Patani in 1786 and 1791, were settled along the capital's northeastern perimeter (Sites 14 and 15); a later convoy, from Kedah in 1808, was consigned to a site far downriver (Site 16). The distancing between those initial Patani and Kedah captive cohorts at opposite ends of the capital's purlieu was likely a preventive measure against their possible collaboration in fomenting insurrection.

The later years of the Second Reign saw a resurgence in the South's resistance to Siamese hegemony. In 1818, Kedah was ordered to force the recalcitrant sultan of Perak to accept Siamese suzerainty, and when Kedah resisted that command, Siam in 1821 mobilized a punitive expedition. Entire villages of the Kedah populace were rounded up and trundled off to Bangkok (Damrong 1993, p. 8). Most was settled in the undeveloped scrublands of Thung Kraboe (Sansani 1994, p. 121; Wat Sunthon 1990, pp. 12–13), along the northern bank of the Mahanak Canal well beyond the city wall. Nothing further is known of those settlements, most likely because the transformation of the entire district with the digging of the Phadung Krung Kasem Canal in 1851–1852, followed by the introduction of a welter of Lao, Mon, Vietnamese, and Chinese settlements, impelled the Muslim villages' relocation to the newly established Malay districts further east along the Saen Saep Canal. The remaining vestiges of Muslim settlement were eradicated by the subsequent comprehensive redevelopment of the district around the turn of the twentieth century to accommodate a cluster of princely palaces and noblemen's villas, served by Lan Luang Road. While the Malay presence in the former Thung Kraboe district has been obliterated, several closely related settlements (Sites 14 and 15) dating from the First and Second Reigns have survived.

Site 14: *Bang Lamphu (Willow Tree Village)* — Upon the conclusion of Siam's 1785 military offensive to remove the lingering Burmese presence from the Peninsula, the First Reign viceroy mobilized a supplementary campaign to return Patani to Thai suzerainty (Wenk 1968, pp. 62, 101; Thipakorawong 2009*b*, pp. 95–96). As a result, a body of Patani aristocrats and artisans was transported to Bangkok as surety for the sultanate's continued loyalty. They were assigned a settlement site near the mouth of the Banglamphu Canal, within the city wall, under the viceroy's direct supervision (Wenk 1968, pp. 100–102; Damrong 1993, p. 2). There they joined a small Malay fishermen's village apparently dating back to Ayutthaya days (Surin 2002). That village of war captives within the city wall was a unique — and probably contentious — exception to the convention that war captives be prohibited from *intramuros* residence. Their community centre was known as the Bang Lamphu Mosque until around 1900, when Chakraphong Road was laid out alongside, leading to its name change to Chakraphong Mosque. In the 1960s, traditional Malay goldsmiths could still be found plying their trade out of wayside stalls along Bang Lamphu's back alleys, and today the neighbourhood continues to boast restaurants and food stalls serving traditional Malay dishes, unperturbed by the cultural dissonance of the area's Buddhist temples, Sino-Thai marketplace, and rowdy tourist traffic.

Site 15: *Ban Tani (Patani Village)* — Despite Siam's brutal Southern expedition of 1785–1886, Patani soon refused again to submit to Thai suzerainty. Repeated assaults mounted by Bangkok's Southern minions culminated in the transport of a second convoy of Patani war prisoners to Bangkok around 1790/91 (Damrong 1993, p. 2; Thipakorawong 1978, pp. 167–68). There, hostages drawn from the Patani ruling circle were consigned to Thung Kraboe, where they founded Ban Tani and its Mahanak Mosque along the southern shore of the Mahanak Canal. They were joined by a further contingent of Patani hostages sent to Bangkok in 1792 after the suppression of renewed Southern unrest (Damrong 1993, pp. 3–4). No further record of Ban Tani's history exists until the digging of the Phadung Krung Kasem Canal early in the Fourth Reign. With that development, Ban Tani found itself situated at the confluence of two major waterways, the Phadung Krung Kasem Canal and Mahanak/Saen Saep Canal, which prompted the emergence of a lively floating market from which the local Muslim community profited greatly. An influx of Indian textile merchants on the canal's opposite bank during the twentieth century added the Bobae Market to the neighbourhood and provided Ban Tani with further income opportunities.

Site 16: *Ban Suan Luang (Village in the Royal Plantations)* — A detachment of war captives arriving at Bangkok from Kedah around 1808 was relegated to a remote tract along the east bank of the river some five kilometres downstream from the walled city. Their settlement, which may have been referred to originally as Ban Kedah, comprised the elite element of a sizeable consignment of Malay captives (Damrong 1993, p. 8) deliberately separated from the bulk of their cohort to prevent insurrection. The peasant component of that captive convoy was settled further downstream (outside the area of this study) in the isolated marshlands of Thung Khru (Water Basket Tract, so named for the area's depressed, waterlogged topography), a remote exurb that today boasts a cluster of nine mosques. One of the first actions of the Ban Suan Luang settlers was to link their secluded village site with the river and provide it with a drainage and irrigation base by digging the Suan Luang Canal, reaching more than a kilometre into the deltaic jungle. Second was the construction of the settlement's linchpin mosque, today known as the al-Athik (Old, Ancient, Antique, or Original) Mosque. After several generations of isolation and deprivation, the settlement's prospects were greatly improved in the 1860s with the extension of New Road, Bangkok's first major thoroughfare, downriver to Bang Ko Laem (Land's End). That development brought a stream of new employment opportunities to the local Muslim community with the establishment of square-rigger and tramp steamer docks, a bevy of Western rice and timber export firms (foremost among them the Borneo Company, 1856; Clarke and Co., 1882; and the East Asiatic Company, 1897), the Siam Electric Company's downriver tram terminus (1894), the Bangkok municipal abattoir (1899), and not long thereafter one of Bangkok's first coal-fired electric generating plants.

The Third Reign

Renewed unrest in the South starting around 1830 was met in 1832 by a robust Siamese military response. Under the impetus of the Third Reign's vigorous development policy, the resultant Malay defeat led to the deportation to Bangkok of some 4,000–5,000 war captives (Vella 1955*b*, pp. 68–70; Moor 1968, pp. 201–202), a number that likely refers to households rather than individuals. Again in 1838–1839, mounting disorder in the rebellious South prompted a punitive Thai expedition that led to the forced migration of even greater numbers of Malay households to the Centre. Most of the captives were consigned to the hinterlands along the "Eastern Corridor" (outside the area of this study) extending far east from the capital beyond the Mahanak Canal past Bang Kapi and Hua Mak to Minburi and Nong Chok, a vast waterlogged wilderness known as the uninhabitable Saen Saep tract since Ayutthaya times. The Malay war prisoners gradually domesticated those extensive swamplands for paddy cultivation. The 56-kilometre-long Saen Saep/Bang Khanak Canal, extending from Bangkok to the Bang Pakong River, was dug between 1837 and 1839; the addition of a web of tributary canals to drain the extensive wetlands required a further decade's labour. The project aimed initially to cut the travel time of troops and supplies to the eastern front during Siam's 1830s–1840s warfare against Vietnam, but it succeeded ultimately in the far greater achievement of taming and populating a previously inaccessible, pestilential wilderness for paddy farming (Vella 1955*b*, pp. 71–77; Hanks 1972, pp. 72–74; Skinner and Corfield 1993, pp. 181–83). Under the loose supervision of Siam's Ministry of Lands (*krom na*), the Malay captives relegated to that wasteland were left to their own devices so long as they maintained a low political profile while meeting their annual rice tax quotas for the royal granaries. Only after the mid-twentieth century did the extension of modern land transport and the penetration of modern mass communications introduce any appreciable tendencies to Thai cultural integration in that Malay Muslim hinterland.

Few traces of the Third Reign exodus of Malay war captives from the South to the Centre remain evident today within Bangkok proper. Though there is virtually no reference in the historical records to the numbers or dispersal of the hostage elites, nor to any special treatment accorded them, it is well known that the standard procedure was to settle them close to the city while assigning the captive peasant masses to the more distant hinterlands. The only clear-cut case, parallel in many respects to the earlier examples of Bang Lamphu (Site 14) and Ban Tani (Site 15), is the following:

Site 17: *Ban Khaek Sai Kai (Muslim Village on the Sai Kai Canal), later known as Ban Khaek Ban Somdet (Muslim Village near the Regent's Residence)* — During the Third Reign, Chaophraya Prayurawong (Dit) and his younger brother Phraya Si Phiphat (That, later raised to Chaophraya Phichaiyat) each in turn led a military expedition against the rebellious South, Dit in 1832 and That in 1838. As reward for their services, they each received for their personal retinues a consignment of captive Malay artisans — Patani and Kelantan goldsmiths, silversmiths, silk weavers, and the like (Saowani 2001, p. 97; Winyu 2014, p. 9). To accommodate them, Ban Khaek Sai Kai with its mosque and graveyard was established shortly after 1832 along the Sai Kai Canal, behind Dit's estate, and a lesser settlement, sometimes referred to as Ban Chang Thong (Goldsmiths' Village), was created around 1840 behind That's estate nearby. Ban Khaek Sai Kai prospered under the patronage of Dit and then his son, Chaophraya Si Suriyawong (Chuang), who rose to the unparalleled rank of Regent of Siam and built himself a princely retreat nearby known as Ban Somdet Chaophraya (the Regent's Residence) — and thus the village name was changed to Ban Khaek Ban Somdet. For obscure reasons, however, the smaller Malay community behind That's estate failed to flourish. It neither built a mosque nor laid out a burial ground, nor did it ever adopt an individuating name, and so it never attained full-fledged village status. Over the following century, the residents of Ban Chang Thong were largely absorbed into Ban Khaek Ban Somdet. At the same time, the addition of considerable numbers of Indian Muslim immigrants — peddlers, shopkeepers, handicraft producers, petty moneylenders and the like — transformed the character of Ban Khaek Ban Somdet from an isolated Malay village to one of Bangkok's most cosmopolitan Muslim neighbourhoods.

The Fourth and Fifth Reigns

Bangkok's increasingly buoyant economy under the free-trade regime introduced by the Bowring Treaty offered a wealth of new employment opportunities for the city's various Muslim communities. Among the Sunni Muslim settlements of the Khlong San district and downstream west bank of the river, the assimilative influence of Malay employment in the many small Indian trading firms that had set up shop in the later nineteenth century — compounded by their adjacent habitation, shared religious ritual and education, and intermarriage — formed an emerging amalgam of Indo-Malay commercial neighbourhoods. For the east-bank Malay villages strung along lower New Road, reaching from Bang Rak to Bang Ko Laem, a new convention of wage employment materialized with the establishment of Western sawmilling, rice milling, and shipping firms, though the local Malay villagers did not adapt easily to the regimentation imposed by day-wage labour (Phanni 2012). Cheap, swift, and safe tramp steamer transport inspired not only an inflow of Indians via Singapore but also a mounting trickle of Peninsular Malays, who took up a diversity of petty occupations and employments. At the same time, and through the same process, the cultural distancing between the "modernizing" Malays of urban Bangkok and the "traditionalist" Malays of the eastern hinterlands gained ground. The following two village sites exemplify the process.

Site 18: *Bang Uthit (Donated Village)* — A 500-metre Yan Nawa riverfront tract extending from the Khwang Canal down to the Suan Luang Canal was in the 1840s ceded by King Rama III to Prince Isaret Rangsan (Chutamani, the later Fourth Reign viceroy) for the development of a shipyard to support the naval campaigns then underway against Vietnam. The site was dominated by an imposing temple, Wat Phraya Krai, and came to be known by that name throughout its subsequent turbulent history of commercial exploitation (Phanni and Aphinya 2013). After the close of the Vietnam conflict, the start of the Fourth Reign, and the investiture of Chutamani as Phra Pin Klao, King Mongkut's viceroy, the riverside site was converted to support Thai royal participation in the lucrative China trade. Initially staffed by a contingent of Chutamani's bondsmen, that arrangement fell into abeyance during the troubled tenure of his son and successor, Prince Bowon Wichaichan (Yot-yingyot), the Fifth Reign viceroy. After Wichaichan's death in 1885, his factotum, Phraya Isaranuphap (Iam), claimed that the tract had been bequeathed to him and attempted to revive the shipyard as his own. To secure a reliable labour force he extended his patronage to the nearby Malay village of Ban Suan Luang (Site 16) by providing a new settlement site at the rear of the tract to accommodate the village households willing to accept his offer of regular employment. In recognition of that endowment the new site was named Bang Uthit (Donated Village). Iam's business venture did not last long, however, as his undocumented claim to the tract was soon contested by the Crown, and he was required to return the site to the Crown Property Office, though the Malay village of Bang Uthit was allowed to remain. Shortly thereafter, in 1897, the riverside tract was leased by the Crown to the East Asiatic Company (E.A.C.), and the Malay workers found ready employment at the newly established E.A.C. dockyard, rice mill, and sawmill. In 1915, Bang Uthit attained formal independence from its parent village of Ban Suan Luang with the founding of its own mosque. It continued to prosper there until 1945, when Allied bombing destroyed the E.A.C. riverfront facilities. Today the former E.A.C. site is occupied by the popular Asiatique shopping and recreation complex, with Bang Uthit enduring nearby.

Site 19: *Ban Trok Mo (Village on Missionary Alley)* — Trok Mo — *mo* here being an abbreviation of *mo sasana*, or "missionary" — likely received its name from John Chandler, an American Baptist missionary who built an imposing riverside residence at the foot of the lane and lived there from 1856 to 1865, not far from the Bang Ko Laem Baptist Chapel. Like Bang Uthit (Site 18), Ban Trok Mo emerged along lower New Road as an offshoot of Ban Suan Luang (Site 16) during the boom years around the turn of the twentieth century. It was situated within easy walking distance of the day-labour offered by the Western business firms and residences that invaded the Bang Ko Laem district with the upgrading of lower New Road and the turn-of-the-century addition of a tramline linking Land's End with the inner city. Initially, the Ban Trok Mo households continued to attend prayer sessions in their ancestral village mosque at Ban Suan Luang. With the expanding, increasingly diverse Muslim population drawn to the favourable employment opportunities at Land's End over the early decades of the twentieth century, the new settlement soon established its own mosque, giving Ban Trok Mo an independent village identity. Over the course of the twentieth century and continuing to the present day, this village's as-Salafiya Mosque, along with Ban Suan Luang's nearby al-Athik Mosque, gained a reputation among Bangkok's Muslim population for its fundamentalist reform teachings.

INDONESIAN WANDERERS

It has been estimated — surely seriously underestimated — that, as of 1910, as few as a thousand Muslims of "Javanese" origin (*chaw yawa*, Thai vernacular for Indonesians in general, "Indonesian" here serving as a convenient trope for the diversity of closely associated ethnic groups populating the Indonesian archipelago) were residing at Bangkok, rising to around 2,000 by 1915 (Thailand, Ministry of Interior 1910, p. 142; Samai 2012, p. 62). They consisted of four distinct groups: descendants of seafaring Malay-speaking Indonesian fisherfolk who had settled along the Chaophraya riverbank over the course of earlier generations; Javanese gardeners who had been recruited around the turn of the twentieth century to landscape Bangkok's royal precincts; Buginese fugitives from Dutch colonial custody who had arrived at Bangkok shortly thereafter; and a smattering of well-heeled entrepreneurs operating tramp steamer services between Bangkok, Singapore, and the Javanese ports of Batavia and Semarang.

Seafaring Fisherfolk

An ancient practice among the seafaring peoples of the Southeast Asian island world, known for their navigational skills and trading prowess no less than for their piratic bent, was to voyage far and wide in search of hospitable anchorages as chance dictated. That wanderlust imprinted a certain cultural uniformity upon the Malay-speaking world stretching from present-day Indonesia and the southern Philippines to the seaboard reaches of the Southeast Asian mainland. During the late Ayutthaya period, the ambit of migration for those voyagers extended to the Gulf of Siam and up the Chaophraya River to the Thai capital itself, a process of maritime dispersal that reappeared in the nineteenth century. The following two village biographies exemplify the manner in which a scattering of Indonesian fisherfolk, possibly from Borneo and the Sulu islands, are believed to have established themselves at Bangkok as early as the Third Reign, and possibly earlier.

> **Site 20: *Ban U (Boatyard Village)*** — Local memory has it that the Ban U Mosque, along Bangkok's eastern riverbank directly downriver from Bang Rak, dates back to the Fourth Reign, but it is likely that the settlement originated somewhat earlier. The village was apparently founded by a band of Indonesian fisherfolk who had formerly moored their boats at the Chaophraya River estuary, where the fishing was bountiful (as were opportunities for pilferage and piracy). The boat people of Ban U introduced a regular practice of selling their catches to the ragtag community of Western seamen and merchants settled along the Bang Rak waterfront — a boisterous quarter that grew dramatically in the years following the signing of the Bowring Treaty (see Chapter 7, section on "*Farang*"). During the Fifth Reign, the economic status of Ban U was further enhanced with the establishment of a formal fresh food market — the Luang Nawa Market named after its Sino-Thai landowner, Luang Nawa Kenikon (Sui-beng Posaya-chinda), later known as the Bang Rak Market — along New Road directly behind the Indonesian settlement. With the village men off fishing, the women rented fish vendors' stalls in the marketplace, and incomes rose as the market's popularity soared. Later in the Fifth Reign, the riverside stretch along which this little community was situated came to be known for its many shipyards (*u roea*, from which Ban U took its name), among them the marine workshops of Aaron Westervelt and Charles Allen, Howarth Erskine, Ltd., Captain John Bush's Bangkok Dock Company, and the Chinese-owned Taphao Dockyard. There is no evidence that

any of the Ban U fishermen sought or gained employment at those shipyards, but some did take up a new calling as lightermen, handling ship-to-shore cargo for the nearby European shipping firms represented most prominently by Windsor Rose and Company, and A. Markwald and Company. Reflecting Ban U's stabilized presence and its shift from an aquatic to an increasingly terrestrial orientation, the village mosque was rebuilt in 1919 on a plot some 100 metres inland from its former shoreline location.

Site 21: *Ban Khaek Lang (Muslim Village Downstream), later Ban Suwanaphumi (Village in the Golden Land)* — A band of Indonesian seafarers from the Thai fishing port of Trat, bordering Cambodia, is said to have established this village along the west bank of the river during the Third Reign (Saowani 2001, p. 99). It occupied a sparsely populated stretch of riverbank about half a kilometre downstream from the mouth of the San Canal, at that time marking the urban area's downriver limit. In Siam's liberalized economic environment after the Bowring Treaty of 1855, the river's right bank, opposite the square-rigger berths and mid-river anchorage stretching from Bang Rak down to Yan Nawa, came to be stippled with the unobtrusive docks, warehouses, and premises of Indian Muslim merchants, many of them associated with Singapore-based "native" trading houses. With no religious leader of their own, those merchants attended weekly prayer sessions at Ban Khaek Lang, and several formed marriage bonds with the village. Early in the Fourth Reign they sponsored a reconstruction of the village prayer house, which — at the personal suggestion of King Mongkut, it is said — was renamed the Suwanaphumi Mosque, after the nearby, newly built Wat Suwan Ubasit. Like the men of Ban U (Site 20), many of the Ban Khaek Lang villagers found work as lightermen, conveying cargo between ship and shore for the cross-river Western shipping companies; others collaborated with the district's Indian merchants in dealing in the cargoes purchased or otherwise acquired from the many Western freighters queued along the mid-river anchorage.

Javanese Gardeners

In stark contrast to the footloose inclinations of Indonesia's coastal fisherfolk was the powerful hold of the land on Indonesia's — especially Java's — agrarian populace. That was underlined by the Javanese peasantry's cultural focus on intensive wet-rice cultivation, supported by their extraordinary emphasis on village solidarity. With their refined sense of communal integration, mutual support, and cloistered settlement, the Javanese villages that appeared in Bangkok around the start of twentieth century showed clear traces of that tradition. They displayed a high degree of ethnic insularity and endogamy, thereby maintaining a discreet social distance from neighbouring Muslim communities. On the other hand, they adapted easily to Bangkok's labour needs, meeting a ready demand for their horticultural skills and uncomplaining willingness to take up ill-paid itinerant trades and day labour. A residuum of those qualities can still be glimpsed among their descendants today.

Three times during the course of his reign, King Chulalongkorn departed Bangkok with a sizeable royal entourage on a voyage to the Netherlands East Indies. The first occasion, in 1871, when he was eighteen years of age, opened his eyes to a wide range of Western technological, administrative, and educational advances, which greatly influenced his subsequent policy reforms. His second and third visits, in 1896 and 1901, both ostensibly "private", were "in search of peace and quiet ... , and for health reasons" (Brummelhuis 1987, pp. 88, 90). But even after three decades on the throne, Chulalongkorn continued to rely on his overseas travels as unrivalled opportunities to introduce to Siam the refinements of "higher civilization" (*siwilai*). One relatively minor cultural borrowing arose out of his admiration for the ornate plantings and topiary at the Dutch East Indies' Governor-General's estate at Buitenzorg (later Bogor), prompting him to seek a consignment of Javanese horticulturists for Bangkok's royal precincts. Thus, not long after the royal visit of 1896, a party of Javanese gardeners arrived at Bangkok to improve the grounds of the Grand Palace and neighbouring royal precincts, and soon after the king's 1901 visit a second group of skilled workers showed up to help landscape the newly laid-out Dusit Palace (initially called the Dusit *Garden* Palace).

Site 22: *Ban Toek Din (Powder Mill Village)* — This little Muslim neighbourhood of Javanese origin, dating from the closing years of the nineteenth century, is today situated incongruously on a sliver of crown property hemmed in between the multi-story commercial buildings lining Rachadamnoen Avenue (the King's Promenade) and the rear wall of Wat Bowon Niwet, one of the most royal of Bangkok's many Buddhist temples. Its unusual name arose from Toek Din (Powder Mill), formerly the government's main munitions production facility, located on Dinso Road (near the present-day Democracy Monument and Bangkok Municipal Headquarters), less than 200 metres distant from the Javanese village. There is no evidence, however, that the village ever provided any workers to that facility. They were recruited exclusively to tend the royal gardens at the nearby Grand Palace, Saranrom Palace, and Saranrom Garden, as well as the double rows of newly planted tamarind trees encircling the expanse of Sanam Luang (the Royal Esplanade) and lining the 3.8-kilometre-long Rachadamnoen Avenue leading from the Grand Palace to the Dusit Palace. Royal interest in those grandiose urban development projects gradually waned over the following decades, after the enthronement of King Wachirawut (Rama VI). With the fiscal problems that plagued the Sixth and Seventh Reigns, the government cut back on the Ban Toek Din gardeners' employment, leading many of the Javanese immigrants to move to the city's sparsely populated southern outskirts and relegating those who remained to such petty employments as food hawkers and domestic servants. Ban Toek Din thus lingers on as a relic of a former era, though its residents scarcely recall (or are willing to recall) their forebears' past menial service to the Crown.

Site 23: *Ban Khaek Bang Kraboe (Muslim Village near the Buffalo Village), or simply Ban Khaek Kraboe* — Located between the river and Samsen Road about two kilometres north of the Dusit Palace, the initial occupants of this unsung Javanese village appeared in Bangkok in the immediate aftermath of King Chulalongkorn's 1901 visit to Java, several years after its better-known counterpart, Ban Toek Din. The village workforce was hired to landscape the grounds of the Dusit Palace (built 1898–1909), the neighbouring Sunantha Garden (laid out in 1908), and various other newly built palaces and villas of the Dusit district. With their discharge as royal gardeners during the Sixth Reign (1910–1925), those members of the Ban Khaek Kraboe workforce who did not depart for a new life along the city's downstream periphery turned for employment to the Siamese Tramway Company, a royally sponsored but perennially financially strained tramline that ran down Samsen Road from a point near Bang Kraboe past the Dusit Palace and across the City Moat to the Front Palace ferry landing (*tha chang wang na*) (Wright and Breakspear 1908, p. 192). Though passing through some of the city's wealthiest neighbourhoods, that tramline never managed to earn a respectable profit and sought to conserve funds with repeated employment cutbacks, until it finally closed down in the 1950s. Those of the unemployed local Javanese villagers who did not then move away took up work as pedicab drivers, food hawkers, and other itinerant employments. With continued attrition, the village is today little more than a secluded hamlet boasting a small mosque, with many of its remaining men working in nearby motor-vehicle repair shops and as taxi drivers.

Sites 24 and 25: *Ban Kruay (Village along the Funnel Canal) and Ban Khwang (Village along the Broad Canal)* — Amid the turmoil of the sweeping financial cutbacks of the Sixth Reign (Greene 1999, pp. 55–60, 63–65), most of the Javanese gardeners of Ban Toek Din and Ban Khaek Kraboe were released from royal employment. As a sop toward relieving their growing distress, they were in 1912 offered a tract of undeveloped crown property land along lower New Road reaching from the Kruay Canal to the Khwang Canal, stretching inland behind New Road and the Yan Nawa riverfront. There the Javanese gardeners established two independent villages, Ban Kruay and Ban Khwang, each with its own mosque and graveyard; local informants express no knowledge as to which of the two villages derives from Ban Toek Din and which from Ban Khaek Kraboe. Today the two villages are separated by Chan Lane (recently upgraded to Chan Road) running inland from New Road; Ban Kruay occupies the upriver side and Ban Khwang stretches downstream. Over the course of the twentieth century, segments of both villages hived off to start several new Javanese hamlets (Ban Rong Nam Khaeng, Ban Khaek Yawa, and Ban Indonesia) discreetly hidden behind Bangkok's upscale Sathon, Silom, and Withayu districts, serving those posh residential neighbourhoods as gardeners and domestic servants. Today, with their separate Darul Abidin and Bayan Mosques only about 100 metres apart and sharing a close relationship through their common ethnicity and intermarriage, Ban Kruay and Ban Khwang form a single bustling neighbourhood bordering Bangkok's heavily travelled New Road.

Buginese Fugitives

Inhabiting the southern reaches of the Indonesian island of Celebes (today Sulawesi) as subjects of the Sultan of Makassar, the Buginese people had a celebrated seafaring tradition and an equally storied history of resistance to Dutch colonial rule. In its persistent defiance of the Dutch "forward movement", Makassar suffered repeated defeats, the first ending with the Dutch conquest of 1660–1669, which drove many Buginese warriors into overseas exile. Aside from their diaspora to Malacca, Johor, Sulu, and Mindanao in the mid-1660s, a sizeable Makassar émigré community emerged at Ayutthaya. Their Ayutthaya presence proved tumultuous and

culminated in 1686 in an armed uprising, which was ruthlessly put down
(Turpin 1997, pp. 33–40; Reid 2000, p. 37). Nothing further is known of
any Buginese presence in Siam until the early twentieth century, in the
wake of a latter-day revival of the sporadic Makassar resistance to Dutch
rule. Upon the defeat of that final armed uprising in 1905 many rebel
families were banished by the Dutch to the desolate Riau islands off the
east coast of Sumatra. Some managed to escape that internment by sailing
off in improvised watercraft to Singapore and neighbouring mainland
territories. One element of that jury-rigged flotilla somehow found its
way to Bangkok.

Site 26: *Ban Makkasan (Makassar Village)* — Several elders of this
sequestered Bangkok village boast — spuriously in my estimation
— direct descent from the Buginese settlers of seventeenth-century
Ayutthaya; at least one, however, recalls that his immigrant grandparents
had been "invited" to Bangkok during the Fifth Reign. On the basis of
that recollection, an estimate that the original residents of this village
arrived during the first decade of the twentieth century coincides neatly
with the Dutch suppression of the last Makassar rebellion. Lacking
further testimony, it can only be conjectured that an impoverished
party of Buginese refugees from the 1905 Makassar defeat, having
been accorded an unheralded asylum in Siam, accepted the offer of
an inferior residential tract along Bangkok's eastern outskirts only
because they were at the end of their tether. Their new village occupied
for decades a dengue-infested marsh that served as a flood catchment
basin between the Samsen and Saen Saep Canals — the so-called
Macassar Swamp (Boeng Makkasan) — until in the second half of
the twentieth century the area was improved with proper drainage,
potable water, public sanitation, and a paved road. In their nostalgia
for their lost past the refugees named their new settlement after their
ancestral homeland, and the name "Makkasan" has continued to be
associated with the area ever since (Sansani 1994, pp. 265–66). Their
assignment to this waterlogged tract was apparently orchestrated by
officials of Siam's state railways, at that time under the jurisdiction of
the Ministry of Public Works. The Railway Department was under
persistent financial pressure, and with the available supply of Chinese
coolie labour fully occupied in extending the state railways to the North
and Northeast, two new projects — the construction in 1908 of a rail
line reaching from the capital's eastern outskirts to Chanthaburi, and
at the same time the construction of workshops for the maintenance

of the railways' rolling stock (Wright and Breakspear 1908, p. 81) — impelled the Railways Department to search for alternative sources of cheap labour. The Buginese refugees were provided their village site directly alongside the planned rail yards and train terminus, evidently with the promise of continuing employment at those labour-intensive facilities. However, the inhospitable locale and the unremitting hardship associated with the arduous and underpaid work, compounded by wage and employment retrenchments in the subsequent austerity years, led to the gradual attrition of the village population through outmigration. Many of those who stayed on became politically radicalized during the turbulent post-Revolution years of the 1930s–1960s and as labour activists were harassed, dismissed, jailed, and worse (information on file at the Thai Labour Museum, Makkasan, Bangkok). With that, Ban Makkasan faded into obscurity, only to be revitalized in recent decades with new wage work opportunities in the nearby Pratu Nam shopping district. Among the improvements to the village infrastructure allowed by that employment revival is Ban Makkasan's recently rebuilt Niamatul Islam Mosque, its glittering stainless-steel-plated domes reminding motorists passing along the nearby urban expressway of Bangkok's vigorous Muslim presence.

... To *Thai Isalam*

Consequent to the refashioning of Siam's feudal realm into a nation-state, a process that has been underway since the late nineteenth century, it has been said that the "distinctions of Mon, Lao, Malay, Khmer, and other local identities [have been] submerged within the ideology of a seamless 'Thai' people" (Pasuk and Baker 2002, p. 256). For Bangkok's Muslim community, however, the outcome of that extended process of cultural transformation has not been quite so seamless. Today, after more than a century of modernization, Bangkok's Muslims are still commonly referred to not as "Thai" but as "*thai isalam*" (Muslim Thai). The alien designation "*khaek isalam*" (Muslim guests) has been largely discarded in favour of the newer form, but the implication of Otherness remains. Nor is that epithet imposed on the Muslims by the national majority alone; it reflects the general self-perception within the Muslim community itself. Both from "outside" and "inside", the clearcut ethnic distinctiveness of Bangkok's Muslim community remains, but it is a new pseudo-ethnicity founded on religious criteria alone in the wake of the Cham-Persian-Arab-Indian-Malay-Indonesian "ethnic cleansing" of the past century's nation-building project. In the aftermath of the fundamental reshaping of Siam's-now-Thailand's collective consciousness under the nationalist impulse, the generality of Bangkok's Muslim residents are said to have adjusted well to the new reality.

[They have become] outwardly indistinguishable in many ways from their Thai-Buddhist fellow citizens. Indeed, by and large, they accept Thai as their native tongue [, and] in terms of their general educational background, media exposure, food and dress habits, recent social and political experiences and collective historical memory, they tend to differ very little from the other Thais (Bajunid 1992, p. 20).

Yet, they remain Others, for reasons to be briefly explored below.

With the inner city's ever-increasing population density and commercial tumult, a substantial portion of the younger cohorts of Bangkok's old Muslim village population has found work in white-collar employments and moved to the burgeoning tenements, townhouses, condominiums, and housing estates of the Bangkok metropolitan region's rising suburbs and satellite towns. Their dispersal has distanced them from the village mosque and its tight-knit social nexus and thus has loosened for many the routines of Islamic ritual and customary behaviour. Most evident is their frequent abandonment of the traditional headdress (*takiyah* and *hijab*) and sarong at school and at work and their easy association with non-Muslim friends at non-*halal* social gatherings — with the opponents of such broad-minded behaviour taking exactly the opposite course of action. A natural consequence has been the cultural integration of the Muslim progressives into the Thai national fabric, with the corollary effect of increasing secularism, potentially quantifiable in reduced mosque attendance as well as increased rates of intermarriage and religious conversion.

Such Muslim cultural integration into the Bangkok scene is a convincing perception if viewed from "without", from the perspective of the broader metropolitan community; viewed from "within", however, the distinctive Muslim village culture has held on resolutely. With the past century's continuing urbanization, many of Bangkok's old Muslim villages have been threatened by an intensifying encroachment of commercially disparate neighbourhoods. The casual observer today would be hard-pressed, for instance, to find the Chakraphong and Toek Din mosques within the congested Bang Lamphu market quarter; or the Harun and Ban U mosques along the clamorous backstreets of the thriving Bang Rak district; or the Kudi Khaw, Charoenphat, or Suan Phlu mosques along the secluded byways edging Thonburi's Bang Luang Canal. Yet, nearly all the old city's twenty-six Muslim villages have survived, tucked away within its new "seamlessly Thai" precincts. Furthermore, Bangkok's urban core has gained an expanded Muslim presence, much of it of South Asian origin, as confirmed by fifteen new mosques, most of post-World War II vintage, spread across the Bang Rak, Pathumwan, Silom-Sathon, and Sukhumvit districts, while the congregations of many of the old inner-city mosques have been replenished by new Muslim arrivals from the provinces as well as from overseas.

The tensions embroiling cultural, national, and religious identity within Bangkok's Muslim community have fomented contending compulsions of ideology and lifestyle. They have contributed to a mixed response to modern secularism, an ambiguity of "multiple identities" (Winyu 2014, pp. 12–13). The secular tendencies among those who have opted for cultural accommodation, including outmigration, are opposed by those who have chosen to remain as strict observers in their ancestral villages. In the inner-city village, strict adherence to Islamic principle and practice has come to serve as "an escape route for people mired in the negative morass of modernity" (Spira 2004, p. 250). Stripped of their former ethnic multiplicity, Bangkok's Muslim villages have increasingly redefined themselves along sectarian lines — traditionalist (liberal) versus reformist (fundamentalist). Under that emerging ideological divide, Islamic fervour has been on the rise. A striking visual indicator is Bangkok's increasingly assertive, sometimes pretentious mosque architecture (Adis 2008, pp. 121–32). From the former humble wood-plank prayer houses fitting their villages like yolk-in-egg, many of Bangkok's mosques have been rebuilt as increasingly prominent brick-and mortar edifices, with their bulging Ottoman-style onion domes, soaring minarets, and impressive newly minted Arabic names looming as an incongruous presence over their modest village settings.

Application of the sacred precept of Muslim brotherhood (*ikwat*) as a broad, supra-ethnic imperative of Islam has waxed and waned over Islam's fourteen-century history. In Old Bangkok, that integrative ideal struggled against the everyday reality of ethnic diversity. More recently, it has come to be challenged by the dialectic of imported Islamic militancy versus indigenous Islamic traditions of moderation in thought and deed (Scupin 1980; Scupin 1998; Winyu 2014, pp. 16–20). Mirroring the global Islamic resurgence, the past century has seen an intensification of religious ferment within Bangkok's Muslim community. Eased conditions of overseas travel — on the haj, and for education, employment, business, and tourism — and the rise of mass communications — newsprint, radio, television, and most recently the Internet — have encouraged, in Bangkok as elsewhere, a popular surge in Muslim sectarian zeal, just as it has contributed to the obverse decline in ethnic insularity (Muzaffar 1986). Contrasting with the secularization and assimilation pursued by segments of Bangkok's Muslim citizenry, the pan-Islamic movement has generated "a very strong Islamic reformist movement in the metropolis" — "reformist" here referring to the ideological injunctions associated with fundamentalist (*salafi*) thought (Bajunid 1992, p. 21; Scupin 1980). As elsewhere, that reformist agenda is in Bangkok largely a reaction against the seductive pull of secularism in a culturally dynamic, economically progressive urban setting. Though it is averred that such liberal-conservative tensions are intensifying, Muslim community elders steadfastly maintain that the character of Islamic fundamentalism in Bangkok remains resolutely apolitical.

Having discarded much of their former ethnicity under the several-generations-old impulse of national integration, Bangkok's Muslims today continue to grapple with an existential dialectic — the quest for attainment of material aspirations in the "outer", Thai-Buddhist world versus aspirations for spiritual fulfilment in the "inner", Muslim-village world. Efforts to accommodate both those contending worldviews have given rise to the tensions of double identity, which remain one of the fundamental realities of everyday life among Bangkok's "Thai Islam" — a term which itself connotes a sense of ethnic bifurcation. That dichotomy has replaced the former ethnic diversity of Old Bangkok's Muslim community with a new, ideologically contentious, theologically based pseudo-ethnic minority within the modern nation-state.

6

Taming The Dragon:
Chinese Rivalries

From China to Siam

The thickly populated, culturally dynamic Chinese littoral extending from Taiwan to Hainan follows a great southwestward-bending arc toward the Southeast Asian landmass. Along that thousand-kilometre seaboard have resided for millennia a string of Chinese ethnic minorities — the Hokkien, Taechiu, Cantonese, Hakka, and Hainanese — commonly referred to as Chinese "speech groups" in recognition of their most prominent individuating culture trait. Over the course of innumerable generations up to the nineteenth–twentieth centuries they were gradually but never fully absorbed into the dominant Han culture. It was only in the past century or so that the cultural distinctions among those various ethnic subspecies, most readily distinguishable in terms of habitat, dialect, and mutual antipathies, were sharply attenuated under the compulsions of Chinese nationalism, Communist ideology, and rampant industrialization.

Among that regional cluster of ethnic minorities, the Taechiu (or Teochew, Chiuchow, or Chaozhou, among other transliterations) historically occupied a comparatively inconsequential position. Inhabiting the resource-poor, flood- and famine-prone Chaoshan Plain and Han River delta, a lonely prefecture straddling the borderlands between southern Fujian Province (the Hokkien heartland) and central Kwangtung (the Cantonese cradle), they may well have been among the region's autochthonous lowland peoples, pressed by later intruders into that relatively inhospitable ecological zone. Considered impoverished country bumpkins by their more sophisticated Hokkien and Cantonese neighbours, they eked out a living as peasant agriculturalists, sea-salt farmers, fisherfolk, food processors, and coastal traders (Chang 1991, pp. 29–31). Their intrepid maritime skills, coupled with their stubborn defiance of imperial Chinese rule, earned them a lasting reputation in government circles as recalcitrant smugglers, pirates, and renegades (Antony 2003, pp. 19–53; Supang 1991a). As one early nineteenth-century Western observer candidly noted:

> [The inhabitants of] Chaou-chow-foo, the most eastern department of Canton province, ... are, in general, mean, uncleanly, avaricious, but affable and fond of strangers... . Being neighbours to the inhabitants of Fuhkeen, the dialects of the two people are very similar, but in their manners there is a great difference. This dissimilarity in their customs, joined to the similarity of their pursuits, has given rise to considerable rivalry, which frequently results in open hostility. But the Fuhkeen men have gained the ascendency, and use all their influence to destroy the trade of their competitors (Gutzlaff 1834, pp. 84–85).

Overseas trade opportunities had been drawing junks from southern China to Southeast Asia for centuries. Emigration to the Nan Yang (the South Seas) was a perennial option also for political dissidents, particularly in the decades following the fall of the Ming dynasty (1644). Imperial efforts to suppress smuggling, piracy, and emigration, and cope with the persistent threat of exile-fed rebellion along China's southern coastlands during the early decades of the Ching dynasty, included the closing of the southern ports and prohibition of private maritime trade. The great ports of Canton (Guangzhou) and Amoy (Xiamen) suffered less in being allowed limited trade under close supervision. The smaller ports, such as the Taechiu prefecture's Changlin, did not share such privileges. Only after 1727, in the face of recurring crop failures and famines, were the draconian restrictions rescinded, allowing the Taechiu homeland, among other southern China hinterlands, to revive its overseas trade and transport connections (Sarasin 1977, pp. 28–57, 70–75; Swi 1991, pp. 37–50).

In the wake of the Ching victory over the Ming, waves of Hokkien political dissidents evaded the state's travel restrictions to flee the mainland for Taiwan and the Nan Yang. A number of those activists joined the old Hokkien trading community at Ayutthaya, linking with the regional network of Amoy-centred trading posts stretching along the shores of the South China Sea from Vietnam to the Malay Peninsula, East Indies, and Philippines. Over the succeeding decades their leaders rose to high office in the Siamese state as court merchants and royal junk fleet operators, capturing control of Siam's thriving state trade with China (Sarasin 1977, pp. 160–63). Operating in the shadow of that Hokkien trade supremacy after 1727, Taechiu coastal traders sailing smaller junks managed to find shelter and trading opportunities at the lesser ports along Siam's eastern seaboard, where they established a string of small outposts, led by Chanthaburi and Chonburi, that developed the pepper, sugar, tobacco, and cotton export trades (Wanwipa 1991, pp. 92–94). A Taechiu presence also emerged at Ayutthaya in the lee of the city's robust Hokkien settlement. The Hokkien merchant-officials had been permitted to establish their residences, warehouses, and a popular marketplace in the southeastern quarter within the city wall; the less well-connected, less affluent Taechiu seafarers were relegated to the rowdy, disreputable port district at Suan Phlu, across the river downstream from the capital (Map 2.2; Van Roy 2007*b*).

Just as the Taechiu community at Ayutthaya was beginning to consolidate a profitable position in the coastal traffic, dealing in bulk commodities — as distinct from the Hokkien role in the royal tribute trade at Canton and Amoy, which dealt primarily in luxury goods — the Burmese invasions of the 1760s annihilated their hard-earned gains. From the sparse evidence, it can be inferred that many of the Hokkien survivors of Ayutthaya's destruction fled south by junk to the peninsular ports of Surat Thani, Nakhon Si Thammarat, Songkhla, and Pattalung, whereas the Taechiu sailed east to find sanctuary at Chonburi, Rayong, Chanthaburi, and Trat. The epic flight of Phraya Taksin (the later parvenu king of Thonburi) from beleaguered Ayutthaya followed a similar eastward route to the Taechiu coastal settlements, though by land. His subsequent astonishing military successes and revival of the Siamese state at Thonburi afforded the Teachiu settlers a second chance. Through the influence of his father, a Taechiu immigrant merchant with divers business interests along Siam's seaboard ports, Taksin favoured the Taechiu community over the Hokkien. Their unique dialect and customs were familiar to him, and equally, their unstinting support from the very inception of his rise to power warranted his sustained patronage. It would not be too much to say that without Taechiu backing Taksin would not have succeeded.

During the Thonburi kingdom's early famine years, King Taksin sought the aid of both the Taechiu and Hokkien merchants in acquiring urgently needed rice stocks. The Hokkien traders, fearing that they would go unpaid, equivocated on the spurious grounds that rice cargos were not readily available. The Taechiu, however, brought in rice shipments from their eastern seaboard warehouses, and they later supplied Taksin with desperately sought-after arms to deal with the continuing threat of Burmese aggression and the challenge posed by various pretenders to the throne

(Sarasin 1977, pp. 144–45). Taksin bought time to consolidate his position by offering them long-term credit arrangements and other inducements, such as monopoly privileges over various lucrative trades. He hired their junk fleets as troop carriers to extend his sway over the southern and eastern seaboards. And he devised with them an arrangement whereby impoverished Taechiu youths were indentured at Changlin (the main junk port of the Taechiu homeland) and transported to Thonburi to provide a reliable force of military conscripts.

Military campaigns against Thonburi's rising rivals — Khorat, Uttaradit, Nakhon Si Thammarat — were an early preoccupation of the new regime. An additional threat rose from Hatien, a Cantonese mercantile outpost along the Cochinchina shoreline. Animosities over trade routes, rice consignments, and spheres of influence culminated in a Thai naval expedition, a pitched battle resulting in Hatien's destruction, and the relocation of the Hatien ruling elite to Thonburi (Chen 1977; Sakurai and Kitagawa 1999, pp. 203–204; Sellers 1983, pp. 71–75). There, the self-styled prince of Hatien was awarded a rank in the Thai nobility and provided with a residential compound near Wat Photharam (Map 6.1, sites 2 and 4). His approximately 1,000-person entourage was assigned a village site along the east bank of the river directly downstream from the "East Thonburi" city wall (Map 6.1, site C). So, Thonburi's Chinese populace was diversified to include a substantial representation of three distinct speech groups.

Under Taksin's patronage, Thonburi's Taechiu community grew and prospered — at the expense of the formerly dominant Hokkien nobility, and much to their resentment, while the Cantonese settlement kept a low profile (Nidhi 1996, p. 285). It can be speculated that Bangkok's Taechiu-Hokkien population ratio, as a result of Taksin's efforts, may have risen from near equality to two-to-one over the course of his fifteen-year reign, the total more than doubling from less than 10,000 to over 20,000. Kudi Chin, the Hokkien settlement along the river's west bank at the confluence of the Bang Luang Canal (otherwise known as the Bangkok Yai Canal), directly downstream from the Thonburi Grand Palace, languished (Map 6.1, site B). Hokkien ostracism under Taksin was further indicated by the infringement on the Kudi Chin settlement's bounds by a Portuguese refugee village, Santa Cruz (Map 6.1, site D). All that while the left bank of the river directly across from the Thonburi Grand Palace — "East Thonburi," circled by its own city wall and moat (Map 6.1, site A) — allotted to the Taechiu merchants and seamen and the many indentured immigrants who arrived under their protection, prospered. The Taechiu merchants' dwellings, warehouses, and docks lined

MAP 6.1

Thonburi: Chinese and other minority settlements, pre-1782

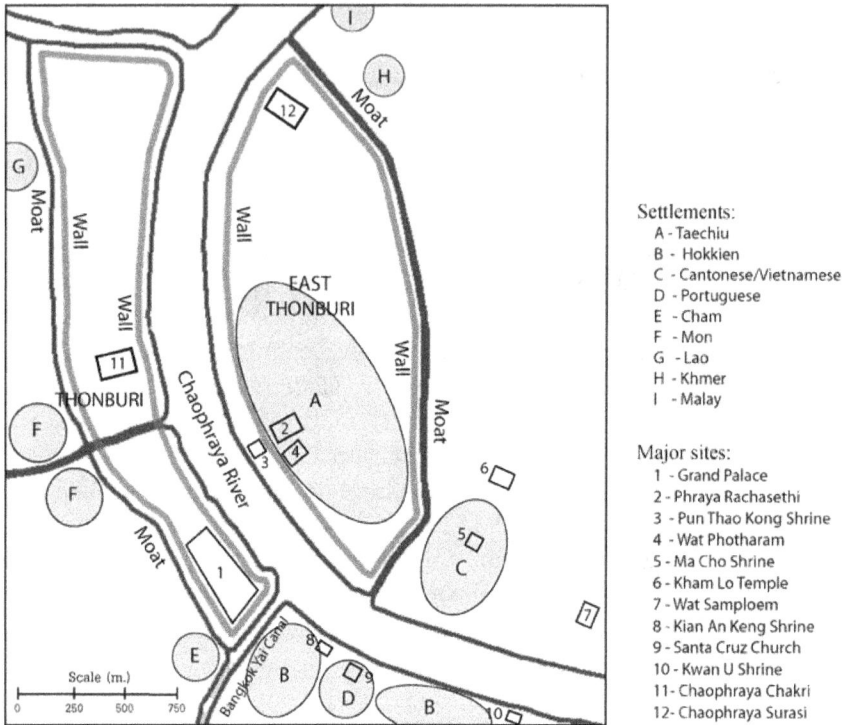

Settlements:
A - Taechiu
B - Hokkien
C - Cantonese/Vietnamese
D - Portuguese
E - Cham
F - Mon
G - Lao
H - Khmer
I - Malay

Major sites:
1 - Grand Palace
2 - Phraya Rachasethi
3 - Pun Thao Kong Shrine
4 - Wat Photharam
5 - Ma Cho Shrine
6 - Kham Lo Temple
7 - Wat Samploem
8 - Kian An Keng Shrine
9 - Santa Cruz Church
10 - Kwan U Shrine
11 - Chaophraya Chakri
12 - Chaophraya Surasi

the East Thonburi riverbank, with the workers' shanties behind, spread from the imposing, centrally situated compound occupied by the Taechiu headman, Phraya Rachasethi, and the settlement's chief Daoist shrine directly alongside the old Buddhist temple of Wat Photharam (later rebuilt as Wat Phra Chetuphon). By 1782, the Thonburi capital's Taechiu precinct was functioning as a well-established, thriving junk port. But in that year the Thonburi regime fell to a coup d'état engineered by a powerful military faction. Taksin's abdication and execution facilitated the installation of his two chief ministers and commanding generals — the brothers Chaophraya Chakri (Thong-duang) and Chaophraya Surasi (Bunma) — as the founding king and viceroy of the Chakri dynasty. With that dynastic overthrow the scales of royal preference and privilege swung back to the old, Ayutthaya-based Thai aristocracy and their Hokkien associates.

Sampheng, Founded in Adversity

One of the new regime's first decisions was to relocate the citadel, including the Grand Palace, from the Thonburi citadel to the opposite bank of the river. That, according to the royal chronicles, required the removal of the east-bank Taechiu community, which under Taksin had occupied the area designated for the new city centre (Thipakorawong 2009a, p. 6). Yet, several other ethnic minorities (Cantonese-Vietnamese, Malay, Khmer) already settled within the new riparian city's precincts and yet others (Hokkien, Cantonese, Portuguese, Mon, Lao, Cham, Persian) situated along its immediate outskirts, were not required to relocate. The Taechiu, as close associates and supporters of the *ancien régime*, were suspect and thus warranted exclusion. That point was glossed over in the official record: the Taechiu "were asked [sic] to transfer their residence to the 'gardens' [sic] beyond the future heart of the city" (Wenk 1968, p. 18). Stated more graphically, they were exiled to the waterlogged precincts of Sampheng, a riverside tract several kilometres downstream from the new city centre, well distanced from the new city wall and moat, a district demarcated by Wat Samploem (later renamed Wat Chakrawat) and its canal as the upstream boundary and Wat Sampheng (later renamed Wat Pathum Khongkha) and its canal on the downstream side (Map 6.2, sites 7 and 17). The Sampheng district likely gained its name from the latter of those temples, which stood as the juncture of three riverside paths (*sam praeng*). The most important of them, the old elephant track leading downriver from the walled city, came gradually to be lined with Chinese shophouses and gained the name Sampheng Lane (later known as Soi Wanit, or Commercial Lane). Alternatively, it has been averred that Ayutthaya's rowdy Taechiu port district, which had housed many of the city's brothels, had been popularly known as Sampheng (*sampheng* deriving from *sophani*, the Khmer term for prostitute), and that that name was carried over to Bangkok's new Taechiu quarter (Reynolds 1987, p. 134).

The Taechiu eviction from the "East Thonburi" port could not have been a happy event. While great effort was expended by the Chakri regime to build the new riparian capital of Ratanakosin, the Taechiu community of perhaps 15,000 souls was left entirely to its own devices in laying out its new downriver settlement. The designated site was a riverside mire, so inhospitable that an old neighbouring temple was popularly known as the Lanka Island Temple (Wat Ko Lankaram (Map 6.2, site 16), later rebuilt as Wat Samphanthawong) for its location in the midst of a brackish, flood-prone backswamp. Access to Sampheng from Ratanakosin through the

MAP 6.2
Sampheng and environs, 1782–1868

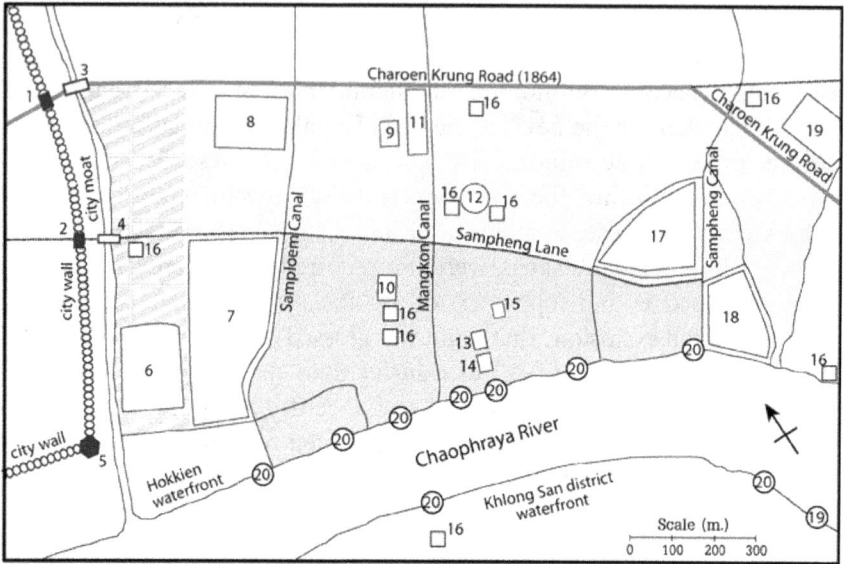

1 - Sam Yot Gate
2 - Saphan Han Gate
3 - Damrong-sathit Bridge
4 - Swivel Bridge
5 - Chakraphat Bastiom
6 - Wat Bophit Phimuk
7 - Wat Samploem
8 - Wat Toek
9 - Wat Chun Heng Yi (Mahayana)
10 - Wat Bien Proek Kroe (Mahayana)
11 - Wat Kan Maturayam (Thammayut)
12 - Market
13 - Phraya Rachasethi
14 - Lao Pun Thao Kong Shrine
15 - Cheng Huang Shrine
16 - Other major shrines
17 - Wat Ko Lankaram
18 - Wat Pathum Khongkha
19 - Wat Sam Chin
20 - Major docks

Original Taechiu settlement (1782)

Expanded Taechiu settlement (c.1868)

Buffer zone

city wall and across the City Moat (*khu moeang*) was limited to a single unpaved footpath passing through a well-guarded gate and over a rickety pedestrian bridge (later improved to a heavily trafficked swivel bridge, Saphan Han). Taechiu junks were initially prohibited from sailing upriver beyond the confluence of the City Moat, guarded by the Chakraphet Bastion, whereas Hokkien junks could sail a kilometre further upstream to their settlement at the mouth of the Bang Luang Canal, under the protective guns of the Thonburi citadel's Wichai Prasit Bastion. Furthermore, the roughly 300-metre-wide buffer zone between the city and Sampheng was assigned to senior army and police officials (for example, the sequence of ministers of the capital and chiefs of the municipal police, titled Chaophraya Yomarat) for their residential use and the bivouacking of their troops. In the third Chakri reign (1824–1851), a great monument, some 44 metres high, was erected by one of those military commanders (Chaophraya Bodin Decha) at Wat Samploem, Sampheng's upstream boundary temple, to commemorate a great military victory over the Lao (Van Roy 2007*a*, pp. 279–89); it also served as a vivid reminder to the Taechiu of their perennially precarious, suspect status as Others within their designated settlement bounds at the periphery of the Thai capital. It still stands there today, though its former significance has long been forgotten.

The downfall of King Taksin and rise of the Chakri dynasty demonstrated the tenuous position of the Taechiu sojourners within the Siamese state. In one fell swoop, livelihood- and even life-threatening ethnic tensions replaced the former climate of close collaboration. The problem was twofold. Thai-Taechiu distancing, though inter-ethnic in effect, was not a direct result of ethnic antipathies; rather, it sprang from specific circumstances of political factionalism. The more deep-seated enmity lay between the Taechiu and Hokkien. From the start of the new dynasty, the balance of power in the Taechiu-Hokkien rivalry gravitated back to the latter. Hokkien memories of their former favoured position at Ayutthaya, followed by their fall from grace during the Thonburi period, were compounded by the new dynasty's Hokkien links — through the Hokkien mother of King Rama I and his viceroy — compounded by its latent fear of Taechiu insurrection.

From the outset, Sampheng was firmly identified with the Taechiu sojourners, who settled there *en masse*. The continued immigration of indigent Taechiu labourers eventually crowded the Sampheng port area and turned the outskirts of the original riverside settlement into a sprawling shanty town. Even if the Taechiu had been permitted to settle in more dispersed hamlets they would not have wished to do so, for they would have found themselves socially — linguistically, occupationally, defensively — isolated. The Hokkien were settled cross-river and upstream, primarily along the opposite bank at Kudi Chin, nearer the centre of power. By the Third Reign, the most prominent among them, all stemming from Ayutthaya's old Hokkien merchant community, were the Kalayanamit (*sae* Oeng), Krairoek (*sae* Lim), Phisonbut (*sae* Lao), Ratanakun (*sae* Ong), and Sethabut (*sae* Tae) lineages — *sae* being the Chinese for "lineage name" or "clan name", with the abovementioned Thai surnames being introduced under Thai law only in 1913. The residences of those trading magnates came to line the west-bank waterfront downstream from Kudi Chin, with outliers dispersed along the east bank upstream and downstream from Sampheng (Map 6.3, site B). Though fewer in numbers than the Taechiu, they pursued more lucrative lines of business, held more prestigious government posts, occupied more luxurious quarters, and were more firmly integrated into Thai elite society. Exceptional were the few Taechiu merchant families — notably the Posayanon (*sae* Kim) and Phisanbut (*sae* Ko) lineages — that managed to rise into the nobility as early as the Third and Fourth Reigns and were awarded residential sites along the west bank directly across from Sampheng, downstream from the focus of Hokkien settlement. In later reigns, direct purchase of such estates became the norm as the government relaxed its landholding restrictions. Thus, in the later nineteenth century, as Sampheng's population overflowed its bounds under the economic boom induced by the free trade regime installed during the Fourth Reign, significant Taechiu offshoot settlements began to appear. The principal branches emerged along the Sampheng periphery, in the downriver Yan Nawa port district, and along the inland Bangkok Yai Canal transport hub crowding the mouth of the Phasi Charoen Canal (Map 3.2), which had been excavated by Chinese wage labour — financed and directed between 1866 and 1872 at the king's request by Phraya Phison Sombat Boribun (Yim *sae* Lao), a leading tax farmer of the time.

THE ERA OF BENIGN NEGLECT

The Siamese state had a long-standing policy of recognizing the autonomous status of Bangkok's respective ethnic minorities and assigning jurisdiction over their internal affairs to ethnically kindred "governors", "shahbandars", or "kapitans" serving under the patronage of Chaophraya Phra Khlang, head of the Ministry of Trade and Foreign Affairs (*krom phra khlang*). The Taechiu, however, were accorded no formal leader of their own. Instead, authority over all of Bangkok's Chinese residents was assigned to a functionary serving as director of the Eastern Trade Department (*krom tha sai*) and carrying the rank and title of Phraya Chodoek Rachasethi. From 1782 to 1932, when the nobility was abolished, a series of ten prominent Chinese tycoons occupied that post, all but one of them Hokkien — the single exception being a Hakka. Despite comprising the overwhelming majority of Bangkok's Chinese population, the Taechiu were thus systematically excluded from that prestigious position and were formally governed by a series of non-Taechiu "mayors" all of whom resided in Hokkien-dominated villages, neighbourhoods, and districts outside Sampheng.

Even if not intended as an outright snub or insult, the unremitting Hokkien mayoral reign over Bangkok's Taechiu community proved a provocative policy, and one bound to fail. That was evident in at least two ways. First, as director of the Eastern Trade Department within the Ministry of Trade and Foreign Affairs, Phraya Chodoek shouldered responsibility for the state's frequent tribute missions to China (until Siam's tributary status to China was abrogated by King Rama IV in 1852). Those missions, involving junk fleets carrying tax-free and unblocked trade goods far exceeding the king's tributary offerings, proved exceptionally profitable (Sarasin 1977, pp. 121–59). The series of Phraya Chodoek naturally ensured that the transport contracts fell to their Hokkien kindreds and ethnic fellows, while the Taechiu were excluded. Second, as one of their principal mayoral duties, the series of Phraya Chodoek were charged with maintaining law and order among Bangkok's Chinese residents. They had the powers of arrest and detention, of judge, jury, and jailer over wrongdoers within their jurisdiction. But in this regard their concerns lay primarily with maintaining peaceful *external* relations between the Chinese and Bangkok's other ethnic communities, particularly in the port area. *Internally*, within Sampheng, they had little interest or influence, and their subordinates found themselves essentially impotent. Within Sampheng, issues of public order were dealt with independently, by other means, with the implicit approval of the Siamese state.

In the absence of effective formal governance, the Sampheng citizenry turned for security and social justice to their own *de facto* leadership, concentrated in the Taechiu community's secret societies (or "triads", known as "*ang-yi*" in the Taechiu dialect); such communal arrangements also developed among the other Chinese speech groups in their separate settlements. Such illicit social syndicates had thrived in the rebellious provinces of southern China for centuries, originally having been formed in opposition to imperial despotism. In the eighteenth and nineteenth centuries those widely dispersed fraternities gained spiritual strength from their unremitting devotion to the anti-Ching/pro-Ming cause, fortified by their elaborate, quasi-religious rituals. They were organized in the mould of *kongsi*, the traditional socially embedded, profit-sharing, family-networking form of business enterprise prevailing in the southern Chinese seaboard provinces (Brown 1995, pp. 7ff). Like *kongsi*, they functioned as brotherhoods, divided into lodges, shared their gains and losses, and emphasized fictive kinship relationships and terminology, with the presiding officer ("*tua-hia*", a Taechiu term meaning "elder brother") serving as *primus inter pares* (Baffie 2007, pp. 11–14). Though originally formed in China for purposes of political resistance, their functions as mutual aid societies predominated in Bangkok. Each speech group developed its own network of secret society lodges — commonly operating under cover of neighbourhood clubs, clan associations, occupational guilds, religious cults, charitable societies, and the like — with the dominant Taechiu cluster of lodges headquartered in Sampheng's numerous neighbourhood Daoist shrines and Mahayana Buddhist temples.

Of overriding importance among the functions of Bangkok's secret societies was the delicate task of negotiating peaceful relations among the respective speech groups; collectively, they were sworn to protect the public security interests of the Chinese community at large, though their very presence was generally sufficient to prevent any need for collaborative defence. Of more practical everyday relevance, the secret societies were expected to afford their members such forms of social sustenance as employment, housing, subsistence, fellowship, and spiritual support (including funerary arrangements). In practice, however, they generally fell far short of achieving those ideals. Increasingly, their revenues came to be diverted to ends eclipsing the well-being of their communal constituencies. Much has been made of the racketeering role of the secret societies, and that certainly came to be a growing aspect of their activities in the increasingly mercenary social environment of the late nineteenth century. But in the early generations of Bangkok's Chinese community's struggle toward prosperity, in the absence of effective state support, their social welfare functions predominated.

The social sway of the secret societies over Bangkok's Chinese populace, particularly in Sampheng, was greatly enhanced by their active sponsorship of the religious rituals, seasonal celebrations, and physical facilities of the city's many Daoist shrines and Mahayana Buddhist temples (Maps 6.2 and 6.3), most of which have survived to the present day. In turn, the shrines served as cover for the secret societies' lodge meetings and numerous nefarious activities. The best known of Sampheng's Daoist shrines in the early Bangkok period was the Old Pun Thao Kong Shrine (Sanchao Lao Pun Thao Kong (Map 6.2, site 14), moved to Sampheng in 1782 from its former site in "East Thonburi"), located directly behind the Old Shrine Dock (Tha Sanchao Kao), close by the residence of Phraya Rachasethi (the Taechiu leader under Taksin who had been exiled downriver by the new regime), in the very midst of the original Sampheng settlement (Map 6.2, site 13; Van Roy 2007a, pp. 193–202). There, the neighbourhood elders gathered regularly to perform their rituals in front of Pun Thao Kong, the quintessentially Taechiu guardian deity, to stage fireworks displays and Chinese operas, to sponsor weddings and funerals, to welcome distinguished visitors, to distribute charity to indigents, to administer justice within their local territory and among its residents. On another nearby Sampheng lane stood the Cheng Huang (Siang Oeng Kong) Shrine, where Sampheng's births and deaths were ritually "registered" with the gods. Across the river, at Kudi Chin, the Kian An Keng Shrine (dedicated to Kwan Im, the Bodhisatta Avalokitesvara), dating from the Ayutthaya era, played a similar role for the Hokkien community. As the Chinese population continued to grow in the later half of the nineteenth century and into the twentieth, dozens more such shrines, most of them speech-group specific, sprang up in Sampheng's emerging Hakka, Hainanese, and Cantonese neighbourhoods and across the wider city (Ho 1995).

The Thai state's perennial sensitivities regarding Sampheng were highlighted by two incidents associated with the building of Charoen Krung Road (New Road), Bangkok's first major thoroughfare (built 1862–1864), an 8.6 kilometres-long route stretching from the citadel through the walled city, then bypassing Sampheng and continuing downstream past the Western port district of Bang Rak and the rice mills, sawmills, and lime kilns of Yan Nawa to the downriver anchorage at Bang Ko Laem. The first of those incidents was the issuance of a royal proclamation (Mongkut 1964, vol. 4, p. 795) that the section of New Road passing behind Sampheng would be paid for with the revenues collected from the triennial Chinese head tax, set at the quite substantial rate of four baht, then equivalent to about 100 kilograms of milled rice. In earmarking Chinese tax revenues for Sampheng, the state appears to have been offering a conciliatory response to the chronic complaints of the Taechiu — shades of their resistance to Chinese imperial exactions — over the imposition of such an arbitrary impost. Equally telling in its suggestion of lingering Thai anxieties over the chance of Taechiu insurrection was the second incident, a military proposal of 1862 that the section of New Road running past Sampheng should be cut wide and straight to provide a clear line of sight for the army's artillery in the event of Chinese civil disturbance, with a sharp bend at the bridge crossing the City Moat to provide a defensive position against enemy fire. The consequent realignment of New Road and repositioning of its bridge and city gate required by that cautionary proposal was ultimately carried out, though fortunately never put to the test (Nit 1964).

Over the later half of the nineteenth century, Bangkok's Chinese population expanded at an accelerating pace (Skinner 1957, pp. 87–88). Political turmoil and deteriorating economic conditions along the southern

Chinese seaboard, coupled with the buoyant labour demand generated by Siam's commodities export boom, spurred Chinese immigration to new heights. Construction of the Taechiu deep-sea port of Swatow (1856–1858) to replace the old silted-up junk port of Changlin greatly quickened the flow of coolie labour from the Taechiu Prefecture to Bangkok by steamer transport (Supang 2006a, pp. 80–89 *infra*). The labour recruitment practices that had been innovated under the Thonburi regime were elaborated into a full-scale coolie transport trade supplying Taechiu workers to the Bangkok docks and mills and the sugar and pepper plantations of the eastern seaboard provinces. Grasping opportunity by the throat, leading Sampheng-based entrepreneurs — many of them doubling as secret society elders — developed diversified interests in labour recruitment, transport, and contracting. They compounded their profits from the coolie trade with such highly remunerative services as moneylending and remittance forwarding as well as opium and spirits trafficking and sponsorship of gambling and prostitution. With their ready access to Sampheng's workers, the labour contractors supplied coolie contingents for a broad array of state-sponsored infrastructure projects, including fortifications, palaces, and temples, canal excavation and land reclamation, and the construction of roads, telegraph lines, and railways (Piyanat 2006, pp. 5–11).

Beyond the accelerating Taechiu immigration flow, Hokkien, Hakka, and Hainanese migration to Siam became significant contributors to the kingdom's wage labour force as the century wore on. But a persistent distancing was maintained between the different speech groups, to the extent that they refused to work together under the same employers or in the same projects. Hokkien residence at Bangkok avoided the Taechiu centre at Sampheng, concentrating along the west bank of the river and along the east bank upstream and downstream from Sampheng (Map 6.3, site B). By and large, the Hokkien coolie traffic bypassed Bangkok, proceeding directly via Singapore, Penang, and Phuket to supply the Peninsula's west-coast tin and lead mines, and later its rubber smallholdings. Most of the Hainanese (Hailam speech group) immigrants dispersed upcountry as small-scale traders and peddlers, dealing in metal implements, salt, provincial luxuries, and the like, and shipping boatloads of rice, timber, hides, and other bulk commodities downriver to Bangkok. The Taechiu may have been shrewder businessmen, but the Hainanese were considered more adventurous (Skinner 1957, p. 89). At Bangkok, the Hainanese kept to themselves in self-segregated settlements along the urban periphery. Their earliest-known Bangkok village, dating from the 1840s or before, was situated along the river at Samsen, well upstream from the city. Not long thereafter, another village arose far downstream, at the present-day mouth of the Sathon Canal, below Bang Rak. A third village emerged after mid-century at Ban Khao Lam, along the Phadung Krung Kasem Canal at the Sampheng periphery near Talat Noi (Map 6.3, site D). Unlike the many neighbourhood Pun Thao Kong shrines erected by the Taechiu, the Hainanese built at each of their settlements a single large shrine devoted to Tian Fa, Empress of Heaven and protector of seamen (known to the Thai as Mae Thabthim, the Ruby Mother). Bangkok's Hakka (or Khae) community, on the other hand, proved more eclectic in their choice of deities, though they favoured Kwan U, the warrior god of integrity, enterprise, and wealth. Like the Hainanese, they established their villages along the urban periphery (Map 6.3, site C). The first, dating from the 1840s, was sited on the west bank of the river across from Sampheng but was soon pushed back into the Khlong San district interior to make way for riverside Taechiu rice mills, docks, and warehouses. A later Hakka concentration emerged in the 1890s along the Sampheng outskirts at Phlabphlachai. Hakka coolies complemented the dominant Taechiu workforce by gaining employment at some of Bangkok's smaller rice mills and sawmills that had difficulty recruiting sufficient labour. They also made a name for themselves in the leather tanning industry and through that specialty came to control the footwear trades, establishing a small commercial enclave for that trade in mid-Sampheng.

Revenue farming — the outsourcing of various public revenue collections to private bidders — served Siam's administratively weak government as a key fiscal instrument (Hong 1984, pp. 75–110). Similarly, until the introduction of a free trade regime with the promulgation of the Bowring Treaty (1855), the provisioning of export goods remained largely a royal monopoly, with the China trade being administered by the Ministry of Trade and Foreign Affairs in close cooperation with Hokkien merchant houses and junk fleets. Sampheng's Taechiu merchants faced continuing obstruction in gaining access to those commercial opportunities. Marginalized from those lucrative options, they turned to such alternative lines as sugar refining and alcohol distilling, rice- and saw-milling, coastal transport and trade, and opium smuggling (until its legalization as a government monopoly in 1851, after which they legitimized their operations by gaining control of the opium farm). In the early Bangkok period that system was dominated by Hokkien merchants, who had the social connections, financial backing, and organizational resources necessary to secure such challenging but lucrative opportunities. Among the capital's early Hokkien tycoons, the Lim lineage, forebears of the royally connected

MAP 6.3
Sampheng and environs: Chinese speech groups, 1910

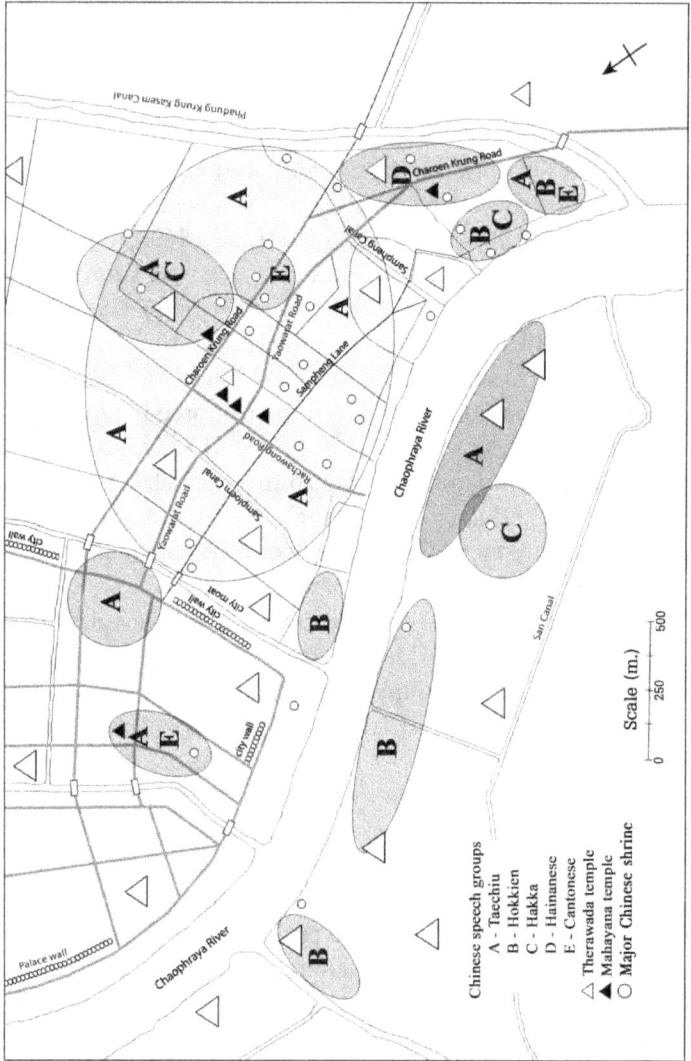

Chinese speech groups
A - Taechiu
B - Hokkien
C - Hakka
D - Hainanese
E - Cantonese
△ Therawada temple
▲ Mahayana temple
○ Major Chinese shrine

Scale (m.)
0   250   500

Krairoek family, held the lottery monopoly, as well as the tax farms for raw
and granulated sugar; they owned a number of sugar refineries and with
their junk fleet participated in the China trade. The Oeng lineage, forebears
of the Kalayanamit family, dominated the Hokkien junk trade from their
Kudi Chin base and toward the close of the Third Reign attained control of
the Ministry of Civil Affairs (*krom mahadthai*). Under the crown's standard
practice of awarding noble titles to its career officials and contract personnel,
the inferior status of the Taechiu merchants versus their Hokkien rivals was
apparent in the early reigns in the fewer numbers and lesser rankings of
their titles. Also indicative of their inferior standing was the near absence
of Taechiu daughters accepted as concubines by the notably polygynous
Thai aristocracy and senior nobility.

The Hokkien-Taechiu rivalry was profoundly affected by the Fourth
Reign abandonment of administered trade under British pressure to extend
competitive parity to Western firms in Siam's import-export markets.
Not only Western firms but also the Taechiu merchants were suddenly
lifted to a competitive position by that trade opening, and they took full
advantage. The free trade environment also led indirectly to the elimination
of tax farming in the Fifth Reign (1868–1910) under the direction of a
shrewd, royally favoured Hakka official, Thian *sae* Lao (Phraya Chodoek
Rachasethi, forebear of the Chotikasathian family), further undermining
the privileged Hokkien economic base. While most of the broad assortment
of farmed-out excise taxes (*phasi*) were gradually discontinued or reverted
to the state, a select group of state monopolies (*akon*) rose to prominence.
Those sinecures were auctioned off to the highest bidders, most of them
Taechiu syndicates closely associated with the secret societies. (Two major
exceptions were the South's tin mining and bird's nest monopolies, both
retained by Hokkien consortiums.) The most important of those franchises
were opium, gambling, the lottery, and spirits, which together contributed
as much as 30–40 per cent of total government revenues toward the end of
the nineteenth century, half of that from opium alone (Hong 1984, p. 127).
The monopoly profits from those highly lucrative vice-based industries
provided much of the seed money for the later Taechiu investments in
steam milling, maritime transport, banking, and property development.

Sampheng flourished under the liberalized commercial environment of
the Fourth and Fifth Reigns, though its teeming coolie underclass continued
to suffer acute deprivation. Accelerated growth in rice and timber exports
as well as consumer goods imports during the closing decades of the
nineteenth century fed a Taechiu-led investment boom most noticeable
in the proliferation of steam rice mills and sawmills, warehouses, docks,

and shipyards lining both riverbanks downstream from the urban centre (Phanni 2002, pp. 32–46). Complementing the investment boom was a continued upsurge in coolie immigration, now adding appreciable numbers of destitute Hakka, Hainanese, and Cantonese workers to the continuing Taechiu inflow, fed by the extreme poverty and repeated famines afflicting the southern Chinese seaboard provinces as the Ching dynasty lost its grip in the chaotic decades following the Taiping Rebellion (1850–1864). Taechiu immigrants flocked to Sampheng with the promise of wage labour on the docks and in the mills, drawn by the quest for good fortune in the knowledge that they would at least be among their own. But Sampheng's congested, unhygienic, disorderly conditions provided little comfort for that swarming rabble of overworked, underpaid, desolate, homesick coolies. Unfortunately, the lack of social support marking the Siamese state's policy of benign neglect was never adequately compensated by the increasingly self-serving secret societies.

By the start of the twentieth century, overcrowded Sampheng was, according to a fastidious Western observer, housing an estimated population of 200,000 in appalling circumstances:

> [The district comprises] a dense agglomeration of small wooden huts, some floating, some on piles, [swarming] in a shameless promiscuity and a filthiness without name…. [It] is a good reproduction of a city of the Middle Kingdom, with its narrow, unhealthy, twisting alleys, with its rough and slippery pavement. The alleys are only two or three meters wide; every house is a stall where mostly foods, spices, tea, tobacco and opium are displayed…. In the vicinity of the river, the quarter projects on stilts, above a miry swamp. One moves on shaky footbridges, attached to the houses with light beams. One cannot imagine a more unhealthy living environment…. [than] this quagmire, a sickening receptacle of refuse, a collection of detritus (Buls 1901, pp. 72, 86).

Given those overcrowded, unsavoury conditions it is understandable that Sampheng had, well before the turn of the century, broken its bounds, with new Taechiu neighbourhoods sprawling across the former buffer zone into the walled city and with many of the more affluent households moving to the surrounding Talat Noi and Plabphlachai neighbourhoods and cross-river into the Khlong San "suburbs".

THE TRANSITION TO ACTIVE INTERVENTION

The second half of the nineteenth century witnessed an epic struggle by the weak Siamese state against the threat of Western colonialism.

After years of circumspect deliberation, negotiation, procrastination, and concession, Siam's government in 1892 engineered a comprehensive bureaucratic reorganization aimed at meeting the West's criticisms of Siam's lingering feudalism (Mead 2004). Sampheng was not excluded from that transformation. Under the new arrangement, the district was initially divided into neighbourhoods, or communes (*tambon*), headed by local luminaries (Piyanat 1993*b*, pp. 28–29). Then, in 1895, the old "mayoral" post of Phraya Chodoek Rachasethi was transferred from the new Ministry of Foreign Affairs (*krasuang tang prathet*) to the Ministry of the Capital (*krasuang nakhonban*), exercising direct executive superintendence of several appointed district chiefs (*nai amphoe*) (Amphoe Phra Nakhon 1961). That new administrative arrangement immediately found itself in confrontation with Sampheng's secret societies. Over the following years, the municipal government sought to bring the secret societies to heel through registration requirements and strict oversight of neighbourhood leaders, community associations, and public gatherings. The district's unabating crime problem was confronted with regular police patrols and undercover surveillance, a magistrate's court, severe legal penalties including extradition, and such preventive measures as street lighting and random identity checks. A police hospital was established at the Sampheng outskirts to deal with crime victims, the rampant incidence of venereal diseases, and sporadic outbreaks of cholera, typhoid, plague, tuberculosis, and other epidemic diseases. Every brothel was required to submit to periodic inspection and publicly announce its trade by hanging a green lantern outside its front door.

The government's intervention into Sampheng's inner workings generated much resistance from the secret societies. As the state proceeded to exert its sovereignty with the centralization and professionalization of its bureaucratic apparatus, its traditional reliance on Sampheng's self-governance receded. An initial turning point came in 1889 with a forceful government response to an outbreak of gang warfare — one of a number of such instances of "Chinese rioting" — between Taechiu and Hokkien secret society lodges over the control of coolie labour at the downriver rice mills (Pasuk and Baker 2002, pp. 190, 233–34; Skinner 1957, pp. 143–45). Such internecine strife had been growing increasingly frequent and violent as the takings to be raked off from the booming export economy rose. More than a thousand gang members were involved, with twenty killed and over a hundred seriously injured. When government injunctions were ignored, a 700-man Thai military force under the command of Western officers was sent in. Several thousand purported gang members — many more than the original bands of rioters — were arrested in the government crackdown; about 900 were imprisoned, with their leaders being beheaded and most of the rest being caned and eventually released. Following a further outbreak of internecine fighting in 1895, a royal decree, the Secret Societies Act (1897), was issued requiring the registration of all Chinese association leaders, who were then placed under close observation by a special police branch.

The state's campaign to suppress the secret societies proceeded with the imposition of a series of constraints on their major revenue sources. Restrictions on pawnshop operations (closely connected with petty crime) were introduced in 1901. The opium farm was reorganized as a government department in 1908, and the spirits farm in 1909. The gambling and lottery farms were terminated in 1917. Brothels, teahouses, bars, and dance halls were placed under increasingly strict control. The free-wheeling pay-off schemes whereby the authorities were induced to turn a blind eye to infractions of the law were themselves sufficiently costly to rein in some of the excesses. Despite the government's efforts, at least thirty secret society lodges were still operating in Bangkok as of 1907, with two-thirds of them located in and around Sampheng (Piyanat 1993b, pp. 31–32). Not recognized in the government's suppression campaign were the many charitable, community-service functions that the secret societies had been sponsoring. Deprived of revenues, many of the secret societies were driven underground and otherwise weakened. To fill the social welfare vacuum left by their reduced presence, a number of new philanthropic organizations, most of them closely affiliated with or operating as sublimated versions of the old multipurpose associations, were founded — chambers of commerce, trade guilds, workers' associations, funeral societies, hospital foundations, indigents' hospices, school boards, and so forth. In a major departure from past practice, many of those new organizations came to be served by directorates involving the participation of all five of Bangkok's major Chinese dialect groups. Though the secret societies had not been fully eradicated, the old speech group rivalries had been quashed.

Quite different in intent and effect, but no less disruptive of the old order, was the government's programme to criss-cross Sampheng with a grid of metalled roads (Map 6.3). The much-publicized aim was to improve access, ventilation, sanitation, fire control, and public safety in Sampheng's cramped quarters (Piyanat 1993a, pp. 68–70; Van Roy 2006, pp. 37–44). The initial idea was to upgrade Sampheng Lane to a carriageway, but that was found impracticable; even today that ever-crowded pedestrian byway remains too narrow for any conveyance larger than a handcart or motor scooter. Instead, a broad new thoroughfare, Yaowarat Road, was laid out along a parallel course roughly halfway between Sampheng Lane and New Road. Crossing that major route were Chakrawat Road, Rachawong Road, and Yaowaphanit Road, and along the river paralleling Sampheng Lane and Yaowarat Road were Anuwong Road and Songwat Road. In all, eighteen new roads were laid out to modernize the district's transport network. But that ambitious road-building programme soon ran into difficulties. Construction of Yaowarat Road (Map 6.3), less than two kilometres long, took a decade (1891–1900) to complete and resulted in a strangely winding route to avoid the resistance of wealthy Taechiu landowners as well as the threat of mass protest by the district's slum dwellers against the expropriation of their rat-infested tenements and squalid hovels. During the initial stage of land acquisition (1892–1895), a number of smallholders transferred their property to Chinese land speculators holding extraterritorial (foreign subject) status. Exempt from the Siamese state's jurisdiction under the kingdom's trade treaties with the Western powers, those protected property owners demanded high prices for the release of their land to the state. To curtail that problem, the Ministry of the Capital prohibited local smallholders from mortgaging or selling their land to foreign subjects. A group of Sampheng residents then petitioned the king seeking "fair price" indemnity at the same rate as was being accorded to individuals holding extraterritorial protection. The Crown eventually acceded to that request, but not before serious tensions had arisen between the Sampheng citizenry and the Ministry of the Capital, preoccupied with the eviction of landowners occupying the right-of-way, and the Ministry of Public Works, struggling to complete its construction assignments by deadline (Piyanat 1993a, pp. 72–75; Van Roy 2006, pp. 30–31).

Complicating the matter was the government's policy of laying out the new roads and lanes with a right-of-way wide enough to serve as firebreaks and accommodate improved frontage. In the event, much of the expropriated frontage was acquired by the Crown Property Office (*krom phra khlang khang thi*), the royal household's investment arm, to build multi-storey rowhouses for rental purposes. The Privy Purse thus became one of Sampheng's major landlords. That added to the process of royal encroachment on Sampheng's crowded confines that had started in the Fourth Reign, following the construction of Charoen Krung Road, with the award of undeveloped roadside tracts as investment legacies to a number of princes. Considerable tumult arose in Sampheng during the 1890s–1900s over the procedure whereby expropriated land holdings designated as right-of-way for new roads ended up as crown property.

Siamese state intervention in the kingdom's Chinese affairs reached a critical juncture in 1910 following the government's decision to revise the Chinese capitation tax. Not that the government did not have ample justification for revising the tax structure. Rather, it was the ill-timed moment and provocative manner in which the decision was activated that warrants attention. The Chinese had traditionally been exempted from the *corvée*, the annual labour conscription that all able-bodied male commoners owed the state. Instead, all adult Chinese males were subject to a 4.25 baht head tax — a basic four baht tax plus a 0.25 baht administration fee — payable every three years. Upon the abolition of the *corvée* in 1899, the Thai citizenry became subject to a head tax of about six baht per year. In 1909 the government decided to eliminate the old triennial Chinese head tax and include the Chinese population under the annually payable Thai tax. That decision more than quadrupled the tax rate imposed on the Chinese, but it went unnoticed in 1909, which was the triennial year in which the Chinese had traditionally been paying the 4.25 baht tax. When the new annual six baht tax had to be paid in 1910, however, Sampheng exploded in protest (Piyanat 1993*b*, pp. 34–38; Skinner 1957, pp. 162–65). The secret societies responded to the announcement of the tax increase by organizing a general strike, the most comprehensive and widely coordinated Chinese political action in Siam to date. It closed down Sampheng and severely disrupted the broader Bangkok economy, including the city's docks, mills, and markets. Sampheng's wage earners refused to work and shopkeepers refused to open their doors, causing great inconvenience and resentment among the non-Chinese public, who found themselves unable to buy food and other household staples. After three days of turmoil, the strike was broken by military units brought in by tram to calm the situation. Anyone found to be inciting unrest was jailed, and a number of the strike leaders were deported on charges of sedition. For the first time, strident anti-Chinese sentiments were voiced among the Thai ruling elite.

In 1913, anti-Chinese vitriol intensified among the Thai elite as well as among the public-at-large following the collapse of the international rice market and its generation of a broad decline in the Thai economy (Sia 2004, pp. 8–10). Several leading members of the royal family had been enticed, during the turn-of-the-century boom years, to invest heavily in a series of speculative Chinese-led business ventures carrying promise of high returns. But in 1913 the tide turned, the firms failed, and in the aftermath blame was meted out in a fury of resentment, despite the fact that the Chinese shareholders were the biggest losers. The Siam Rice Milling Company, a consortium of thirty-four mills, had been founded in 1910 by a group of leading Bangkok-based Chinese mill-owners. The new conglomerate had quickly become Siam's largest rice exporter, accounting for 40 per cent of the kingdom's rice exports in 1912. It had joined an upstart bank (the Chino-Siam Bank) and a shipping company (the Chino-Siam Mail Shipping Company), both founded in 1908, in a concerted effort to support the efforts of Bangkok's Chinese entrepreneurs in competing effectively with the increasingly dominant Western banks, shipping lines, and agency houses. The house of cards started its tumble with a sudden drop in the rice forward-trading price on the London exchange. By mid-December 1913, all thirty-four mills participating in the Siam Rice Milling consortium had stopped buying paddy, threatening the very survival of the kingdom's agro-economy. In turn, the collapse of the Chino-Siam Bank under the weight of the scores of unsecured overdrafts it had fraudulently drawn on the royal-family-held Siam Commercial Bank sparked a broad financial crisis. A number of Bangkok's leading Chinese merchants, along with many lesser actors, were driven to bankruptcy — among them Kiang-sam Sophanodon (Luang Sophon Phecharat), son of the renowned Akon Teng (Tia U-teng), holder of extensive teak concessions and a major player in the opium farm syndicate; Thomya Rongkhawanit (Luang Chit Chamnongwanit), owner of many of the mills linked to the Siam Rice Milling consortium and heir to the Sathon development tract; Chim Phisonbut (Luang Chai Chamnan-nit), son of the royally connected Yom *sae* Lao (Luang Sathon Rachayut) and himself a rice mill owner, import export trader, and land speculator; and Yu Seng-heng (Chalong Nayanat), managing director of the Chino-Siam Bank and manager of the Domestic Department of the Siam Commercial Bank, convicted for embezzlement and sentenced to ten years in prison and loss of all his swindled wealth. The Chino-Siam Bank, Chino-Siam Mail Shipping Co., and Siam Rice Milling Company, among many lesser local firms, were swept from history (Brown 1988, pp. 136–43; Greene 1999, pp. 84–86).

In the immediate aftermath, an anonymous member of the Chotikasathien lineage (*sae* Lao), a leading Sino-Thai family badly bruised by the financial debacle, composed a wistful poem lamenting the hazards of commerce and his family's fall from grace (Anon., c.1913 (translated from Thai)):

The history of former generations *Reminds us of the whims of fortune.*
We who are alive today *As a result of past good fortune, say:*
Remember, when you fall near bankrupt, *Retaining little of former fortune,*
Stand steady on your own firm ground, *Stand not on the shifting sands of*
fortune.

It took a generation and more for some of the affected families to recover from the disaster; some never did. In the vacuum, a new circle of tycoons emerged. They were, in turn, severely affected by a series of subsequent capitalist crises as Siam tied its fate ever more firmly to the volatile global economy.

FROM ETHNICITY TO IDEOLOGY

By the end of the Fifth Reign (1910), on the eve of the Chinese Revolution (1911) and the subsequent escalation of Siam's project to assimilate its Chinese community into the emerging Thai nation-state, the composition and distribution of Bangkok's five main Chinese speech groups, totalling some 400,000 individuals, was approximately as follows (spatial distribution shown in Map 6.3; percentages based on Supang 1991, p. 21, citing National Archives, R 5 N 30/9, census of Bangkok, SK 128 (1910)):

Taechiu — 60 per cent	Centred in the Sampheng locale, with major offshoots in the "City", along Thonburi's Bang Luang Canal, and in the downriver Yan Nawa district.
Hokkien — 15 per cent	Concentrated along the west bank of the river, particularly in the Khlong San district, as well as along the east bank around the mouth of the City Moat and in the Talat Noi precinct.
Hakka — 10 per cent	Scattered along the Sampheng inland periphery (the Plabphlachai district) and in the cross-river Khlong San district.
Hainanese — 10 per cent	Divided among three distinct settlements along the Phadung Krung Kasem Canal, upstream near the mouth of the Samsen Canal, and downstream at the mouth of the Sathon Canal.
Cantonese — 5 per cent	Concentrated in central Sampheng.

Among the Chinese business elite, however, ethnic distinctions were becoming increasingly ambiguous as mercantile rivalries were being tamed through intermarriage, both among Chinese speech groups and between Chinese and other ethnic groups.

Siam's struggle to refashion itself as a Thai nation-state required that Bangkok's multiplicity of ethnic constituencies, particularly its five Chinese speech groups, be infused with a unifying sense of Thai nationalism, or patriotism. As a visceral consequence of that policy there emerged an insidious strain of Thai ultra-nationalism, nurturing "racist" sentiments

(Barmé 1993, pp. 21–34; Kasian 1997). During the Sixth Reign (1910–1925), that attitude culminated in a number of "carrot-and-stick" measures to disparage "Chinese-ness" and advance Chinese political integration and cultural assimilation into the Thai national fold; thereafter, the policy mix increasingly emphasized the "stick". The Naturalization Act of 1913 eased the path to Thai citizenship, but the Family Name Act of that same year introduced a counteracting disincentive by requiring the adoption of Thai surnames upon naturalization. The Associations Act of 1914 compelled all Chinese clubs, societies, guilds, and other organizations to desist from overtly political activity. The Private Schools Act of 1919 extended government control over the Chinese schools, requiring them to teach, at least part-time, in the Thai language and include courses in Thai history; the National Education Act of 1921 carried those regulations further (Skinner 1957, pp. 164–65; Supang 1997, pp. 235–36).

Under the Local Government Act of 1915 the administrative structure of Sampheng was further formalized with the incorporation of the Bangkok Municipality into the nationwide "*thesaphiban*" system of centralized administration (Amphoe Phra Nakhon 1961). Through that bureaucratic reorganization, Sampheng was divided among four new administrative districts (*amphoe*): Chakrawat, Samphanthawong, Sam Yaek (later dissolved), and the southern periphery of Pomprap Satruphai (later redefined as Plabphlachai). That political landscape was further fragmented with the superimposition of a patchwork of police districts (*sathani tamruat khet*) that overlapped the administrative districts. The affect, as evidently intended, was to dismember the community's organic integrity. Sampheng's political standing was reduced a further notch in 1922 with the downgrading of the Bangkok Municipality from ministerial autonomy to departmental status within the Ministry of Interior. With those adjustments, it was expected that Bangkok's "Chinese problem" would be effectively delinked from Sampheng. In other words, the government sought, through its administrative fragmentation of Siam's chief Chinese commercial, political, and demographic centre, to assert effective control over Chinese public affairs throughout the kingdom.

A related spate of relatively draconian legal reforms aimed at the Chinese were enacted in 1927–1928, including revisions of the Criminal Act, Military Criminal Act, Printing Act, Immigration Act, and Private Schools Act, and the imposition of more stringent controls on the establishment and activities of Chinese associations of all sorts. Following the Revolution of 1932 and particularly during the chauvinistic decade following 1938, the rising tide of Thai xenophobia prompted efforts to eradicate Chinese schools, newspapers, secret societies, and remittance agencies. A number of Chinese community leaders and political activists were arrested and deported; highly restrictive quotas were set on Chinese immigration; a variety of petty trades and semi-skilled occupations were reserved for Thai nationals; Chinese signboards were required to be rewritten in Thai, with any accompanying Chinese text to be of small size; Chinese economic dominance in the domestic wholesale, food processing, and import-export trades was countered with the establishment of several state-owned trading companies operating under advantageous competitive conditions (Pasuk and Baker 2002, pp. 122–23, 275–76; Skinner 1957, pp. 261–72; Supang 1997, pp. 240–43; Stowe 1991, pp. 118–20, 132–33). In the presence of that flood of discriminatory measures, the only options left to those Chinese unwilling to adopt Thai citizenship were to suffer increasing marginalization or sell out and depart. Nor was Thai citizenship a particularly viable option, as those who accepted naturalization continued to suffer arbitrary harassment.

However, that series of increasingly restrictive measures did not occur in a vacuum. The rise of Thai nationalism was paralleled — some would say incited — by a countervailing process on the Chinese side. During the closing decades of the nineteenth century the long-standing populist movement against China's Ching dynasty had modulated into a more coordinated campaign to replace the Ching empire with a republican nation-state. Sun Yat-sen, a charismatic leader of that nationalist revolt and hero of the secret societies, visited Sampheng four times during his travels to mobilize overseas Chinese political and financial support for his cause (Sia 2004, pp. 6–11; Van Roy 2007a, pp. 137–45). During his 1908 Sampheng visit he gave a stirring public address on behalf of the revolution, so well remembered years later that the site of the speech came to be known in the Taechiu dialect as the Oration Intersection, with a memorial arch being erected nearby in later years. Thai government concern over the influence of that revolutionist agitator prompted the close monitoring of his subsequent visit in 1910 and restricted him to private meetings with local businessmen and intellectuals on an individual basis only. King Chulalongkorn assigned the Crown Prince (soon to be elevated to King Rama VI) to personally oversee Sun's surveillance and requested that he seek to expedite his departure; he met with him secretly in person to affect that end. The government's subsequent plethora of policies aimed at controlling Siam's Chinese community can be traced back to Prince Wachirawut's hostile opinion of that anti-royalist firebrand and his generally negative impression of the local Chinese politics surrounding Sun's four Bangkok visits (Sia 2004, pp. 6–15).

The moment of truth for Bangkok's Chinese residents came in 1911 with the overthrow of the Ching dynasty and proclamation of a Chinese Republic, with Sun Yat-sen proclaimed its first president. In an outburst of popular enthusiasm for the Chinese Revolution, Sampheng's male population cut off their queues, formerly a proud emblem of their Chineseness, now a detested symbol of the *ancien régime* (Kasian 1992). The new Republic of China received unfettered support from all elements of Bangkok's Chinese community, irrespective of class, vocation, or ethnicity. The surging spirit of Chinese nationalism marking those transitional years brought together Bangkok's formerly feuding Chinese speech groups to form a broad-ranging assortment of multi-ethnic public service associations. Most notable among them was the Chinese Chamber of Commerce (founded 1908), headquartered in a fine mansion along South Sathon Road, some 3.5 kilometres across town from Sampheng. That major new institution, representing Bangkok's unified Chinese business community, symbolized the end of the traditional Hokkien-Taechiu rivalry. Other important examples of the new attitude transcending the old speech-group insularity were the Tian Fa Hospital (1906), Po Tek Toeng Charity Foundation (initially founded as the Tai Hong Kong Association, 1911), Rice Merchants' Association (1919), and Pey Ing School (1920) (Van Roy 2007*a*, pp. 55–68, 183–92, 226–29).

As the political situation in China fragmented into regional warlordism during the 1920s, Chinese nationalism within Bangkok's Chinese community divided between the Kuomintang and Communist causes. Japanese aggression against China, culminating in 1937 in the Sino-Japanese War, furnished only a brief unifying respite between those perennially warring camps (Sia 2004, pp. 41–87). Even within the Chinese Chamber of Commerce, the quasi-official voice of Bangkok's now ethnically non-partisan Chinese community, ideological factions became increasingly apparent, with the chairmanship swinging between the pro-Kuomintang faction led by Tan Siu-meng and the pro-Communist wing led by Hia Kwong-iam. Hia Kwong-iam (1879–1939, founder of the Iamsuri lineage) was a first-generation Taechiu immigrant, a self-made man who rose meteorically from coolie to labour organizer to shipping tycoon, in the process developing close secret society ties. Along the way he served as a leader of Sampheng's politically roused youth and organizer of Sampheng's boycotts against Japanese trade. In 1936 he was elected chairman of the Chinese Chamber of Commerce and was still holding that position in November 1939 when he was gunned down on Yaowarat Road by an unknown hand (Amphon 2005; Murashima 1996, pp. 38–42,

125–27, 137–38, 187–89). By contrast, Tan Siu-meng (1904–1945, Wang Lee lineage), fifth-generation scion of a leading Bangkok Taechiu family, inherited a thriving rice milling, maritime transport, banking, and insurance empire. He served as chairman of the Chinese Chamber of Commerce from 1932 to 1936 and was again appointed to that position in 1942. During the course of the Sino-Japanese War (1937–1945) he served as Thai government representative to the several contending Chinese governments, including the pro-Japanese Nanking regime, for the negotiation of rice export contracts. In August 1945, on the day after Japan's capitulation, while still serving as chairman of the Chinese Chamber of Commerce, he was murdered by unknown assailants in front of his office on Captain Bush Lane, Bang Rak District (Chamnongsi 1998, pp. 175–201; Murashima 1996, pp. 29–46). The strangely parallel careers and tragically paired deaths of those two rival Taechiu business leaders form a remarkable parable of Sampheng's transformation from ethnic solidarity to ideological factionalism.

Closure was brought to this period of contending nationalisms in 1949 with the Chinese Communist victory on the mainland and the Chinese Nationalist flight to Taiwan. Mainland China's ensuing decades of self-imposed international isolation, prohibiting emigration and home visits, disallowing remittance inflows, and disdaining foreign aid, virtually cut off contact between Bangkok's Chinese residents and their mainland China kin. In Sampheng, the old dream of temporary overseas sojourn, of making one's fortune in Siam/Thailand and eventually returning to the ancestral homeland in blissful retirement or at least for honourable burial, withered away (Coughlin 1960, pp. 199–202). Nothing could have provided more compelling encouragement to the accelerated political naturalization and cultural assimilation of Thailand's overseas Chinese, as well as the easing of formal restrictions on the local Chinese community. So it is that a close observer of Thailand's Chinese community can remark that "most of the Siamese-Chinese of the mid-twentieth century have ... become Thai citizens, and the appropriate term for them should [today] be 'Thais of Chinese descent'" (Supang 1997, p. 254), while another states that "the large majority of Thai Chinese are [today] Sino-Thai and their fierce loyalty to the social [and political] structure in which they have a large stake is not doubted" (Wang 1991, p. 296). That process of Chinese assimilative diffusion has been paralleled nationwide; in fact, a national-level regional-systems model points to the catalytic role of the "Chinese as agents of Thailand's national integration during the latter two-thirds of the twentieth century" (Montesano 2005). With Siam's inexorable modernization, the assimilation

— or at least integration, suggesting the retention of a residual strain of ethnic self-awareness — of Bangkok's Chinese community into the Thai national mainstream proceeds apace (Supang 1997; Wanwipa 2001). With that process well underway, the terms "Thais of Chinese descent" and "Sino-Thai" have become graphic references to the discernible waning of the old speech-group affiliations within the ideological melting pot of Thai nationalism.

7

Along the Margins:
Some Other Minorities

urther to the ethnohistories of Old Bangkok's five major minority groups presented in the preceding chapters, this chapter deals with five of the city's smaller ethnic communities. Those groups — Khmer, Vietnamese, Thai Yuan, Sikh, and *farang* (Westerners) — are given relatively brief attention here because they constituted an often-peripheral presence, in terms of both their small numbers and physical location, and in most cases — with the notable exception of the *farang* — because we lack much essential historical information about them. Together, those five ethnic groups as of 1910 are estimated to have accounted for no more than 20,000 — 2.5 per cent — of Bangkok's total resident population of 800,000: 10,000 Khmer; 7,000 Vietnamese; 2,000 *farang*; and fewer than 1,000 Thai Yuan and Sikhs (Tables 1.3 and 1.5). Other than the Khmer, the bulk of those groups arrived on the scene relatively late. Nevertheless, each enriched the city's political, economic, and cultural evolution in ways that can still be observed today. They established new neighbourhoods and stretched the city bounds, introduced new products and handiworks into the urban market, enhanced the capital's cosmopolitan pluralism, and linked its destiny more intimately to distant lands and cultures. This chapter presents capsule biographies of those five marginal minorities, referring in particular to their origins, residential assignments, political positions, social status, economic specializations, and cultural legacies, as an auxiliary contribution to Old Bangkok's broader ethnohistory.

Khmer

Thai-Khmer relations at both the capital of Ayutthaya and later at Thonburi/
Bangkok proceeded along parallel lines — connections between the
Thai and Khmer ruling elites, and Thai dealings with Khmer commoner
communities. Repeated Siamese military incursions into Cambodia date
back to well before the climactic conquest of Angkor in 1431 (Wyatt 1984,
pp. 68–70). That Thai triumph and many further armed expeditions into
Cambodia over the following centuries carried off large numbers of Khmer
captives into Siamese territory. Select groups of captured commoners
were assigned to the outskirts of Ayutthaya to farm premium rice for the
royal granaries, and some of those war captives (or their descendants)
in turn fled the Burmese attack of 1767 to end up at Thonburi. At the
same time, the eighteenth century was a particularly dark period within
Cambodia, a time of recurring turmoil, bloodshed, and devastation that
saw frequent reign changes (Chandler 2000, pp. 94–97). Repeatedly, the
ousted royal family and its noble entourage turned to Ayutthaya as refuge
and sponsor of their efforts at reinstatement. Under those circumstances, a
substantial Khmer exile circle grew at the court of Ayutthaya, accompanied
by an influx of Khmer royal language, custom, patron-client networks,
and intermarriage. That royal tradition was carried over into Thonburi/
Bangkok, where a dual Khmer commoner and Khmer elite presence was
discernible from the outset.

Ban Klang Na (Village Amidst the Rice Fields)
Among the scattering of refugees finding their way to shelter at Thonburi
in the wake of the Ayutthaya disaster of 1767 was a dispossessed Khmer
peasant rabble. No information survives on their numbers, but most likely
they were, like the disparate groups of Lao, Mon, and Malay refugees
arriving at Thonburi, a tiny remnant of Ayutthaya's sizeable population
of war captives, who had long made the old capital's agrarian hinterlands
their home in forced exile. At Thonburi they were assigned a settlement site
(Ban Klang Na) along the left bank of the river directly downstream from
Bang Lamphu (see Chapter 5, section on "Malay Captives: The First and
Second Reigns"), with their rice fields behind, the village temple carrying
the name Wat Klang Na (Temple Amidst the Rice Fields (Map 7.1, site 3),
later rebuilt as Wat Chana Songkhram). Some years later, after the 1782
Chakri coup, they were evicted from that prime riverside tract to make
way for the installation of Chaophraya Mahayotha (Cheng) and his Mon
militiamen, a company of Front Palace partisans under whose tenure the

MAP 7.1
Bangkok: Major Khmer sites, 1782–1910

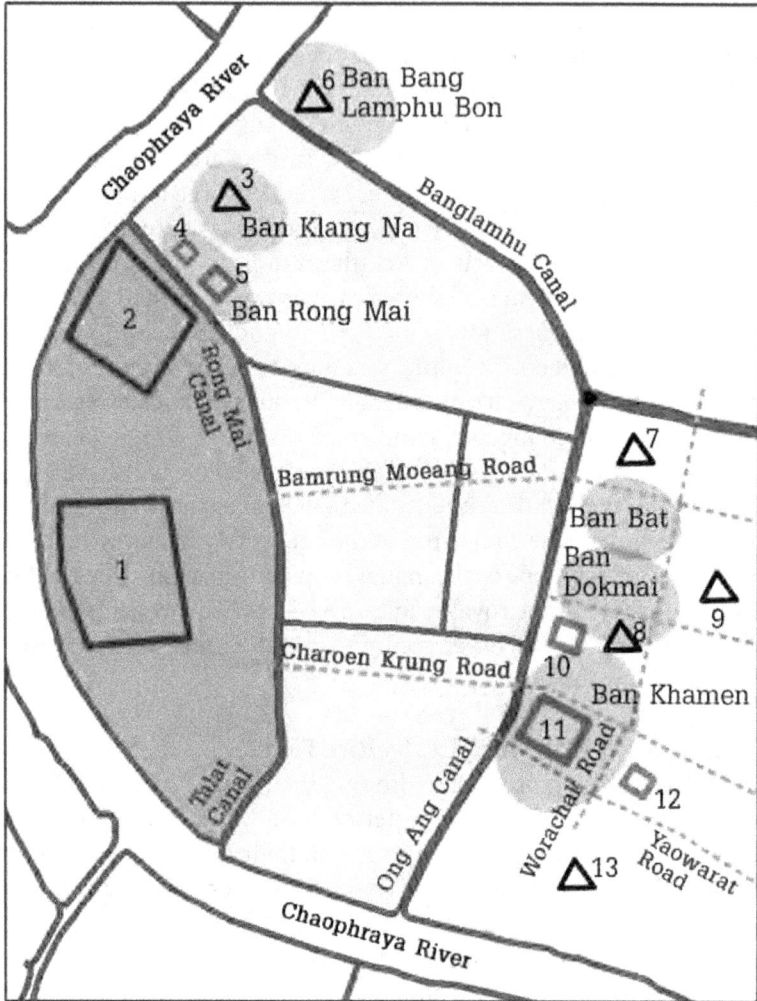

1. Grand Palace
2. Front Palace
3. Wat Klang Na
4. Silk Sheds
5. Prince Eng Palace
6. Wat Bang Lamphu
7. Wat Saket

8. Wat Phra Phiren
9. Wat Changwang Dit
10. Wang Chao Khamen
11. Woeng Nakhon Kasem
12. Chaophraya Bodin Decha res.
13. Wat Samploem

site became known as Ban Phra Athit (after a nearby Front Palace bastion) (see Chapter 3, subsection on "Ban Phra Athit").

The Khmer refugees evicted from Ban Klang Na were assigned a new settlement site adjacent to Wat Saket (Map 7.1, site 2), outside the city wall along the eastern segment of Bangkok's newly dug City Moat. There they joined the contingents of Khmer war captives who had recently been conscripted to help dig the moat and erect a number of the city's other prominent lineaments (see "Ban Khamen" below). The displaced Ban Klang Na settlers were apparently the founders of Ban Bat (Alms Bowl Village), they or their descendants taking up the fashioning of monks' alms bowls as their communal occupation, having lost their rice fields and lacking new ones in the inhospitable marshlands east of the walled city.

The Khmer Royal Presence at the Front Palace

During the eighteenth century, Siam's ancient adversarial relationship with Cambodia was set on a new, more complicated course with Vietnam's efforts to extend its control over Cambodia from the east. After decades of sporadic skirmishing between the two aggressor states, a dynastic crisis was provoked in 1779 with the assassination of Cambodia's Thai-backed King Rama Racha (Non) and his sons by Vietnamese partisans, and their replacement by a Vietnamese-backed regent (Thipakorawong 2009a, pp. 31–33; Chitrasing 2009, pp. 127–65). Siam responded with a major military intervention led by Taksin's senior commanders, Generals Chakri (Thong-duang) and Surasi (Bunma). They took into custody the principal pretender to the throne, Prince Eng (age six, son of the former King Narai Racha, Rama Racha's predecessor), his mother (Dowager-Queen Maen) and three sisters (Princesses Ang, Ee, and Phao), and their sizeable entourage of retainers. All of them were carried off to Bangkok by General Surasi (now raised to Prince Surasinghanat, the First Reign viceroy) upon his return from the Cambodia campaign in mid-1782 (Manich 2001, pp. 69–70). The exiled Cambodian royal household received sanctuary in Bangkok's Front Palace under the viceroy's patronage, with their entourage being consigned to a settlement site named Ban Rong Mai (discussed in the following subsection), located in the noble quarter directly across the Inner City Moat. The viceroy accepted Eng's three sisters as his concubines, and over the ensuing years he fathered by them four daughters.

Upon puberty (c.1783), Eng, as required by ancient custom, left his mother's side within the Front Palace and moved to a new royal residence (Map 7.1, site 5) at Sanam Kraboe (the Buffalo Meadows) alongside Ban Rong Mai. Then, in 1786, King Rama I awarded him a more elaborate palace, later known as Wang Chao Khamen (The Khmer Royal Palace), in the Khmer settlement zone along the outer perimeter of the City Moat (Thipakorawong 2009a, p. 96). The First Reign king and viceroy continued to sponsor his struggle for the Cambodian throne, and with their support he finally secured the throne at Udong, the Cambodian capital, in 1794 as King Narai Rama. With his death soon thereafter, in 1796, the Siamese-Vietnamese struggle for Cambodian suzerainty was reignited. In keeping with the Thai royal-hostage tradition, Eng's mother and sisters and their retainers had stayed behind at Bangkok, and after his death they remained in Bangkok exile for the rest of their lives.

Ban Rong Mai (Silk Sheds Village) and Bang Lamphu Bon (Upper Willow Tree Village)

Accompanying the exile Khmer royal family was a sizeable entourage of nobles, lesser functionaries, household servants, artisans, foot soldiers, and their dependants. The whole of that contingent was split spatially between royalty, nobility, and commons in accordance with the mandala template that defined the Bangkok cityscape (and that was a fundament of Khmer culture as well). While the royal household was accommodated within the Bangkok citadel's Front Palace, the bulk of their retainers were provided quarters outside the citadel — the nobility at Ban Rong Mai in the precincts across the Inner City Moat directly north of the Front Palace, and the commons in an extramural tract further north, directly across the City Moat from Bang Lamphu, a settlement that came to be known as Bang Lamphu Bon (Upper Bang Lamphu) (Map 7.1). There, early in the first Reign, they built Wat Bang Lamphu (rebuilt some eight decades later as Wat Sangwet) (Map 7.1, site 6), which served for the remainder of the First Reign as Bangkok's principal Khmer communal cremation site, highlighted in due course by the funerals of Cambodia's dowager queen and other members of the exiled Cambodian royal family and nobility.

The stretch of the Inner City Moat directly north of the Front Palace, separating the walled city's noble precinct from the citadel, was called the Rong Mai Canal (Silk Sheds Canal). Alongside it were situated the Front Palace's textile manufactories (Map 7.1, site 4), simple thatch-roofed structures providing shade for the handlooms that produced the colourful, graceful silk sarongs and breast cloths that were the royal women's aristocratic perquisite. Silk spinning, dying, and weaving were skills in which many elite Khmer women, like their Lao counterparts, excelled. Ban Rong Mai, the adjoining Khmer noble settlement, provided the Front Palace weavers and their families social connectivity and shelter. (A parallel

Grand Palace textile production facility stood along the Inner City Moat further downstream, on the site of the later Ministry of War, apparently staffed by Lao silk weavers.)

Upon Thai-Vietnamese rapprochement, followed by the attainment of Prince Eng's majority in 1794, Eng and his retainers were permitted to return to Cambodia for his coronation as King Narai Racha. The reduced tract along the Inner City Moat that had housed the Khmer nobility at Ban Rong Mai was then infiltrated by a line of viceroys' sons' palaces and Thai nobles' mansions, though enough of the weavers stayed on at Ban Rong Mai to ensure the survival of the Front Palace silk textile industry. The Khmer settlement at Bang Lamphu Bon also declined. In later years, the leftovers, no longer playing a supportive role for the Khmer royals at the Front Palace, moved to the growing Khmer precinct of Ban Khamen along the east bank of the City Moat (Map 7.1).

Ban Khamen

Large numbers of Khmer war captives were in mid-1782 carried off to Siam by Bunma (the former Chaophraya Surasi), the newly appointed but not yet installed First Reign viceroy, upon his return from the Thai invasion of Cambodia following the 1779 assassination of King Rama Racha (Non). A reported 10,000 of those captives — likely a sizeable exaggeration — were force-marched on to Bangkok to serve as manual labour in the construction of Bangkok's City Moat and other key urban features (Thipakorawong 2009a, pp. 59–60). They were assigned residential quarters along what would become the eastern perimeter of the City Moat (later known as the Ong Ang Canal). That Khmer village was joined in 1786 by Wang Chao Khamen (Prince Eng's new palace), and then by Ban Bat (Alms Bowl Village) and Ban Dokmai (or Ban Tham Dokmai Phloeng, Fireworks Producing Village) (Map 7.1). Together, those settlements came to be known as Ban Khamen (the Khmer Village[s]). A notable occupation taken up by the Ban Khamen villagers was the staging of dance drama performances (*lakhon*), featuring epic recitations accompanied by acrobatic ballet, song, and instrumental music requiring life-long training and the production of elaborate dance masks, costumes, and musical instruments. Equally well known were the Khmer settlers' religiously affiliated vocations, including the production of monastic goods (including alms bowls), funerary paraphernalia (particularly fireworks), spiritual charms (mystical symbols inscribed on cloths, on votive tablets, as tattoos, and on sundry other receptive surfaces), and the shamanistic practice of black magic (*mon dam*), centred at Wat Phra Phiren (also referred to as Wat Ban Khamen) (Map 7.1, site 8), later joined by

Wat Changwang Dit (Map 7.1, site 9). The occult powers (*saksit, sayasat*) practised by Khmer shamans (*mo phi*) were as much sought after as they were feared by the Bangkok Thai (McDaniel 2011, p. 35), and they thus played an aggravating role in the social tensions that perennially roiled relations between the Thai and Khmer commoner communities. Or, it could be argued in reverse, the Thai stigmatized their Khmer neighbours with the charge of supernatural malice as a means of social distancing; "In the minds of many Buddhists in central Thailand …. 'Khmer' often has negative connotations connected to black magic" (McDaniel 2011, p. 35).

Ban Khamen's reputation rose significantly in the 1840s, toward the end of the Thai-Vietnamese War, with the arrival of some of the many war captives carried off to Siam by the Third Reign's leading military commander, Chaophraya Bodin Decha (Sing, minister of civil affairs), whose residence (Map 7.1, site 12) stood directly behind Ban Khamen, as if to watch over it. Among those he brought into Bangkok exile was the pretender to Cambodia's throne, Prince Duang (who was elevated to King-in-Exile Harirak Rama soon after his arrival in 1841) and his two senior sons, Princes Rachawat (later King Norodom) and Sisawat (later King Harirak). For their Bangkok residence they were provided a fine compound including a handsome brick mansion (Map 7.1, site 10) replacing the crumbling teak First Reign Wang Chao Khamen (Khmer Palace) nearby but retaining the old name. The new Wang Chao Khamen quickly became the Khmer community's social and cultural centre, reflecting the patron-client bonds of the Khmer social hierarchy just like those fusing the Thai system. Though King Harirak Rama (Duang) returned to Cambodia to reign at Udong in 1848, his sons remained behind at Wang Chao Khamen as royal hostages to continue Bangkok's Khmer royal presence until 1858 (Thipakorawong 2009*b*, pp. 131–33; Manich 2001, p. 147). Thereafter, following the two princes' return to Cambodia, the Khmer royal presence at Bangkok waned with their replacement by lesser Khmer royals. The conversion of Cambodia to a French protectorate in 1863 proved to be the final undoing of Wang Chao Khamen as a home for Khmer royalty in exile and started a swift decline of Ban Khamen toward privation and cultural degradation. The downturn was reinforced by the reduced demand for the traditional Khmer arts and crafts that accompanied Bangkok's modernization. By the turn of the century, the entire moat-side stretch of Khmer neighbourhoods reaching from Bamrung Moeang Road to Charoen Krung Road had become a sprawling slum rather dismissively referred to as Yan Khamen (the Khmer District). Its spatial spread — the range of Khmer habitation, intensive Khmer social networking, and Khmer self-administration — extended along the outer reaches of the City Moat from Wat Saket on the one side (Map 7.1, site 7) to Wat Samploem on the other (Map 7.1, site 13), reaching eastward toward Sampheng behind.

Action was taken during Bangkok's turn-of-the-century street-building boom to splinter Yan Khamen with the cut-throughs of Worachak Road (1898), Yaowarat Road (1900), and Luang Road (c.1904), accompanied by land expropriation for right-of-way and commercial construction. With royal backing, the heart of the Khmer community alongside the former Khmer Palace was replaced by a commercial project known as Woeng Nakhon Kasem (the Happy City Clearing) (Map 7.1, site 11), founded c.1910 in the wake of a fire that had ravaged — i.e., fortuitously "cleared" — the local slum. The area was redeveloped as a grid of Chinese shophouse-lined lanes that gained popularity for its kitchenware, household furnishings, artifacts and curios, and second-hand (i.e., stolen) merchandise. In a further adverse allusion to the locality, Bangkok's *farang* community came to refer to that shopping area as the "Thieves' Market". As the butt of all that negative attention, much of the local Khmer population found it expedient to assimilate into the Thai cultural mainstream. Such steps were evidently considered by them to be less traumatic than continued ethnic rigidity in the face of Thai social hostility. As the twentieth century wore on, the Khmer character of the area thus melted into the broader Bangkok scene, accompanied by a gathering Taechiu mercantile intrusion. Today, scarcely a trace is left of the former Khmer presence, except for a continuing link between Wat Phra Phiren, shamanism, and the tradition of dance mask production, as well as a network of tenement-lined alleys following the contours of the former Wang Chao Khamen.

VIETNAMESE

Central and southern Vietnam, with Hué as the capital and a budding Saigon seaport, was by the late eighteenth century generally known as Annam. However, the people were generally referred to by the Thai as "Yuan" — apparently, it has been suggested, because an early Thai mapmaker had confused Annam's location with "Yonok", an ancient name for the Thai North's Lan Na region, home of the Thai Yuan (Surachit 2002, p. 106). Thai interaction with Vietnam's southward spreading "Yuan" increased from the seventeenth century on, waxing and waning with the escalating competition between Siam and Vietnam for economic and political hegemony over the lower Mekong River basin (Li 2004). That confrontation first simmered during Cambodia's dynastic turmoil of the seventeenth–eighteenth centuries, then boiled over upon the Siamese invasion of Cambodia in 1779–1780, and finally exploded with the Siamese-Vietnamese war of 1831–1841. In each of those cases Siam received Vietnamese refugees as well as a far greater number of Vietnamese war prisoners (while also losing many of its own troops), with a direct impact on Bangkok's multi-ethnic cityscape.

Ban Yuan (Pak Khlong Talat)

During 1777–1778, Vietnam's Tay Son peasant rebellion against the Nguyen overlords overran the Mekong Delta. In the process, they forced the evacuation of Hatien (or Ha Tien), a trade-based city-state situated along the Vietnam-Cambodia coastal boundary in the lee of the Ca Mau Peninsula. Mac Thien-tu, the Cantonese-Vietnamese ruler of that principality, escaped by sea with his followers to Thonburi, where they formed an additional minority group among the capital's growing ethnic diversity (Sellers 1983, p. 75; Sakurai and Takako 1999, p. 204). They arrived at the start of 1778 on a flotilla of crowded junks and were assigned a settlement site along the east bank of the river directly downstream from the "East Thonburi" wall and moat, at Pak Khlong Talat (Mouth of the Market Canal). There, with their small junk fleet, they gradually built up an import-export base in weak competition with Thonburi's well-established Hokkien and Taechiu merchant communities.

King Taksin awarded Mac Thien-tu the rank and title of Phraya Rachasethi Yuan, with the promise of eventual reinstatement over his former domain. In return, Mac presented one of his daughters in concubinage to Taksin, establishing firm patron-client bonds with the Siamese throne. He was accordingly presented a nobleman's residence (Map 7.4, site 1) alongside Wat Pho (later rebuilt as Wat Phra Chetuphon), within the walled precinct of "East Thonburi" directly across the river from the Thonburi Grand Palace. (Generations later, during the 1860s, a stretch of boatyards fronting Mac Thien-tu's former residence burned down, leading to that riverside tract being referred to by the Thai term "Tha Tien" (Cleared Landing); that term is today commonly misunderstood as a play on "Ha Tien," supporting the specious claim that the entire Vietnamese exile community was situated within the city wall (contradicting the city's mandala principles), directly across the river from Taksin's palace.) In 1780, Mac Thien-tu committed suicide while thirty-six family members and seventeen of his senior officers were executed by order of King Taksin on charges of collaboration in a suspected Tay Son plot against Thonburi (Sellers 1983, pp. 81–83; Sakurai and Takako 1999, p. 205). But the remainder of the Vietnamese community was reprieved from punishment and allowed to stay on. During the First

Reign the community's new leader, Phraya Phakdi Nuchit (Ong Wang-tai, or Ong Toeng) solidified relations with his Thai overlords by presenting his daughter Chui in concubinage to Rama I. She bore Prince Wasukri (1790–1853), who chose the monkhood as his life's vocation and ultimately rose to the exalted rank and title of Somdet Phra Parama Nuchit Chinorot, abbot of Wat Phra Chetuphon and supreme patriarch of the Thai Buddhist monastic order. In the Second and Third Reigns, Chui attained the senior Grand Palace rank and title of Thaw Songkandan, with the function of overseeing the king's personal treasury (*phra khlang nai*). So the local Vietnamese connection to the Siamese throne continued.

The village at the mouth of the Market Canal grew over the subsequent years with the arrival of additional Cantonese-Vietnamese refugees. It long demonstrated its ethnicity through its religious institutions as well as its artisanal traditions. From the start it was marked by a Daoist shrine (today known as Sanchao Ban Mo, dedicated to the deity Pun Thao Kong, with the later addition of Kwan U) (Map 7.4, site 2) and a Mahayana Buddhist temple (Wat Sam Lo Thoen, or Wat Kham Lo Yi) (Map 7.4, site 3) practising Vietnamese rites. The temple was abandoned in the Third Reign and then re-established in the Fifth Reign as Wat Thipawari, a Chinese rites Mahayana temple serving the Taechiu community that dominates the area today. The transformation of that shrine and temple from Vietnamese to Chinese cult status reflects the incursion of Taechiu tradesmen into the neighbourhood in the later decades of the nineteenth century with the opening up of the old city to commercialization. In the same period, the community's Cantonese-Vietnamese craftsmen developed specialties in such decorative arts as mother-of-pearl inlay, niello glazing, glass making, and jade and ivory carving. Early in the Fifth Reign, Prince Worachak Tharanuphap (Pramot, 1817–1872) became patron of the community's artisans in his capacity as royal overseer of the Mirrorers Department (*krom chang kloeap*), Glassmakers Department (*krom krachok*), and Jade Carvers Department (*krom yuan yok*). Confirming that artisans' tradition, the government early in the twentieth century established in the neighbourhood a celebrated Arts and Crafts School (the Pho Chang School, (Map 7.4, site 4)). With that school setting the local tone, the neighbourhood survives today as a centre of Bangkok's Sino-Thai jewelry and gems trade.

Ban Yuan (Ton Samrong)

An aspirant to the throne of Annam, Prince Nguyen Anh (referred to in the Thai annals as Prince Chiang-soe), was in 1785/86 cornered by the Tayson rebels on a remote island off Vietnam's Ca Mau Peninsula.

Through the intervention of Catholic missionary priests, he received sanctuary for himself and his retinue of fighting men at Bangkok. The only information on the numbers in his party is that they filled five Chinese junks (a large seafaring junk has a capacity of over 100 passengers). King Rama I provided him with residential quarters at Ban Yuan (Pak Khlong Talat) but assigned his troops an isolated riverside tract about three kilometres downstream, below the Portuguese settlement at Rosario (also known as Ton Samrong), occupying the approximate site of the later Portuguese consulate (Map 7.3, site 9; Thipakorawong 2009a, pp. 40–41; Sakurai and Takako 2002, p. 263). In gratitude, Prince Nguyen Anh presented his sister as a consort to King Rama I. Though a favoured royal concubine, she bore no children.

Abandoning his troops to their fate, Nguyen Anh slipped away on a Chinese trading vessel a year later (1786) to return to the Vietnamese civil war. In so doing, he flouted the customary protocol for leave-taking of his host, earning him fierce opprobrium from the First Reign viceroy and many others. But Rama I took no retaliatory action. Instead, he moved the stranded Vietnamese troops to a more secure site at Bang Pho, about eleven kilometres upstream from the Bangkok citadel, and included them in his military forces. The Vietnamese princess-concubine continued to represent Nguyen Anh's deserted men at court and sponsored the construction of a Vietnamese Mahayana Buddhist temple for them at Bang Pho. Nguyen Anh himself eventually went on to vanquish the Tayson rebels, unite Vietnam, and proclaim himself Emperor Gia Long, first reign of a rejuvenated Nguyen dynasty, apparently with no further thought to his lost Bangkok-based regiment.

Ban Yuan (Bang Pho)

The Chakri kings had great confidence in the fighting skills of their Vietnamese regiment quartered at Bang Pho, but those soldiers appear to have been sparingly used. For fear of their defection in battle against their countrymen, they were not deployed in the Thai-Vietnamese wars of 1831–1845, nor did they see active service in Siam's Southern expeditions of the 1830s. Thus, the community's military role withered, and the men turned to the supplementary occupations of timber dealing and manual sawmilling, and then steam-powered rice milling and sawmilling in the late nineteenth century. In the late twentieth century, several of those old sawmills, fully refurbished, were still operating along the river at Bang Pho. Further defining the settlement's integrity was Wat Annam Nikayaram, founded in 1787 under the patronage of Nguyen Anh's sister, the First Reign concubine (Poole 1970, p. 32, ft. 3). Though the local community has over the generations been thoroughly integrated into the Thai national mainstream, that temple remains today a remarkable example of the persistence of Vietnamese identity along Bangkok's urban fringe, advertising its ethnic roots in its Vietnamese rooflines, prominent Vietnamese calligraphy, statuary of Vietnamese military heroes, numerous miniature-pagoda-marked burial plots representing the Vietnamese Buddhist preference for interment over cremation, and local denizens eager to expound on the community's Vietnamese roots.

Ban Yuan (Samsen)

The mounting Siamese-Vietnamese rivalry in Cambodia culminated in a protracted conflict lasting from 1831 to 1841, settled by treaty in 1845 (Vella 1955*b*, pp. 95–106; Chitrasing 2009, pp. 185–89). In the course of that war, some 15,000 captured Vietnamese troops were carried off to Siam from the Cambodian battlefields by Siam's great military commander, Chaophraya Bodin Decha (Sing). Most of them were relegated to the remote frontier province of Kanchanaburi, ostensibly to help guard Siam's western border. With the war well behind them and a new king of Siam installed in 1851, one of the captive contingents, said to consist of about 500 artillerymen, 300 of them Mahayana Buddhists and the other 200 Roman Catholic converts (though that may be a gross underestimate, especially if their dependants are counted in), petitioned the Thai court for an end to their nearly two-decades purgatory. King Mongkut took pity and agreed to resettle them along the Bangkok outskirts. The Catholic soldiers and the many dependants they had accumulated over the course of their exile were assigned a settlement site at Samsen, alongside the well-established Catholic community of Ban Portuket (Pallegoix 2000, pp. 407–408; see Chapter 2, subsection on "Ban Portuket (Samsen)"). There they were placed under the patronage of Phra Pin Klao, the Fourth Reign viceroy. Their leader was awarded the rank and title of Phraya Narong Rithikosa in the Front Palace Artillery Corps (*krom poen yai wang na*).

Despite their religious commonality, the differing languages and everyday customs of the neighbouring Portuguese and Vietnamese at Samsen prevented them from forming a unified Catholic parish. So the Vietnamese erected a new church on the site of Wat Somkliang, an old, abandoned Mon temple. King Mongkut's discovery that the Catholic Vietnamese had demolished that temple and desecrated its sanctified bounds occasioned a fierce royal reprimand (Pussadee 1998, pp. 131–37). Phra Pin Klao was held responsible and was ordered to replace Wat Somkliang with a new temple alongside (Wat Rachaphat, established around 1857), contributing to the deepening rift between the two royal brothers, king and viceroy, that ultimately led to the abolition of the viceroy's post some two decades later. In any case, the Vietnamese settlers established the St. Francis Xavier Church and cemetery (both founded around 1863) as their community's hallmarks, and there they still stand. Further demonstrating their ethnic pride, the Catholic Vietnamese settlers at Samsen adapted to Thailand "in a way that was almost exactly opposite to that of the eighteenth-century [Vietnamese] Buddhist immigrants [at Bang Pho; they did not allow] their children to marry non-Vietnamese, and many still [as of the 1960s] use the Vietnamese language among themselves and in religious worship" (Poole 1970, p. 28).

Ban Yuan (Saphan Khaw)

The approximately 300 Buddhist members of the captive Vietnamese artillerymen's Kanchanaburi contingent were around 1854 settled under the king's patronage along the outer bank of the newly dug "Outer City Moat" (the Phadung Krung Kasem Canal), near the soon-to-be-built Wat Somanat. There they founded Wat Saman Annam Borihan (Temple Attended by Annamese Commoners) as their community centre. Their leader was awarded the rank and title of Luang Annam Nikonrit, captain in the Grand Palace Artillery Corps (*krom poen yai*). With their military duties defunct in the warless years of the Fourth and Fifth Reigns (after Siam's disastrous Kengtung expedition of 1852–1854), Luang Annam led his fellow villagers in setting up a canal-boat building business dealing primarily in cargo barges (Akin 1978, p. 4) and apparently also leased out their services as bargemen for local transport.

The closing decades of the Fifth Reign brought many changes to the area. Fruit peddlers frequenting the nearby Mahanak floating market (see Chapter 5, subsection on "Ban Tani") took to mooring their boats along the Phadung Krung Kasem Canal and its side channels in the vicinity of Ban Yuan. Some of those tradespeople eventually settled on vacant land bordering the canal, building small, insubstantial stilted shacks. Though they abutted on Ban Yuan, no one bothered them because the canal-side land had no market value. In time, those peddlers formed a local fruit market, which survives today at Saphan Khaw (White Bridge). The Vietnamese settlement was also infringed upon, around 1900, by the building of Lan Luang Road and Saphan Khaw. The princely palaces and noble mansions lining Lan Luang Road placed Ban Yuan in a subservient position, damping the natural exuberance of village life. The looming royal presence was intensified by the expropriation of village land for the building of Phisanulok Road and installation of the 100-acre Ban Bantomsin (today known as Ban Phisanulok), the palatial residence of the Sixth Reign favourite, Phraya Anirut Thewa (Foen Phoengbun) and later the official residence of Thailand's prime minister. To accommodate the changing circumstances, the Vietnamese villagers built tenements for rent to itinerant workmen and their families; many of the tenants were construction workers engaged in building the palaces and mansions of the newly emerging Dusit district, specialists in tile-laying, plastering, carpentry, and indoor plumbing, which subsequently became featured occupations at Ban Yuan (Akin 1978, p. 8) and continue to be represented in the shop-fronts strewn along the nearby Lan Luang Road and Krung Kasem Road today. And so, the descendants of the original villagers entered Bangkok's middle class as landlords, and many of them moved out to better neighbourhoods, leaving behind them the old Mahayana temple and a much-diminished Vietnamese presence.

"Vietnamese" Mahayana Buddhist Temples

As of 1910, Bangkok contained seven Vietnamese-sect (*annam nikai*) Mahayana Buddhist temples, all still functioning today. (Several others, not listed here, had by that date been abandoned or had — like Wat Thipawari, near Pak Khlong Talat, mentioned above — been reconstituted as Chinese-sect Mahayana temples):

Wat Annam Nikayaram (Quang Phuoc)	Bang Pho
Wat Saman Annam Borihan (Canh Phuoc)	Saphan Khaw
Wat Kuson Samakom (Pho Phuoc)	Central Sampheng
Wat Mongkhon Samakom (Khanh Hoi)	Central Sampheng
Wat Lok Anukrao (Tu Te)	Central Sampheng
Wat Chaiyaphum (Tuy Ngan)	Central Sampheng
Wat Aphai Racha Bamrung (Khran Van)	Talat Noi (downstream Sampheng)

A common misunderstanding among observers of the Sino-Thai scene advances the proposition that Bangkok's "Vietnamese" Mahayana temples — discernably different in their ritual practices from the city's majority of "Chinese" Mahayana temples — were all built by and continue to serve the local Vietnamese community (Map 6.3; Poole 1970, pp. 25–27; Thawi 2002). However, the origin of those temples does not bespeak Vietnamese congregations. Rather, with the exception of the first two listed (and mentioned in earlier subsections of this chapter), their founders and later parishioners were entirely Taechiu. In times of financial constraint, they were founded by Sampheng's Taechiu community with Taechiu-speaking Mahayana monks imported from Vietnam, a far more convenient and cost-efficient option than sending to Canton or further afield for China-based monks. In requital, however, the local congregants were exposed to the Vietnamese Mahayana liturgy, which soon gained popularity and lingers on today. Today, those temples — a cultural borrowing bereft of its ethnic context — continue to serve their entirely Taechiu congregations with not a glimmer of Vietnamese ethnic membership.

THAI YUAN

After two centuries of Burmese vassalage, the mandala-style confederacy of Thai Yuan states collectively known as Lan Na — today Northern Thailand, with its capital at Chiangmai — switched allegiance in 1775 from Ava to Thonburi. That political realignment was orchestrated through a major Siamese military campaign led by King Taksin and his two chief generals, Chaophraya Chakri (Thong-duang) and Chaophraya Surasi (Bunma). "Reversing a centuries-old policy, Lan Na princes now agreed to place themselves under the king of Siam" (Penth 1994, pp. 28–29). The specifics of that feudal realignment do not survive, but it can be surmised that the rulers of Chiangmai and the associated Thai Yuan principalities agreed, under considerable pressure, to become Siam's vassals, with all the tributary duties that such status would entail; in turn, they were given plausible assurances that they would be backed by their Siamese patrons in consolidating power within Lan Na and in receiving military backing against Burmese aggression whenever the need should arise. That pact was validated by a number of ritual practices, including marital arrangements between the respective dynasties; the exchange of Buddha images, monastic delegations, and temple sponsorships; and the periodic submission of obeisance and tribute by the Thai Yuan rulers to the Siamese king and viceroy at Bangkok. Yet, the Thai and Thai Yuan retained a mutual cultural distancing: "The Lan Na people had closer [cultural] ties with the Burmese, Shan, Lue, and Lao than with the Thai. They felt little in common with the Siamese, who felt likewise about their northern neighbours" (Sarassawadee 2005, p. 210). Despite that sense of ethnic dissociation, the feudal relationship between Siam and Lan Na survived for over a century, to the benefit of both ruling elites. It confirmed the rising political might of the Siamese state within the Mainland Southeast Asian political order while also allowing for the pacification and gradual political, economic, and cultural integration of Lan Na into the Siamese orbit.

With the intensifying British and French colonial encroachment upon the Siam-Lan Na entente in the closing decades of the nineteenth century, an enhanced integrative strategy was initiated by the Bangkok-based ruling elite. That process led — not without considerable impotent resentment among both the Thai Yuan elite and commons — to the absorption of the North into the emerging Siamese nation-state through the effective dismantling of Lan Na independence: first with a Bangkok-imposed royal commissioner starting in 1874, then with the North's administrative reorganization as Monthon Phayap (Northern Mandala) in 1893, and finally with Siam's effective annexation of Lan Na through imposition of the provincial (*thesaphiban*) governance system in 1899 (Penth 1994, pp. 34–36; Sarassawadee 2005, pp. 180–213). Through all that, Lan Na's increasingly ineffectual ruling elite maintained a small but culturally significant presence at Bangkok.

The Thai Yuan Royal Presence at Bangkok

In the several Thai military expeditions sent to draw Lan Na from Burmese to Siamese suzerainty during the decade following the destruction of Ayutthaya, a pivotal role was played by King Taksin's generals, Chaophraya Chakri (Thong-duang) and Chaophraya Surasi (Bunma) — the brothers who in 1782 usurped the throne of Siam as King Rama I and his viceroy. After the culminating victory against the Burmese in 1775, Chao Kawila, ruler of the North, pledged to Bunma his undying friendship, and Bunma swore in kind. To affirm that alliance, Kawila presented Bunma with his younger sister, Chao Rocha, to wife. When Bunma left on another military expedition in 1779 to conquer the Lao capital of Vientiane, Rocha was left behind to supervise their Thonburi household. During his absence the Thonburi "disturbances" that spelled the end of King Taksin's reign broke out, and in that episode Rocha helped mobilize the military forces that guaranteed the success of the Chakri coup of 1782. For that great service she was elevated to queen of the First Reign viceroy (Bunma) with the title of Siri Rochana. That contribution by a Thai Yuan royal to the establishment of the Chakri dynasty was not forgotten in the subsequent cordial relations between Siam and Lan Na.

As an additional affirmation of his vassalage, Kawila presented to Bunma around 1780 a Phra Sihing (Sinhalese-style) Buddha image, claimed to be the palladium of Chiangmai — and, it is said, centuries earlier the palladium of Sukhothai (Phiset 2003; Gosling 1991, p. 69). (It must surely have been a copy or replica (*rup chamlong*) of Chiangmai's palladium, as "*the*" Phra Sihing Buddha image versus "*a*" Phra Sihing Buddha image was never a serious issue among the Thai, unlike the Western obsession with "original versions" and "first editions" (Phiset 2003).) The viceroy installed the icon in the Front Palace's main throne hall, fronting his residential quarters. There, gracing the viceroy's royal audiences, it represented a dramatic counterpoint to the Grand Palace's presiding Emerald Buddha image. The Front Palace installation of the revered Sihing icon affirmed the equivalence of the viceroy's mystical power or charisma (*saksit, barami*) with that of the king, raising a highly provocative issue between Grand Palace and Front Palace. (The fact that the Sihing image was situated, along with the Emerald Buddha, precisely on the citadel's longitudinal axis (Map 1.3) was surely no coincidence.) After the First Reign viceroy's death, the Sihing image was moved to the Grand Palace Chapel Royal as a means of removing any spiritual support it might otherwise have exerted over the next viceroy's efforts at aggrandizement. During the Fourth Reign it was returned to the Front Palace and installed in the newly built Front Palace Chapel Royal (Wat Phra Kaew Wang Na), signalling King Mongkut's desire to placate the royal pretensions of his younger brother, the Fourth Reign viceroy.

It became an established practice for each successive ruler of Lan Na to present a daughter — or in the absence of a presentable daughter, a ranking niece — in concubinage to the reigning king of Siam. (Parallel evidence of such a practice at the Front Palace is lacking.) The tale of two Chiangmai princesses, Chao Tipa Keson and Chao Dara Rasami, at Bangkok's Grand Palace during the Fifth Reign is a case in point (Chirachati 2008). Tipa Keson (c.1869–1908) was a daughter of Chao Suriya, a senior prince of Lan Na's royal dynasty. She was presented to King Chulalongkorn as a consort around 1882 and several years later bore Prince Dilok Noparat (1884–1914). It may have been Tipa Keson's lonely, friendless life as an "alien" in Bangkok's Grand Palace that decided Chao Intha Wichayanon, the new ruler of Lan Na, to present to King Chulalongkorn his daughter Dara Rasami, accompanied by a retinue of over a hundred female retainers, as companion to Tipa Keson. Dara Rasami (1873–1933) was the eleventh and youngest child of Chao Intha, but as she was the daughter of his senior wife in the polygynous royal household, she was first in royal precedence (though she was excluded from the all-male line of succession). In 1886, at age thirteen, she was sent to Bangkok and presented to King Chulalongkorn. Three years later she bore a daughter, Princess Wimon Nakhanaphisi, who died at age three, and Dara bore no further children. Dara's main distractions at the Bangkok court after that personal tragedy were the popularization of Northern culture and the care and rearing of her nephew, Prince Dilok. After Tipa Keson's death in 1908, Dara took on the role of Dilok's surrogate mother, and in that capacity she commissioned the construction of his palace and selected his Thai Yuan wife from among the Chiangmai royalty. Dara performed her royal duties faithfully and was in 1909 formally elevated to "royal wife" (*phra racha chaya*). Dilok proved his worth by earning a doctoral degree (in agricultural economics from Germany's Tübingen University) in 1907 — the only Chakri prince ever to have attained that academic distinction and only the second Thai to have done so. After Dilok's death in 1914 Dara was permitted to return to Chiangmai, where she spent the remainder of her life promoting the advancement of her people. Dilok's empty palace (Map 7.2, site 5) near the mouth of the Samsen Canal, at what was then Bangkok's northern purlieu, survives as a melancholy reminder of the close of that chapter in Chiangmai-Bangkok relations.

The Front Palace Guest House

As with most other states engaged in foreign diplomacy, an ancient tradition of official Siamese hospitality was the provision of guest facilities to visiting foreign dignitaries. Well remembered today is the brick Government Guest House (*ban rachathut*, formerly the home of the British merchant, Robert Hunter) located on the west bank of the river alongside the estate of Siam's minister of foreign affairs. After Hunter's expulsion in 1844, the residence was appropriated to lodge the series of British officials who visited Siam during the late 1840s and 1850s to regularize trade relations between the two kingdoms (Phusadi 2002, vol. 2, pp. 162–65). The dwellings that were provided to the exiled Sino-Vietnamese ruler of Hatien in 1778, the Lao hostage princes in 1780, the Cambodian king and princes during the 1850s–1860s, and a number of favoured Western medical missionaries, ministerial staff, and royal advisors during the 1850s–1900s offer other notable examples of that traditional form of royal hospitality. Yet another memorable case was the use of the magnificent Saranrom Palace, a few minutes' walk from the Grand Palace, to accommodate visiting European royalty in the closing years of the nineteenth century.

Similarly, in his role as royal overseer of the North, the viceroy maintained a guesthouse for the obligatory periodic tributary visits to Bangkok of the successive rulers and senior officials of Lan Na. The Front Palace Guest House (Map 7.2, site 2) was originally situated along the river directly upstream from the Front Palace elephant landing (*tha chang wang na*, today covered by the Pin Klao Bridge). Its auxiliary residences were intermittently occupied by lesser officials and traders visiting from the North. There the visiting dignitaries could recover from their arduous weeks-long journey from Chiangmai, and there they could store their

MAP 7.2
Bangkok: Thai Yuan sites, 1782–1910

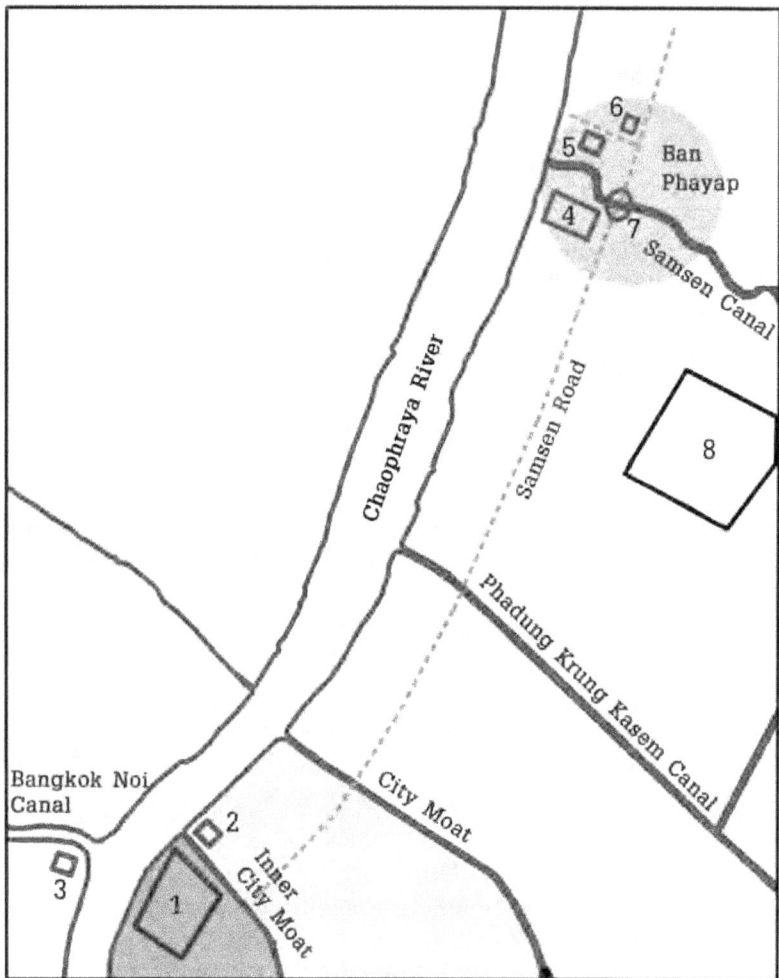

1. Front Palace
2. Front Palace Guesthouse
3. Northern "Palace"
4. Akon Teng residence
5. Prince Dilok palace
6. Phayap Road Guesthouse
7. Akon Teng Bridge
8. Dusit Palace

tributary gifts — the prescribed gold and silver trees, plus auspicious elephants, precious artifacts, rare forest products, and slaves — as well as trade goods. Particularly important were teak consignments, with the largest logs reserved for the erection of royal funerary monuments (*phra meru* and associated structures); a memorable instance was the cremation of Prince Sirirat in 1888, following which King Chulalongkorn donated the funerary site's massive teak timbers for the construction of Sirirat Hospital, built across the river nearby.

The Front Palace Guest House was abandoned in the late 1880s, after the last viceroy's death. With the intent of maintaining Lan Na's tradition of periodic state visits to Bangkok despite the abolition of the viceregal mandate, a new Northern-style "palace" (Map 7.2, site 3) was built around 1894 for Chao Intha Wichayanon (1873–1896) along the Bangkok Noi Canal in front of Wat Amarin, near the canal's confluence with the Chaophraya River (Sarassawadee 2005, p. 242). The mansion was built for the Lan Na ruler by Akon Teng (U-teng *sae* Tia, 1842–1919), a leading Taechiu timber baron. For that service, Teng was awarded the lucrative Chiangmai tax farms (*phasi-akon*) for pigs, cattle, tobacco, opium, betel leaves, and coconuts (Sarassawadee 2005, pp. 241, 242). After Chao Intha's death, the residence was converted to Bangkok's opium tax office (Phusadi 2002, vol. 2, p. 160), before being demolished around 1903 to make way for the Thonburi railway terminus, which occupies the site today.

Ban Phayap

In 1911, a new state guesthouse (Map 7.2, site 6) for visiting Thai Yuan officials was built upstream, at the intersection of Samsen Road and Phayap Road ("Northern" Road), near the mouth of the Samsen Canal (Phusadi 2002, vol. 3, pp. 19–21). Across the street stood the recently erected palace of Prince Dilok (Map 7.2, site 5), son of King Chulalongkorn and maternal grandson of Chao Intha. On the opposite canal bank stood the mansion and business premises of Akon Teng (Map 7.2, site 4). As one of Bangkok's leading business personalities and investment operatives for the Crown, Akon Teng carried the noble title of Luang Udon Phanphanit. In the management of his firm, Kim Seng Lee, he was partnered and succeeded by his son, Ki-ang-sam, who rose to the rank and title of Phra Sophon Phecharat (Thai surname Sophonodon). Teng had made his fortune in the North in the 1880s and remained for the rest of his life a great Bangkok patron of the Northern traders (Wright and Breakspear 1908, p. 161; Skinner 1957, p. 137). However, like many other Bangkok-based tycoons of the day, his rice speculations led to bankruptcy in Siam's financial crisis of 1913, forcing him to divest his Samsen-based business headquarters and mansion to the Crown Property Office (*krom phra khlang khang thi*) (Yibphan 2002, pp. 11–12). It was soon thereafter converted to the Sukhothai Palace (for Prince Prachatipok Sakdidat, later elevated to Rama VII). Today, comprehensively rebuilt, that palace continues to dominate the local scene.

The close connection between Akon Teng, Chao Intha, and the Thai Yuan settlement at Samsen illustrates the emergence of close Taechiu-Thai Yuan relations in Siam's dynamic decades of nation building. That connection played a largely unrecognized role in the economic development of the North as the twentieth century proceeded. Among his many gestures in support of Bangkok's Thai Yuan community, Akon Teng sponsored the construction of a vehicular bridge spanning the Samsen Canal — first built as the teak-timber Akon Teng Bridge in 1898, rebuilt of reinforced concrete as the Kim Seng Lee Bridge in 1904, and some time after the firm's bankruptcy a decade later renamed the Sophon Bridge (Map 7.2, site 7) — to allow the passage of horse-drawn carriages and later automotive and tram traffic between Ban Phayap and the nearby Dusit Palace, and on downriver into the city's commercial districts. That transport link helped greatly in promoting Ban Phayap as the residential center for Bangkok's small community of Thai Yuan officials, traders, and artisans. But today, a century later, following the cultural integration of Ban Phayap into the Bangkok metropolitan fold, no suggestion of that former colourful minority presence remains.

SIKHS

Conditions in India's Punjab region, the centre of Sikh civilization, grew increasingly difficult for the local population under British colonialism, starting in 1845 with the British East India Company's military occupation of the region, intensifying in 1849 with the Company's annexation of the region as a province of British India, deepening after the Sepoy Mutiny of 1857 (despite Sikh military assistance to the Company against the insurgency), and then introducing further hardship with the province's conversion to British government administration in 1859. Seeking relief from the restrictive colonial rules and regulations as well as adverse demographic and ecological developments, some adventurous Sikhs abandoned their farms and emigrated to other Asian lands, where they found subaltern work in the British civil service and in the military, and as shopkeepers and itinerant tradesmen. Singapore and the Malay States were prime Sikh destinations, and in time some of those sojourners moved on to Siam.

The Bangkok Police Constabulary

The initial arrival at Bangkok of a substantial group of Sikh immigrants has been lost to common memory. It occurred during the Fourth Reign, when the Ministry of the Capital (*krom nakhonban*) decided to establish a police presence in the city's increasingly disorderly Chinese and *farang* precincts. Captain S.J.B. Ames, a British army officer billeted at Singapore, was in 1862 recruited to serve as the first commissioner of a newly created Bangkok Police Constabulary (*krom kong trawen*). In need of a body of strong, reliable, non-partisan officers, Ames and his successors in turn brought to Bangkok from Singapore several contingents of Indian patrolmen, including a number of Sikhs. Police headquarters and the adjacent police barracks (Map 7.3, site 4) were initially located near the Phithaya Sathian Bridge along Charoen Krung Road (better known as New Road) spanning the Phadung Krung Kasem Canal to link the Chinese centre at Sampheng and Bang Rak's *farang* quarter. By 1885 they had moved from that site (which was then converted to accommodate the stables of Nai Loet's horse-drawn bus line), dividing the constabulary between the Talat Noi police post, located at the foot of the bastion behind the Calvary Church (Map 7.3, sites 2 and 3), and the Bang Rak police post (Map 7.3, site 16), located on Customs House Lane off Charoen Krung Road. As of 1900, the Bangkok Police Constabulary included fifty-six Sikh and Hindu patrolmen plus 124 Pathan Muslims, aside from its majority Mon-Thai force, which was deployed to other Bangkok districts (see Chapter 3, section on "The Fading of Mon Ethnicity"). Upon promulgation of the Nationality Act in 1913, all the *khaek* (South Asian) policemen who wished to continue in service were required to adopt Siamese nationality (Mani 1993, p. 914). Among them, the Sikh police and their families gradually merged into the local Sikh business community, eventually shedding their former occupational status.

Ban Mo and Pahurat

Disregarding the Sikh police patrolmen's 1860s arrival, local lore has it that the first Sikh to establish residence at Bangkok was an itinerant Punjabi textile trader who arrived in 1884 via Singapore. Within a decade he managed to accumulate sufficient savings to return home and convince his extended family to join him. Learning of Siam's tolerant political climate and the opportunities for earning a decent living at Bangkok, others followed (Sidhu 1993, p. 1). The Thai classified them as *khaek india* (as distinct from *khaek isalam* (see Chapter 5, section on "*Khaek Isalam*")), grouping them indiscriminately with the city's Indian Hindus and Muslims. Though

MAP 7.3
Bangkok: Major sites at Bang Rak, 1855–1910

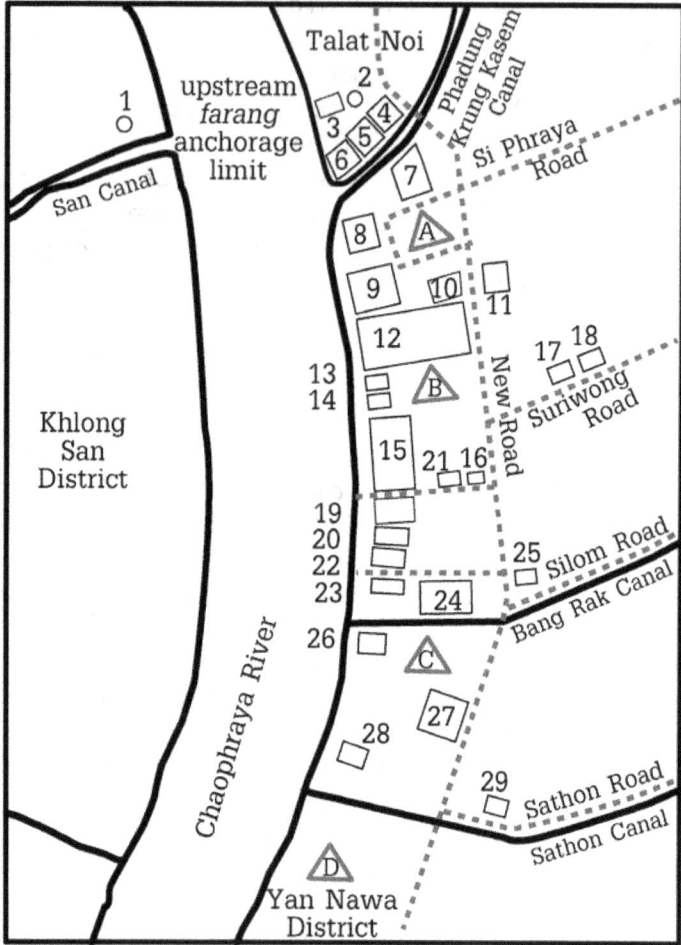

1. Pong Pachamit Bastion	13. Netherlands Consulate	25. Banque de L'Indochine
2. Pit Pachanoek Bastion	14. American Consulate	26. Howarth Erskine boatyard
3. Calvary Church	15. New Customs House	27. Bang Rak Market
4. Police Hq./bus stables	16. Bang Rak police post	28. Westervelt and Allen boatyard
5. Bangkok Mfg. Co.	17. German Club	29. New Baptist Mission
6. Markwald and Co. hq.	18. German Consulate	
7. Concordia Club	19. French Consulate	A. Wat Khrua (demolished c.1907)
8. Old Customs House	20. Mercantile Bank	B. Wat Muang Khae
9. Portuguese Consulate	21. Chartered Bank	C. Wat Suan Phlu
10. Post Office No. 2	22. Oriental Hotel	D. Wat Yannawa
11. (Baptist) Sailors' Rest	23. E.A.C. Co. hq.	
12. British Consulate	24. Assumptiom Cathedral	

farmers by background, the newcomers followed the example set by their forerunner and set themselves up as peddlers and marketplace vendors in the piece-goods textile trade. The parvenu Sikh textile dealers presented an interesting contrast with the established Indian Muslim textile merchants (Inthira 2004; see also Chapter 5, section on "Indian Traders"). Whereas the Muslims had earlier dealt primarily in high-quality textiles catering to the elite market, the Sikhs specialized from the start in less costly piece-goods directed at the mass market. And unlike the Indian textile merchants, still concentrated along the river's west bank with branches spreading cross-river to Sampheng's Rachawong financial centre, the Sikhs established their businesses along Ban Mo Road (the riverward extension of Foeang Nakhon Road) and Pahurat Road, in Bangkok's most upscale turn-of-the-century shopping district, the "City", within the city wall (Mani 1993, pp. 914, 918; Theingi and Thiengi 2011, pp. 226–29). By 1912–1913, Bangkok's Sikh community had grown large enough to warrant the conversion of a residence along Ban Mo Road, alongside the original office of the Siam Commercial Bank (Map 7.4, site 5), for use as a prayer house. A few years later that facility was moved to a house in the nearby Pahurat market area (Map 7.4, site 6; Sidhu 1993, p. 94). In 1932, a larger, permanent Sikh temple (gurudwara) (Map 7.4, site 7) was built off Chakraphet Road alongside the Pahurat market (Mani 1993, pp. 914, 925; Theingi and Thiengi 2011, p. 224). Over the subsequent decades their increasingly crowded neighbourhood led a substantial share of the community to hive off to a new Sikh neighbourhood on the Thonburi side of the river, near Si Yaek Ban Khaek (the Khaek Village Crossroads), a sprawling Indian (Muslim, Hindu, Sikh) district along the Sai Kai Canal (Map 5.1).

With Bangkok's continuing population growth and buoyant consumer goods market as the twentieth century proceeded, the Sikh shops in the "City's" Pahurat neighbourhood eventually spilled across the City Moat via Saphan Han (the Turning Bridge) into upper Sampheng Lane, known as Hua Met (named after the wooden posts that insulated Wat Samploem from that stretch of Sampheng Lane) and Khlong Thom Lane (a narrow path set upon the course of a filled-in drainage canal passing alongside Wat Chakrawat) (Mani 1993, pp. 916–17). That considerable extension of the original Sikh textile market toward Sampheng denoted the continued growth and economic achievement of the Sikh trading community. It was intensive ethnic networking — featuring the intra-communal creation of social capital though goodwill, information sharing, apprenticeship,

MAP 7.4
Bangkok: Major Vietnamese, Sikh, and *farang* sites in the walled city, 1910

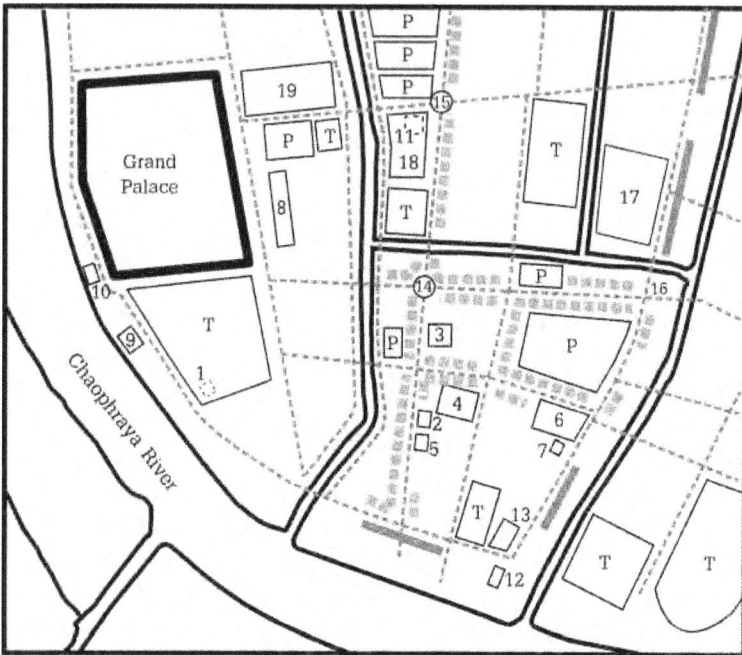

Vietnamese (and related sites)
1. Mac Thien-tu res. (1778-1780)
2. Daoist Shrine
3. Wat Sam Lo Thoen/Wat Thipawari
4. Arts and Crafts School

Sikh (and related sites)
5. SCB (original office)
6. Pahurat Market
7. Gurudwara

Farang (and related sites)
8. Parade Ground rowhouses (1862-c.1878)
9. Tha Tien *farang* staff res. (c.1878-c.1900)
10. Thai Sanom *farang* staff res. (c.1900-c.1910)
11. Ramsay and Co.
12. Post Office No.1
13. Bangkok Electric Co./power plant
14. Phraya Si Intersection
15. Saphan Chang Rong Si Intersection
16. Sam Yot Gate (demolished)
17. Prison
18. Ministry of Interior
19. Ministry of War

```
━━━   City wall remnamts
T     Buddhist temple
P     Palace
▓▓▓   Farang shopping district
      (mixed Chinese, Indian, farang shops)
```

and low-interest lending, supported by strict cultural conformity and a preference for endogamy — that lay at the heart of that success (Theingi and Thiengi 2011, pp. 223-36). The Pahurat — Saphan Han — Hua Met — Khlong Thom market area with its multitude of textile wholesalers and its imposing Sri Guru Singh Sabha Gurudwara remains today the heart of Thailand's vigourous Sikh community, which has grown over the course of the last century to a total population of 70,000, with perhaps half that number residing in Bangkok.

FARANG

Bang Rak, Old Bangkok's *farang* (Western) enclave, housed no more than 2,000 Western residents as of 1910, one of the city's smallest ethnic minorities and yet its most influential and most meticulously documented. More historical surveys and interpretive studies have been written on that rowdy, quarrelsome, nationalistically and religiously fractured community than about all the city's other ethnic groups combined (a selective listing: Anake 2006; Bateson 1976; Bradley 1981; Bristowe 1976; Brummelhuis 1987; Damrong 1962; Harrison and Jackson 2010; Khumsupha 2010; McFarland 1999; Pirasi 2005; Siwali 2006; Sulak 1995; Thailand, Ministry of Foreign Affairs 2008; Thanet 2009; Vella 1955a). The writings on Bangkok's *farang* ethnohistory are as inflated as the research on the city's far larger non-Western minorities is sparse, making for such distortions in Thai ethnographic insight as the common exaggeration that the *farang* community dominated Bangkok social life. Furthermore, an immediate side-issue arises in speaking of the city's *farang* minority: was it, like Bangkok's five Chinese speech groups or the city's six Muslim groups, one broad ethnic constituency or many? In the cultural cauldron of Old Bangkok, could the West's ethnic identity be considered unitary despite its multiplicity of languages, nationalities, religious denominations, and idiosyncratic customs? Or was all that *je ne sais quoi* distinguishing Brits from French, Americans from Germans, Danes from Iberians, and so forth inconsequential in the face of the larger East-West cultural chasm? That issue remains unanswered in the present telling and continues to haunt its shadows.

Reference to "*farang*" (Western people, artifacts, ideas, attitudes) in Thai history can be conceived of as "a blurred [Thai] ethnocultural reference to Western otherness" (Pattana 2005, p. 5). It is in that perspective very much a collective, indiscriminate referent to a wide variety of cultures and nationalities featuring certain defining commonalities: "white" skin,

"Christian" religion, "advanced" civilization, "imperialist" power. Like the ethnically encapsulating taxonomies "*chin*" and "*chek*" (Chinese), "*khaek*" (swarthy South and Southeast Asians), and "*lao*" (most non-Thai Tai-speaking peoples), each of which is often meant to disparage those broad groupings in Thai parlance, "*farang*" also covers a host of national and cultural variations and can also carry derogatory implications, but the term more commonly conveys undertones of admiration, wonder, and even a hint of envy (Pattana 2005, pp. 7–12). So much has been written on the influence of *farang* on Siamese polity, economy, society, and culture that the primary purpose of this brief survey is simply to identify the shifting spatial presence of the *farang* ethnic minority within Old Bangkok's multi-ethnic setting. In passing, the account inevitably touches on the influence of Old Bangkok's small *farang* community on the city's rapidly changing social and political character.

What the evolving relationship between Siam and the West taught Old Bangkok's ruling elite — based on their memory of the *farang* at Ayutthaya, their observations of current events in China, Burmese India, the Dutch East Indies, Indochina, the Malay States, and the Philippines, not to mention their ever-intensifying, ever-fraught interaction with the *farang* community at Bangkok — was the need for persistent scepticism, distrust, distancing, and selective dealings. As interpreted by one rather dyspeptic Thai commentator, "The more Siam has adopted *farang* ways, the less has it been able to retain the Buddha's Dhammic principles" (Sulak 1997, p. 24; quoted in Pattana 2005, p. 39 (rev. trans.)). Bespeaking that awareness of the cultural fragility of Thai-*farang* relations, King Mongkut (Rama IV), inserted into a royal proclamation of 1855 the following pragmatic warning:

> Be it brought to the attention of the people that business with British, European [and] American merchants should be conducted by the people in public, in front of their houses or shops, where the same may be witnessed by citizens, and care should always be taken to prevent such aliens from trespassing into their home where violence may be committed as a result of commercial dispute (Mongkut 1987, p. 45).

Elaborating for his subjects on that delicately penned instruction, King Mongkut' son Chulalongkorn (Rama V) several decades later wrote rather more pointedly:

> [I]t is not easy to hire *farang* and encourage them to work. Their trustworthiness and loyalty are always questionable. Their aim is only

to make money and go home. Having said so is unfair, because there are some knowledgeable and reliable [*farang*], who have built up their reputation and decent career. They are very helpful. Nonetheless, almost all *farang* must be counted as "fake, not true friends" (*phuen kin mai chai phuen tai*) (Chulalongkorn 1997, p. 49, quoted in Pattana 2005, p. 26).

And again, King Chulalongkorn's son Wachirawut (Rama VI) maintained that "Thais should not hate foreigners [which suggests, of course, that many did], but should just not trust them completely" (Thailand, National Archives 1913, p. 256, cited in Pattana 2005, p. 28).

From the viewpoint of the Thai ruling elite, the *farang* presence at Bangkok posed a unique dilemma: the enticements of Western material culture were inextricably paired with the threat of Western political hegemony. In a studied attempt to square that circle, the Thai ruling elite sought to temper their interaction with the *farang* community through a continuing policy of compromise — initially emphasizing spatial containment but turning increasingly to more subtle approaches to political and social accommodation-at-a-distance. Even the recruitment of *farang* as government staff and then advisors contributed to that containment effort, allowing the selective adoption, adaptation, and assimilation of Western knowledge and its associated refinements under controlled conditions, subtly drawing their cultural benefactors/adversaries into the Thai social ambit while guarding their own political independence.

Precursors

Western contact with Siam can be traced far back in history. An Eastern Mediterranean oil lamp dating from the fifth–sixth centuries has been found at Pong Tuk, not far from Nakhon Pathom, attesting to Western contact with Dvaravati (a Mon-ruled precursor state to Thai-ruled Ayutthaya) over a millennium ago (Borell 2008). Marco Polo's thirteenth-century account of his travels across Asia refer to Lavo (Lopburi), an ancient Dvaravati capital some sixty kilometres upriver from later-day Ayutthaya (Rong 1977, p. 3). During its heyday some four centuries later, Ayutthaya boasted the presence of a variety of *farang* residents (see Chapter 2, section on "Merchants, Mercenaries, Missionaries, Mestizos"). Ayutthaya's violent anti-Western outburst of 1688 led to a century of reduced contact; the destruction of Ayutthaya in 1767, followed by Europe's Napoleonic wars, extended that hiatus into the nineteenth century. But thereafter, Siam saw a steady revival in Western interest. Without putting a fine point on the matter, it can be said that the *farang* presence at Old Bangkok grew through a cumulative series of overlapping phases — initially a drizzle of seafaring adventurers and missionaries, followed after mid-century by a gathering storm of diplomats, technicians, and shopkeepers — each infusion adding to the increasingly tempestuous expatriate brew.

A *farang* presence at Bangkok first emerged with the arrival of transient mariners and longer staying missionaries. From early on, occasional visiting Western vessels brought with them agents (supercargoes) who sought to develop trade relations, particularly in such high-value, often-illicit imports as arms and opium in exchange for rice, spices, and forest products. With few exceptions, those visitors were kept at a physical and social distance by being obliged to live shipboard or on shore-side house-rafts in the absence of permission to establish dry-land residence. A more troublesome intrusion was the post-Ayutthaya return of Catholic missionaries associated primarily with the local Portuguese-Thai community (see Chapter 2, subsection on "Survivors at Thonburi"). Goaded to distraction by the Catholic priests' defiant dogmatism, King Taksin had them imprisoned and then expelled; the more forbearing King Rama I allowed their return under condition that they abide by prescribed regulations and restrict their preaching to their parishioners (Pallegoix 2000, pp. 386–98). The arrival of a gaggle of Protestant missionaries — Congregational, Baptist, and Presbyterian — during the Third Reign greatly complicated the issue (McFarland 1999, pp. 1–50). Under carefully controlled conditions, they were assigned small sites along the urban outskirts for their chapels, schools, clinics, residences, and graveyards. They and their wives proved to be colourful characters, indulged by the local authorities as much for their personal eccentricities, cultural pratfalls, and baffling doctrinal rivalries as they were respected for their scientific expertise and contributions to the citizenry's wellbeing (Bradley 1981; Bristowe 1976, pp. 13–22). Despite the Protestant missionaries' strenuous efforts, their local converts never exceeded more than a few destitute men, abandoned women, and orphaned children drawn from the Chinese and other ethnic minorities. The influence of both mariners and missionaries did not far outreach their small numbers, which in the decades preceding the Bowring Treaty never rose beyond a few dozen at any one time and was additionally characterized by high turnover, a paucity abetted by Rama III's abiding anti-*farang* bias (Vella 1955*a*, p. 332; Vella 1955*b*, p. 126). Only with the accelerated influx of *farang* residents in the decades following the Bowring Treaty did the magnitude and ramifications of the *farang* presence, centred at Bang Rak and progressively penetrating the walled city, rise to a level of serious political concern.

Bang Rak

Policy matters! Decisions have consequences! Individuals make a difference! Those timeworn tropes are nowhere better illustrated than in the amicable negotiations — defusing an implicit threat of raw colonial coercion — between King Mongkut and Sir John Bowring (post-Opium War governor of Hong Kong, British emissary to Siam), aided by their capable subordinates, that culminated in the 1855 "Treaty of Friendship and Commerce between the British Empire and the Kingdom of Siam". Its terms and conditions were in short order extended through a series of nearly identical pacts with thirteen additional Western trading powers. All that opened the Siamese market to free trade and regularized *farang* residence. It also introduced preferential expatriate legal status. The treaties' trade provisions "did away with the age-old privileges enjoyed by the Sino-Siamese junk trade" (Sarasin 1977, p. 238) and thus allowed *farang* merchants to compete effectively with the dominant Chinese presence of the day. Their residency clauses provided for the establishment of Western consulates and the rental and purchase of residential and commercial properties, and thereby initiated an amplified *farang* presence at Bangkok. They also included a clause providing for extraterritorial privileges for the nationals and subjects of the treaty powers, a devilish provision that came to haunt the Thai ruling elite with its shielding of the treaty powers' nationals and their Asian colonial protégées from Siamese law (Hooker 1988; Hong 2004).

At Thai insistence, the treaty provisions included a clause prohibiting any foreign national or subject from purchasing land at Bangkok within some four miles (about 200 *sen*) of the walled city until he had lived in Siam for ten years (Mongkut 1987, p. 44). At the same time, royal pressure was brought to bear on local landowners to desist from renting property to *farang* within about three kilometres of the walled city. Those restrictions created a strong impulse to concentrate *farang* settlement at its primary locus, the downstream square-rigger anchorage at Bang Rak, some three–four kilometres from the walled city. There, the Crown established a Customs House at the residence of Captain Bush, the later Harbormaster (Map 7.3, site 8) and provided sites for the treaty powers' consulates. The concentration of *farang* settlement at Bang Rak was further reinforced with the harbour master's restriction of Bangkok's *farang* anchorage to the river channel downstream from the opposing mouths of the Phadung Krung Kasem Canal and San Canal, marked by the soaring flagstaffs of the well-gunned Pong Pachamit and Pit Pachanoek Bastions (Map 7.3, sites 1 and 2). That regulation instituted a strict demarcation between

Old Bangkok's Western and Chinese ports, preventing untoward inter-communal incidents.

Bang Rak grew rapidly over the decades following promulgation of the Bowring Treaty (1855). Adding to the pre-existing Assumption Church (since c.1811) (Map 7.3, site 24) and Portuguese consulate (since 1821) (Map 7.3, site 9), the shoreline quickly came to be marked by a row of additional Western consulates (Map 7.3, sites 12, 13, 14, 19, plus inland site 17) and in 1884 a splendid new Customs House (Map 7.3, site 15), located between the British and French consulates, replacing a squalid stretch of misused shoreline (see Chapter 5, section on "Ban Khaek Bang Rak"). More than its administrative role, the *farang* settlement at Bang Rak was from the outset unabashedly commercial. Arriving Western brigs and barques offloaded there a jetsam of seafarers and footloose adventurers bent on turning their sundry skills to profitable purpose. Residential turnover was high, but some *farang* merchants, tradesmen, and technicians managed to hang on, and with time others joined them. And so emerged a multiplicity of firms and related facilities (Map 7.3, selected sites): towing, lightering, pilots, dockyards, and warehouses; shipwrights, sail-makers, rope-makers, iron founders, and ships' chandlers; general provisioners, grocers, bakers, tailors, and livery stables; boardinghouses and hotels, saloons and dancehalls, opium dens and bawdy houses; printing shops and publishing offices; agency houses, banks, auctioneers, and insurance brokers; rice millers, saw millers, and teak concessionaires; shipping companies (sail, and increasingly from the 1880s steam); and independent professionals such as engineers, architects, pharmacists, physicians, lawyers, and teachers.

The densely occupied Bang Rak shoreline persuaded the consuls and leading businessmen around 1863 to petition the king for a metalled carriageway to serve the *farang* community; that audacious request resulted in a singular act of *noblesse oblige* — a downstream extension of Charoen Krung Road (New Road) running from Talat Noi to the Bang Rak Canal (Silom Canal), not long thereafter extended further downstream to Yan Nawa and Land's End (Bang Ko Laem) (Map 5.1). Further expansion of Bang Rak in the closing decades of the Fifth Reign prompted the construction of a series of brick-paved and rubble-metalled (later macadamized) roadways running inland off New Road: Silom Road, Surawong Road, Sathon Road, and Si Phraya Road. With the introduction of that extension of roadways plus a horse-drawn tramway via New Road in 1889 (electrified in 1894), Bang Rak's *farang* community was effectively linked with the heart of the capital — the walled city of Ratanakosin — by the turn of the century.

Yan Nawa to Land's End

In anticipation of war with Vietnam, Rama III around 1828–1830 ordered a line of Royal Navy shipyards to be built downstream from Wat Khok Kraboe (renamed Wat Yannawa in honour of that Third Reign naval presence), some four kilometres downstream from the walled city (Map 4.4; also see Chapter 3, subsection on "Ban Tawai;" Chapter 4, subsection on "Ban Kruay"). Following the downscaling of the Thai-Vietnamese war in the early 1840s, those facilities encountered years of abandonment. In the decades following the Bowring Treaty, however, that waterfront staged a strong recovery with the incursion of a number of dockyards, rice mills, sawmills, warehouses, and shipping firms under *farang* management. Among the well-known operations lining that river stretch by the turn of the century (their head offices located nearly without exception at Bang Rak) were the Bangkok Dock Company, the Borneo Company, A. Markwald and Company, Windsor and Company, the East Asiatic Company, and Clarke and Company, with Denny, Mott and Dickson (later Louis Leonowens and Company) on the opposite shore (Map 4.4; Wright and Breakspear 1908, pp. 263–81). Under Crown sponsorship, an inter-denominational Union Chapel (the congregation of *farang* Protestants too small to support separate sectarian parishes) was established along the Yan Nawa waterfront in 1861, with an interdenominational *farang* cemetery further downriver; the chapel was moved in 1904 to North Sathon Road and renamed Christ Church, which continues to function at that site today.

With the extension of New Road downstream past Yan Nawa to Land's End (Map 5.1), and with the addition of an electric tram line from the city centre by the turn of the century, the small resident *farang* community at the downriver anchorage at Land's End also developed an expanded presence of seafarers, import-export agents, and rice mills and sawmills, which made largely unsuccessful efforts to add the plentiful but generally unwilling supply of local Malay villagers to their limited Chinese, Mon, and Lao work forces (see Chapter 5, subsections on "Ban Suan Luang," "Bang Uthit," and "Ban Trok Mo"). Such persistent labour constraints, plus the distance from the city centre, prevented that downriver commercial settlement from attaining more than peripheral urban status.

Missionaries along the Urban Periphery

Unlike the clustering of Bangkok's many ethnic groups — including the *farang* — in distinct villages, neighbourhoods, and districts, the Protestant missionaries, most of them Americans, purposely scattered their proselytizing activities widely along the urban periphery, seeking out vulnerable minority communities that they thought to be ripe for conversion. In that strategy they were singularly unsuccessful. Their hardy independence ensured that their often-strained relations amongst themselves (frequently for obscure doctrinal reasons) extended well into the twentieth century (McFarland 1999; Thanet 2009). At Bang Rak, the Baptists in the 1840s set up a mission from which they hoped to convert neighbouring Sampheng's Chinese coolies. A devastating fire in 1853 led them to move their premises far downstream, to Land's End, where their little church has survived to the present day. While the Baptists settled along the east bank of the river, the Presbyterians and allied groups established themselves at a series of secluded sites: along the west bank at Samre, across from Yan Nawa, where the Rev. Stephen Mattoon and his wife established one of the first mission schools; alongside Santa Cruz, where a series of newcomer missionaries acclimated themselves to the Thai milieu under the close purview of the minister of foreign affairs; along the Bang Luang Canal, where the best-known of the missionaries, the Rev. Dan Bradley, practised medicine and ran a popular printing press in the shadow of the Thonburi Palace wall till his death in 1873; in the Nantha Uthayan Palace grounds, near Ban Mon and the Mon Canal, where the Rev. Sam McFarland ran the Suan Anand School in the 1880s; and along the Rear Palace riverside, where the Rev. Samuel House established a girls' school in 1875 which survives today along Sukhumvit Road as the Wathana Withayalai Academy. All those marginal sites were assigned to missionary use by the successive kings in recognition of the valuable medical, educational, and other ad hoc services rendered by the Protestant preachers and their wives.

Penetrating the Walled City

The reformist, revisionist King Mongkut in 1862 took a bold first step to challenge the city's mandala template by introducing a privileged *farang* residential presence within the walled city — in fact, within the sacrosanct Citadel itself. Preparing to recruit a series of *farang* experts as royal staff, he ordered in 1862 the construction of a line of brick, tile-roofed, two-storey rowhouses (Map 7.4, site 8), forty units long, fronting the eastern wall of the Grand Palace across Parade Ground Road (Sanam Chai Road) and its broad grassy verge. Those premises were quickly occupied by a small group of the king's *farang* staff, prominent among them royal tutors (e.g., Anna Leonowens), military instructors (e.g., E. Lamache), mechanical engineers (e.g., John Chandler), and surveyors (e.g., Henry Alabaster), while the remaining residential units were rented out to privileged *farang* and *khaek* purveyors to the royal household. Additional rowhouses of the same type were later added alongside to serve as officers' billets for the Western-trained Palace Guard. A smaller, replica facility was built by the Fourth-Reign viceroy along the Front Palace Parade Ground Road (Sanam Chai Wang Na Road).

The facilities along the Grand Palace Parade Ground were demolished around 1878 for the construction of the Saranrom Garden. In their place, King Chulalongkorn ordered the construction of a residential compound of *farang*-style dwellings along the river at Tha Tien (Map 7.4, site 9), directly behind Wat Phra Chetuphon. The brick residences at that site initially served as ambassadorial guesthouses and then were assigned to *farang* royal staff. Among the residents at one time or another over the following years were: Henry Alabaster (Superintendent of Roads), John Clunis and his son Henry (royal architects), Captain Andre Richelieu and Admiral Louis Richelieu (officers in the Royal Navy), James McCarthy (Director of the Royal Survey Department), Captains Gustav Schau and G.E. Gerini (consecutive Directors of the Royal Military Academy), Professor Otto Frankfurter (Conservator of the Royal Library and Curator of the Grand Palace Museum), and Drs. Peter Gowan and Eugene Reytter (successive royal physicians). Later in the reign another *farang* residential compound was laid out 100 metres upstream, near the rear of the Grand Palace, at Thai Sanom (Map 7.4, site 10). There, additional guesthouses were built for newly arrived *farang* staff and advisors, and there Dr. Reytter established a pharmacy and clinic serving the Thai elite.

Complementing the penetration into the citadel by *farang* staff and advisors to the king and his government was the escalating encroachment of *farang* shopkeepers and tradesmen into the walled city's old noble quarter, which came to be known as the "City" as its commercial, middle-class character became manifest. Along Bamrung Moeang (Developing City) Road, Foeang Nakhon (Dominant Metropolis) Road, and Charoen Krung (Prosperous Capital) Road, King Mongkut in the 1860s built rows of brick single-storey leasehold shophouses fronted with roofed walkways for protection against sun and rain. Most of those streets were widened and their roadside structures rebuilt by King Chulalongkorn during the 1880s as improved two-storey shophouses for rental to Chinese, Indian, and *farang* merchants, and many more were added during the 1890s–1900s along Ban Mo Road, Triphet Road, Pahurat Road, and other inner city carriageways, a project that extended down New Road and Yaowarat Road through Chinatown and Bang Rak.

During his 1872 excursion to India, King Chulalongkorn invited a Calcutta-based British haberdasher, Richard Ramsay, to open a Bangkok branch to serve the royal household. Ramsay accepted the invitation and was provided with facilities in a vacant royal mansion (Map 7.4, site 11) on Bamrung Moeang Road near the Ministry of War, becoming the official supplier of military uniforms as well as a major importer of arms to the Thai army. The firm expanded operations (at the same location) in 1882 as a department store, Messrs Ramsay, Wakefield and Co., selling fashionable men's and women's wear and accessories, as well as household furnishings. Other department stores followed, chief among them Harry A. Badman and Co. (from 1884) and John Sampson and Son (from 1899); as of 1910, both those firms occupied prominent crown-property premises along Rachadamnoen Avenue. A diverse assortment of other *farang*-run retail establishments lining the "City's" shopping streets — centring on the Phraya Si and Saphan Chang Rong Si Intersections and the Sam Yot city gate neighbourhood (Map 7.4, sites 14, 15, and 16) came to cater to the aristocracy's limitless appetite for conspicuous consumption, followed by the rising infatuation (otherwise known as "commodity fetishism") of Bangkok's emerging middle class with Western consumer fashions — wearables, accessories, household furnishings, baubles of all sorts — all intended to demonstrate their familiarity with, if not identity with, the *beau monde* of the West (Tomosugi 1993, pp. 211–23; Pellegi 2002, pp. 39–43).

That transformation of much of Ratanakosin's old noble quarter into Bangkok's premier shopping district in the closing decades of the Fifth Reign was mirrored in the dismantling of the walled city's physical, political, and social bounds (see Chapter 1, subsection on "Dismantling Ratanakosin"). On the one hand, the expanding Thai elite and its increasing wealth, demanding public ostentation, pressed outward, bursting the seams of the walled city's restrictive bounds. On the other, Bangkok's ambitious *farang* bourgeoisie, abetted by its Chinese and Indian commercial counterparts, found the opportunity to set up shop on the very doorstep of their moneyed clientele an irresistible attraction. Contributing further to the "City's" ethnic diversity was a cluster of Thai-ized Lao, Mon, and Khmer working-class communities (Map 4.2; see Chapter 3, subsection on "Pottery Marketplaces," and Chapter 4, subsections on "Ban Kraba" and "Ban Ti Thong"). Close inter-ethnic proximity in those densely occupied precincts reinforced the bevy of new policies and programmes promoting the Thai nation-state. The outcome was the emergence of an ethnic melting pot that broke all the rules of Old Bangkok's mandala template, contributing to Siam's twentieth-century ethno-national metamorphosis (see Chapter 1, subsection on "Thai ethno-nationalism").

8

Retrospect: Contextualizing Some Contentious Concepts

Ethnohistory unites ethnography and history. As ethnography, this book is the product of several decades of on-site interactive observation of local communities, is based on inductive methods of data gathering and analysis, and adopts a holistic, multifaceted approach to an account of Old Bangkok's spatial, political, and social order. As history, it is retrospective in outlook, takes a narrative form, and relies on a diversity of time-worn data sources, including unstructured oral histories, surviving primary-source documentation, and the scattered physical remnants of the Old Bangkok cityscape. In both its ethnographic and historical guises, the book seeks to place its subject in broad perspective by ranging somewhat more widely, now and again, across space and time than the urban landscape of Old Bangkok per se.

Beyond ethnography, the book ventures into the rather more rarified reaches of ethnology. As interpretation naturally follows observation, so is ethnology the child of ethnography. While ethnography is conventionally defined as rigorously objective single-society observation, description, and explication, ethnology delves more profoundly and expansively into the mysteries of the cultural landscape "to reconstitute the deeper structures out of which [the surface patterns] are built, and to classify those structures, once reconstituted, into an analytical scheme" (Geertz 1973, p. 351). Thus, ethnographic research is by inclination empirically small-scale and expository, whereas ethnology tends to take on conceptually large-scale and interpretive dimensions, emphasizing generalization, abstraction, and comparative analysis, exploring broad cross-cultural themes and theories.

The ethnography–ethnology distinction is useful here as an opportunity to explore briefly several ethnological themes that infuse the book's ethnographic discussion: *Ethnicity*, a means of identifying and differentiating socio-cultural groups; *feudalism*, the political form of premodern, ethnically diverse, emerging states; *the plural society*, which historically served as the organizational mode of Southeast Asia's port-cities; and *the mandala*, the spatial template upon which that world region's traditional political systems, and particularly its urban social orders, were imprinted. Each of those themes is itself a contentious concept, subject to long-standing scholarly, ideologically tinted debate. Yet, their conceptual plausibility is enhanced by the fact that they are closely linked, and mutually reinforcing. Jointly, they hold considerable explanatory power. Together, they form an analytical framework within which the temporal logic of Old Bangkok's ethnically diverse social order can be cogently expressed. Conversely, the book's ethnohistory of Old Bangkok may be considered an exercise in defense of those several contentious concepts.

ETHNICITY AND ITS CULTURAL CONTENT

The first fact of ethnicity is the application of systematic distinctions between insiders and outsiders; between Us and Them (Eriksen 2010, p. 23).

Born over two-and-a-half millennia ago in the multi-cultural cauldron of the Mediterranean Levant, the term "*ethnos*" and its modern derivatives centring on "ethnicity" have evolved over the past six decades or so from technical obscurity to increasingly popular usage. Though "ethnicity" is of ancient pedigree, having in former days commonly been associated with such crude abstractions as "race", "nation", "people", and "culture", the archaic notions conveyed by all those terms have diverged to take on altered, refined meaning today. That has allowed "ethnicity", "ethnic group", "ethnic identity", and the like to take on their own specific meanings, though the core concept they represent continues to be a subject of spirited debate. Ethnicity does not, as is all too often supposed, constitute some immutable, primordial given, an identity stamped on the soul. Rooted in culture, not biology, it is not a euphemism for race. Unlike the genetics of race, ethnicity is an aspect of learned behaviour. It is a highly malleable social construct, referring essentially to communal sodality. Though ethnic groups are almost invariably organized on a scale so broad that their members cannot possibly all know one another individually, membership dictates that they all share similar customs, beliefs, and values, have collaborative means of expressing their unity, and nurture a common image of their communal affinity.

Ultimately, ethnicity is simply a matter of the social group's self-identification, its imagined individuality, its distinction from the Other. It arises out of a society's struggle, internally, to organize itself and, externally, to differentiate itself from its neighbours, in pursuit of its collective self-preservation and well-being. Without its sense of common identity, the ethnic collectivity would not long survive, though its individual members well might, under other guise. Yet, as a product of humankind's inventive powers, ethnic identity is situationally adaptive; individuals crossing ethnic boundaries readily adjust their social behaviour and expressed beliefs to fit different cultural contexts. In ethnically complex societies, the frequently encountered circumstances of "ethnic flux", "ethnic porosity", and "double (or multiple) ethnic identity" thus play an important part.

But the concept and its application are not quite so straightforward. Efforts to place ethnicity in broad analytical perspective invariably encounter perplexing problems (Jenkins 1997; Eriksen 2010; Fenton 2010). The overriding issue in nearly all cases is that "in ethnicity and its practical consequences … what ultimately matters is not what exists but what people believe to be true" (Spira 2004, p. 255). In identifying an ethnic group, no amount of intellectual gymnastics can overcome the logical conundrum implicit in attempts to marry the studied "objectivity" imposed by the alien observer with the intuitive "subjectivity" evinced by the indigenous participant. Efforts toward consensus on the specific parameters of ethnicity in specific cases more often than not descend into confusion or controversy. For example, a noted Southeast Asian scholar-statesman on the overseas Chinese, in seeking to apply an interdisciplinary methodology to the issue of ethnic identity in the region's Chinese diaspora, delicately describes the derivation of a general, consensual approach as "elusive" (Wang 1991).

Similar difficulties reside in the long-standing debate between the proponents of social (or "behavioural") and cultural (or "symbolic") criteria as constituting the elemental determinants of ethnic identity. That distinction has been dogged by an abiding dispute between the European (social anthropology) and American (cultural anthropology) schools of thought (Dianteill 2012), as if academia had somehow curiously decided to invent its own pair of contending ethnicities. Cultural anthropologists focus on ethnic groups' distinctive means of symbolic expression, their culture, ranging across a vast tapestry of traits (Geertz 1973, pp. 3–30; Marcus and Fischer 1999). By contrast, social anthropologists and sociologists regard ethnic differentiation as the product of social interaction and organization

(Barth 1969; Sanders 2002). But focusing on the differences between social and cultural criteria obscures their inherent complementarity as "socio-cultural" process and content, with the members of each culture favouring social intercourse within their own community, just as members of a single society prefer to deal with practitioners of their own culture.

A half-century ago a pioneering cross-cultural research project was mounted to map the exceptionally complex ethnic landscape of mainland Southeast Asia (LeBar 1964) and subsequently to produce a parallel atlas for insular Southeast Asia (LeBar 1972). As a result, Southeast Asian ethnic studies were placed "on the map", so to speak. The mainland atlas alone lists a total of 146 distinct ethnic groups, classified across four ethnolinguistic zones: Sino-Tibetan (including Tibeto-Burman); Austro-Asiatic (mainly Mon-Khmer); Tai-Kadai (dominated by Siamese Tai, or Thai); and Malayo-Polynesian (represented by Cham and Malay). Somewhat naively, perhaps, the project's regional maps and accompanying gazetteers were designed to identify and territorially demarcate individual ethnic groups in terms of their linguistic features alone, with no more than secondary support being provided by such other major cultural factors as settlement pattern, kinship structure, religious system, sociopolitical organization, and economic institutions. But no culture trait, no matter how imposing, can claim to define an entire ethnicity.

Moreover, as some of the project's principal collaborators — Lucien Hanks, Jane Hanks, Lauriston Sharp, Georges Condominas — themselves informally acknowledged, the rising intensity of inter-communal relations and growing affinity of cultural features among many of the region's ethnic groups in the presence of rapid modernization prevented the project from clearly delimiting the respective groups' rapidly fading territorial bounds or pinpointing specific localities of intensive cross-cultural contact (traditionally confined to transport junctions, market places, administrative centers, cult sanctuaries, and the like). Not only was that problem closely associated with the project's narrowly defined parameters of ethnic identification, it was compounded by an upsurge of ethnic flux under mid-twentieth-century Southeast Asia's burst of post-colonial nation-building. Ideologically infected nationalism was swiftly extending its influence cross-culturally from the nascent nation-states' political centres to their newly delineated political boundaries. Under the thrust of military-sponsored regimes, the nation-state was fast supplanting the ethnic group as the primary guarantor of communal security and prosperity, however flawed its ability to deliver on its promises. With the ascendency of national political integration, featuring the imposition of official languages and state ideologies, the old cultural criteria for ethnic identification and demarcation were fast losing relevance. The region's traditional ethnic diversity, widely held to derive from an age-old southward flow of human migrations still ongoing today, was being rapidly diluted under the gathering momentum of nationalism. It is telling, in that regard, that each of mainland Southeast Asia's new nation-states appropriated the name of its dominant ethnicity, leaving the region's multitude of less commanding ethnic groups to accommodate to the new political realities as best they could.

The issues of ethnic identification (detecting key culture markers), ethnic differentiation (tracing social boundaries), and ethnic flux (gauging social porosity and cultural adaptation), as exemplified by the ethnic atlas of mainland Southeast Asia, stand out as particularly problematic. First, the selection of specific *objective* cultural markers as means of ethnic identification and classification gives rise to unavoidable ambiguities and inconsistencies. It is not uncommon for a particular culture trait to be shared by communities considered in other respects to be of quite different ethnicity, while another may divide communities otherwise believed to share the same ethnicity. While vagaries of linguistic affiliation stand out as perhaps the most egregious example, none of the many other culture markers that have attracted particular interest, ranging across such disparate features as, for instance, child-rearing practice, death ritual, architectural style, culinary preference, and textile design, can be said to have individually provided definitive markers of ethnic identity. Even the apparently straightforward *subjective* indicator of voluntarily expressed ethnic self-identification has proved a notoriously unreliable guide, as self-identification has been found to vary widely with passing circumstance and changing context.

The delineation of ethnic boundaries constitutes a second, closely related issue. While ethnic bounds are commonly visualized in territorial terms, they actually appear wherever insiders and outsiders reveal their mutual differences in social interaction. The social distinctions between ethnic groups thus often penetrate their individual cultural precincts, creating enigmatic social-cultural inconsistencies. That is plainly evident in the special case of close physical proximity. In Old Bangkok, for instance, the various ethnic groups mingled openly in such unrestricted, inter-communal venues as market places, public entertainments, and ceremonial events. Despite such close ethnic juxtaposition, neither cultural distinctions nor social individualities were compromised. The Thai ruling elite, ever watchful for hints of disaffection, recognized that factor in its policy and practice of interspersing the different ethnic minority settlements along the urban periphery and beyond to deter possibilities of political collusion and civil unrest.

The third highlighted ethnographic problem concerns ethnic flux under conditions of intensified cross-cultural contact — accompanying war, forced migration, manpower exploitation, mercantile intrusion, and the like. In modern times, the most dramatic instance of ethnic flux under intensified cross-cultural contact, accommodation, and assimilation has been the rise of nationalism. "Nationalism [has] provided an ideological means, following the collapse of feudalism and absolutism, for the modern incorporation of elites and masses into the same political space, the nation-state." (Jenkins 1997, p. 144). In Siam, during the decades crossing the nineteenth–twentieth century divide, the kingdom's diverse ethnicities were consolidated — at least superficially — through a deliberate, carefully orchestrated political project pursued under the twin banners of opposing Western imperialism and promoting Thai nationalism. Under that proto-chauvinistic impulse emerged a variety of "post-ethnic" or "supra-ethnic" ideological alliances — affiliations of class, religion, locality, and political faction. Accompanying that reshaping of group coalitions was a process of minority ethnic attrition in the presence of majority Thai-ification. Only with the advent of nationalism and its accompanying process of cultural accommodation and assimilation during the decades crossing into the twentieth century did those traditional social divisions begin to fade, though vestiges linger on a century later. In view of its homogenizing power, nationalism has been succinctly described as "ethnicity writ large" (Eriksen 2010, p. 118). Whether the transformation from ethnic diversity to political and social integration in Siam/Thailand — and, more directly to the point here, Bangkok — has erased traditional communal distinctions or, alternatively, has simply raised ethnicity to a higher level of collective abstraction remains an issue for future studies to deal with.

Feudalism in Comparative Perspective

Has there been more than one feudalism? ... It is a question of the deepest interest whether there have been other societies [than Europe], in other times and in other parts of the world, whose social structures in their fundamental characteristics have sufficiently resembled that of our Western feudalism to justify us in applying the term "feudal" to them as well (Bloch 2014, pp. xvi, 463).

As a generic concept in *political* history, feudalism may be described as the incipient stage of state making. As a *social* system, it can be characterized as a sharply stratified social hierarchy of royals, nobles, and lessers set upon a fragile foundation of patron–client reciprocities. In its *economic* guise it centres on an agrarian mode of production constrained by a relatively primitive land- and labour-intensive technology, with distribution of the output sharply favouring the ruling elite. With the exception of several pioneering forays (Coulbourne 1965; Leach 1985), that heuristic vision of feudalism as a broadly applicable phase of history rather than a unique European experience remains to be rigorously investigated (*pace* the loose-fitting universalist schools deriving from Oswald Spengler, Arnold Toynbee, Fernand Braudel, and the like). In moving beyond the idiosyncratic European case, the complex and highly variable content of feudalism across cultures requires a definition that is sufficiently flexible to accommodate a broad range of empirical configurations. It is possibly the very breadth of the topic that has inhibited in-depth analysis, as the cross-cultural conceptualization of feudalism appears to defy strict conformity to any binding archetype.

Some decades ago it was widely held that, with the decline of the ancient empires, protracted periods of feudalism appeared repeatedly in history; the cases of Japan, China, the Indian subcontinent, and Byzantium, among others, were often called to attention in that regard. Though that theory of world history has fallen from favour in recent years, the comparative dynamics of medieval Europe and premodern Siam (and other Southeast Asian kingdoms) are suggestive of their continued relevance. European feudalism emerged initially out of the Germanic incursions into the weakened Roman heartland (Bloch 2014, p. 465). Similarly, Thai feudalism appeared as a product of Tai tribal infiltration into the Mon-Khmer culture zone (Somsamai 1987, pp. 70–75; Wales 1965, pp. 144–45, 151–52). In both cases the old order succumbed, leaving the invaders to devise successor polities of much-diminished sophistication, an imperfect fusion of two very different cultures. That oft-repeated historical experience has prompted the view that feudalism is a mode of revival from political and social collapse in the wake of catastrophic external shock, an interstitial development stage that may endure indefinitely (Coulbourne 1965, p. 364). The loosely structured, manpower-hungry, multi-ethnic kingdom of Siam, for example, filled a void but could not manage, over the course of more than five centuries until well into the nineteenth century, to exceed a population of some three million souls despite the magnificent mirage of its showcase capital so widely acclaimed by passing visitors.

Feudalism is customarily referred to in Thai studies as *sakdi-na* (power over the fields, alternatively translated as "landed power"). The critical economic factor in traditional Siam was the scarcity of manpower, which meant a "shortage of labour to cultivate the land, to fight enemy invasions, and to make up the work-force for construction projects...." The king remedied that scarcity by "foreign conquest, enticement, and compulsion". The *sakdi-na* system evolved out of that land-labour-power reality (Hong 1984, pp. 9–10). "The point at issue is not so much whether it was the control of land or that of men which was more important but rather how labour was controlled and compelled to work on the land" (Chaiyan 1994, p. 60). Despite that correlative usage, application of the term "feudalism" as a descriptor of premodern Siam's cultural setting has generally been found wanting on several grounds. It is said, for one thing, to be no more than a populist label, a loose, imprecise, even careless gloss begging too many questions to fit the many changing centuries of Siam's cultural history (Reynolds 2006*a*, pp. 102, 120). It is claimed, secondly, to mistakenly transpose to the unique Thai historical record the incommensurable culture of medieval Europe: in the words of one strident critic, "[t]he ancient Thai social system was Thai, the ancient Western social system was Western; they were entirely distinct from one another" (Kukrit 2000, p. 5). In the predominately conservative world of Thai studies it is contended, furthermore, that to speak of Thai feudalism is to misinterpret the country's history within what is widely proclaimed to be an ideologically blinkered, intellectually perverse Marxist framework (Reynolds 1987, pp. 149–69).

Here I present in brief the counter-argument that each of those criticisms is misguided or inadequate in its objection to "Thai feudalism". To dismiss the conceptual status of feudalism on grounds of ambiguity is unjustifiable, as many other political mega-concepts — democracy, class, revolution, modernity, nationalism, etc. — are widely and profitably used as cultural descriptors despite being equally subject to the sin of definitional ambiguity. To discard its application to the Thai historical setting for the incompatibility of certain superficial Thai cultural features with the European case seems simplistic, excessively judgmental, and short-sighted. To reject it for its affinity to Marxist dogma is to jettison an alluring historical metaphor simply for having been co-opted by a particular (unpopular) political ideology. Better to make the most of it rather than throw out the baby with the bathwater.

Beneath the essentially heuristic amalgam of political, social, and economic institutions that together define feudalism, the historical reality emphasized a fundamental reciprocity — as was so clear in the case of Siam — between the embrace of protection from above and the provision of material wealth from below. That equivalence was layered into a progression of hierarchical relationships ultimately joining ruler and ruled. "The characteristic human bond was the subordinate's link with the nearby chief. From one level to another the ties thus formed — like so many chains branching out indefinitely — joined the smallest to the greatest" (Bloch 2014, p. 466). The weak king, reigning over a soft state or barely any state at all, relied on his vassals for their military support just as they depended on his devolution of power through the distribution of benefices, the fief being the most notable. It was a system of dispersed, parcelized political control, a division of despotism between centre and periphery, realm and fiefdom, monarch and nobility, lord and liege. Such a dispersal of sovereign power has often been witnessed in history, ranging from such varying feudal instances as the "desmesnes" of medieval Europe (Bloch 2014, p. 253) and the "segmentary states" of multi-tribal Africa (Southall 1988) to the "galactic polities" of mainland Southeast Asia (Tambiah 1977). A dominant warrior class, a subjugated peasantry, dependence on the fief in exchange for fealty, fragmentation of authority — these are the fundamental political features of feudalism (Bloch 2014, pp. 467–68). "Not citizen to state but vassal to lord was the bond that underlay political structure. The [integrated, territorial] state was still struggling to be born" (Tuchman 1978, pp. 5–6).

That feudal reality was as evident in thirteenth–nineteenth century Siam as in ninth–thirteenth century Europe. In the Thai feudal state, fiefdoms were demarcated in terms of population rather than territory, and power devolved upon them in keeping with manpower allotments rather than land. The king's ambit of authority was restricted; rarely did he countermand the administrative jurisdiction of his vassals, and equally rarely did he leave the security of his capital. In turn, the largely unchecked political authority dispersed among the kingdom's fragmented fiefdoms, governed by oft-rapacious princelings and nobles, ensured a perpetually impoverished, subservient peasantry. The distinction between taxpaying, appointed provincial governors and tribute-tendering subject rulers was blurred and volatile. The outer dependencies, though charged with regular revenue contributions (far more often in kind than in cash) and defence of the kingdom's heartland, often failed fully or faithfully to comply. Vows of fealty were frequently neglected in favour of more immediate, local concerns. "Loyalty …, as a permanent social bond designed to unite the various groups at all levels, … showed itself decidedly ineffective" (Bloch 2014, p. 467). Dispersed militias rather than a unified standing army, decentralized revenue collections (tax and tribute) lacking strict accountability, inadequacies of administrative oversight in the face of transport and communication obstacles, popular resistance to bureaucratic intervention in communal affairs — all those and other issues raised stiff barriers against the rise of the centralized, sovereign state.

Complementary with feudal Siam's divisive political tensions stood its integrative social impulse. A numerical scale of *sakdi-na* ranks, accompanied by an elaborate ordering of titles, formed the basis of Siam's rigid social hierarchy (Akin 1996, pp. 115–34; Englehart 2001, pp. 26–27). That rank ordering featured distinct estates of the body politic — a hereditary aristocracy, a conferred nobility, a consigned commons — supported by elaborate rituals of allegiance, arranged marriage, religious patronage, and the registration (and indelible marking) of commoners. The relations between individuals of differing rank along the *sakdi-na* scale were formally fixed as a master–minion (*nai–phrai*) pecking order. Modulating that rigid chain of command was a resilient grading of informal patron-client arrangements, which undermined the formal status hierarchy. Those unregulated, pliant alliances, or entourages, reinforced the fragmentation of power by supporting lower class, local autonomy from ruling class, centralized control (Akin 1975, pp. 113–23). In the aftermath of Siam's feudal past, such informal patron-client relations persist as a fundamental feature of modern Thai society (Hanks 1975).

In Siam as in Europe, though the village economy under feudalism was supported (from below) by the nexus of informal patronage relations, it was firmly subordinated (from above) to the ruling elite (Bloch 2014, pp. 159–61; Chatthip 1999, pp. 16–43). Three master–minion features predominated in the Thai village world: first, many villages fell under the king's direct jurisdiction, and many more were allotted to lesser royals and high-ranking officials as their fiefs; though often referred to as freemen or yeomen, the peasantry under those masters actually occupied a serf-like status. Second, the cultivators were permitted to farm the land in usufruct but had no right of ownership; they thus occupied their plots at the mercy of their masters. Third, the imposition of taxes and tribute as well as annual labour contributions to state projects ensured that the peasants' lifestyle was persistently pressed to subsistence level. With land and labour serving as complementary inputs, a standard land–labour equivalent was applied under the *sakdi-na* status hierarchy. The *sakdi-na* rank for a single peasant stood at four acres (equivalent to ten *rai*) and eight to ten acres (twenty to twenty-five *rai*) for a peasant household, a landholding scarcely sufficient to maintain its occupants, given the primitive technology of the times. In addition to land allotments approaching that restrictive benchmark, the annual imposition of months of mandatory state servitude plus heavy tax and tribute exactions created often-insuperable burdens. Under those circumstances, radical critiques of Thai feudalism (e.g., Somsamai 1987; Chatthip 1999) have over the years certainly raised a pertinent point in arguing that the reciprocity between the elite's protection and peasantry's production was a spurious equivalence, amounting to little more than extortion. The contrary view that stresses "the vitality and flexibility of the system" in its response to the opening up of the Thai economy over the course of the nineteenth century suggests that the peasantry under Thai feudalism may not have been so seriously downtrodden after all (Hong 1984, p. 150).

With the rise of a commercial, monetized economy in Europe, the sovereign power acquired new revenue sources, and thus greater access to both administrative and military specialists. The central state's reduced dependence on the services of its loosely affiliated, fickle vassals allowed its principal retainers, the emerging gentry, to gain in wealth and influence, an outgrowth sometimes referred to as bastard feudalism (Hicks 1995; Coss 2003). Similarly, the spread of commerce and monetization in nineteenth-century Siam, expedited to no small extent by the royal monopoly trade ventures of the king, viceroy, and select coterie of lesser princes in collaboration with Chinese merchant adventurers, led to their increased wealth and administrative power, ultimately separating them from the rank and file of the nobility and reshaping the latter into little more than a corps of professional bureaucrats (Sarasin 1977, pp. 181–89; Englehart 2001, pp. 94–103). That Siamese version of bastard capitalism contributed greatly to the ultimate transformation of Siam from fragmented, feudal kingdom to absolute monarchy and nation-state.

Such similarities between the European and Siamese cases are evocative. In sum, "it is by no means impossible that societies different from our own should have passed through a phase closely resembling [medieval Europe]. If so, it is legitimate to call them feudal during that phase" (Bloch 2014, p. 468). On the basis of the evidence alluded to here, pre-modern Siam — and Old Bangkok as its spatial, political, and social centre of gravity — certainly stands eligible for that designation. It is in that context that references in earlier chapters to the feudal character of Old Bangkok's social hierarchy should be understood.

THE PORT-CITY'S PLURAL SOCIETY

In [the Southeast Asian port-city] probably the first thing that strikes the visitor is the medley of peoples — European, Chinese, Indian and native. Each group holds by its own religion, its own culture and language, its own ideas and ways. As individuals they meet, but only in the market-place, in buying and selling. There is a plural society, with different sections of the community living side by side, but separately, within the same political unit. Even in the economic sphere there is a division of labour along racial [or rather, ethnic] lines (Furnivall 1956, pp. 304–305).

Some two millennia ago the Greco-Roman historian Lucius Mestrius Plutarchus observed that among the peoples — that is, the ethnic groups — inhabiting the known world of his day the hill dwellers favoured democracy, the lowlanders were subjected to oligarchy, and those who dwelt along the seashore practiced a mixed form of government (Plutarch 2001, vol. 1, p. 114). Plutarch's insight remains cogent today as a convenient trope for examining Southeast Asia's premodern cultural landscape. His observation has, in fact, been rediscovered in contemporary Southeast Asian historical studies to speak incisively of the region's contrasting cultural configurations. It has been asserted, for instance, that Southeast Asian history traditionally revolved around the contending interests of the anarchic uplands, the manpower states of the wet-rice growing lowlands, and the creole (i.e., racially and ethnically diverse) metropolitan centres (Scott 2009). Similarly, the Thai world, in approximate equivalence to Plutarch's tripartite dissection, is said to have historically drawn sharp moral distinctions between the palpably different inhabitants of wilderness (*pa*), countryside (*ban-nok*), and town (*moeang*) (Thongchai 2000*b*). That proposition has helped validate the idea of a three-tiered Southeast Asian political economy: first, subjugation of the region's upland tribes by the neighbouring lowland states through a blatantly coercive, slave-raiding process that provided the lowlanders with much-needed manpower. Second, interaction between the plains peoples and port-cities through a state-sanctioned system of ritual aggrandizement and exploitative agrarian taxation supportive of the urban ruling elite. And third, commercial linkages between the port-cities and the overseas world through mercantile mechanisms that favored the region's aristocracies.

Southeast Asia's lowland kingdoms and colonial dependencies, as manpower states bent on the redistribution of wealth from the hinterlands to the cosmopolitan emporiums, historically ignored the striking cultural distinctions among their inhabitants. "Such states had great incentives to incorporate whomever they could and to invent cultural, ethnic, and religious formulas that would allow them to do so"; each of the lowland states at its core was thus "a social and political invention, an alloy, an amalgam [of ethnic constituencies bearing] traces of ingathering from many diverse sources" (Scott 2009, p. 79). Situated at the vital juncture of Southeast Asia's resource-rich hinterlands and the far-flung reach of cosmopolitan mercantilism, the region's principal urban centres — the port-cities — with their unique political economy encapsulated that ethnic diversity. The porous nature of the region's leading port-cities — Rangoon, Batavia, Saigon and Hanoi, Manila, Singapore, Bangkok — posed persistent challenges to the centripetal and homogenizing tendencies of the multi-ethnic states (colonial or otherwise), yet their vibrant ethnic diversity provided an essential contribution to the wealth and power of the state itself. In retrospect, the historically vexed relations between the region's port-cities — Plutarch's "seaside" — and its lowland and upland hinterlands have been submerged in modern thought beneath such more immediate concerns as methods of resource extraction, institutions of land occupancy and management, policies of wealth appropriation, issues of social status and class relations, and the exigencies of state-making, military prowess, dynastic legitimation, and colonialism in a volatile world of perpetually contending empires. As a result, "in much of the existing literature, [Southeast Asia's] ports hover like disembodied spirits over their own countrysides" (Lieberman 2009, pp. 112–13). For good or bad, the historical development of the ethnically exuberant Southeast Asian port-city has thus come to be viewed as a separate and distinct unit of analysis (Kathirithamby-Wells 1990; Murphy 1989; Falkus 2010).

It was the port-city's very ethnic porosity, in fact, that ensured its intimate association with both the agrarian hinterlands, on the one hand, and overseas markets, on the other. As the domestic economy's redistributive centre, the port-city drew to itself, through the lure of its markets, representation of the inlands' sundry ethnic elites. As the inlands' vent for external trade, it attracted enterprising migrants from overseas. While that interstitial role between the region's inner and outer worlds was the essential source of the port-city's continuing prosperity, its political realization pivoted over the course of the past several centuries: originally a *pre-colonial*, ethnically conjoined plural society; then a *colonial*, imperial, ethnically fragmented plural society; and finally a *post-colonial* national society striving toward ethnic integration and, hopefully, full assimilation. In that volatile history, Bangkok stands out as the exception that proves the rule. (It is worth noting in that regard that, while Thai feudalism lasted longer than in the colonies, the new paradigm of [official] nationalism in the late nineteenth and early twentieth centuries also came earlier to Siam than to the colonies. So Bangkok is the exception that proves the rule in a second respect, too.) Due to its unique nineteenth-century circumstances as an indigenous buffer state between contesting colonial spheres of interest, Bangkok bypassed the explicitly colonial phase of Southeast Asian urban development. In the absence of colonial rule, the kingdom's traditional feudal polity and its well-articulated plural society continued to prevail under the command of the Thai ruling elite. Only with the waning of Thai feudalism upon the centralization of the kingdom's political power in the decades linking the nineteenth and twentieth centuries did the plural society succumb to the new paradigm of Thai nationalism.

Ethnic diversity was so pervasive and intrinsic a feature of the Southeast Asian port-city that it was largely disregarded as a research issue until J.S. Furnivall, in the closing days of the colonial era, brought it into focus in his analysis of Southeast Asian colonial society (Furnivall 1956). His iconic study of Southeast Asian colonial policy and practice attributes to the "plural society" (as he vividly exemplifies in the British and Dutch colonial port-cities of Rangoon and Batavia) several essential properties. "On looking at a plural society in its political aspect", he states, "one can distinguish three characteristic features: the society as a whole comprises separate racial [i.e., ethnic] sections; each section is an aggregate of individuals rather than a corporate or organic whole; and as individuals their life is incomplete" (Furnivall 1956, p. 306). He maintains that unlike the harmonious multi-ethnic social configuration of pre-colonial Southeast Asia, the plural society under Western colonialism featured a confluence of ethnic groups each separately suffering a degree of anomie. It was, in Furnivall's words, "a social structure quite distinct in its political and economic properties" from both the region's indigenous, "medieval", loosely articulated feudal entities and the homogeneous, politically integrated national societies of the West (Furnivall 1956, p. 306).

The plural society of Southeast Asia's colonial port-cities was, in Furnivall's view, dysfunctional, sustainable only through the blatantly coercive measures imposed by the colonial rulers. "There was a racial [sic] division of labour. All the various peoples met in the economic sphere, the market place; but they lived apart and continually tended to fall apart unless held together [by the colonial overlords]" (Furnivall 1956, p. 123). And again: "The urban population was ... divided into separate [ethnic] communities, with very different and often conflicting interests, different ideas of welfare, and few wants in common.... [Self-government] was impossible because there was no self to govern itself" (Furnivall 1956, p. 149). The various urban ethnic communities under colonialism were territorially compartmentalized and segmented, stagnant in their lack of economic opportunity and competitive diversification, polarized in their mutual antipathies, and thus incapable of the "social will" necessary for self-rule. Furnivall noted the political problem associated with that ethnic fragmentation, but in his blinkered perspective as a British colonial civil servant he reversed cause and effect. The aforementioned elements of anomie that he observed among the port-city's ethnic constituencies were not, as he envisaged, the conditions that colonial policy sought to remedy. Rather, they were the product of that very policy, which sought to control the subject populations through such divide-and-rule tactics as social distancing, social undermining, and social marginalization — not to mention political disenfranchisement and economic exploitation.

Despite its analytical shortcomings, Furnivall's study is useful for considering the exceptional case of Bangkok. Of all Southeast Asia's port-cities, nineteenth-century Bangkok was the only one to successfully withstand Western colonial rule. It thereby avoided, by and large, the socially disruptive impact of the colonial policy environment. Unlike Furnivall's "tropical dependencies", the social lives of Bangkok's ethnically diverse residents were not "incomplete". Siam's primate port-city thus continued to function relatively smoothly as a feudal, "medieval" (Furnivall's term), non-colonial social plurality. Its much-debated semi-, quasi-, pseudo-, crypto-, auto-, or informal colonialism under the umbrella of nineteenth-century Western imperialism (Harrison and Jackson 2009; Hong 2003; Hong 2004; Thongchai 2011, p. 27; plus the various articles contained in Harrison and Jackson 2010) appears in this perspective a semantic red herring. Even reading the penetration of Western imperialism into Siam back to the Bowring Treaty of 1855, Great Britain's first gentle foray into Siamese intervention, does not change the picture. The explosive growth of the world market and with it the rapid expansion of Siam's agrarian mono-cultures (led by rice, sugar, and later rubber) and extractive industries (primarily teak and tin) in the wake of the Bowring Treaty brought an intensified mingling of ethnic groups to Bangkok, but it did not change the elemental feudal structure of the port-city's plural society. That development had to await the advent of the absolute monarchy of the late-nineteenth century, followed directly by Siamese state-sponsored nationalism, the emergence of Thai national identity, and the crystallization of the Siamese/Thai nation-state.

THE MANDALA AS URBAN TEMPLATE

The study of such specific "spatial phenomena" as the distribution of particular camps, the layout of towns, the network of roads, "permits us to grasp the natives'" own conception of their social structure; and, through our examination of the gaps and contradictions, the real structure, which is often very different from the natives' conception, becomes accessible" (Kuper 2003, p. 249, citing Lévi-Strauss 1967, p. 328).

Humankind has always and everywhere hungered for security, and in that quest it has ever sought to impose order — unity, stability, continuity — on its otherwise chaotic universe. All science, all civilization may be said to arise from that primordial urge. Among the many conscious and subconscious devices that have been invented to satisfy that ever-present, ever-troubling human predilection is the mandala (*monthon* in Thai), a rigorously symmetrical mental construct, a geometric archetype that builds on the deeply psychological aesthetics of centricity, boundedness, radiation, axiality, dualism, congruence, replication, orientation, and hierarchy. Embedded as a rational abstraction in the collective human consciousness, the mandala provides a cognitive image that bestows a gratifying integrity, harmony, and logic on the cosmos in space and time (Jung 1964, pp. 230–35, 266–73).

Though examples of the mandala as a powerful cognitive image have been noted worldwide (Arguelles 1972, and the sources cited therein) the concept has historically been examined and applied most thoroughly and with most far-reaching implications in South Asia, where it was in ancient days elaborated as a formative element in Brahman cosmology, insight meditation, social ethics, and even political organization. In conformity with its use as an instrument for mental discipline, spiritual vision, and religious ritual demarcating the consecrated space within which supplicants entered into communion with the gods (Tucci 1961, p. 35), the mandala traditionally provided an architectonic blueprint whereby the structure of the cosmos could be replicated on earth not only to glorify the might of the sovereign state and justify the political reach of contending kingdoms but to mandate the social construction of urban space.

Rigorous application of the mandala as a template for state and city planning was explored over two millennia ago by the Indian statesman, Kautilya (c.350–275 BCE), in his authoritative pre-Machiavellian treatise on governance, *Artasastra* (Dutt 1925, p. 8; Lannoy 1971, pp. 314–23). Eventually, that pragmatic vision was transmitted to Southeast Asia, where it was adapted to fit the indigenous political landscape. It came to serve, in due course, as a mystic metaphor for the structure of Southeast Asian and Chinese kingdoms and capitals (Heine-Geldern 1956; Tambiah 1977; Eck 1987; Sunait 1990; Wheatley 2008; Wolters 1999). "The … premodern [Southeast Asian] kingdoms, including those in Thailand, were quite self-consciously constituted as microcosms in which the main lineaments of the cosmography and the hierarchical, merit-determined order of the cosmos were replicated at the level of human social organizations" (Reynolds and Reynolds 1982, p. 23). That vision is described in graphic detail in the mid-fourteenth century Thai metaphysical treatise, *Discourse on the Three Worlds* (Thammapricha 1977–78; Reynolds and Reynolds 1982; Lithai 1985).

Premodern Siam was replete with examples of cultural borrowing and adaptation from the Brahman tradition of South Asia. In Old Bangkok, the heir to that tradition examined in this book, application of the mandala as the template of symmetrical urban space was tacitly accepted. Rigorous application of the mandala's aesthetic elements identified the city's ceremonial centre, the *axis mundi*, by the precise midpoint positioning of its guardian spirit shrine, sheltering the sacred *omphalos*. The city bounds, dividing inner order from outer chaos, were delineated by an encircling wall, bastions, shuttered gates, and moat. Sanctity, status, and sumptuousness radiated in diminishing gradations from the city centre to the periphery and beyond. The city's palaces, temples, and lesser landmarks were graded from the centre outward, aligned along the cardinal axes, and oriented to the auspicious east. Its principal precincts were systematically bifurcated between inner and outer, superior and inferior, north and south, east and west. Replication was evident in the structural equivalence of the city's major elements and the nesting of congruent sites of progressively lesser scale but increasing sanctity. The mandala's emphasis on hierarchy was exemplified in the soaring rooflines and tapering towers punctuating the city skyline as allusions to the cosmic order itself. At the same time, the city's populace was distributed radially from centre to periphery and beyond in keeping with considerations of status and power, and was divided north and south of the centre in keeping with aspects of royal patronage.

One of the urban mandala's last appearances in Southeast Asian history — the very last being the eponymous city of Mandalay, founded in 1857 — was in the design and construction of Bangkok, founded only seventy-five years earlier. Though often contested, there can be no doubt, upon close examination of Bangkok's architectonic detail, that the mandala provided the essential template for the city's original physical structure and social organization (Map 1.2; Van Roy 2010*b*; Van Roy 2011). Over the subsequent generations, the evolving Bangkok cityscape diverged progressively from its original design for a myriad petty pragmatic reasons, obscuring its metaphoric image and culminating, around the turn of the twentieth century, in the dismantling of its traditional infrastructure and social plan in favour of a new urban morphology patterned after Western prototypes. That physical and social transformation of Bangkok's symbolic cityscape formed an integral element of Siam's transition from premodern feudal polity to modern nation-state, a process that remains incomplete to the present day.

Reliance on the mandala as an organizing principle in Old Bangkok's urban design was clearly supported by universal human predilections for spatial harmony. Its role in framing the city's social organization is perhaps less apparent. "The correlations between 'spatial configurations' and 'social structures' may in some cases be obvious, in others evident but not clear, and in others 'extremely difficult to discover'" (Kuper 2003, p. 249). But close analysis demonstrates the link. The mandala template underlying Bangkok's cityscape was not simply some sort of subliminal, psychological demiurge directing the planners' conscious thoughts and actions, nor was it simply an esoteric formula providing a mystic patina to mundane events; rather, it had an immediate practical purpose in defining the ruling elite's command over the capital's social resources. In the case of Old Bangkok, we can go one step further by examining the nexus between the city's evolving physical structure and social organization from its eighteenth century inception into its twentieth century transformation. Among the many questions that arise in examining that urban history with direct reference to the sacred symbolism of the mandala are the role that the mandala motif played in Bangkok's planning and construction; the manner in which the mandala's aesthetic principles expressed themselves in Bangkok's physical design; the means whereby the mandala informed the city's social organization, including the polarities between its Thai ruling elite and its various ethnic minorities; the progressive entropy that caused the capital's mandala template to atrophy over the course of the city's two-centuries-long history; and the ways in which the city's structural transformation interacted with the kingdom's transition from multi-ethnic feudality to integrated nation-state.

Such questions animate the contentious concept of the urban mandala. They redirect attention from the blunt assertions that "after [twelfth-century] Angkor, it is hard to identify a Southeast Asian city in which the *mandala* is a strong influence" (Sunait and Baker 2002, p. 172) and that "even the most cursory glance at the layout of the walled and moated city of Bangkok shows that it lacks the sophisticated symmetry required to fulfill its role as the center of the cosmos" (Englehart 2001, p. 81). Similarly, they challenge the view that "the layout of [Old Bangkok] showed an obvious lack of concern for the correct arrangement of the Indic ritual space [viz., the mandala] in which to carry into effect the performative form of government that Clifford Geertz has famously termed (with reference to Bali) the 'theater state'" (Peleggi 2002, p. 78). Instead, they build on the recognition that Bangkok's founder "attempted to microcosmically recapitulate the macrocosm in the physical structure of his capital .... [Bangkok was built as] an artificial mountain representing Mt. Meru ... which was laid out in a series of concentric circles symbolically identifying cosmos and kingdom" (Kirsch 1978, p. 57)).

* * *

Bangkok was for the span of its existence as "Old" Bangkok — here identified as the period covering the first five reigns of the Chakri dynasty (1782–1910) — a vibrant centre of ethnic diversity. The city's disparate minority ethnic constituencies of refugees, captives, and sojourners drawn from near and far were, in fact, one of its defining features. Unlike the scattering of isolated community studies that form the bread and butter of traditional ethnography — in mainland Southeast Asia ordinarily oriented to an examination of the peasant hinterlands and the splintered cultures of the upland frontiers — the preceding chapters have sought to illuminate the staying power of the multiplicity of cultures inhabiting urban Bangkok, the very core of one of the region's dominant states. Remarkably, Bangkok's diverse citizenry thrived within the city's close quarters under a political regime that affected a traditionally complacent, even neglectful attitude toward its diversity of ethnic groupings. Equally remarkably, the city's ethnic heterogeneity intensified steadily while remaining peaceably intact for well over a century after the 1767 abandonment of Ayutthaya for the downstream Thonburi anchorage, the capital's cross-river move to Bangkok, and the subsequent generations of turbulent growth. If nothing else, this book has offered a synoptic description of that notable achievement.

It was Old Bangkok's distinctive spatial, political, and social construction that provided the supportive institutional base for that cosmopolitan citizenry: the mandala template that segmented the city among its ethnic gradients; the feudal hierarchy that linked the respective ethnic groups with the Thai ruling elite though a chain of dyadic master-minion relations; the communal "benign neglect" that allowed the separate ethnic constituencies a high degree of internal autonomy in exchange for their fealty to the Siamese state. Through those mechanisms the urban whole transcended the sum of the city's many individual ethnic parts. At the root of those integrative mechanisms lie the contentious concepts that continue to enliven the ongoing debate over the nature of Siam's — and Bangkok's — premodern history.

In the process of reconnoitering the ethnic landscape of Old Bangkok, this study has delineated various regularities that defined that urban terrain. And so, the study has moved from enthnography to ethnology. One of the distinctions of contemporary social analysis is its consistent avoidance of macro-theory. But broad theoretical preconceptions inevitably underlie even the narrowest of empirical studies. By closing this ethnographic survey of Old Bangkok's multi-cultural panorama with a brief gathering-together of certain implicit analytical issues, I have sought to bring to light some key elements of the study's underlying frame-of-reference. An explicit recognition of those predilections is essential to combatting the many prejudices to which Thai ethnohistorical studies are persistently prone.

Bibliography

Adis Idris Raksamani (2008). "Multicultural Aspects of Mosques in Bangkok". *Manusya: Journal of Humanities*, special issue no. 16, pp. 114–34.

Akin Rabibhadana (1975). "Clientship and Class Structure in the Early Bangkok Period". In *Change and Persistence in Thai Society*, edited by G. William Skinner and A. Thomas Kirsch. Ithaca, NY: Cornell University Press, pp. 93–124.

—— (1978). "Rise and Fall of a Bangkok Slum". Bangkok: Thai Khadi Research Institute, Thammasat University.

—— (1996 [1969]). *The Organization of Thai Society in the Early Bangkok Period, 1782–1873*. 2nd ed. Bangkok: Amarin.

Alisa Ramkomut, ed. (1999). *Ko kret: withi chiwit chumchon mon rim nam chaophraya* [Ko Kret: Life of a Mon Community Along the Chaophraya River]. Bangkok: Department of Fine Arts.

Amphan Kitngam (1994). "*Naew kamphaeng moeang kao samai krung ratanakosin*" [The Course of the Old City Wall During the Ratanakosin Period]. *Silpakon* 37, no. 6, pp. 44–62.

Amphoe Phra Nakhon (1961). *Kwamru roeangton kiawkap amphoe phra nakhon* [Introduction to the Phra Nakhon District]. Bangkok: Sammit.

Amphon Iamsuri (2005). *Hia kwongiam: Chiwa prawat chut pap* [Hia Kwong-iam: An Illustrated Biography]. Bangkok: Hun Suan.

Anake Nawigamune (2006). *Farang thi kiaw khong kap siam* [*Farang* Who Had Connections With Siam]. Bangkok: Saengdao.

Andaya, Leonard Y. (1999). "Ayutthaya and the Persian and Indian Muslim Connection". In *From Japan to Arabia: Ayutthaya's Maritime Relations with Asia*, edited by Kennon Breazeale. Bangkok: Foundation for the Promotion of Social Sciences and Humanities Textbooks Project, pp. 119–136.

Anon. (c.1913). "*Prawat sakun chotikasathien*" [History of the Chotikasathien lineage]. Privately printed.

Antonio, J. (1997 [1904]). *The 1904 Traveller's Guide to Bangkok and Siam*. Bangkok: White Lotus.

Antony, Robert (2003). *Like Froth On the Sea: The World of Pirates and Seafarers in Late Imperial South China*. Berkeley: University of California, Institute of East Asian Studies.

Arguelles, José and Miriam (1972). *Mandala*. Boulder, CO: Shambala.

Aruwan Lowira and J. Baffie (1992). "*Ban khrua: adit an rungrot roe anakot cha dap sun?*" [Ban Khrua: A Rich Past but an Empty Future?]. *Silpa Wathanatham* 13, no. 10, pp. 176–86.

Assumption Cathedral (1995). *Wachara sompot asan wihan assamchan, 1919–1994* [Anniversary Celebration of Assumption Cathedral, 1919–1994]. Bangkok: Assumption Press.

Baffie, Jean (2007). "The Ang-yi or Chinese Secret Societies of Thailand, Understanding a Total Social Phenomenon". In *Investigating the Grey Areas of the Chinese Communities in Southeast Asia*, edited by Arnaud Leveau. Bangkok: Research Institute on Contemporary Southeast Asia, pp. 11–30.

Bajunid, Omar Farouk (1992). "The Other Side of Bangkok: A Survey of Muslim Presence in Buddhist Thailand's Capital City". In *The Formation of Urban Civilization in Southeast Asia*, edited by Yoshihiro Tsubouchi. Kyoto: Kyoto University, Center of Southeast Asian Studies, pp. 11–42.

Bang-on Piyabhan (1998). *Lao nai krung ratanakosin* [The Lao in (the) Ratanakosin (Kingdom)]. Bangkok: Thailand Research Fund Foundation for the Promotion of Social science and Humanities Textbook Project.

Barmé, Scot (1993). *Luang Wichit Wathakan and the Creation of a Thai Identity*. Singapore: Institute of Southeast Asian Studies.

Barth, Frederik (1969). "Introduction". In *Ethnic Groups and Boundaries: The Social Organization of Culture Difference*, edited by *idem*. Oslo: Universitetsforlaget, pp. 9–38.

Bateson, Benjamin A. (1976). "American Diplomats in Southeast Asia in the Nineteenth Century: The Case of Siam". *Journal of the Siam Society* 64, part 2, pp. 39–111.

Battye, Noel A. (1974). "The Military, Government and Society in Siam, 1868–1910: Politics and Military Reform during the Reign of King Chulalongkorn". Doctoral dissertation. Ithaca, NY: Cornell University.

Bauer, Christian (1990). "Language and Ethnicity: The Mon in Burma and Thailand". In *Ethnic Groups across National Boundaries in Mainland Southeast Asia*, edited by Gehan Wijeyewardene. Singapore: Institute of Southeast Asian Studies, pp. 14–47.

Bidya Sriwattanasarn (1998). "*Chumchon chaw portuket nai samai krung ayutthaya pho. so. 2059-2310*" [The Portuguese Community During the Ayutthaya Period, 1516–1767]. Ph.D. thesis. Bangkok: Chulalongkorn University.

Bloch, Marc (2014 [1940]). *Feudal Society*. London and New York: Routledge.

Borel, Brigitte (2008). "The Early Byzantine Lamp from Pong Tuk". *Journal of the Siam Society* 96, pp. 1–26.

Bowring, Sir John (1969 [1857]). *The Kingdom and People of Siam*. 2 vols. Kuala Lumpur: Oxford University Press.

Boxer, C. R. (1963). *Race Relations in the Portuguese Colonial Empire, 1415–1825*. Oxford: Clarendon Press.

——— (1965). "Asian Potentates and European Artillery in the 16th-18th Centuries". *Journal of the Malayan Branch of the Royal Asiatic Society* 37, part 2, pp. 156–72.

——— (1969). *The Portuguese Seaborne Empire 1415–1835*. New York: Alfred A. Knopf.

Bradley, William L. (1981). *Siam Then: The Foreign Colony in Bangkok Before and After Anna*. Pasadena, CA: William Carey Library.

Breazeale, Kennon (1999). "Thai Maritime Trade and the Ministry Responsible". In

From Japan to Arabia: Ayutthaya's Maritime Relations with Asia, edited by *idem*. Bangkok: Foundation for the Promotion of Social Sciences and Humanities Textbooks Project, pp. 1–54.

—— (2002). "The Lao – Tay-son Alliance, 1792 and 1793". In *Breaking New Ground in Lao History: Essays on the Seventh to Twentieth Centuries*, edited by Mayoury Ngaosyvathn and Kennon Breazeale. Chiangmai: Silkworm Books, pp. 261–80.

Bristowe, W.S. (1976). *Louis and the King of Siam*. New York: Thai-American Publishers.

Brown, Ian G. (1988). *The Elite and the Economy of Siam c. 1890-1920*. Singapore: Oxford University Press.

—— (1992). *The Creation of the Modern Ministry of Finance in Siam, 1885-1910*. London: Macmillan.

Brown, R.A., ed. (1995). *Chinese Business Enterprise in Asia*. London: Routledge.

Brummelhuis, Han ten (1987). *Merchant, Courtier and Diplomat: A History of the Contacts Between the Netherlands and Thailand*. Gent: Uitgeversmaatschappij de Tijdstroom.

Buls, Charles (trans. from French) (1901). *Siamese Sketches*. Brussels: Georges Balat.

Bunchuay, Phra Maha (So. Cho. Wano) (1979). *Khana song raman nai prathet thai* [The Raman Monastic Order in Thailand]. Bangkok: Khiriwan.

Bunnag, Jane (1973). *Buddhist Monk, Buddhist Layman: A Study of Urban Monastic Organization in Central Thailand*. Cambridge: Cambridge University Press.

Campos, Joaquim de (1959 [1940]). "Early Portuguese Accounts of Thailand". In *Selected Articles from the Siam Society Journal, Vol. VII, Relationship With Portugal, Holland, and the Vatican*. Bangkok: Siam Society, pp. 211–37.

Chaen Pachachusanon (1966). *Prawat kan thahan roea thai* [History of the Thai Navy]. Bangkok.

Chaiyan Rajchagool (1994). *The Rise and Fall of the Thai Absolute Monarchy: Foundations of the Modern Thai State from Feudalism to Peripheral Capitalism*. Bangkok: White Lotus.

Chamnongsri Ratnin (1998). *Dut nawa klang mahasamut* [Like a Ship Afloat Upon the Ocean]. Bangkok: Nanmi Books.

Chandler, David P. (2000). *A History of Cambodia*. 3rd ed. Chiangmai: Silkworm Books.

Chang Ian-chiu (1991). "*Kan ophayop ma prathet thai khong chaw chianghai*" [The Migration of Chianghai People to Thailand]. In *Chaw chin taechiu nai prathet thai lae nai pumisamnao doem thi chaosan ... (2310-2393)* [The Taechiu Chinese in Thailand and In Their Former Homeland in Chaosan ... (1767-1850)], edited by Supang Chanthawanit. Bangkok: Institute of Asian Studies, Chulalongkorn University, pp. 27–35.

Charney, Michael W. (2004). *Southeast Asian Warfare, 1300-1900*. Leiden: Brill.

Chatchai Panananon (1982). "Siamese 'Slavery': The Institution and Its Abolition." Doctoral dissertation, Ann Arbor, MI: University of Michigan.

—— (1988). "*Phrai*, Neither Free Nor Bonded". *Asian Review 1988*, vol. 2, pp. 1–22.

Chatri Prakitnonthakan (2012). "Rattanakosin Charter: The Thai Cultural Charter for Conservation". *Journal of the Siam Society* 100, pp. 123–48.

——— (2013). *Sanyalak lae kan ok baep wat arun rachawararam* [Symbolism and Design of Wat Arun Rachawararam]. Bangkok: Amarin.

Chatthip Nartsupha (Chris Baker and Pasuk Phongpaichit, trans.) (1999 [1984]). *The Thai Village Economy in the Past*. Chiangmai: Silkworm Books.

Chen, Chingho A. (1977). "Mac Thien Tu and Phraya Taksin: A Survey on Their Political Stand, Conflicts and Background". *Proceedings of the Seventh Conference of the International Association of Historians of Asia*, vol. 2, Bangkok, pp. 1534–75.

Chirachati Santiyot (2008). "*Phra racha chaya chao dara rasami: kap kansang khwamsongcham duay phiphipthaphan lae anusawari*" [Royal Wife Chao Dara Rasami: and the Construction of Her Museum and Memorial Monument]. *Silpa Wathanatham* 25, no. 11, pp. 79–101.

Chitrasing Piyachat (2009). *Prawatisat songkhram thai rop khamen* [History of the Wars Between the Thai and the Khmer]. Bangkok: Yip Si.

Chokchai Wongtani (2011). "*Malayu Bangkok/nayu bakoi: kan phochonphai nai paendin syam/siyae*" [The Bangkok Malays/Nayu Bakoi: Adventures in Siam/Siyae). *Rubaiyat: Journal of Asian Studies* 2, no. 3, pp. 402–73.

Chuan Khroeawichanyachan (1994). *Withi chiwit chaw mon* [The Way of Life of the Mon People]. Bangkok: Moeang Boran.

Chulalongkorn, King (1989 [1888]). "*Phra rachadamrat nai phrabat somdet phra chula chom klao chao yu hua song thalaeng phra rachathibai kae khai kan pok khrong phaendin*" [Proclamation of King Chulalongkorn Explaining Improvements in the Kingdom's Administration]. In *Ekasan kan moeang kan pok khrong thai (B.E. 2417-2577)* [Thai Political and Administrative Documents (1874-1934)], edited by Chai-anan Samudavanija and Khatthiya Kanasut. Bangkok: Social Science Association of Thailand, pp. 72–99.

——— (1997 [n.d.]). "*Khat khon*" [Lacking of Manpower]. In *Nangsoe sanuk* [A Book of Readings for Pleasure], compiled by Sulak Sivaraksa. Bangkok: Kled Thai, pp. 47–54.

Conversi, Daniele, ed. (2004). *Ethnonationalism in the Contemporary World*. London: Routledge.

Coss, Peter (2003). *The Origins of the British Gentry*. Cambridge: Cambridge University Press.

Coughlin, Richard J. (1960). *Double Identity: The Chinese in Modern Thailand*. Hong Kong: Hong Kong University Press.

Coulborn, Rushton, ed. (1965 [1956]). *Feudalism in History*. Hamden, Conn.: Archon Books.

Crawfurd, John (1967 [1828]). *Journal of an Embassy to the Courts of Siam and Cochin China*. Kuala Lumpur: Oxford University Press.

Cruikshank, R. B. (1975). "Slavery in Nineteenth Century Siam". *Journal of the Siam Society* 63, part 1, pp. 316–33.

Cushman, Jennifer W. (1981). "Siamese State Trade and the Chinese Go-between, 1767–1855". *Journal of Southeast Asian Studies* 12, no. 1, pp. 46–61.

Cushman, Richard D. (2000). *The Royal Chronicles of Ayutthaya*. Bangkok: Siam Society.

Damrong Rachanuphap, Prince, ed. (1937). "*Phra racha phongsawadan krung thonburi, chabap phan chanthanamat (choem)*" [The Royal Chronicle of Krung Thonburi, Phan Chanthanumat (Choem) Edition]. In *Prachum phongsawadan, pak thi 65* [Collected Chronicles, Volume 65], edited by idem. Bangkok: Daily Mail.

—— (1939). *Lamdap sakun khochaseni lae borankhadi mon* [The Generations of the Khochaseni Family and Its Mon Antiquity]. Bangkok: Privately published cremation volume.

—— (1962 [1926]). "The Introduction of Western Culture in Siam". In *Miscellaneous Articles Written for the Journal of the Siam Society by His Late Royal Highness Prince Damrong*, edited by Dhani Nivat. Bangkok: Siam Society, pp. 107–114.

—— (1964 [1922]). "*Roeang tamnan wang kao*" [Concerning the History of Old Palaces]. In *Prachum phongsawadan phak thi 26* (Collected Chronicles, Part 26). Bangkok: Khurusapha, pp. 61–209.

—— (1993 [1906]). "Historical Background to the Dispatches of Luang Udomsombat". In *Rama III and the Siamese Expedition to Kedah in 1839: The Dispatches of Luang Udomsombat*, translated by Cyril Skinner and edited by Justin Corfield (1993). Clayton: Monash University, Centre of Southeast Asian Studies, pp. 1–31.

—— (2001 [1917]). *Our Wars With the Burmese: Thai-Burmese Conflict 1539–1767*. Bangkok: White Lotus.

—— (2008). *A Biography of King Naresuan the Great*, translated and edited by Kennon Breazeale. Bangkok: Toyota Thailand Foundation and Foundation for the Promotion of Social Science and Humanities Textbooks Project.

D'Ávila Lourido, Rui (1996). "European Trade Between Macao and Siam, From the Beginnings to 1663". *Journal of the Siam Society* 84, Part 2, pp. 75–10.

Dhida Saraya (1999). *(Sri) Dvaravati: The Initial Phase of Siam's History*. Bangkok: Moeang Boran.

Dianteill, Erwan (2012). "Anthropologie Culturelle ou Anthropologie Sociale? Une Dispute Transatlantique". *L'Année Sociologique* 62, no. 1, pp. 93–122.

Dutt, Binode Behari (1925). *Town Planning in Ancient India*. Calcutta: Thacker, Spink and Co.

Eck, Diana L. (1987). "The City as a Sacred Center". In *The City as Sacred Center: Essays on Six Asian Contexts*, edited by Bardwell Smith and H.B. Reynolds. Leiden: Brill, pp. 1–11.

Englehart, Neil A. (2001). *Culture and Power in Traditional Siamese Government*. Ithaca, NY: Cornell University, Southeast Asia Program.

Eriksen, Thomas Hylland (2010). *Ethnicity and Nationalism: Anthropological Perspectives*. 3rd ed. London: Pluto Press.

Evers, Hans-Dieter, ed. (1969). *Loosely Structured Social Systems: Thailand in Comparative Perspective*. New Haven, CT: Yale University Southeast Asia Studies.

Falkus, Malcolm (2010). "Bangkok in the Nineteenth and Twentieth Centuries: The Dynamics and Limits of Port Primacy". In *Gateways of Asia: Port Cities of Asia in the 13th–20th Centuries,* edited by Frank Broeze. New ed. Oxford: Routledge, pp. 211–32.

Fenton, Steve (2010). *Ethnicity.* 2nd ed. Cambridge, U.K.: Polity Press.

Ferrand, Gabriel (1920). "Les Poids, Mesures et Monnies des Mers du Sud aux XVIe et XVIe Siècles". *Journal Asiatique* 16, pp. 5–150, 193–312.

Finlayson, George (1988 [1826]). *The Mission to Siam and Hué 1821–1822.* Singapore: Oxford University Press.

Foster, Brian Lee (1973). "Ethnic Identity of the Mons in Thailand". *Journal of the Siam Society* 61, part 1, pp. 203–26.

Francis Xavier Anurat na Songkhla, Fr., ed. (1999). *Wat sangtakhrut wat kudi chin* [Santa Cruz Church, Kudi Chin Church]. Bangkok: J.A.S. International.

Furnivall, J.S. (1956 [1948]). *Colonial Policy and Practice: A Comparative Study of Burma and Netherlands India.* New York: New York University Press.

Geertz, Clifford (1973). *The Interpretation of Cultures.* New York: Basic Books.

Gosling, Betty (1991). *Sukhothai: Its History, Culture and Art.* Singapore: Oxford University Press.

Goss, Frederick B. (2008). "'*Anucha*': The Younger Brother in *Ramakien* and Thai Historical Narratives". *Rian Thai: International Journal of Thai Studies* 1, no. 1, pp. 26–51.

Greene, Stephen L.W. (1999). *Absolute Dreams: Thai Government Under Rama VI, 1910–1925.* Bangkok: White Lotus.

Grabowsky, Volker (1996). "The Thai Census of 1904: Translation and Analysis". *Journal of the Siam Society* 84, part I, pp. 49–85.

Guillon, E. (1999). *The Mons: A Civilization of Southeast Asia.* Bangkok: Siam Society.

Gutzlaff, Charles (1834). *Journal of Three Voyages Along the Coast of China in 1831, 1832, and 1833.* London: Frederick Westley and A.H. Davis.

Halliday, Robert (1913). "The Immigration of the Mons into Siam". *Journal of the Siam Society* 10, no. 3, pp. 1–15.

——— (1922). "The Mons in Siam". *Journal of the Burma Research Society* 12, no. 2, pp. 69–79.

Hanks, Lucien M. (1972). *Rice and Man: Agricultural Ecology in Southeast Asia,* Honolulu: University of Hawaii Press.

——— (1975). "The Thai Social Order as Entourage and Circle". In *Change and Persistence in Thai Society,* edited by G. William Skinner and A. Thomas Kirsch. Ithaca, NY: Cornell University Press, pp. 197–218.

Harris, P.M.G. (2001). *The History of Human Populations, Vol. 1: Forms of Growth and Decline.* Homewood, Illinois: Praeger.

Harrison, Rachel V. and Peter A. Jackson (2009). "Siam's/Thailand's Constructions of Modernity Under the Influence of the Colonial West". *South East Asia Research* 17, no. 13, pp. 325–60.

———, eds. (2010). *The Ambiguous Allure of the West: Traces of the Colonial in Thailand.* Hong Kong: Hong Kong University Press.

Harvey, G.E. (1925). *History of Burma From the Earliest Times to 10 March 1824, the Beginning of the English Conquest*. London: Thomas Nelson.

Heine-Geldern, Robert (1956 [1942]). "Conceptions of State and Kingship in Southeast Asia" (Data Paper No. 18). Ithaca: Cornell University Southeast Asia Program.

Hicks, Michael (1995). *Bastard Feudalism*. London: Routledge.

Historical Publications Committee (1971). *Tamnan phoen moeang chiangmai* [Local History of Chiangmai]. Bangkok.

Ho, Chuimei (1995). "Chinese Temples in Bangkok: Sources of Data for 19th-Century Sino-Thai Communities". *Journal of the Siam Society* 83, parts 1 and 2, pp. 25–43.

Hogendorn, Jan, and Marion Johnson (1986). *The Shell Money of the Slave Trade*. Cambridge: Cambridge University Press.

Holm-Peterson, F. (1979). *Windjammers Under the Old Elephant Flag: Notes About the Old Siamese Merchant Navy 1824–1900*. Troense, Denmark: The Maritime Museum.

Hong Lysa (1984). *Thailand in the Nineteenth Century: Evolution of the Economy and Society*. Singapore: Institute of Southeast Asian Studies.

——— (2003). "Extraterritoriality in Bangkok in the Reign of Chulalongkorn, 1868–1910: The Cacophony of Semi-colonial Cosmopolitanism". *Itinerario: European Journal on the History of European Expansion* 27, no. 2, pp. 25–46.

——— (2004). "'Stranger Within the Gates': Knowing Semi-Colonial Siam as Extraterritorials". *Modern Asian Studies* 38, no. 2, pp. 327–54.

Hooker, M.B. (1988). "The 'Europeanization' of Siam's Law 1855–1908". In *The Laws of South-East Asia. Vol. II: European Laws in South-East Asia*, edited by idem. Singapore: Butterworth and Co. (Asia), 1988, pp. 531–77.

Hudson, Roy (1983). "Lineage of Constance Phaulcon". Letters to the Editor, *Bangkok Post*, 4 October, p. 8A.

Imanaga, Seiji (2000). *Islam in Southeast Asia*. Hiroshima: Keisuisha.

Inthira Sahee (2004). "The Network of Indian Textile Merchants in Thai Society". *Asian Review* 17, pp. 39–57.

Ishii, Yoneo (1986a). *Sangha, State and Society: Thai Buddhism in History*. Honolulu: University of Hawaii Press.

——— (1986b). "The Thai Thammasat". In *The Laws of South-East Asia. Vol. I: The Pre-Modern Texts*, edited by M.B. Hooker. Singapore: Butterworth (Asia), pp. 143–203.

——— (2012). "A Note on the Cham Diaspora in the Ayutthayan Kingdom". In *Anthony Reid and the Study of the Southeast Asian Past*, edited by Geoff Wade and Li Tana. Singapore: Institute of Southeast Asian Studies, pp. 242–45.

Ivarsson, Søren (1995). "The Study of *Traiphum Phra Ruang*: Some Considerations". In *Thai Literary Traditions*, edited by Manas Chitakasem. Bangkok: Chulalongkorn University, pp. 56–85.

Jenkins, Richard (1997). *Rethinking Ethnicity: Arguments and Explorations*. London: Sage.

Johnson, Samuel (1755). *Preface to a Dictionary of the English Language*. Amazon Digital Services LLC (Kindle Edition): Public Domain Book.

Joseph Wuthiloet Haelom, Fr., ed. (1997). *100 pi si kalawa,1897–1997* [100 Years: Sri-Calvary, 1897–1997]. Bangkok: Holy Rosary Church.

Jottrand, Emile and Denise (W.J. Tips, trans. from French) (1996 [1905]). *In Siam: The Diary of a Legal Adviser of King Chulalongkorn's Government*. Bangkok: White Lotus.

Julisphong Chularatana (2003). *Khunnang krom tha khwa* [Nobles of the Western Trade Department]. Bangkok: Chulalongkorn University, Faculty of History.

—— (2008). "The Shi'ite Muslims in Thailand from [the] Ayutthaya Period to the Present". *Manusya: Journal of Humanities*, special issue no. 16, pp. 37–58.

Jung, Carl. G., ed. (1964). *Man and His Symbols*. London: Aldus.

Kalayani Wathana, Princess (1980). *Mae lao hai fang* [What My Mother Told Me]. Chiangmai: Suriwong Book Center.

Kaplan, Yosef (1992). "The Formation of the Western Sephardic Diaspora". In *The Sephardic Journey, 1492–1992*, edited by Sylvia A. Herskowitz. New York: Yeshiva University Museum, pp. 136–55.

Kasian Tejapira (1992). "Pigtail: A Pre-History of Chineseness in Siam". *Sojourn: Journal of Social Issues in Southeast Asia* 7, no. 1, pp. 95–122.

—— (1997). "Imagined Uncommunity: The *Lookjin* Middle Class and Thai Official Nationalism". In *Essential Outsiders*, edited by Daniel Chirot and Anthony Reid. Seattle: University of Washington Press, pp. 75–98.

—— (2001). *Commodifying Marxism: The Formation of Modern Thai Radical Culture, 1927–1958*. Kyoto: Kyoto University Press.

Kathirithamby-Wells, J. (1990). "Introduction: An Overview". In *The Southeast Asian Port and Polity: Rise and Decline*, edited by J. Kathirithamby-Wells and John Villiers. Singapore: Institute for Southeast Asian Studies, pp. 1–16.

Keyes, Charles (2008–2009). "Muslim 'Others' in Buddhist Thailand". *Thammasat Review* 13, no. 1, pp. 19–42.

Khachon Sukhaphanit (1976). *Thanandon phrai* [The Status of Phrai]. Bangkok: Si Nakharin Wirot University.

Khumsupha, Malinee (2010). "Changing Bangkok 1855–1909: The Effects of European Settlers and Their Subjects". *Rian Thai: International Journal of Thai Studies* 3, pp. 65–96.

Kirsch, A. Thomas (1978). "Modernizing Implications of Nineteenth Century Reforms in the Thai Sangha". In *Religion and Legitimation of Power in Thailand, Laos and Burma*, edited by Bardwell Smith. Chambersburg, Penn.: Anima, pp. 52–65.

Kukrit Pramot (2000). *Farang sakdina* [Western Feudalism]. Bangkok: Dokya.

Kuper, Hilda (2003 [1972]). "The Language of Sites in the Politics of Space". In *The Anthropology of Space and Place: Locating Culture*, edited by Setha M. Low and Denise Lawrence-Zuñiga. Oxford: Blackwell, pp. 247–63.

La Loubère, Simon de (1969 [c.1700]). *The Kingdom of Siam*. Kuala Lumpur: Oxford University Press.

Lannoy, Richard (1971). *The Speaking Tree: A Study of Indian Culture and Society*. London: Oxford University Press.

Lazara, Leopoldo Ferri de and Paolo Piazzardi (1996). *Italians at the Court of Siam*. Bangkok: Amarin.

Leach, Edmund R., et al (1985). *Feudalism: Comparative Studies*. Sydney: Sydney Association for Studies in Society and Culture.

LeBar, Frank M., ed. (1972). *Ethnic Groups of Insular Southeast Asia*. New Haven, Conn.: Human Relations Area Files Press.

——, et al. (1964). *Ethnic Groups of Mainland Southeast Asia*. New Haven, Conn.: Human Relations Area Files Press.

Lévy-Strauss, Claude (1967). *Structural Anthropology*. New York: Basic Books.

Li Tana (2004). "The Late-Eighteenth- and Early-Nineteenth-Century Mekong Delta in the Regional Trade System". In *Water Frontier: Commerce and the Chinese in the Lower Mekong Region, 1750–1880*, edited by Nola Cooke and Li Tana. Singapore: National University of Singapore, pp. 71–84.

Lieberman, Victor (2003). *Strange Parallels: Southeast Asia in Global Context, c. 800–1830*. 2 vols. Cambridge: Cambridge University Press.

—— (2009). "Mainland Southeast Asia and the World Beyond, c. 800–1825: Rethinking Assumptions". *Journal of Asian History* 43, no. 2, pp. 103–36.

Lithai, King (Kullasap Gesmankit et al., trans.) (1985 [c. 1360]). *Traibhumikatha: The Story of the Three Planes of Existence*. Bangkok: Amarin.

Loos, Tamara (2005). "Sex and the Inner City: The Fidelity between Sex and Politics in Siam". *Journal of Asian Studies* 64, no. 4, pp. 881–909.

Mani, A. (1993). "Indians in Thailand". In *Indian Communities in Southeast Asia*, edited by K.S. Sandhu and A. Mani. Singapore: Institute of Southeast Asian Studies and Times Academic Press, pp. 910–49.

Manich Jumsai (1972). *Popular History of Thailand*. Bangkok: Chalermnit.

—— (2001). *History of Thailand and Cambodia*. 7th revised ed. Bangkok: Chalermnit.

Marcus, George E. and Michael M.J. Fischer (1999). *Anthropology as Cultural Critique: An Experimental Moment in the Human Sciences*. 2nd ed. Chicago: University of Chicago Press.

Matichon (2005). *Wang na chana songkhram: chalong pha pa...* [The Front Palace (and Wat) Chana Songkhram: Celebratory Offering of Monks' Robes ...]. Bangkok: Matichon.

Mayoury and Pheuiphanh Ngaosyvathn (1994). *Kith and Kin Politics: The Relationship Between Laos and Thailand*. Manila: Journal of Contemporary Asia Publishers.

—— (1998). *Paths to Conflagration: Fifty Years of Diplomacy and Warfare in Laos, Thailand and Vietnam, 1778–1828*. Ithaca: Cornell University, Southeast Asia Program.

McDaniel, Justin (2011). *The Lovelorn Ghost and the Magical Monk: Practicing Buddhism in Modern Thailand*. New York: Columbia University Press.

McFarland, George B., ed. (1999 [1928]). *Historical Sketch of Protestant Missions in Siam, 1828–1928*. Bangkok: White Lotus.

Mead, Kullada Kesboonchoo (2004). *The Rise and Decline of Thai Absolutism*. London: Routledge Curzon.

Mendonça e Cunha, Hélder de (1976 [1971]). "The 1820 Land Concession to the Portuguese". In *Collected Articles in Memory of HRH Prince Wan Waithayakorn*. Bangkok: Siam Society, pp. 142–47.

Mongkut, King (1964 [1851–1868]). *Prachum prakat rachakan thi 4* [Collected Proclamations of King Rama IV]. Bangkok: Phrae Phithaya.

—— (1987 [c.1857]). "Proclamation Concerning Treaty Farangs". In *A King of Siam Speaks*, edited and translated by Seni Pramoj and Kukrit Pramoj. Bangkok: Siam Society, pp. 42–46.

Montesano, Michael J. (2005). "Beyond the Assimilation Fixation: Skinner and the Possibility of a Spatial Approach to Twentieth-Century Thai History". *Journal of Chinese Overseas* 1, no. 2, pp. 184–216.

Moor, J. H. (1968 [1837]). *Notices of the Indian Archipelago, and Adjacent Countries*. London: Frank Cass and Co.

Moore, R. Addy (1914–1915). "An Early British Merchant in Bangkok". *Journal of the Siam Society* 11, part 2, pp. 21–39.

Morbey, Jorge (2006). *A Heritage Home in Bangkok — The Portuguese Ambassador's Residence*. Bangkok: Embassy of Portugal.

Murashima, Aichi (1996). *Kan moeang chin siam kan khloean wai tang kan moeang chaw chin phon thale nai prathet thai kh. s. 1924–1941* [Sino-Chinese Politics: Political Movements of the Overseas Chinese in Thailand, 1924–1941]. Bangkok: Institute of Asian Studies, Chinese Studies Center, Chulalongkorn University.

Murphy, Rhoads (1989). "On the Evolution of the Port City". In *Brides of the Sea: Port Cities of Asia from the 16th–20th Centuries*, edited by Frank Broeze. Honolulu: University of Hawaii Press, pp. 223–45.

Muzaffar, Chandra (1986). "Islamic Resurgence: A Global View". In *Islam and Society in Southeast Asia*, edited by Taufik Abdullah and Sharon Siddique. Singapore: Institute of Southeast Asian Studies, pp. 5–39.

N. na Paknam (1999). *Tham top: silpa thai* [Questions and Answers: Thai Art]. Bangkok: Sarakhadi.

Naengnoi Saksri et al. (1991). *Ong prakop thang kai phap krung ratanakosin* [Physical Aspects of the City of Ratanakosin]. Bangkok: Chulalongkorn University Press.

Neale, F.A. (1852). *Narrative of a Residence in Siam*. London: National Illustrated Library.

Nidhi Eosiwong (1996). *Kan-moeang thai samai phrachao krung thonburi* [Thai Politics During the Reign of the King of Thonburi]. 4th ed. Bangkok: Silpa Wathanatham.

—— (2002). "Niphan Wang Na" [Death of the (First-Reign) Viceroy]. *Silpa Wathanatham* 23, no. 3, pp. 106–11.

Nit Hinchiranan (1964). "*Adit kap pachuban: thanon charoen krung ton sam yaek*" [Past and Present: Charoen Krung Road to Sam Yaek]. *Warasan Thesaban Nakhon Krungthep* [Bangkok Municipality Journal], no. 46, pp. 30–31.

O'Connor, Richard A. (1978). "Urbanism and Religion: Community, Hierarchy, and Sanctity in Urban Thai Buddhist Temples". Doctoral dissertation. Ithaca, NY: Cornell University.

Ong Banchun (2007). *Ying mon: amnat lae rachasamnak* [Mon Women: Power and the Royal Court]. Bangkok: Matichon.

Ornanong Noriwong Benbournenane (2012). *Political Integration Policies of the Thai Government Toward the Ethnic Malay-Muslims of Southernmost Thailand (1973-2000)*. Chulalongkorn University, Institute of Asian Studies.

Pallegoix, Msgr. Jean-Baptiste (2000 [1854]). *Description of the Thai Kingdom of Siam: Thailand under King Mongkut*. Bangkok: White Lotus.

Parate Attavipach (2008). "*Botbat khong chon chat mon to prawatisat lae sangkhom khong thai*" [Role of the Mon in Thai History and Society]. *Silpa Wathanatham* 29, no. 6, pp. 91–104.

Pasuk Phongpaichit and Chris Baker (2002). *Thailand: Economy and Politics*. 2nd ed. Selangor Darul Ehsan, Malaysia: Oxford University Press.

Pattana Kitiarsa (2005). "*Farang* as Siamese Occidentalism". Singapore: University of Singapore, Asia Research Institute Working Paper Series No. 49. (Reworked as Pattana Kitiarsa (2010). "An Ambiguous Intimacy: *Farang* as Siamese Occidentalism". In *The Ambiguous Allure of the West: Traces of the Colonial in Thailand*, edited by Rachel V. Harrison and Peter A. Jackson. Ithaca and Hong Kong: Hong Kong University Press, pp. 57–74.)

Peleggi, Maurizio (2002). *Lords of Things: The Fashioning of the Siamese Monarchy's Modern Image*. Honolulu: University of Hawaii.

Penchan Phoborisut (2008). "Understanding the Identity of the Thai Muslim Community of Kudi Khao in Thonburi, Bangkok". *Manusya: Journal of Humanities*, special issue no. 16, pp. 68–81.

Penth, Hans (1994). *A Brief History of Lan Na: Civilizations of North Thailand*. Chiangmai: Silkworm.

Phanni Bualek (2002). *Laksana khong nai thun thai nai chuang rawang 2457-2482* [Features of Thai Capitalists, 1914-1929]. Bangkok: Panthakit.

——— (2012). "*Chumchon musalim bang ko laem*" [The Muslim Communities at Bang Ko Laem]. *Moeang Boran* 28, no. 4, pp. 25–33.

——— and Aphinya Nonnat (2013). "*Wat phraya krai*" [Wat Phraya Krai]. *Moeang Boran* 39, no. 2, pp. 52–57.

Phathara Khan (2007). "*Wan wan 3 samai masyit ton son*" [Three Different Periods (in the History) of the Ton Son Mosque]. *Warasan aksonsat: Khaek thai — khaek thet kham khet khwamru* [Liberal Arts Journal: (Special Issue on) Thai Muslims — Foreign Muslims Across Various Areas of Knowledge] [Chulalongkorn University, Faculty of Arts] 36, no. 1, pp. 128–72.

Phibul Choompolpaisal (2013). "Tai-Burmese-Lao Buddhisms in the 'Modernizing' of Ban Thawai (Bangkok): The Dynamic Interaction Between Ethnic Minority Religion and British–Siamese Centralization in the Late Nineteenth/Early Twentieth Centuries". *Contemporary Buddhism* 14, no. 1, pp. 94–115.

——— (2015). "Political Buddhism and the Modernisation of Thai Monastic Education: From Wachirayan to Phimonlatham (1880s–1960s)". *Contemporary Buddhism* 16, no. 2, pp. 428–50.

Phiset Choey-chanphong (2003). *Phra phutha sihing: "ching" thuk ong mai mi "plom" tae mai dai ma chak langka.* [The Phra Sihing Buddha Image: Every Image is "Real", There is No "Imitation", But None Comes from Sri Lanka]. Bangkok: Matichon.

Phobun Wibulo, Phra Maha (2003). "Prawat wat sam phraya, phra aram luang chan tri chanit saman" [History of Wat Sam Phraya, Third Class Royal Temple of the Common Type]. Unpublished manuscript.

Phromphong Phairiran (2004). *Chumchon chang haeng krung ratanakosin* [Artisans' Communities in Bangkok]. Bangkok: Wanchana.

Phum, Khun (1922 [1869]). *Nirat wang bang yi-khan* [Elegy on the Bang Yi-khan Palace Community]. Bangkok: Sophonphiphit.

Phusadi Thiphathat (2002). *Ban nai krung ratanakosin* [Houses in Bangkok]. 4 vols. Bangkok: Chulalongkorn University Press.

Pinto, Fernão Mendes (1989 [1614]). *The Travels of Mendes Pinto.* Chicago: University of Chicago Press.

Pirasi Povatong (2005). *Chang farang nai krung siam* [Western Artisans (Architects) in the Kingdom of Siam (in the Fifth Reign)]. Bangkok: Chulalongkorn University Press.

Pisarn Boonphook (2007). *Khroeang pan din phao nonthaburi* [Fired Earthenware of Nonthaburi]. Bangkok: Sukhothai Thammathirat University.

Piyanat Bunnag (1993a). "*Sampheng: Kwampen ma lae kan plianplaeng (ph. s. 2325 – ph. s. 2475)*" [Sampheng: Origin and Change (1782–1932)], [Part I]. *Warasan rachabanthit sathan* [Royal Library Journal] 18, no. 3, pp. 63–81.

———— (1993b). "*Sampheng: Kwampen ma lae kan plianplaeng (ph. s. 2325 – ph. s. 2435)*" [Sampheng: Origin and Change (1782–1932)], [Part II]. *Warasan rachabanthit sathan* [Royal Library Journal] 18, no. 4, pp. 28–50.

———— (unattributed) (1999). "*Thin-than ban roean khong sakun bunnag*" [Locations of the Homes of the Bunnag Lineage]. In *Sakun Bunnak* [The Bunnak Lineage], by Banchop Bunnag et al., vol. 1. Bangkok: Thai Wathana Phanit, pp. 340–59.

———— (2006). "*Sampheng: Prawatisat chumchon chaw chin nai krungthep maha nakhon*" [Sampheng: History of a Chinese Community in Bangkok]. In *Sampheng: Prawatisat chumchon chaw chin nai krungthep* [Sampheng: History of a Chinese Community in Bangkok], edited by Supang Chanthawanit. Bangkok: Institute of Asian Studies, Chulalongkorn University, pp. 1–22.

Plutarch (2001 [c.110 C.E.]). *Plutarch's Lives.* 2 vols. New York: The Modern Library.

Poole, Peter A. (1970). *The Vietnamese in Thailand: A Historical Perspective.* Ithaca, NY: Cornell University Press.

Porphant Ouyyanont (2013). "The Bangkok Economy in 1937/38". In *Essays on Thailand's Economy and Society*, edited by Pasuk Phongpaichit and Chris Baker. Bangkok: Sangsan, pp. 157–74.

Pramuan Wichaphun, Phraya (1939). *Phongsawadan moeang lan chang lae lamdap sakun sithisaribut rachasakun lan chang wiangchan* [The Chronicles of Lan Chang and the Genealogy of the Sithisaribut Royal Lineage of Vientiane, Lan Chang]. Bangkok: Private printing.

Prani Klamsam (2002). *Yan kao nai krungthep* [Old Neighbourhoods in Bangkok]. Bangkok: Moeang Boran.

Praphatson Phosithong (2007). *"Phokha musalim kap kankha pha india nai na prawatisat thai"* [Muslim Merchants and the Trade in Indian Textiles in Thai History]. *Warasan aksonsat: Khaek thai — khaek thet kham khet khwamru* [Liberal Arts Journal: (Special Issue on) Thai Muslims — Foreign Muslims Across Various Areas of Knowledge], 36, no. 1, pp. 173–88.

Pussadee Chandavimol (1998). *Vietnam nai moeang thai* [The Vietnamese in Thailand]. Bangkok: Thailand Research Fund.

Reid, Anthony (2000). *Charting the Shape of Early Modern Southeast Asia.* Singapore: Institute of Southeast Asian Studies.

Reynolds, Craig J. (1972). "The Buddhist Monkhood in Nineteenth Century Thailand". Doctoral dissertation. Ithaca, NY: Cornell University.

——— (1987). *Thai Radical Discourse: The Real Face of Thai Feudalism Today.* Ithaca: Cornell University, Southeast Asia Program.

——— (2006*a* [1985]). "Feudalism as a Trope for the Past". In *Seditious Histories: Contesting Thai and Southeast Asian Pasts,* edited by idem. Seattle: University of Washington Press, pp. 102–21.

——— (2006*b* [1979]). "Religious Historical Writing in Early Bangkok". In *Seditious Histories: Contesting Thai and Southeast Asian Pasts,* edited by idem. Seattle: University of Washington, pp. 143–60.

Reynolds, Frank E. and Mani B. Reynolds, trans. and ed. (1982). Three *Worlds According to King Ruang: A Thai Buddhist Cosmology.* Berkeley: University of California Press.

Rong Syamananda (1977). *A History of Thailand.* Bngkok: Chulalongkorn University/ Thai Wathana Panich.

S. [Sombat] Plainoi (2002). *"Lao bangkok"* [The Bangkok Lao]. *Silpa Wathanatham* 23, no. 3, pp. 98–103.

Saichon Sathayanurak (2003). *Somdet krom phraya damrong rachanuphap kansang athalak "moeang thai" lae "chan" khong chaw sayam* [Prince Damrong Rachanuphap's Construction of the Identities of the "Thai State" and the "Classes" of the Siamese People]. Bangkok: Silpa Wathanatham.

Sakurai, Yumio and Takako Kitagawa (1999). "Ha Tien or Banteay Meas in the Time of the Fall of Ayutthaya". In *From Japan to Arabia: Ayutthaya's Maritime Relations with Asia,* edited by Kennon Breazeale. Bangkok: Foundation for the Promotion of Social Sciences and Humanities Textbooks Project, pp. 150–217.

Samai Charoenchang (2012). *Yon roi … muslim siam* [Tracing Back … the Muslims of Siam]. Bangkok: Foundation for the Development of Young People for Leadership.

San Thongpan (2000). *"Dan khanon"* [Military Inspection Posts and Transit Tax Stations]. *Moeang Boran* 26, no. 4, pp. 60–65.

Sanders, Jimy M. (2002). "Ethnic Boundaries and Identity in Plural Societies". *Annual Review of Sociology* 28, pp. 327–57.

Sansani Wirasilchai (1994). *Choe ban nam moeang nai krungthep* [Place Names in Bangkok]. Bangkok: Matichon.

—— (2007). *Luk than lan thoe thi yu boeang kwam samret nai racha samnak* [Royal Family Members (Women) Who Stood Behind the Success of the Royal Household]. Rev. ed. Bangkok: Mathichon.

Saowani Jitmoud (2001). *"Klum chat phan musalim nai thonburi"* [Muslim Ethnic Groups in Thonburi]. In *Musalim masyit ton son kap banphachon sam yut samai* [The Muslims of the Ton Son Mosque and Their Forebears over Three Eras], edited by idem. Bangkok: Chira Rachakan, pp. 89–102.

Sarasin Viraphol (1977). *Tribute and Profit: Sino-Siamese Trade, 1652–1853*. Cambridge, Mass.: Council of East Asian Studies, Harvard University.

Sarassawadee Ongsakul (2005). *History of Lan Na*. Chiangmai: Silkworm Books.

Schmitt, Joseph (1904). "Les Thavais" [The Tavoyans]. *Revue Indochinoise, 2e semestre*, pp. 443–44.

Scott, James C. (2009). *The Art of Not Being Governed: An Anarchist History of Upland Southeast Asia*. New Haven: Yale University Press.

Scupin, Raymond (1980). "Islamic Reformism in Thailand". *Journal of the Siam Society* 68, part 2, pp. 1–10.

—— (1998). "Muslim Accommodation in Thai Society". *Journal of Islamic Studies* 9, no. 2, pp. 229–58.

Seabra, Leonor de (2005). *The Embassy of Pero Vaz de Siqueira to Siam (1684–1686)*. Macao: University of Macau.

Seidenfaden, Erik (1927). *Guide to Bangkok*. Bangkok: Royal State Railways of Siam.

Sellers, Nicholas (1983). *The Princes of Ha-Tien (1682–1867)*. Brussels: Thanh-Long.

Sia Kuang (Chow Phongphichit, trans. from Chinese) (2004). *Kichakam thang kan moeng khong chaw chin phon thale nai prathet thai (kh. s. 1906–1939)* [Political Affairs of the Overseas Chinese in Thailand, 1906–1939]. Bangkok: Chinese Studies Center, Institute of Asian Studies, Chulalongkorn University.

Sidhu, Manjit S. (1993). *Sikhs in Thailand*. Bangkok: Institute of Asian Studies, Chulalongkorn University, 1993.

Silva, Beatriz da (1997). *Cronologia da História de Macau* [Chronology of the History of Macao]. 5 vols., 2nd ed. Macao: Direcção dos Serviços de Educação e Juventude.

Silva Rego, Antonio da (1982). "A Short Survey of Luso-Siamese Relations from 1511 to Modern Times". In *Thailand and Portugal, 470 Years of Friendship*, by anonymous, Lisbon: Calouste Gulbenkian Foundation, pp. 7–27.

Sirichai Narumit (1977). *Old Bridges of Bangkok*. Bangkok: The Siam Society.

Sisak Walliphodom (1996). *"Sai sakun sultan sulaiman sha"* [The Lineage of Sultan Sulaiman Shah]. In *Musalim nai prathet thai* [Muslims in Thailand], by Prayunsak Chalayandecha. Bangkok: Amarin, pp. 73–137.

—— (2000). *Phumisat-phumilak: tang ban paeng moeang* [Physiographic Features: Layout of the Country]. Bangkok: Moeang Boran.

—— (2004). *"Lum nam maeklong mi khon yut hin pen banaphachan khun yut pachuban"* [The Meklong River Basin had Stone Age People Who Were the

Ancestors of the Present-day People]. In *Lum nam maeklong: prawatisat chatiphan "khroeayat" mon* [The Meklong Basin: History of Our Mon "Kin"], edited by Suchit Wongthet. Bangkok: Matichon, pp. 27–79.

Siwali Phuphet, ed. (2006). *Chiwaprawat lae kanngan khong farang nai moeang thai* [Biographies and Work of *Farang* in Thailand]. 2 vols. Bangkok: Thailand, Department of Fine Arts.

Skinner, Cyril, trans., and Justin Corfield, ed. (1993). *Rama III and the Siamese Expedition to Kedah in 1839: The Dispatches of Luang Udomsombat.* Clayton: Monash University, Centre of Southeast Asian Studies.

Skinner, G.W. (1957). *Chinese Society in Thailand: An Analytical History.* Ithaca, NY: Cornell University Press.

Smith, Bardwell, ed. (1978). *Religion and Legitimation of Power in Thailand, Laos and Burma.* Chambersburg, PA: Anima Books.

Smithies, Michael (1972). "Village Mons of Bangkok". *Journal of the Siam Society* 61, part 1, 307–32.

Snit Smuckarn and Kennon Breazeale (1988). *A Culture in Search of Survival: The Phuan of Thailand and Laos.* New Haven: Yale University Southeast Asia Studies.

Somsamai Srisudravarna [Jit Poumisak] (1987 [1957]). "The Real Face of Thai Saktina Today". In *Thai Radical Discourse: The Real Face of Thai Feudalism Today*, by Craig J. Reynolds. Ithaca, NY: Cornell University, Southeast Asia Program, pp. 43–148.

Sorayut Choenphakdi (2001). *"Musalim masyit ton son kap banphaburut sam samai"* [The Muslims of the Ton Son Mosque and Their Ancestors over Three Eras]. In *Musalim masyit ton son kap banphachon sam yut samai* [The Muslims of the Ton Son Mosque and Their Forebears over Three Eras], edited by Saowani Jitmoud. Bangkok: Chira Rachakan, pp. 1–32.

Sorayut Cholthira (2007). *"Thai musalim choeasai cham"* [The Thai Muslims of Cham Ancestry]. *Warasan aksonsat: Khaek thai — khaek thet kham khet khwamru* [Liberal Arts Journal: (Special Issue on) Thai Muslims — Foreign Muslims Across Various Areas of Knowledge], 36, no. 1, pp. 112-127.

South, Ashley (2003). *Mon Nationalism and Civil War in Burma: The Golden Sheldrake.* London: Routledge Curzon.

Southall, Aidan (1988). "The Segmentary State in Africa and Asia". *Comparative Studies in Society and History* 30, no. 1, pp. 52–82.

Spira, Thomas (2004). "Ethnicity and Nationality: The Twin Matrices of Nationalism". In *Ethnonationalism in the Contemporary World*, edited by Daniele Conversi. London: Routledge, pp. 248–68.

Stengs, Irene (2009). *Worshipping the Great Modernizer: King Chulalongkorn, Patron Saint of the Thai Middle Class.* Singapore: National University of Singapore.

Sternstein, Larry (1982). "City of Magnificent Distances". In *Portrait of Bangkok*, edited by idem. Bangkok: Bangkok Metropolitan Administration, pp. 65–85.

——— (1984). "The Growth of the Population of the World's Pre-eminent 'Primate City': Bangkok at its Bicentenary". *Journal of Southeast Asian Studies* 15, no. 1, pp. 43–68.

Sthirakoses (Phraya Anuman Rachathon) (1992). *Looking Back: Book One*. Bangkok: Chulalongkorn University Press.

────── (2002). *Looking Back: Book Three*. Bangkok: Chulalongkorn University Press.

Stowe, Judith A. (1991). *Siam Becomes Thailand: A Story of Intrigue*. London: Hurst.

Streckfuss, David (1993). "The Mixed Colonial Legacy in Siam: Origins of Thai Racialist Thought, 1890–1910". In *Autonomous Histories, Particular Truths: Essays in Honor of John Smail*, edited by Laurie Sears. Madison: University of Wisconsin, Center for Southeast Asian Studies, pp. 123–53.

Suchaw Phloychum (2001). *Khana song raman nai prathet thai* [The Raman Monastic Order in Thailand]. Bangkok: Mahamakut Rachawithayalai.

Suchit Wongthet, ed. (2002). *Wiang wang fang thon: chumchon chaw siam* [The City and Palaces on the Thonburi Side: a Siamese Community]. Bangkok: Matichon.

────── (2005). *Krungthep ma chak nai, Bangkok: The Historical Background* [What are Bangkok's Origins? The Historical Background]. Bangkok: Matichon.

Suehiro, Akira (1989). *Capital Accumulation in Thailand 1855–1985*. Tokyo: Centre for East Asian Cultural Studies.

Sujaritlak Deepadung et al. (1983). *Botbat nai dan sangkhom wathanatham lae kanmoeang khong khon klum noi nai krung ratanakosin: khwampenma lae khwamplianplaeng nai rop 200 pi: mon* [Social, Cultural, and Political Roles of a Minority Group in Bangkok: Origins and Changes over 200 Years: The Mon]. Mimeographed. Bangkok: Chulalongkorn University.

Sulak Sivaraksa (1995). *Thai khadi soeksa kap ongruam haeng khwamru* [Thai Studies and the Whole Body of Knowledge]. Bangkok: Semasikhalai.

────── (1997). *Wathanatham lae ithiphon khwamkit baep farang to kanplianplaeng khong sangkhom thai* [The Influence of *Farang* Thought and Culture on Change in Thai Society]. Bangkok: Semasikhalai.

Sunait Chutintaranond (1990). "'Mandala', 'Segmentary State' and Politics of Centralization in Medieval Ayudhya". *Journal of the Siam Society* 78, no. 1, pp. 89–100.

────── (1999). "Mergui and Tenasserim as Leading Port Cities in the Context of Autonomous History". In *From Japan to Arabia: Ayutthaya's Maritime Relations with Asia*, edited by Kennon Breazeale. Bangkok: Foundation for the Promotion of Social Sciences and Humanities Textbooks Project, pp. 104–18.

────── and Chris Baker (2002). *Recalling Local Pasts: Autonomous History in Southeast Asia*. Chiangmai: Silkworm Books.

Supang Chanthawanit (1991). "*Tin kamnoet khong chao chin taechiu bai prathet chin*" [The Place of Origin of Thailand's Chinese Taechiu People]. In *Chaw chin taechiu nai prathet thai lae nai pumisamnao doem thi chaosan ... (2310–2393)* [The Taechiu Chinese in Thailand and In Their Former Homeland in Chaosan ... (1767–1850)], edited by idem. Bangkok: Institute of Asian Studies, Chulalongkorn University, pp. 1–18.

────── (1997). "From Siamese Chinese to Chinese-Thai: Political Conditions and Identity

Shifts Among the Chinese in Thailand". In *Ethnic Chinese as Southeast Asians*, edited by Leo Suryadinata. Singapore: Institute of Southeast Asian Studies, pp. 232–66.

—— (2006). "*Kanka lae kan khonsong nai yan sampheng: Ak tha roea sampao su tha roea konfai*" [Trade and Shipping in the Sampheng District: From Junk Port to Steamship Port]. In *Sampheng: Prawatisat chumchon chaw chin nai krungthep* [Sampheng: History of a Chinese Community in Bangkok], edited by idem. Bangkok: Institute of Asian Studies, Chulalongkorn University, pp. 67–92.

Suporn Ocharoen (1998). *Mon nai moeang thai* [The Mon in Thailand]. Bangkok: Thammasat University Press.

Surachit Chantharasakha (2002). "*Yuan (wietnam) ophayop*" [Yuan (Vietnamese) Migrations]. *Silpa Wathanatham* 23, no. 7, pp. 106–15.

Surin Mukhsi (2002). "*Krung thonburi nai phaenthi phama*" [Thonburi in a Burmese Map]. In *Wiang wang fang thon: chumchon chaw siam* [City and Palaces on the Thonburi Side: Siamese Communities], edited by Suchit Wongthet. Bangkok: Matichon, pp. 105–15.

Suthachai Yimprasert (1999). "The Portuguese in Siam and Pegu". *Asian Review 1999–2000*, 13, pp. 37–59.

Suthiwarapiwat, Phra Khru (2006). *Wat Suthi-wararam* [Wat Suthi-wararam]. Bangkok.

Swi Saw-lin (Sawai Wisawanan, trans. from Chinese) (1991). "*Nayobai chaw chin phon thale khong rachawong ching*" [Ching Dynasty Policies Concerning the Overseas Chinese]. In *Chaw chin taechiu nai prathet thai lae nai pumisamnao doem thi chaosan … (2310–2393)* [The Taechiu Chinese in Thailand and In Their Former Homeland in Chaosan … (1767–1850)], edited by Supang Chanthawanit. Bangkok: Institute of Asian Studies, Chulalongkorn University, pp. 36–87.

Tambiah, Stanley Jeyaraja (1976). *World Conqueror and World Renouncer: A Study of Buddhism and Polity in Thailand Against a Historical Background*. Cambridge: Cambridge University.

—— (1977). "The Galactic Polity: The Structure of Traditional Kingdoms in Southeast Asia". *Annals of the New York Academy of Sciences*, no. 293, pp. 69–97.

Tanabe, Shigeharu (1978). "Land Reclamation in the Chao Phraya Delta". In *Thailand: A Rice-Growing Society*, edited by Yoneo Ishii. Honolulu: University Press of Hawaii, pp. 40–82.

Tanya Phonanan (1984). *Bangkok Street Directory*. Bangkok: Executive Resource (Thailand).

Terweil, B.J. (2005). *Thailand's Political History: From the Fall of Ayutthaya to Recent Times*. Bangkok: River Books.

Thailand, Department of the Army (2004). *Tamnan thahan mahadlek* [History of the Royal Pages Bodyguard]. Bangkok.

Thailand, Department of Fine Arts (1963). *Prachum phongsawadan pak thi 62 wa duai roeang thut farang samai krung ratanakosin* [Collected Chronicles, Part 62: Western Embassies During the Ratanakosin Period], vol. 34. Bangkok: Kurusapha.

Thailand, Ministry of Culture, Department of Religious Affairs, Muslim Affairs Bureau (n.d. [1988?]). *"Prachachon khon isalam lae masjit nai prathet thai, BE 2531"* [Muslim Population and Mosques in Thailand, 1988]. Unpublished mimeograph. Bangkok.

Thailand, Ministry of Foreign Affairs (2008). *Foreign Residents in Siam* [excerpts from Dan Bradley, *The Bangkok Calendar, 1859-1872*]. Bangkok.

Thailand, Ministry of Interior (1910). [Untitled summary of data from the 1909/10 census], *Thesaphiban*, no. 10 (special issue), pp. 138-212.

Thailand, National Archives (1913). "An Additional Memo". Bangkok [quoted in Stephen Greene (1970), "King Wachirawut's Policy on Nationalism". In *In Memoriam: Phya Anuman Rajadhon*, edited by Tej Bunnag and Michael Smithies. Bangkok: Siam Society.]

Thailand, National Muslim Center, Office of the Islamic Committee of the Bangkok Municipality (n.d. [2011?]). Unpublished computer printout.

Thailand, Post and Telegraph Department (1883). *Sarabanchi [krom praisani thoralek], chulasakarat 1245* ([Post and Telegraph Department] Directory, 1883). 4 vols. Bangkok.

Thailand, Royal Institute (2007). *Wat sangkhrachai worawihan* [Wat Sangkhrachai Worawihan]. Printed on the occasion of a royal presentation of monks' robes. Bangkok.

Thailand, Royal Railway Department (n.d. [1903?]). *Tiraloek chalong sathapana thang rotfai pak tai* [Souvenir of the Inauguration of the (First Stage of the) Southern Railway Line]. Bangkok.

Thammapricha (Kaew), Phraya (1977-1978 [1802]). *Traiphumi lok winichai katha chabap thi 2* [Consideration of the Three Worlds Discourse, Second Edition]. 3 vols. Bangkok: Department of Fine Arts.

Thanet Aphornsuvan (2009). "The West and Siam's Quest for Modernity: Siamese Responses to Nineteenth Century American Missionaries". *South East Asian Research* 17, no. 3, pp. 401-431.

Thawi Sawangpanyangkun (2002). "*16 wat annam nikai nai thai*" [16 Annamese Temples in Thailand], *Silpa Wathanatham* 23, no. 11, pp. 100-102.

Theingi, Hla and Theinghi (2011). "Sikh Business Community in Thailand". In *Sikhs in Southeast Asia: Negotiating an Identity*, edited by Shamsul AB and Arunajeet Kaur. Singapore: Institute of Southeast Asian Studies, pp. 221-40.

Thipakorawong, Chaophraya (1995 [c. 1870]). *Phra racha phongsawadan krung ratanakosin rachakan thi 3* [The Royal Chronicles of Krung Ratanakosin, Third Reign]. 6th ed. Bangkok: Royal Thai Government, Department of Fine Arts.

——— (2005 [c.1870]). *Phra rachaphongsawadan krung ratanakosin rachakan thi 2* [The Royal Chronicles of Krung Ratanakosin, the Second Reign], edited by Narimon Thirawat and Nithi Auesriwongse. Bangkok: Amarin Printing.

——— (2009a [c.1870]). *Phra racha phongsawadan krung ratanakosin rachakan thi 1* [The Royal Chronicles of Krung Ratanakosin: First Reign]. Bangkok: Amarin (for Wat Phra Chetuphon Wiman Mangkhalaram).

—— (2009*b* [c.1870]). *Phra racha phongsawadan krung ratanakosin rachakan thi 4* [The Royal Chronicles of Krung Ratanakosin: Fourth Reign]. Bangkok: Amarin Printing.

Thipakosa, Maha Amat Tri Phraya (Son Lohanan) (1985 [1930]). *Prawat somdet phra phuthachan to phromrangsi* [Biography of Somdet Phra Phuthachan (To Phromrangsi)]. Bangkok.

Thongchai Winichakul (2000*a*). "The Others Within: Travel and Ethno-spatial Differentiation of Siamese Subjects, 1885–1910". In *Civility and Savagery: Social Identity in Tai States*, edited by Andrew Turton. Richmond, Surrey: Curzon, pp. 38–62.

—— (2000*b*). "The Quest for 'Siwilai': A Geographical Discourse of Civilizational Thinking in the Late Nineteenth and Early Twentieth-Century Siam". *Journal of Asian Studies* 59, no. 3, pp. 528–49.

—— (2011). "Siam's Colonial Conditions and the Birth of Thai History". In *Unraveling Myths in Southeast Asian Historiography*, edited by Volker Grabowsky. Bangkok: River Books, pp. 20–41.

Tomosugi, Takashi (1991). *Rethinking the Substantive Economy in Southeast Asia*. Tokyo: University of Tokyo, Institute of Oriental Culture.

—— (1993). *Reminiscences of Old Bangkok: Memory and the Identification of a Changing Society*. Tokyo: University of Tokyo, Institute of Oriental Culture.

Tucci, Giuseppe (1961 [1949]). *The Theory and Practice of the Mandala*. London: Rider.

Tuchman, Barbara W. (1978). *A Distant Mirror: The Calamitous 14th Century*. New York: Knopf.

Turpin, F. H. (1997 [1771]). *A History of the Kingdom of Siam up to 1770*. Bangkok: White Lotus.

Turton, Andrew (1980). "Thai Institutions of Slavery". In *Asian and African Systems of Slavery*, edited by J.C. Watson. Oxford: Blackwell, pp. 251–92.

—— (2000). "Introduction". In *Civility and Savagery: Social Identity in Tai States*, edited by idem. London: Curzon.

Van Roy, Edward (2006). "*Ak phoen nam su phaen din ak trok lek su thanon yai: khlong thanon soi saphan lae kan khomanakhom nai sampheng*" [From Water to Land, From Footpaths to Thoroughfares: Canals, Roads, Lanes, Bridges, and Transport in Sampheng]. In *Sampheng: Prawatisat chumchon chaw chin nai krungthep* [Sampheng: History of a Chinese Community in Bangkok], edited by Supang Chanthawanit. Bangkok: Institute of Asian Studies, Chulalongkorn University, pp. 23–56.

—— (2007*a*). *Sampheng: Bangkok's Chinatown Inside Out*. Bangkok: Institute of Asian Studies, Chulalongkorn University.

—— (2007*b*). "Taechiu versus Hokkien in Thai History: Before Bangkok". Siam Society lecture, 15 February 2007, available on disc at the Siam Society Library, Bangkok.

—— (2010*a*). "Prominent Mon Lineages from Late Ayutthaya to Early Bangkok". *Journal of the Siam Society* 98, pp. 205–31.

—— (2010*b*). *"Tan kamnoet 'monthon' khong krungthep"* [On the Origins of the Bangkok "Mandala"]. *Najua* (Gables), (Silpakon University, Bangkok) 7, pp. 1–17.

—— (2011). "Rise and Fall of the Bangkok Mandala". *Journal of Asian History* 45, nos. 1–2, pp. 85–118.

Varah Rochanavibhata (2004). *"Mon krung si"* [Mon of the City of Ayutthaya]. In *Luk chin lan mon nai krungthep* [Children of the Chinese and Grandchildren of the Mon in Bangkok], edited by Pimpraphai Phisanbut. Bangkok: Sarakadi, pp. 153–84.

Vella, Walter F. (1955*a*). *The Impact of the West on Government in Thailand*. Berkeley: University of California Press.

—— (1955*b*). *Siam Under Rama III, 1824–1851*. Locust Valley, NY: J.J. Augustine.

Wakeman, Jr., Frederic (1975). *The Fall of Imperial China*. New York: The Free Press.

Wales, H.G. Quaritch (1931). *Siamese State Ceremonies: Their History and Function*. London: Bernard Quaritch.

—— (1965). *Angkor and Rome: A Historical Comparison*. London: Bernard Quaritch.

Wang Gungwu (1991). "The Study of Chinese Identities in Southeast Asia". In *China and the Overseas Chinese*, edited by idem. Singapore: Times Academic Press, pp. 198–221.

Wanarat, Somdet Phra (1923 [1789]). *Sangitiyavamsa: phongsawadan roeng sangkhayana pra tham winai* [Sangitiyawong: Chronicle of the Great Councils]. Bangkok.

Wanwipa Burutratanaphan (1991). *"Chaw chin taechiu nai sapap sangkhom thai samai thonburi lae ratanakosin ton ton"* [The Standing of the Taechiu Chinese in Thai Society in the Thonburi and Early Ratanakosin Periods]. In *Chaw chin taechiu nai prathet thai lae nai pumisamnao doem thi chaosan … (2310–2393)* [The Taechiu Chinese in Thailand and In Their Former Homeland in Chaosan … (1767–1850)], edited by Supang Chanthawanit. Bangkok: Institute of Asian Studies, Chulalongkorn University, pp. 88–113.

—— (2001). "Preservation of Ethnic Identity and Acculturation". In *Alternate Identities: The Chinese in Contemporary Thailand*, edited by Tong Chee Kiong and Chan Kwok Bun. Singapore: Times Media.

Wat Arun Rachaworaram (1983). *Prawat wat arun rachaworaram* [History of Wat Arun Rachaworaram]. Bangkok: Department of Fine Arts.

Wat Bang Sai Kai (n.d.). *"Prawat wat bang sai kai"* [History of Wat Bang Sai Kai]. Unpublished paper. Thonburi.

Wat Dawadoeng (2004). *Luang pho wat dawadoeng* [Luang Pho (the Abbot) of Wat Dawadoeng]. Privately published cremation volume. Thonburi.

Wat Inthara Wihan (1994). *Wat inthara wihan kap chiwa-prawat somdet phra phuthachan (to phrom-rangsi) nai ngan chitrakham fa-phanang ubosot* [Wat Inthara Wihan and the Biography of Somdet Phra Phuthachan (To Phrom-rangsi), Upon the Celebratory Installation of the Ordination Hall's Wall Murals]. Bangkok.

—— (2001). *Khon khwa ha ma dai: Ekasan samkhan khong wat inthara wihan* [Research Findings: Important Information on Wat Inthara Wihan]. Bangkok.

Wat Nak Klang Worawihan (1997). *"Prawat wat nak klang worawihan"* [History of Wat

Nak Klang Worawihan]. In *Pariyati soeksa wat nak klang worawihan* [Buddhist Scriptural Studies at Wat Nak Klang Worawihan], by Wat Nak Klang Worawihan. Thonburi.

Wat Phraya Tham Worawihan (2007). *Naew khit thang tham: phithi kan — phithi kam* [Ways of Thinking on the Way of the Law: Rites, Ceremonies]. Thonburi.

Wat Sangkhrachai (1990). *Prawat wat sangkhrachai* [History of Wat Sangkhrachai]. Printed on the occasion of the visit of Princess Maha Chakri Sirindhon. Bangkok.

Wat Sunthon Thammathan (1990). *Prawat wat sunthon thammathan* [History of Wat Sunthon Thammathan]. Bangkok.

Wat Yannawa (n.d.). *Prawat wat yannawa* (History of Wat Yannawa). Bangkok.

Weber, Max (2012 [1924]). *General Economic History*. New York: Dover.

Wenk, Klaus (1968). *The Restoration of Thailand under Rama I, 1782–1809*. Tucson: University of Arizona Press.

West, Geoffrey (2011). "The Surprising Math of Cities and Corporations". Post-presentation commentary. Oral presentation. Edinburgh: TEDGlobal Conference, 12 July 2011.

Wheatley, Paul (2008). *The Origins and Character of the Chinese City*. New Brunswick, NJ: Aldine Transactions.

Wilson, Constance M. (1978). "Ethnic Participation in the Export of Thai Rice, 1885-1890". In *Economic Exchange and Social Interaction in Southeast Asia*, edited by K. Hutterer. University of Michigan, Papers on South and Southeast Asia, pp. 245–71.

——— (1989). "Bangkok in 1883: An Economic and Social Profile". *Journal of the Siam Society* 77, part 2, pp. 49–58.

Winyu Ardrugsa (2014). "Bangkok Muslims: Social Otherness and Territorial Conceptions". Paper presented at the 12th International Conference on Thai Studies, 22–24 April 2014, Sydney: University of Sydney.

Wolters, Oliver William (1999). *History, Culture, and Region in Southeast Asian Perspective*. Ithaca, NY: Cornell University Southeast Asia Program.

Wright, Arnold, and Oliver T. Breakspeare (1908). *Twentieth Century Impressions of Siam: Its History, People, Commerce, Industries, and Resources*. London: Lloyd's Greater Britain.

Wyatt, David K. (1984). *Thailand: A Short History*. New Haven: Yale University Press.

——— (1994 [1963]). "Siam and Laos 1767-1827". In *Studies in Thai History*, edited by idem. Chiangmai: Silkworm Books, pp. 185–209.

Yibphan (2002). *Chaosua Yesterday: Sokanatakan nai thun thai* [Tycoons Yesterday: Capitalist Tragedies]. Bangkok: Nation Books.

Yusuf, Imtiyaz (2010). "The Role of the *Chularajmontri* (*Shaykh al-Islam*) in Resolving Ethno-religious Conflict in Southern Thailand". *American Journal of Islamic Social Sciences* 27, no. 1, pp. 31–53.

Index

About the Author

Edward Van Roy arrived in Thailand in 1963 with the Cornell-Bennington Survey of Hill Tribes in Thailand and, in effect, never left. His hill tribe research led to a doctorate in economics, credentialed in economic anthropology (University of Texas, 1965) and a monograph titled *Economic Systems of Northern Thailand* (Cornell University Press, 1971). Bracketed between a tenured appointment with the Department of Economics at the State University of New York at Stony Brook and a visiting appointment with the Center for East Asian Studies at the University of Pennsylvania, he was stationed for some three decades at Bangkok with the United Nations Economic and Social Commission for Asia and the Pacific (ESCAP) as senior economist and then consecutively directed the Development Planning Division, Transport and Communications Division, and Social Development Division. He is grateful for the many opportunities presented by that lengthy, leisurely, lucrative tenure to explore Bangkok's maze of cultural, cross-cultural, intercultural, and multicultural byways. Since his UN retirement in 1997 he has spent much of his time researching Bangkok's ethnic history, producing *Sampheng: Bangkok's Chinatown Inside Out* (Institute of Asian Studies, Chulalongkorn University, 2007) as well as a number of shorter studies, while holding visiting fellowships with Chulalongkorn University's Institute of Asian Studies and Department of History.

www.ingramcontent.com/pod-product-compliance
Lightning Source LLC
Chambersburg PA
CBHW071839270326
41929CB00013B/2050